NEGOTIATING WATER GOVERNANCE

Tackling a critical problem facing society, water governance, the authors of this volume unsettle a concept long fitted uncritically into the analytical toolbox of geographers – scale. By questioning how scale is defined, redefined, and even performed using detailed cases from four continents, this book helps readers to fundamentally re-think how scale is produced to affect the governance of water. Their challenge to reconsider scale in water governance also encourages us to re-think how other, interconnected environmental governance challenges might be addressed.

Maureen G. Reed, University of Saskatchewan, Canada

There has been a lot of talk about how physical matter and socio-political organisation interrelate. Rare are the studies that actually show the dynamic interlacing of socio-political and hydro-physical scales. This is one of them and therefore indispensable reading for those concerned with questions of how water, social power and political space shape hydro-social landscapes.

Erik Swyngedouw, Manchester University, UK

Cutting through debates over the politics of scale and water governance with remarkable skill, this outstanding set of essays demonstrates the conceptual sophistication of research on the politics of water while simultaneously presenting an innovative framework for rethinking scalar processes. With outstanding contributors and a wide-ranging geographical focus, this is a genuinely exciting collection.

Alex Loftus, King's College London, UK

Water touches everything, materially and politically: lives, societies, and ecosystems require it; agriculture, industry, and energy production demand it; and water flows across boundaries are leading sources of conflict and cooperation. Understanding its governance is therefore vital. In this volume, leading researchers demonstrate, empirically and theoretically, that the politics of scale lie at the heart of water governance and indeed all environmental governance.

James McCarthy, Clark University, USA

Ashgate Studies in Environmental Policy and Practice

Series Editor: Adrian McDonald, University of Leeds, UK

Based on the Avebury Studies in Green Research series, this wide-ranging series still covers all aspects of research into environmental change and development. It will now focus primarily on environmental policy, management and implications (such as effects on agriculture, lifestyle, health etc.), and includes both innovative theoretical research and international practical case studies.

Also in the series

Communities in Transition: Protected Nature and Local People in
Eastern and Central Europe
Saska Petrova
ISBN 978 1 4094 4850 1

Sustainability and Short-term Policies
Improving Governance in Spatial Policy Interventions
Edited by Stefan Sjöblom, Kjell Andersson, Terry Marsden and Sarah Skerratt
ISBN 978 1 4094 4677 4

Energy Access, Poverty, and Development
The Governance of Small-Scale Renewable Energy in Developing Asia
Benjamin K. Sovacool and Ira Martina Drupady
ISBN 978 1 4094 4113 7

Tropical Wetland Management
The South-American Pantanal and the International Experience
Edited by Antonio Augusto Rossotto Ioris
ISBN 978 1 4094 1878 8

Rethinking Climate Change Research
Clean Technology, Culture and Communication
Edited by Pernille Almlund, Per Homann Jespersen and Søren Riis
ISBN 978 1 4094 2866 4

A New Agenda for Sustainability
Edited by Kurt Aagaard Nielsen, Bo Elling, Maria Figueroa and Erling Jelsøe
ISBN 978 0 7546 7976 9

Negotiating Water Governance
Why the Politics of Scale Matter

Edited by

EMMA S. NORMAN
Northwest Indian College, USA

CHRISTINA COOK
University of Oxford, UK

ALICE COHEN
Acadia University, Canada

ASHGATE

Published by
Ashgate Publishing Limited
Wey Court East
Union Road
Farnham
Surrey, GU9 7PT
England

Ashgate Publishing Company
110 Cherry Street
Suite 3-1
Burlington, VT 05401-3818
USA

www.ashgate.com

British Library Cataloguing in Publication Data
A catalogue record for this book is available from the British Library

The Library of Congress has cataloged the printed edition as follows:
Negotiating water governance : why the politics of scale matter / [edited] by Emma S. Norman, Christina Cook and Alice Cohen.
  pages cm. — (Ashgate studies in environmental policy and practice)
 Includes bibliographical references and index.
 ISBN 978-1-4094-6790-8 (hardback) – ISBN 978-1-4094-6791-5 (ebook) –
ISBN 978-1-4094-6792-2 (epub) 1. Water-supply–Management. 2. Water resouces development. I. Norman, Emma S. II. Cook, Christina. III. Cohen, Alice.
 HD1691.N444 2014
 333.91–dc23

                                                                2014018356

ISBN 9781409467908 (hbk)
ISBN 9781409467915 (ebk-PDF)
ISBN 9781409467922 (ebk-ePUB)

Printed in the United Kingdom by Henry Ling Limited,
at the Dorset Press, Dorchester, DT1 1HD

Contents

List of Figures

List of Tables

Note on Cover Image

Crescent Moon **(2010) by Polly Spenner**

Polly Spenner is a graduate of Interlochen Art Academy and Rhode Island School of Design. She calls Rhode Island home. Her artwork examines the connection and balance of organic forms found in the natural world with their counterpart human-made objects: oceans and river currents with the patterns of night-time auto headlights on the highway systems; and skyscraper scaffolding with tree trunks, sprawling branches and forest undergrowth. *Crescent Moon* is a collage of cut paper, acrylic, watercolours and oil pastels.

Notes on Contributors

The contributors to this project are leading scholars in their disciplines who actively engage in debates at the nexus of nature–society issues. They are experts in their fields, have written widely on issues of scale and the politics of water governance, and represent a range of disciplines: political and environmental geography, political science, development studies, socio-legal studies, planning and environmental studies.

Karen Bakker is Professor of Geography and Canada Research Chair in Political Ecology at the University of British Columbia (UBC) and Co-Director of the UBC Program on Water Governance.

Christian Brannstrom is Professor of Geography at Texas A&M University.

Jessica Budds is Senior Lecturer in Geography in the School of International Development at the University of East Anglia in the UK.

Afton Clarke-Sather is Assistant Professor of Geography at the University of Delaware.

Alice Cohen is Assistant Professor in the Department of Earth and Environmental Science at Acadia University, Nova Scotia, Canada.

Christina Cook is Researcher at the Centre for Socio-Legal Studies, University of Oxford, UK.

Art Dewulf is Researcher at the International Centre for Integrated Mountain Development (ICIMOD), Kathmandu, Nepal.

Coleen Fox is Visiting Assistant Professor of Geography at Dartmouth College, New Hampshire.

Kathryn Furlong is Assistant Professor of Geography at the Université de Montréal and Canada Research Chair in Water, Urban and Utility Governance.

Leila M. Harris is Associate Professor in the Institute for Resources, Environment and Sustainability and the Institute for Gender, Race, Sexuality and Social Justice at the University of British Columbia and Co-Director of the Program on Water Governance.

Wendy Jepson is Associate Professor of Geography at Texas A&M University.

Corey Johnson is Associate Professor of Geography at the University of North Carolina at Greensboro.

Janwillem Liebrand is a Researcher at the Center for Water and Climate of Wageningen University, the Netherlands.

Lyla Mehta is a Professorial Fellow at the Institute of Development Studies (IDS) and Visiting Professor at Noragric, the Department of International Environment and Development Studies, at the Norwegian University of Life Sciences.

François Molle is Director of Research at the Institut de Recherche pour le Développement (IRD), France.

Emma S. Norman is Chair of the Science Department / Native Environmental Science Program at Northwest Indian College, USA.

Eric Perramond holds a joint appointment in both the Environmental and the Southwest Studies programmes at Colorado College.

Tom Perreault is Professor in the Department of Geography at Syracuse University.

Chris Sneddon is an Associate Professor at Dartmouth College, with a joint appointment in environmental studies and geography.

Andreas Thiel is Temporary Professor of Environmental Governance at Humboldt-Universität zu Berlin.

Martinus Vink is Researcher at the Environmental Sciences Group, Wageningen University, the Netherlands.

Eve Vogel is Assistant Professor of Geography at the University of Massachusetts.

Jeroen Warner is Associate Professor of Disaster Studies with Wageningen University's Social Sciences Group.

Philippus (Flip) Wester is Chief Scientist Water Resources Management at the International Centre for Integrated Mountain Development (ICIMOD) and Affiliated Research Water Governance and Institutional Change at Wageningen University.

Margreet Zwarteveen is Professor of Water Governance at UNESCO-IHE Institute for Water Education at the University of Amsterdam.

Foreword
Rethinking the Watershed: Mobilizing Multiscalar Water Politics for the Twenty-First Century

Karen Bakker

Water has always challenged our conventional notions of politics and of scale – from the local to the global. Indeed, the articulation of multiple scales is a central problematic in water politics. As a flow resource that moves through (and shapes) landscapes in nested watersheds, water transcends geopolitical boundaries, political jurisdictions and property ownership conventions. Pitting upstream users against downstream users, with property rights that are difficult to define, water continually generates conflict. Yet, essential for life and environmental health, it has also engendered more cooperative international governance mechanisms than any other resource (Wolf 1998). The challenge of balancing conflict and cooperation entails the articulation of multiple actors at multiple scales. Water is thus deeply political in a conventional sense.

Water is also simultaneously biopolitical: effective governance of water is central to both human and environmental health, invoking both state oversight and individual self-regulation in the use of water as a source and as a sink for wastes. Water thus plays multiple roles: essential for life, it is simultaneously an economic input, an aesthetic reference, a religious symbol, a public service, a private good, a cornerstone of public health and a biophysical necessity for humans and ecosystems alike.

It is hence unsurprising that the relationship between water and broader environmental issues has become a central concern in water governance debates over the past few decades. This problematic is rapidly evolving in response to broader trends in environmental governance, including globalization, decentralization and cross-scale governance (Lemos and Agrawal 2006). An increasing number of actors and scales must be incorporated and articulated in governance processes if we are to effectively address increasing threats to water security in the context of competing and increased demands for trade-offs within the water–energy–food security nexus.

The focus of this volume is thus particularly timely. First, it usefully probes scale as an analytical lens through which we can shed new light on well-recognized problems. For example, the chapters in Part I deftly 'unpack' the scalar assumptions often associated with the invocation of the watershed, querying the limits and challenging the naturalization of the watershed as the default scale for management. For instance, the focus on the watershed is potentially undermined by the growing importance of 'virtual water' flows – notably those associated with global trade (Allen 2003). Given the multiple scales at which these trade-offs occur, reliance on watershed management alone may be insufficient. This is exacerbated by the fact that neither aquifer/groundwater boundaries – and subsurface hydrological gradients – nor ecological boundaries (e.g. biomes) coincide neatly with watersheds (Sophocleous 2002). One is reminded here of Linton's powerful analysis of the global water crisis. Rather than a singular global water crisis, Linton argues that we should speak of a set of interrelated water crises at multiple scales. The implication, in this volume as in Linton's work, is that both problems and solutions may vary across sites and scales, places and spaces (Linton 2004, 2010).

The editors of this volume thus wisely chose to focus Part II on the question of the rescaling of decision-making *beyond* the watershed. In this – perhaps the most innovative – section of the book, the authors explore the tensions and frictions which arise as actors and organizations embark on scale-jumping, cross-scalar or rescaling trajectories in an attempt to devise innovative approaches that might enhance rather than endanger water security. This ability to connect across scales is, I believe, one of the most ubiquitous, pressing and intractable water governance issues that we face in the twenty-first century.

From this perspective, politics and power are inherently scalar. As explored in Part III, imagining and inventing a (multi-)scalar water politics is a central task for those working in water governance. The authors in this volume are thus correct, in my opinion, to explore the potential of – and limitations to – polycentrism, whereby a broader range of non-governmental actors and stakeholders are playing a role in decision-making, justified by the argument that social learning is enabled and improved through the involvement of a greater diversity of actors in on-the-ground management and decision-making processes (Pahl-Wostl et al. 2007). Polycentrism implies, of course, the involvement of multiple actors at multiple scales; hence the need to explore concrete strategies for multilevel governance – such as multi-stakeholder watershed management platforms – which have been initiated in many jurisdictions for a variety of reasons, including:

- increased emphasis on watershed-based and integrated management of environmental issues;
- awareness of the multilevel causes and impacts of water-related threats (particularly, although not uniquely, with regard to the water-energy-food nexus); and
- concern over the implications of climate change for water resources – the study and mitigation of which is necessarily multiscalar (Warner 2007).

This, in turn, brings us full circle to the opening chapters of the book: the analysis provides a profound challenge to the watershed-focused emphasis of traditional Integrated Water Resources Management (IWRM) governance models. Simply put, this book implies that an emphasis on multiscalar linkages leads to a radical insight: the watershed loses its central role as the primary unit of analysis and water management. In other words, polycentrism challenges the notion that the watershed is the sole or optimal scale from which to address complex water security challenges. The most important (and controversial) insight from this book, in short, may be the claim that a watershed-focused approach is insufficient for adequately addressing the water security challenge: balancing human and environmental water needs in order to safeguard essential ecosystem services and biodiversity across the global water system. This is an important but critical and perhaps controversial argument which opens up many additional questions worth pursuing: an exciting debate that I predict will resonate for many years to come.

References

Allan, J.A. 2003. Virtual water – the water, food, and trade nexus: Useful concept or misleading metaphor? *Water International* 28(1), 106–13.

Lemos, M.C. and Agrawal, A. 2006. Environmental governance. *Annual Review of Environment and Resources* 31, 297–325.

Linton, J. 2010. *What is Water? The History of a Modern Abstraction*. Vancouver: University of British Columbia Press.

Linton, J.I. 2004. Global hydrology and the construction of a water crisis. *Great Lakes Geographer* 11(2), 1–13.

Pahl-Wostl, C., Craps, M., Dewulf, A., Mostert, E., Tabara, D. and Taillieu, T. 2007. Social learning and water resources management. *Ecology and Society* 12(2), 5.

Sophocleous, M. 2002. Interactions between groundwater and surface water: The state of the science. *Hydrogeology Journal* 10(1), 52–67.

Warner, J. 2007. *Multi-Stakeholder Platforms for Integrated Water Management*. Aldershot: Ashgate.

Wolf, A.T. 1998. Conflict and cooperation along international waterways. *Water Policy* 1(2), 251–65.

Acknowledgements

Any book requires much work 'behind the scenes', and this volume is no exception. The three of us met as doctoral students at The University of British Columbia (UBC) in Vancouver, Canada, where we were part of a dynamic group of scholars at the Program on Water Governance. We thank the co-directors of this programme – Drs Karen Bakker and Leila Harris – and our colleagues for thought-provoking conversations that have helped shape us as scholars. Thanks also go to the inspiring faculty and students of the Geography Department and the Institute for Resources and Environmental Sustainability at UBC, as well as to colleagues, mentors and students from all corners of the world.

Thank you to all of the authors whose contributions allowed us to transform an idea into the present volume. We are grateful to work with this outstanding group of scholars and honoured to consider them as colleagues. Thanks in particular to François Molle, whose role as editor of *Water Alternatives* helped us lay the foundation, with a themed section, for what has now become *Negotiating Water Governance*. Thanks also to the participants of the original 'water governance and the politics of scale' sessions at the Association of American Geographers Annual Meeting in Seattle (2011). Their insights and passion provided us with the inspiration and momentum to complete this volume.

Thanks to Katy Crossan at Ashgate Publishing for her confidence in and support for this project. Her dedication to detail, clear communication and good cheer helped move this manuscript from draft to final form. Thanks too to Alex Peace for her thorough work in indexing the volume, and to Tricia Craggs for her editing. We are also grateful to the anonymous reviewer and series editor for their thoughtful insights and suggestions on how to strengthen an earlier version of the manuscript.

We acknowledge with appreciation Michigan Technological University, Northwest Indian College, the Hebrew University of Jerusalem, Acadia University and Clark University for their institutional support. Michigan Technological University and Acadia University helped defer the costs of production. We are grateful for financial support from the Social Sciences and Humanities Research Council of Canada and the Alberman Fellowship at the Hebrew University.

A very special thanks to Emma's sister, Polly Spenner, an amazingly talented artist who generously entrusted us with her collage, *The Crescent Moon*, that appears on the cover of the book.

Lastly, we would like to thank our families for their ongoing support through our years of scholarship, and especially during the final stages of this particular project. Their love and good humour continue to help keep us afloat.

EMMA S. NORMAN, CHRISTINA COOK, ALICE COHEN

Chapter 1

Introduction:
Why the Politics of Scale Matter in the Governance of Water

Emma S. Norman, Christina Cook and Alice Cohen

Humans have used water to make deserts bloom and crops thrive, but consistent access to adequate quality and quantity of water for all is not a reality for many in the twenty-first century. The United Nations estimates that 768 million people do not have access to clean drinking water and that 2.5 billion people (36 per cent of the world's population) have inadequate sanitation services. Despite ongoing efforts to rectify this situation, huge barriers remain to achieving universal access to water and sanitation services. Decisions about who gets water services and how – governance decisions – are wrapped up in the politics of scale: as a flow resource water is simultaneously local and global.

Complicating matters, water crosses boundaries of all kinds – political, social and ecological – and varies by type: ground, surface, fresh, marine, solid, liquid, gas. In addition, decisions about the allocation of and access to water are political decisions often made some distance from the site of either allocation or access, and as part of wider geopolitical processes. To better understand the complexities of governing water, scholars seek to understand the relationship between water and political boundaries through questions such as:

- How and why does water governance fragment across sectors and governmental departments?
- How can we govern shared waters more effectively?
- How do politics and power mediate water governance?

Questions like these have been the subject of both the academic literature and water management practices, where scholars and practitioners have grappled with what it means to integrate water governance systems (Biswas 2004; Mitchell 2004; Warner and Johnson 2007), or how to effectively govern water that crosses international political boundaries (e.g. Wolf 1999; Blatter et al. 2001; Kliot et al 2001; Kaika 2003; Sneddon and Fox 2006; Norman and Bakker 2009; Norman et al. 2013).

We build on this thinking by focusing on a small but growing literature that links the concept of scale (and its associated debates) to water governance. The volume thus contributes to the advancement of both environmental governance and scalar theory: decision-making with respect to water is often, implicitly, about scale and its related politics.

The central argument of this volume is that negotiating water governance requires explicit consideration of the politics of scale. We base this argument on three interrelated points:

1. that hydrologic scales such as river basins or watersheds should not be taken for granted as natural and apolitical scales;
2. that the historical legacies of water governance inform current decision-making, including efforts to rescale water governance;
3. that scales are political tools.

These points provide the foundation for the book's structure, with each point serving as a focal point for each book section. Part I grapples with variegated iterations of 'watershed-scale governance' – a paradigm promoted as an effective model for the governance of complex water systems. In Part II the focus is on the production and mobilization of scale in water governance. In Part III the authors engage with scalar politics and power in water governance.

As a whole, this volume calls for closer attention to the interrelationships between governance, water and social networks, with an emphasis on the role of institutional framings and scalar constructions. The authors of this volume are particularly concerned with the following two questions:

- What can academic scholarship on water governance gain by looking through a scalar lens?
- What does scalar literature gain by looking through a water lens?

Through case studies from around the globe, the chapters in this volume address these questions by exploring and analysing the sociopolitical intersections of environment and policy. The diversity of chapters reveals that there is much room in the social sciences to continue to refine and redefine our understanding of hydrosocial processes and the politics of scale within water governance. That is, approaching the topics from different vantage points – geographically, theoretically and methodologically – opens up a conceptual space in which to consider innovative ways to improve water governance. The chapters present a critical realist perspective on scale: fully aware of the nuances of the social construction of scale, yet cognizant of the material impacts of scale and rescaling processes on water governance.

Water Governance through a Scalar Lens

Broadly speaking, water governance debates address the mechanisms and institutional frameworks though which decisions about water are made. Importantly, we emphasize the distinction between 'government' and 'governance': government often refers to a branch of a political authority (such as a nation, tribe, state or municipality), whereas governance is the process in which multiple actors, including civil servants and stakeholder groups, participate in the decision-making process. Here we highlight the procedural dimensions of governance, as governance is as much about the processes of decision-making as it is about its outcomes.

The distinction between government and governance matters because the chapters herein are concerned with the *processes* used to make decisions about water, as well as with the relationships between governmental and extra-governmental actors in these processes. Moreover, because water is a fluid, boundary-crossing substance, decisions about water are *necessarily* (if often implicitly) decisions about what actions are to be taken, by whom and where.

Many chapters in this volume, for example, explore questions on the centralization or decentralization of decision-making for water. Part I in particular is concerned with the rise of watersheds as scales for water governance. In fact, the rise of watersheds is often seen as an example of rescaled environmental governance – a term used to refer to a shift in the locus of decision-making. This may entail a shifting 'up' from national governments to international organizations; a shifting 'down' from national or provincial/state government to municipalities; and/or a shifting 'out' from government-driven decision-making to more inclusive forms of governance (Cohen and McCarthy 2014; Reed and Bruyneel 2010). Importantly, these three shifts can occur alone, together or in uneven fits and starts as actors within and outside government seek to find governance mechanisms most appropriate to the questions at hand.

Much of the rescaling that has occurred with respect to environmental governance is driven by a search for a solution to the putative 'scalar mismatch' between administrative systems and the ecosystem spaces and processes they are responsible for governing; watersheds are one example of this phenomenon. Part II is particularly concerned with the phenomenon of rescaling as an effort to resolve scalar mismatch. It explores the scalar dimensions of water-related decision-making, and is especially focused on how rescaling efforts are spatially and historically contingent.

Part III is concerned with the power dynamics of rescaling, and explores how certain spaces become nodes in complex hydrosocial networks that are heavily influenced by these power dynamics. Thus, in light of the inherently scalar dimensions of water-related decision-making and the political outcomes arising from particular scalar choices, we suggest that scholarship on scale and the politics of scale are central to understanding water governance processes.

Scale through a Water Lens

For many scholars, 'scale' refers to a physical space.[1] While the term can in other contexts be cartographic, musical or refer to a tool that measures weight, here scale has a specifically *spatial* connotation. The term (and its utility) is the subject of some contention, in large part because of its malleable, nebulous nature. Indeed, it is nearly impossible to determine a single, agreed-upon definition (see Sheppard and McMaster 2004 for an overview of different geographic perspectives on scale). In geography the term is used most often to denote a political space (e.g. a municipality); the scope of a particular programme or problem (e.g. a large-scale problem); or a space delineated by ecosystem phenomena (e.g. the watershed scale).

Importantly, these spaces are murky and not clearly defined. For example, the drinking water sources for New York City – the Catskills and Delaware watersheds that together provide 90 per cent of its water supply – are located outside the city's boundaries. Through a memorandum of understanding signed by the state, watershed towns, villages and communities, and by the city itself, New York City has managed its drinking water supply source and avoided the need to install further filtration infrastructure. This and other examples show that in one sense scales are nested and defined, but in another they are part of complex social, legal, economic and political landscapes. It is not our intention to identify a singular definition of scale that is best suited to water scholarship. Rather, we suggest that the multiplicity of definitions broadens the scope of the volume and its contributions.

New York City and the Catskills provide a concrete example of the way(s) in which human systems exist and interact across political, economic and physical boundaries. Indeed, any environmental decision is a decision about scale (i.e., which set of environmental concerns are being parcelled out for particular attention), and it is for this reason that debates about scale – their ontologies, power structures, boundaries and even their existence – have been central to critical geographic scholarship for more than two decades (Smith 1992; Marston 2000; Swyngedouw and Heynen 2003; Brown and Purcell 2005; Marston et al. 2005; Sayre 2005, 2009; McCarthy 2005; Manson 2008; MacKinnon 2011).

Broadly speaking, scale debates pivot on the following points of contention. The first relates to the ontological status of scales – i.e., do these spaces exist in any real way? Second, scholars query the extent to which particular scales are chosen as analytical units for study, as spatial units for management or governance, or as jurisdictional levels appropriate for resource decision-making. Third, and most relevant to this volume, scholars explore the ways in which particular spatial scales are marshalled in support of political, economic, or social change. In other words, how are specific spatial scales – municipalities, provinces, watersheds, ecosystems, or cultural spaces – used to understand or promote particular notions about authority, effectiveness, efficiency and so on?

---

1   For a more thorough treatment of different types of scale and the relationships between them, see Cash et al. (2006).

The idea that scale is socially produced and contingent on political struggle (Delaney and Leitner 1997) can be credited to the foundational work of Neil Smith, which has been central to the development of a literature theorizing the politics of scale (e.g. Smith 1992, 1993; Swyngedouw 1997, 2004; Marston 2000; Marston et al. 2005; Cox 2002; Perreault 2003). The debate has taken distinct directions over the years that have enriched and expanded our understanding of the politics of scale. For a review of the scale debate, see Brenner (1997, 1998, 2001), Howitt (1998, 2003), Marston (2000), Smith (2000) and Sheppard and McMaster (2004). Brown and Purcell (2005: 609) usefully distil scholarly work on scale into three theoretical principles:

1. Scale is socially constructed.
2. Scale is both fluid and fixed.
3. Scale is fundamentally a relational concept.

In a noteworthy contribution to the scale debate, Marston et al. (2005) argued that scale should be eliminated as an analytical concept because it reifies the hierarchies with which many critical geographers are concerned. Rejoinders to this argument, though varied, maintain that scale is an important tool for the analysis of human–environmental relationships (Brenner 1997; Swyngedouw 1997, 2004; Sayre 2005; Jonas 2006; Leitner and Miller 2007; Kaiser and Nikiforova 2008). Kaiser and Nikiforova, for example, argue that removing scale from the social science lexicon would weaken our ability to analyse power dynamics reliant on scale, through obscuring the processes and discourses whereby scales are constructed (see also Harris and Alatout, 2010).

This productive (albeit at times heated) debate has, if nothing else, identified the need for clearer articulation of how scale was being used and encouraged a wider examination of the power dynamics associated with scale. Indeed, the debate has created an opportunity for more critical analysis of the politics at play in the construction and mobilization of scale especially, and closer attention to whom (or what) is included (and excluded) in constructions of scale. Scholars have become more precise about their use of the concept of scale, and more transparent about how to query how spatial scales are produced and politically mobilized. Seeing scale as constructed and fluid rather than pre-given and fixed opens up conceptual space to frame scale as a *process*.

Water Governance and the Politics of Scale

This volume's focus on the relationship between scale and water governance is a departure from the scalar debate's usual focus on political economy and flows of capital (Brenner 2001; Swyngedouw 2004). Indeed, questions of environmental governance have remained largely excluded from the scale literature (Cohen and

McCarthy 2014), although studies of the relationship between water governance and scale have refined thinking about human–environmental and hydrosocial relations.[2]

Although it is understood in the social sciences that scale is socially constructed, historically contingent and politically contested (Smith 1992; Agnew 1997; Swyngedouw 1997), the mutability of that framing is often lost on the water user (see Perramond, Chapter 10 this volume). Furthermore, systems currently in place to govern water follow (and often reify) socially constructed political demarcations that aim to 'fix' water to a territorial scale for the purposes of management (Molle 2006, 2009; Norman and Bakker 2009; Cohen and Davidson 2011; Norman 2015). The complex interconnections of human–environmental issues (specifically, the interscalar and politically complex nature of flow resources such as water) continue to complicate and challenge current governance systems. In response to such complexity, water governance is often rescaled – a move that can serve to 're-fix' governance to a new scale with limited evidence of improved effectiveness or equity. Here we note that rescaling does not inherently lead to 'better governance'. We suggest instead that, in some cases, rescaling may shift problems to other locations rather than necessarily address them in their entirety. Thus, looking at hydrosocial networks may reveal wider social, economic and political processes that influence water governance.

Explorations of complex hydrosocial relations have been guided by two emerging concepts: 'waterscapes' and 'hybrid constructs'. A growing body of literature employs the concept of waterscape to characterize the complicated interactions that occur within hydrosocial relations. It is an analytical tool to articulate, more explicitly, the linkages between water, power, politics and governance (Swyngedouw 1999, 2004, 2006, 2009; Bakker 2003; Harris 2006; Loftus 2007; Loftus and Lumsden 2008; Budds 2008, 2009; Ekers and Loftus 2008).

Budds and Hinojosa (2012) define a waterscape as the range of 'moments' which are mediated by social and political processes. These include physical flows, patterns of access, technologies, institutions, practices, legislative reforms, governance frameworks and discourses on water. Furthermore, Swyngedouw (2009: 56) explains that the concept of 'hydrosocial' is an attempt to 'transcend the modernist nature–society binaries' to envision 'the circulation of water as a combined physical and social process, as a hybridized socio-natural flow that fuses together nature and society as inseparable manners'. The concept of hybrid construct is somewhat parallel to the waterscape; it offers another means of understanding hydrosocial relations. Viewing water as a hybrid construct or a produced socio-natural entity (Swyngedouw 1999, 2007; Bakker 2003; Loftus 2007; Linton 2010) affords us the opportunity to analyze how water and power

---

2   See Gibbs and Jonas (2001); Liverman (2004); Brown and Purcell (2005); Bulkeley (2005); Fall (2005, 2010); Perreault (2005, 2008); Molle (2006); Vogel (2007, 2011); Norman and Bakker (2009); Bakker (2010); Dore and Lebel (2010); Harris and Alatout (2010); Linton (2010); Cohen and Davidson (2011); Cook (2011); and Norman et al. (2013), among others.

mutually constitute each other. How, for example, are governance structures at newly constructed scales similar to or different from their antecedents, and what material effects might they have?

These ideas are advanced in several of the chapters (see, in particular, Sneddon and Fox, Budds, Mehta and Norman). Engaging in scalar debates provides an opportunity to continue to refine and redefine complex nature–society relationships. Thus, as suggested by scholars such as Jonas (2006) and Harris and Alatout (2010), engagement in the *process* of understanding these relationships is the critical component of the analysis of scalar politics.

Organization of the Volume

The chapters are organized according to the volume's overarching argument: that negotiating water governance requires explicit consideration of the politics of scale. As mentioned, we provide the reader with an opportunity to engage with the main argument through three distinct parts:

I.   Examining Scalar Assumptions: Unpacking the Watershed
II   Beyond the Watershed: Rescaling Decision-Making
III. Scalar Politics, Networks and Power in Water Governance

Of course, the separation into parts is somewhat arbitrary – themes run throughout the volume, and chapters in different parts speak to one another. Nonetheless, the separation of the chapters into these sections helps to unfurl the main argument of the volume. The part introductions play a key role in this regard, pulling main themes through the volume.

Examining Scalar Assumptions: Unpacking the Watershed

Introduced by François Molle, Part I unsettles the watershed scale. Molle remarks on the politics and practicalities of governing at a watershed scale, particularly in relation to the debates around Integrated Water Resources Management.

Alice Cohen's chapter – 'Nature's Scales? Watersheds as a Link between Water Governance and the Politics of Scale' – is a thoughtful analysis of the construction of watersheds. She asks what insights can be gained by looking at water governance through a scalar lens and by looking at scale through a water lens. Cohen suggests that the concept of the watershed can serve as a fulcrum on which water governance and the politics of scale are balanced in three ways. First, they are materially, discursively and conceptually constructed. Second, this construction has political consequences in the sense that rescaling always produces new sets of 'winners' and 'losers'. Third, watersheds become political when their boundaries are conflated with the tools of governance.

Chris Sneddon and Coleen Fox continue to unpack the watershed narrative by exploring the complexity of constructing a unique scalar identity around the ideal of the river basin. In their chapter, 'A Genealogy of the Basin: Scalar Politics and Identity in the Mekong River Basin', they explore divergent constructions by tracing the genealogy of two 'basin narratives' in the Mekong River system from early interventions by water resource experts in the 1950s to more recent efforts by grassroots and regional advocacy networks to reimagine a Mekong-based identity. Weaving in stories of privilege and power, Sneddon and Fox explore the conflicting narratives of this transboundary basin through the implications of large-scale dam projects on different populations to provide insights on how these scalar constructions were discursively produced.

In 'River Basins versus Politics? Patterns and Consequences' Eve Vogel provides an historical political-environmental analysis of the management of the river basin scale to watershed management practices. Vogel examines the impact that organizing water management within river basin institutions has on policy and practice over time. Using the historical development of three North American river basins – the Tennessee, Connecticut and Columbia – as models, she discerns three patterns of governing and their associated outcomes. Vogel argues that in all cases the consequences of river basin organization need to be understood as resulting from the *interaction* between political and policy actions within river basin territories and those within more conventional government territories.

In Chapter 5 Jeroen Warner et al. analyse how fear-based discourses of sea level rise and higher river discharges triggered by climate variability have incited major debates on water management in the low-lying, densely populated Netherlands. Responding to climate change and sea level change has spawned a quest for new policies and interventions. This chapter provides insights on how framing water governance at the 'right scale' is intrinsically linked to invocations of a sense of crisis and insecurity.

Andreas Thiel's chapter completes Part I through an examination of scalar reorganization of water management in the Guadalquivir basin in Spain. He engages in the discussion of scalar reform at the watershed level by examining the processes of scalar reorganization of natural resource governance and the drivers of national water reforms in Europe. Thiel explores how in Spain contingent, national and subnational dynamics, rather than international ones, seemingly shape water management. This chapter engages with one of the main issues raised by the implementation of the European Union Water Framework Directive (WFD) and questioned the world over: finding 'the right geographical scale … for water management' (CEC 2007).

Beyond the Watershed: Rescaling Decision-Making

Introduced by Thomas Perreault, Part II explores rescaling to various scales (not just the watershed) as an effort to resolve scalar mismatches of various kinds. Perreault identifies the key themes in this section as including rescaling as a technique to accommodate a changing hydrosocial cycle; rescaling as an established practice in water governance; technology as a tool with impacts on scalar politics; and scale as mutable.

Christina Cook situates scalar restructuring as an historical process rather than a solely modern phenomenon. She reviews scalar reform in the province of Ontario, Canada, focusing on water supply and wastewater treatment, from pre-Confederation (1840s) until Canada and the United States of America signed the Canada–US Great Lakes Water Quality Agreement (1972). She suggests that although most scale discussions take as their starting point the latter third or so of the twentieth century, the rescaling of water governance is, in fact, a centuries old phenomenon.

In Chapter 8 Kathryn Furlong explores the scalar politics of alternative service delivery (ASD) models for water supply in Ontario. Furlong examines the contestation of ASD reforms largely stemming from sweeping neoliberal reforms in the province under a Conservative government from 1995 to 2004. This analysis finds that rescaling water supply and water governance are important driving forces *and* outcomes of institutional change. Furlong's analysis reveals that ASD is both a product of and a factor in socio-spatial change.

Wendy Jepson and Christian Brannstrom focus on technology systems and devices; they view water governance as a technical practice. The authors examine key moments in the historical development of governance over Rio Grande water in south Texas. Their chapter seeks to delineate the relationship between technology and water, and to identify how technologies influence water governance and what that reveals about scalar politics and power. Specifically, they investigate the ways that conflicts over technical devices and practice intersect with and shape scalar politics of water governance.

In Chapter 10 Eric Perramond illustrates the links between social construction of scale and water rights adjudication in the American state of New Mexico, showing how multiple views of scale (and the utility of scale) are enacted there. He notes that one could argue that the state is omnipresent even at the local level, which adds validity to the flat ontology of scale (see Marston et al. 2005). However, ultimately the use of scale as a socially constructed container of analysis proved useful to his study. Perramond's chapter illustrates how the priorities of the stakeholders influence the different ways that scale is mobilized, and how scalar politics operate in different settings from the individual to the watershed level.

In his chapter, Corey Johnson engages with notions of territoriality, sovereignty and governance while examining the EU WFD. He analyses the de- and re-territorialization of environmental governance and the changing nature of sovereignty in the EU, and sheds light on the interplays between scale and environmental governance by exploring the reconceptualization of the EU as a heterogeneous political-territorial construction rather than just a sum of intergovernmental organizations. Similar to Thiel's arguments presented in Chapter 6, Johnson notes that the EU WFD shifts scale and provides insights into the connection between political rescaling and environmental governance.

Scalar Politics, Networks and Power in Water Governance

Introduced by Leila Harris, this part explores scalar politics with a focus on power dynamics in water governance. Harris links the chapters through their common theme of identifying how power dynamics shape water governance through conceptual tools such as: hydrosocial networks, waterscapes and performativity.

In Chapter 12 Jessica Budds uses the waterscape to characterize the complicated interactions that occur within hydrosocial relations. She argues that the waterscape is a useful framework through which the multiple processes and dynamics that mediate water issues over time and space can be brought together. A waterscape approach suggests that it is the linkages or connections (rather than the scales per se) that allow us to insert power dynamics and contestations more readily into the analysis of water governance. By analysing changing waterscapes through mineral extraction in the Andes, Budds shows how these same processes of water production also counter-shape the nature of mining and present challenges for the expansion of the industry.

In Chapter 13 Lyla Mehta offers a challenge to the scalar politics of water governance: to include sanitation in the waterscape. Mehta analyzes the politics of scale of sanitation – considered one of the most 'off-track' of the United Nations' Millennium Development Goals. Mehta demonstrates the differences between the logics of water and sanitation governance and explores the consequences for the lack of attention to sanitation. She offers key lessons of the Community-Led Total Sanitation (CLTS) project as a possible blueprint for addressing sanitation issues. The CLTS rationale holds that for long-term behaviour change to occur, approaches need to be systematic and include 'scaled-down' solutions to respond to local needs and cultural considerations while addressing risks and uncertainties across multiple scales.

Afton Clarke-Sather explores the rescaling of hydrosocial governance through the analysis of changing agricultural economies in regional China's dynamic food–water nexus. He finds that national agricultural policies – not traditionally considered water governance – have profound impacts on local hydrosocial networks. Thus, he argues for broadening the understanding of scale in hydrosocial relations to capture the complexities of political economies. Clarke-Sather shows how political actors actively *rescale* hydrosocial governance by shifting the scale at which both biophysical processes (i.e. basin management) and socioeconomic processes connecting humans and water occur.

Margreet Zwarteveen and Janwillem Liebrand engage with water governance and the politics of scale through an analysis of performativity of irrigation development in Nepal. They show that the scales that underpin the datasets produced by irrigation policy elites not only both describe and enact irrigation in Nepal, underpinning a particular vision of modernity and development, but also – and simultaneously – help perform a particular 'masculine' irrigation elite. The authors stress that it is critical to keep in mind both the technical and cultural dimensions of performance; similar to the discussions of hydrosocial relations and waterscapes, the performative approach suggests that these dimensions are inseparable and happen simultaneously.

In the final chapter of Part III, Emma Norman uses performativity to help explain how hydrosocial networks are enacted and how networks are created as part of a process of self-empowerment in a transboundary setting. Through an analysis of a new governing body created by indigenous leaders in the Coastal Pacific Salish Sea, this chapter adds to the small body of literature that has linked the politics of scale debates to the issues of transboundary natural resource management.

A Guide to Readers

The chapters in this volume envisage the concept of scale beyond the fixity of territory. The volume asks authors (and readers) to put aside the concept of scales as nested and hierarchical – like Matryoshka dolls – and explore scale as dynamic, complex and, at times, surprising. The fluidity of water helps with this exercise: water continues to redefine and challenge nested scales as it circulates through the hydrologic cycle and, indeed, hydrosocial networks.

As a whole, the volume highlights the need for continued and critical inquiry in discussions of water governance and the politics of scale. The chapters show the need for closer attention to the processes and interrelationships between power and social networks in water governance, with particular reference to both institutional dynamics and scalar constructions.

We invite readers to remain open to possibilities while critically engaging with the chapters as each articulates a relationship between water governance and the politics of scale. Moreover, we encourage readers to reflect on what the scalar approach contributes to these – and their own – studies of water governance. And, we suggest that readers consider how the chapters might answer three questions that permeate the water governance literature: How and why does water governance fragment across sectors and governmental departments? How can we govern shared waters more effectively? How do politics and power mediate water governance?

References

Agnew, J. 1997. The dramaturgy of horizons: Geographical scale in the 'reconstruction of Italy' by the new Italian political parties. *Political Geography*, 16(2), 99–121.

Bakker, K. 2003. From public to private to … mutual? Restructuring water supply governance in England and Wales. *Geoforum*, 34(3), 359–74.

Bakker, K. 2010. *Privatizing Water: Governance Failure and the World's Urban Water Crisis*. Ithaca, NY: Cornell University Press.

Biswas, A.K. 2004. Integrated water resource management: A reassessment. *Water International*, 29(2), 248–56.

Blatter, J., Ingram, H. and Levesque, S.L. 2001. Expanding perspectives on transboundary water. In: Blatter, J. and Ingram, H. (eds), *Reflections on Water: New Approaches to Transboundary Conflicts and Cooperation*. Cambridge, MA: MIT Press.

Brenner, N. 1997. State territorial restructuring and the production of spatial scale: Urban and regional planning in the Federal Republic of Germany, 1960–1990. *Political Geography*, 16(4), 273–306.

Brenner, N. 1998. Between fixity and motion: Accumulation, territorial organization and the historical geography of scales. *Environment and Planning D*, 6(4), 459–81.

Brenner, N. 2001. The limits to scale? Methodological reflection on scalar structuration. *Progress in Human Geography*, 25(4), 591–614.

Brown, C.J. and Purcell, M. 2005. There's nothing inherent about scale: Political ecology, the local trap, and the politics of development in the Brazilian Amazon. *Geoforum*, 36(5), 607–24.

Budds, J. 2008. Whose scarcity? The hydrosocial cycle and the changing waterscape of La Ligua river basin, Chile. In: Goodman, M., Boykoff, M. and Evered, K. (eds), *Contentious Geographies: Environment, Meaning, Scale*. Aldershot: Ashgate.

Budds, J. 2009. Contested H2O: Science, policy and politics in water resources management in Chile. *Geoforum*, 40(3), 418–30.

Budds, J. and Hinojosa, L. 2012. Restructuring and rescaling water governance in mining contexts: The co-production of waterscapes in Peru *Walter Alternatives*, 5(1), 119–37.

Bulkeley, H. 2005. Reconfiguring environmental governance: Towards a politics of scales and networks. *Political Geography*, 24(8), 875–902.

Cash, D.W. et al. 2006. Scale and cross-scale dynamics: Governance and information in a multilevel world. *Ecology and Society*, 11(2), 181–92.

CEC. 2007. *Towards Sustainable Water Management in the European Union: First Stage in the Implementation of the Water Framework Directive*. Working paper. Communication from the Commission to the European Parliament and the Council. Brussels: Commission of the European Communities.

Cohen, A. 2012. Rescaling environmental governance: Watersheds as boundary objects at the intersection of science, neoliberalism, and participation. *Environment and Planning A*, 44(9), 2207–24.

Cohen, A. and Davidson, S. 2011. The watershed approach: Challenges, antecedents, and the transition from technical tool to governance unit. *Water Alternatives*, 4(1), 521–34.

Cohen, A. and Harris, L.M. 2014. Performing scale: Watersheds as 'natural' governance units in the Canadian context. In: Glass, M. and Rose-Redwood, R. (eds), *Performativity, Politics, and the Production of Social Space*. New York: Routledge.

Cohen, A. and McCarthy, J. 2014. Reviewing rescaling: Strengthening the case for environmental considerations. *Progress in Human Geography*, 7 March, doi: 10.1177/0309132514521483.

Cook, C. 2011. *Putting the Pieces Together: Tracing Fragmentation in Ontario Water Governance*. PhD dissertation, University of British Columbia, Vancouver.

Cox, K. 2002. 'Globalization', the 'regulation approach', and the politics of scale. In: Herod, A. and Wright, M.W. (eds), *Geographies of Power: Placing Scale*. Malden, MA: Blackwell.

Delaney, D. and Leitner, H. 1997. The political construction of scale. *Political Geography* 16(2), 93–7.

Dore, J. and Lebel, L. 2010. Deliberation and scale in Mekong region water governance. *Environmental Management*, 46(1), 60–80.

Ekers, M. and Loftus, A, 2008, The power of water: Developing dialogues between Foucault and Gramsci. *Environment and Planning D*, 26(4), 698–718.

Fall, J.J. 2005. *Drawing the Line: Nature, Hybridity and Politics in Transboundary Spaces*. Aldershot: Ashgate.

Fall, J. J. 2010. Artificial States? On the enduring geographical myth of natural borders? *Political Geography*, 29(3), 140–47.

Gibbs D. and Jonas A.E.G. 2001. Rescaling and regional governance: The English Regional Development Agencies and the environment. *Environment and Planning C*, 19(2), 269–88.

Harris, L.M. 2006. Irrigation, gender, and social geographies of the changing waterscapes of southeastern Anatolia. *Environment and Planning D*, 24(2), 187–213.

Harris, L.M. and Alatout, S. 2010. Negotiating hydro-scales, forging states: Comparison of the upper Tigris/Euphrates and Jordan river basins. *Political Geography*, 29(3), 148–56.

Howitt, R. 1998. Scale as relation: Musical metaphors of geographical scale. *Area*, 30(1), 49–58.

Howitt, R. 2002. Scale and the other: Levinas and geography. *Geoforum*, 33(3), 299–313.

Howitt, R. 2003. Scale. In: Agnew, J. Mitchell, K. and Toal, G. (eds), *A Companion to Political Geography*. Malden, MA: Blackwell.

Jonas, A. 2006. Pro scale: Further reflections of the 'scale debate' in human geography. *Transactions of the Institute of British Geographers*, 31(3), 399–406.

Kaika, M. 2003. Constructing scarcity and sensationalising water politics: 170 days that shook Athens. *Antipode*, 35(5), 919–54.

Kaiser, R. and Nikiforova, E. 2008. The performativity of scale: The social construction of scale effects in Narva, Estonia. *Environment and Planning D*, 26(3), 537–62.

Kliot, N., Shmueli, D. and Shamir, U. 2001. Institutions for management of transboundary water resources: Their nature, characteristics and shortcomings. *Water Policy*, 3(3), 229–55.

Leitner, H. and Miller, B. 2007. Scale and the limitations of ontological debate: A commentary on Marston, Jones and Woodward. *Transactions of the Institute of British Geographers*, 32(1), 116–25.

Linton, J. 2010. *What is Water? The History of a Modern Abstraction*. Vancouver: University of British Columbia Press.

Liverman, D. 2004. Who governs, at what scale and at what price? Geography, environmental governance, and the commodification of nature. *Annals of the Association of American Geographers*, 94(4), 734–8.

Loftus, A. 2007. Working the socio-natural relations of the urban waterscape. *International Journal of Urban and Regional Research*, 3(1), 41–59.

Loftus, A. and Lumsden, F. 2008. Reworking hegemony in the urban waterscape. *Transactions of the Institute of British Geographers*, 33(1), 109–26.

MacKinnon, D. 2011. Reconstructing scale: Towards a new scalar politics. *Progress in Human Geography*, 35(1), 21–36.

Manson, S.M. 2008. Does scale exist? An epistemological scale continuum for complex human-environment systems. *Geoforum* 39(2), 776–88.

Marston, S.A. 2000. The social construction of scale. *Progress in Human Geography*, 24(2), 219–42.

Marston, S.A., Jones, J.P. and Woodward, K. 2005. Human geography without scale. *Transactions of the Institute of British Geography*, 30(4), 416–32.

McCarthy, J. 2005. Scale, sovereignty, and strategy in environmental governance. *Antipode*, 37(4), 731–53.

Mitchell, B. 2004. Integrated water resources management: A reassessment. *Water International*, 29(3), 398–99.

Molle, F. 2006. *Planning and Managing Water at the River-Basin Level: Emergence and Evolution of a Concept*. Colombo, Sri Lanka: International Water Management Institute.

Molle, F. 2009. River-basin planning and management: The social life of a concept. *Geoforum* 40(3), 484–94.

Norman, E.S. 2013. Who's counting? Spatial politics, ecocolonisation, and the politics of calculation in Boundary Bay. *Area*, 45(2), 179–87.

Norman, E.S. and Bakker, K. 2009. Transgressing scales: Transboundary water governance across the Canada–U.S. borderland. *Annals of the Association of American Geographers*, 99(1), 99–117.

Norman, E.S., Cohen, A. and Bakker, K. (eds). 2013. *Water without Borders? Canada, the US, and Shared Water*. Toronto: University of Toronto Press.

Norman, E.S. 2015. *Governing Transboundary Waters: Canada, the United States, and Indigenous Communities*. London: Routledge.

Perreault, T. 2003. Making space. *Latin American Perspectives* 30(128), 96–121.

Perreault, T. 2005. State restructuring and the scale politics of rural water governance in Bolivia. *Environment and Planning A*, 37(2), 263–84.

Perreault, T. 2008. Custom and contradiction: Rural water governance and the politics of 'usos y costumbres' in Bolivia's irrigators' movement. *Annals of the Association of American Geographers* 98(4), 835–54.

Reed, M.G. and Bruyneel, S. 2010. Rescaling environmental governance, rethinking the state: A three-dimensional review. *Progress in Human Geography*, 34(5): 646–53.

Sayre, N. 2005. Ecological and geographical scale: Parallels and potential for integration. *Progress in Human Geography*, 29(3), 276–90.

Sayre, N. 2009. Scale. In: Castree, N.D., Liverman, D. and Rhoads, B. (eds), *A Companion to Environmental Geography*. Oxford: Blackwell.

Sheppard, E. and McMaster, R. (eds). 2004. *Scale and Geographic Inquiry: Nature, Society, and Method*. Oxford: Blackwell.

Smith, N. 1992. Geography, difference and the politics of scale. In: Doherty, J., Graham, M. and Malek, M. (eds), *Postmodernism and the Social Sciences*. New York: St. Martin's.

Smith, N. 1993. Homeless/global: scaling places. In: Bird, J. et al. (eds), *Mapping the Futures: Local Cultures, Global Change*. London: Routledge.

Smith, N. 2000. Scale. In: Johnston, R.J. et al. (eds), *The Dictionary of Human Geography* (4th edn). Oxford: Blackwell.

Sneddon, C. and Fox, C. 2006. Rethinking transboundary waters: A critical hydropolitics of the Mekong basin. *Political Geography*, 25(2), 181–202.

Swyngedouw, E. 1997. Neither global nor local: 'Glocalization' and the politics of scale. In: Cox, K. (ed.), *Spaces of Globalization: Reasserting the Power of the Local*. New York: Guilford.

Swyngedouw, E. 1999. Modernity and hybridity: Nature, *regeneracionismo*, and the production of the Spanish waterscape, 1890–1930. *Annals of the Association of American Geographers*, 89(3), 443–65.

Swyngedouw, E. 2004. *Social Power and the Urbanization of Water: Flows of Power*. New York: Oxford University Press.

Swyngedouw, E. 2005. Governance innovation and the citizen: The Janus face of governance-beyond-the-state. *Urban Studies*, 42(11), 1991–2006.

Swyngedouw, E. 2006. Circulations and metabolisms: (Hybrid) natures and (cyborg) cities. *Science as Culture*, 15(2), 105–21.

Swyngedouw, E. 2007. Technonatural revolutions: The scalar politics of Franco's hydro-social dream for Spain, 1939–1975. *Transactions of the Institute of British Geographers*, 32(1), 9–28.

Swyngedouw, E. 2009. The political economy and political ecology of the hydro-social cycle. *Journal of Contemporary Water Research and Education*, (142), 55–60.

Swyngedouw, E. and Heynen, N. 2003. Urban political ecology, justice and the politics of scale. *Antipode*, 35(5), 898–918.

Vogel, E. 2007. Regionalization and democratization through international law: Intertwined jurisdictions, scales and politics in the Columbia River Treaty *Oregon Review of International Law*, 9, 337–88.

Vogel, E. 2011. Defining the Pacific Northwest during the New Deal: The political construction of a region and 'its' river. *Western Historical Quarterly*, 42(1), 29–53.

Warner, J.F. and Johnson, C.L. 2007. 'Virtual water' – real people: Useful concept or prescriptive tool? *Water International*, 32(1), 63–77.

Wolf, A.T. 1999. 'Water wars' and water reality: Conflict and cooperation along international waterways. In: Lonergan, S. (ed.), *Environmental Change, Adaptation, and Human Security*. Dordrecht: Kluwer Academic.

PART I
Examining Scalar Assumptions: Unpacking the Watershed

Introduction to Part I

François Molle

Although they have been branded for almost two centuries as pre-existing natural units, hydrologically defined areas such as watersheds and river basins have, in the past 20 years, become a popular if not hegemonic water policy icon. This popularity arises, at least in part, from the scale's connection to Integrated Water Resource Management (IWRM), a water management paradigm that promotes integrated water governance at the watershed scale. As a result of their connection to IWRM, watersheds express three distinct sets of values:

1. economic development and efficiency, as allowed by the manipulation of the resource itself and its rationalization through basin hydrology;
2. the harmonization of worldviews and social equity as promoted by the participation of all basin stakeholders;
3. environmental sustainability, believed to be more achievable at the scale of a natural or ecological unit.

These three different conceptual spaces are supposed to be reconciled under the auspices of an integrative concept and a single physical space – the watershed. However, as the chapters in Part I show, the definition, delineation and management of spaces labelled as 'watersheds' is far from straightforward. In Chapter 4 Eve Vogel emphasizes that watersheds eventually are what we make of them, and that the way they are projected as a concept or enacted in the material world reflects the values and interests of its particular promoters. More often than not watersheds are used to promote one particular value at the expense of others (Molle 2008). Indeed, a common theme across the chapters in this section is the tension between the issues and interests that are attached to competing scales: the national, provincial, regional, watershed and so on.

Establishing a layer of governance at the river basin level creates two types of tension. The first pits local interests, whether bureaucratic or private, against the claim to manage the basin's resources in a holistic way for the greater good. The second tension is between the basin constituencies and national or federal levels of government, particularly with respect to how water resources and their benefits should be allocated: i.e., should benefits accrue only to the watershed or should these be dispersed more generally? Each of the chapters addresses these tensions to some degree.

Boundary making, whether related to administrative or other kinds of territorial delineation, is a clear expression of political power. However, not all boundaries have the same weight. In Chapter 2, for example, Alice Cohen uses the case of the province of Alberta, Canada, to compare its Watershed Planning and Advisory Councils with the Land Use Planning regions that have been defined to plan developmental activities, showing the much weaker legislative status of the former as compared to the latter – and therefore the potential for economic values to prevail over environmental ones.

That tensions between local and holistic management paradigms can result in relative political weakness of watersheds is not uncommon. Indeed, wherever a river basin organization or a lighter form of coordination or participatory process is established, the prerogatives of this new layer of governance, unless minimal or cosmetic, is bound to conflict with the existing distribution of administrative and political power (Molle and Hoanh 2011). In many cases such organizations are placed under the aegis of a recently formed Ministry of Environment, itself not a very powerful administration. They are endowed with minimal financial and human resources, and confined to minor tasks – typically water quality monitoring, data compilation, awareness-raising etc. (see for example the case of Morocco in Tanouti and Molle, 2014).

Fierce bureaucratic infighting is bound to happen if basin organizations are placed outside the purview of traditional ministries and made responsible for planning at the basin level. Planning includes decisions on large-scale infrastructure development, and therefore on the allocation of major financial resources that traditionally accrue to line agencies and concerned ministries. This is a scenario that is favoured by what has become a standard policy recommendation of 'modern' water management: the separation of the roles of water resources managers and operators (Millington 2000; Lincklaen Arriëns 2004). The manager is meant to ensure *regulation* of the water sector by setting standards, allocating and monitoring water use; establishing environmental protection rules, coordinating planning and so on. Meanwhile the operators – typically line agencies in charge of hydropower or irrigation – take care of structures or reservoirs according to the rules the managers set. The *regulation* functions are believed to be best decentralized to the river basin level and encapsulated in a river basin organization.

However sound this separation of power may appear – in particular as a means of controlling the often unbridled development of irrigation and hydropower – it is unrealistic in contexts where traditional governmental departments or ministries are historically very powerful and not inclined to be stripped of the major attributes of their power just because external donors or development banks have stated that this would be desirable. In practice, any redistribution of power generates bureaucratic turf battles, especially when the mandates attributed to basin organizations or 'regulators' are not paralleled with modifications of the mandates of other agencies or ministries.

Territorialization is far from being a natural or neutral act, as it defines those who are in and those who are out. Socially constructed and politically contested, territories often end up shaping the identity of the societies and human groups that they encompass. A testimony to, and illustration of, identity building is the strong nationalisms that have materialized in some countries after 50 years of independence, despite their having inherited colonial boundaries that cut across and/or pool various and sometimes antagonistic ethnic groups.If 'watersheds are what we make of them', we are also partly what we make of watersheds.

In Chapter 3 Chris Sneddon and Coleen Fox recall how the Mekong River basin was conjured up during the Cold War as a unit which could allow not only shared material development through hydropower dams and large-scale irrigation but also cooperation of and shared planning by countries which – in the view of Western countries – urgently needed to be welded against the communist threat. The much-heralded 'Mekong spirit' which was supposed to infuse these collaborating efforts may have contributed to constructing a common identity – albeit a fragile one when confronted with national interests – and to institutionalizing the Mekong River basin. Indeed, it is little challenged by countries in the region, which largely subscribe to the developmentalist agenda promoted, for example, by the basin development plan of the Mekong River Commission, which precisely refers to the basin as a 'development space'.

Such transboundary basin-wide development planning often resonates little with local perceptions of the basin and its material processes. Local water territories involve social networks closely knitted with their landscapes and waterscapes on which people's livelihoods often depend (see, for example, Jessica Budds's discussion of hydroscapes in Chapter 12). Yet, as Sneddon and Fox suggest, the somewhat hegemonic scale of the Mekong basin has also spurred a scaling up and regionalization of civil society movements, whether human rights oriented or struggling against dams and environmental degradation. Social activists have gradually moved from local struggles to wider regional articulations that take the basin as a scale of action and organization. This 'scaling up' is a recognition that local environmental transformations and impacts are ultimately the result of decisions and processes unfolding at higher scales; but, as a consequence, they are also unconsciously forced to espouse the rhetoric of the Mekong basin and defend 'Mekong fisheries' on 'Mekong livelihoods' (Friend et al. 2009).

In Chapter 5 Jeroen Warner et al.'s contribution focuses on the politics of scale framing, which deals explicitly with tension between issues and interests attached to different interpretations of a particular scale. Scale frames can be considered as 'sense-making devices for understanding reality and organizing actions' and are therefore infused with considerable interests and ideologies pertaining to particular groups or individuals. Warner et al. join other authors in this book in emphasizing the discursive and political power of those in a position to establish and impose particular boundaries. They provide several examples drawn from the Netherlands which illustrate how such boundaries and scale framings cut across various divides: north–south, upstream–downstream, core–periphery, urban–rural, high income–low income, economy–ecological, Hollanders–Limburgers etc.

Scale framing can reveal these divides and, moreover, can lead to oversimplification (including labelling practices). It can empower certain constituencies or decision-making mechanisms; allocate costs and benefits; apportion risk; ascribe blame to particular groups; frame some policy options as natural or inevitable; and use the windows of opportunities opened by crises or shock events to impose certain logics and choices over others. In other words, and metaphorically speaking, one is either inside the polder or out of it.

The scale-framing game around flood protection in the Netherlands is a 'war of backyards': it is about shifting negative externalities spatially and socially out of your own 'backyard', with the assumption – strengthened by framing the problems as national issues – that some (others) must 'accept a degree of sacrifice for the greater good'. Warner et al. show how different stakeholders try to change scale framing by reinterpreting water problems, zooming in and out from the delta to the polder or from the polder to the transboundary level, focusing on land rather than water, emphasizing multifunctionality beyond flood protection, or particular time frames associated with varied senses of urgency. Eventually, negotiations reveal not only the distribution of discursive and political power, but also different values and perceptions of risk and equity, the 'competing interpretations of fairness appear[ing] to be the key to each of the scale frame conflicts'.

It is fascinating to see, as one 'zooms out' from the local to the basin, how problems and differences fade, human diversity is reduced and groups aggregated; benefits are increasingly seen with a macro-perspective, costs tend to be glossed over and minimized, and the environment seems to become more easily amenable to manipulation. This is partly the case because it is inherent in the vision and functioning of the state to simplify the complexity of the physical and social worlds to make them legible and amenable to change (Scott 1998) and because capital investment is by nature blind to the negative social and environmental externalities it generates. But aggregation is also a result of the difficulty to comprehend and anticipate the sheer complexity of cross-scale interactions associated with the movement of water, salts, pollutants and sediments in river basins. As decisions tend to be taken at the upper level, they invariably end up conflicting – when translated at the local scale – with local interests and perceptions. Even if participatory processes are established to try to bridge the gap, there is an irreconcilable opposition and a contradiction of logics. After all, this is nothing more than the familiar core problems of politics: to allow the cohabitation of, if not to reconcile, private and collective goals and interests.

Another noteworthy aspect of these Dutch examples discussed by Warner et al. is the role of infrastructure as 'an important artefact mediating the relationship between nature and society but also power relations in society'. This is perhaps a banality when one thinks of the debates and conflicts raging around large dams across the world, but may serve to highlight the impacts, especially cumulative, of smaller interventions on the water cycle. Here again scale matters, as a small change in dyke height, river channel width or bottom level can have sheer consequences at the micro-level.

In some other cases, however – as strikingly revealed by Andreas Thiel's case study on the Guadalquivir River basin (Chapter 6) – the material consequences of choosing particular administrative or political boundaries to manage water are hardly assessed or discussed. The ephemeral transfer of management competency from the Spanish federal level (and its *Confederaciónes Hidrográficas* in charge of basin management) to the provincial level of Andalucía highlights the overriding predominance of party politics and vote-winning strategies, as well as the tensions between basin-scale governance and national political agendas. Although Thiel does not make reference to the use of the basin scale – whether natural, neutral or integrative – as a political currency, he illustrates the political and bureaucratic struggles around the control of the particular scale of the Guadalquivir basin.

Another interesting aspect of this re-territorialization of a river basin is the way it runs against the hegemonic imposition of river basin management by the European Union (EU) in its search for 'the right geographical scale … for water management' (EEA 2012). As is well known, the 'Europeanization' of approaches to water management has dictated that member countries should divide their territory in hydrologic units which would serve as a basis for planning interventions in the water sector and achieving 'good ecological status' of water bodies. Even though the Guadalquivir basin is almost fully included in the province of Andalucía (and may therefore challenge the relevance of a management under federal control), this provides an illustration of how national politics can trump wider Europeanization processes, perhaps foreshadowing the emergence of a deeper contestation in coming years, as the uniform measures promoted by the EU – the river basin, but maybe even more significantly the 'economic tools' supposed to assist in restoring good ecological status – are faced with the specificities of each locale and the diversity of the real world.

Speaking to the tensions between local and national interests, Vogel analyses the case of the Columbia River basin in the US and highlights the role of the Bonneville Power Administration in contributing to achieving a better balance of local and regional/national interests. The Columbia River basin illustrates what Vogel calls a 'parcelling out' of the watershed: a mode of management akin to polycentric governance that emphasizes coordination with other agencies and jurisdictions; negotiation with traditional political spaces; parcelling out the benefits to different constituencies; and constant mediation of conflicts.

Although not optimal in terms of environmental sustainability or even economic efficiency, this model is contrasted with two other modes of basin management. The first, epitomized by the Tennessee Valley Authority (TVA), represents unified management under authoritarian control and is seen as maximizing macroeconomic gains, with costs externalized onto poor, rural people and the environment. Yet authoritarian river basin organization cannot durably suppress local powers, whether administrative or otherwise; are subject to multilevel institutional bricolage; and only survive in a much-reduced form. The second model, illustrated by the Connecticut River basin, is typical of institutional failure and fragmentation, with ad hoc and minimal coordination, and goals and benefits fragmented across conventional political territories.

Vogel uses these three cases to state that institutions operating within a river basin geography either must overcome them, succumb to them or negotiate with them. However simplified, this distinction might have prompted a reflection on the diversity of river basin organizations: although transboundary basins, federal and national contexts or smaller watersheds are sometimes conflated and jointly treated as 'river basins' (with 'watershed' having maybe a similar role in a North American context), and despite all of them being the 'home' of a particular stream, these are eventually quite different beasts.

Transboundary basins (like the Mekong) – as suggested by the fact that they are a subject of predilection of political geographers and international relations specialists – emphasize issues of geopolitics, sovereignty, regional competition and broad-scale regulation. Large national basins (like the Guadalquivir or Connecticut) will be more likely to feature issues of inter-provincial allocation, national politics or rural–urban divides. Small watersheds will be the home of much closer interactions between stakeholders and exhibit a much larger array of interests and worldviews. The social component of the socio-ecological system will vary greatly, and although the issues at stake may at first glance look similar, the patterns of social interaction and governance that can be envisaged for each case are quite different.

In other words, if 'watersheds' are all about people managing water, seen through the lens of a conventional modernist paradigm where capital, technology and a benevolent state develop water resources for the common good, we may measure how far the diversity and sheer complexity of socio-ecological systems take us from simplistic technocratic views.

To conclude, one may ponder on the illustrations offered by the chapters in this section of the striking diversity of interests and constituencies that have adopted the basin scale as an arena to engage with other groups and to further their agenda. Engineers and water resource developers take the basin as a design geographical unit to run simulation models and transform a stochastic natural phenomenon into infrastructures and macro-level economic benefits. Environmentalists are allured by its natural and ecological gloss and, when contaminated by neo-classical green economics, believe in its potential to conceive of and distribute positive and negative incentives. Libertarian, social activists or people struggling against the power of the (federal) state see in the alleged promotion of participatory processes at the local scale a promise of deliberative democracy (see also Cohen 2012). By promising to deliver 'all these good things' the river basin is an avatar of IWRM, and another example of what I have elsewhere called Nirvana concepts (Molle 2008). As a result, it fulfils the role of boundary concept around which different interest groups and constituencies sharing a common language can engage and interact. Just like for IWRM, however, particular values embedded in the concept are often picked up and promoted singlehandedly, and the symbolic and discursive value of the concept is hijacked by specific groups. Eventually, however, whether it is favouring a particular view or governance pattern or is a discursive Trojan horse, the river basin/watershed scale does not escape the *tensions of scale* that permeate the exercise of power.

References

Cohen, A. 2012. Watersheds as boundary objects: Scale at the intersection of science, neoliberalism, and participation. *Environment and Planning A*, 44(9), 2207–24.

EC (European Commission). 2006. Introduction to the new EU Water Framework Directive. [Online]. Available at http://ec.europa.eu/environment/water/water-framework/info/intro_en.htm (accessed 24 July 2006).

EEA (European Environmental Agency). 2012. *European Waters: Assessment of Status and Pressure*. Brussels: European Union.

Friend, R., Arthur, R.I. and Keskinen, M. 2009. Songs of the doomed: The continued neglect of capture fisheries in hydropower development in the Mekong. In: F. Molle et al. (eds), *Contested Waterscapes in the Mekong Region: Hydropower, Livelihoods and Governance*. London: Earthscan.

GWP and INBO. 2009. *A Handbook for Integrated Water Resources Management in Basins*. Stockholm/Paris: Global Water Partnership/International Network of Basin Organizations.

Lincklaen Arriëns, W.T. 2004. *ADB's Water Policy and the Needs for National Water Sector Apex Bodies*. Manila: Asian Development Bank.

Millington, P. 2000. *River Basin Management: Its Role in Major Water Infrastructure Projects*. Thematic Review V.3. Cape Town: World Commission on Dams.

Molle, F. 2008. Nirvana concepts, narratives and policy models: Insight from the water sector. *Water Alternatives*, 1(1), 131–56.

Molle, F. and Hoanh, C.T. 2011. Implementing integrated river basin management in the Red River basin, Vietnam: A solution looking for a problem? *Water Policy*, 13(4), 518–34.

Scott, J. 1998. *Seeing Like a State: How Certain Schemes to Improve the Human Condition Have Failed*. New Haven: Yale University Press.

Tanouti, O. and Molle, F. 2014. Surexploitation et réappropriation de l'eau dans le bassin du Tensift (Maroc). *Etudes Rurales*, 192.

UNESCO. 2009. *IWRM Guidelines at River Basin Level – Part 1: Principles*. Paris: UNESCO.

Chapter 2
Nature's Scales?
Watersheds as a Link between
Water Governance and the Politics of Scale

Alice Cohen

What insights can be gained by looking at water governance through a scalar lens, and by looking at scale through a water lens? This chapter grapples with the book's overarching questions about what the scalar literature and water governance literature have to offer one another, suggesting that the answer to both questions relates to the politics of scale. As such, it explores the ways in which boundaries used to delineate water governance boundaries – in particular, watershed boundaries – function as political boundaries.

Watersheds are most commonly defined as areas of land that drain into a common body of water such as a lake or river. They are typically framed as the 'best' scale at which to carry out water governance activities (e.g. GWP and INBO 2009; Mitchell 1990; Montgomery et al. 1995; Parkes et al. 2010). This framing is grounded in a number of (often implicit) assumptions or assertions. The first of these is the assumption that, by governing water on a watershed basis, all upstream and downstream factors will be accounted for – thereby leading to better environmental outcomes (e.g. Vogel 2012). A second assumption is that the public is more likely to relate to and participate in governance initiatives undertaken at a watershed scale; that is, that watersheds are more conducive to public participation than their jurisdictional counterparts (Blomquist and Schlager 2005; Griffin 1999; Sabatier et al. 2005). Third, watersheds are promoted on the basis that, because they cut across conventional jurisdictional boundaries, they will compel actors from different jurisdictions to cooperate with one another in order to meet watershed-scale targets (Cohen and Davidson 2011; Vogel 2012).

Yet, as human geographers have been demonstrating for decades, spatial scales can be constructed. State or municipal boundaries, for example, are not pre-given units, but are in a constant state of evolution that reflects social contestation and political struggle. More recently, geography scholarship has extended the constructivist perspective to spaces typically framed as 'natural', such as watersheds, ecosystems and so on (Biro 2007; Blomquist and Schlager 2005; Cohen and Davidson 2011; Cohen 2012; Fall 2002; Norman and Bakker 2009; Swyngedouw 1999, 2003). It is the goal of this chapter, then, to parse the ways in which watersheds can serve as a concept on which two primary questions of this book pivot – that is, what can scale debates learn from water governance and what can water governance learn from the scale debates? In so doing, I suggest that there are three ways in which watersheds serve as a fulcrum on which water governance and the politics of scale are balanced. First, watersheds are materially, discursively and conceptually constructed. Second, this construction has political consequences in the sense that rescaling produces new sets of 'winners' and 'losers', and is often politically driven – i.e., by policy, legislation, and so on. And third, watersheds become political when their boundaries are conflated with the tools of governance; that is, that when a set of hydrologic boundaries (namely, watershed boundaries) become synonymous with participation, integration, decentralization or other governance concepts the boundaries can become politicized. Each of these channels linking water and the politics of scale are explored below.

Construction in Action: Watersheds as Spatial, Ecological and Social Scales

The first of these moments is scalar construction. As is pointed out elsewhere (e.g. Biro 2007; Norman and Bakker 2009; Warner et al 2008; Wester and Warner 2002), watersheds – like all scales – are constructed. Critical scholarship on scale points out that scales (of all kinds) are not pre-given, but are constructed and re-constructed through power struggles, discourses and social contestation (e.g. Cox 1996; Delaney and Leitner 1997; Smith 1992; Swyngedouw 1997). Just as scales are constructed through power struggle and social contestation, Whitehead et al. (2007: 14) suggest that states and nature, too, are in a constant evolution, dependent on each other through 'complex system[s] of mutual co-evolution'. That is, just as the materialities of space shape state structure and function, states shape nature – at least in part – through the territorialization (and re-territorialization) of space. In other words, states influence how we conceive of, manage and understand natural spaces and processes through – among other things – boundary drawing and the rescaling of governance processes.

Here, Erik Swyngedouw's insights into the production of scale are especially useful. Swyngedouw summarizes the following points about the social and material production of scale. First, all scales are 'always already a result of' the perpetual evolution of scales and spaces. As such, 'spatial scales are never fixed', but are in a constant state of definition and redefinition. This constant state of flux means that the question of process – that is, the 'mechanisms of scale transformation through social conflict and political-economic struggle' – are central to understanding the ways in which scales get (re)configured (Swyngedouw 2004: 132–4). Most importantly to the constructionist approach used here, Swyngedouw asserts that:

> The condition of everyday life resides in the twin condition of the essential transformation of nature (place) on the one hand and socio-spatial relations through which this transformation is organized and controlled on the other. (ibid.: 134)

With this perspective in mind, it is clear that watersheds are constructed scales, both in the sense that we are physically changing flow regimes through the construction of infrastructure such as municipal supply pipes, ditches for irrigation and drainage, hydropower infrastructure etc. (Blomquist and Schlager 2005) and through the political construction of new governance spaces through, for example, policy discourse, mapping practices and funding arrangements. This chapter (and volume) is primarily concerned with the latter form of construction, and emphasizes the constructedness of watersheds and the politics involved in this construction.

The constructivist perspective on watersheds is not a new idea. Andrew Biro, for example, discusses how certain ideas of the 'natural' – in the form of bioregions such as watersheds – are both reflected and deployed in the projects of regional and national identities, arguing that 'Naturalized scales such as watersheds are the product of political contestation and struggle. Just as national identity can be deconstructed and denaturalized but not entirely done away with, so too can bioregions' (Biro 2007: 26). Norman and Bakker examine the move towards the increasingly popular 'watershed approach' with a view to assessing the degree to which local actors have been empowered by – and, relatedly, the degree to which national governments have lost power through – rescaling to the watershed along the Canada–US border. They find that 'although rescaling of transboundary water governance has occurred (i.e., local actors are increasingly present in transboundary governance), greater empowerment (specifically defined as institutional capacity) for local actors has not resulted' (Norman and Bakker 2009: 111). Most relevant to the arguments in this volume, they have put forward the hypothesis that 'all scales are socially constructed' – even apparently 'natural' scales such as the watershed (2009: 112).

Indeed, the interplay between the perceived 'naturalness' of watersheds and their construction constitutes an active discussion in the governance literature. As Blomquist and Schlager note (2005: 103): 'The argument for organizing management around watersheds rests partly on the premise that watersheds are phenomena that exist "out there" in the "real world".' In other words, 'because river basins appear to be well-bounded by what seem to be "natural boundaries", it would seem they are removed from the arbitrariness and mutability of boundaries drawn by humans' (Blomquist and Schlager 2005 in Warner et al. 2008: 123).

Indeed, I suggest here that watersheds have been discursively and materially constructed simultaneously as spatial, ecological and social scales, and explore each of these constructions below.

Watersheds as Spatial Scales

As Cash et al. (2006: 3) point out, there are at least seven different types of scale:

1. spatial (from 'patches' to the globe)
2. temporal (from daily to annual)
3. jurisdictional (from local to inter-governmental)

4. institutional (from operating rules to constitutions)
5. management (from tasks to strategies)
6. networks (from family to trans-society)
7. knowledge (from the specific and contextual to the general and universal).

Smith's definition of geographic scale – 'the dimensions of specific landscapes' (2000: 725) – is narrower, but inclusive of almost any conceivable dimension within rubric of nature–society relations. The broadness of these definitions highlights the importance of defining which *kind* of scale is being discussed. I argue that watersheds serve as (at least) three kinds of scale.

The first of these is spatial: that is, watersheds occupy a physical space. Of course, this space is shared with and overlaps with many other built and 'natural' features such as buildings, cities, migratory paths, private property and so on. Importantly, the key distinction between water and water*sheds* is that the latter includes land. Indeed, as Savenije and van de Zaag (2000) note in the case of international transboundary relations, the UN Convention on the Law of Non-Navigational Uses of International Watercourses (1997) chose not to adopt the land-inclusive language found in the Helsinki Rules on the Uses of the Waters of International Rivers (1966), which define watercourses as inclusive of land:

> Most states prefer to use the term watercourse rather than river basin, since the latter concept comprises land areas which are also governed by administrative, land use and other laws. Letting land areas be governed by a water law might lead to legal complexities. (Savenije and van de Zaag 2000: 23)

As such, the very act of delineating watersheds is an act which parcels off a particular physical, hydrologically defined space – a specific area of land – and labels it as a watershed. Moreover, watersheds can be materially constructed through the use of water-related infrastructure such as dams, irrigation channels and other types of physical modification. Thus, watersheds are 'created' not only through discursive tools such as cartography, policy discourse and financial restructuring (i.e., the creation of and financial support for watershed-scale governance institutions), but also through physical and material structures that (re)direct the flow of water.

Watersheds as Ecological Scales

Second, watersheds are ecological scales. That is, unlike most jurisdictional boundaries or property boundaries, watersheds are defined (at least to some extent) by hydrologic flow. Importantly, hydrologic flow is not the only form of natural boundary. Omernik and Bailey (1997), for example, make distinctions between watersheds and ecosystems. Similar arguments have been made about the incongruence between watersheds and airsheds (Jaworski et al. 1997; Paerl et al. 2002), as well as watersheds and groundwater flow (Winter et al. 2003). Moreover, assertions about the importance of ecological scales continue to be made in the watershed context despite frequent disagreement about what constitutes a natural boundary. Meyer and Swank (1996), for example, cite conflicting suggestions for ecologically defined boundaries within the same area: one uses the boundaries associated with benthic invertebrate communities inhabiting a particular set of stream habitats, while the other uses the boundaries of particular plant communities.

Scientific disagreement can also arise within a singular level of government. For example, the United States Geological Survey (USGS) notes that 'while watershed boundaries identify surface-water runoff divides, they often do not represent ground-water flow divides' (USGS 2008). This observation from the USGS is at odds with the United States Environmental Protection Agency's description of a watershed as a 'bounded hydrologic system' (US EPA 2012). Indeed, as Griffin (1999: 509) notes, 'the use of watersheds erroneously assumes that all biotic and abiotic factors are similarly organized'. The key point here is that, in addition to being physical spaces, watersheds are often framed as ecosystem spaces because of their basis in hydrologic reality.

Watersheds as Social Scales

Finally, watersheds are a social scale. A wide range of watershed governance structures exists: from those that are strictly voluntary and operate without any legislative basis or governmental funding, to those that are created through national, provincial or state governments legislation and funded accordingly. Of course, not all watersheds have an associated governance structure, but for those that do, watersheds are a social scale as well. In other words, networks of relationships and hierarchies of power exist in relation to the physical and ecological space as discussed above.

The argument that watersheds are spatial, ecological and social scales is not simply a semantic clarification. As explicated below, the conflation of these three scales, the promotion of one at the expense of the others and the 'branding' of watersheds as natural all play an important role in the politics of scale. Indeed, Jamie Linton's (2010) statement on water seems particularly apt here. In response to the question 'What is water?' he replies that 'water is what we make of it'. Similarly, the types of boundaries and scales we emphasize or de-emphasize through discourses and public debates mean that watersheds are 'what we make of them'.

Watersheds and the Politics of Scale

How, then, do constructed watersheds act as a link between politics of scale and water governance? Using examples from rescaled water governance in Alberta, Canada, I explore below instances in which scales are enacted as political.[1]

---

1   A more detailed exploration of this case study was published in Cohen and Bakker (2014).

One example from the Canadian province of Alberta shows this phenomenon at work. Here, two slightly different interpretations of what constitutes a watershed boundary exist, each with a different purpose. In the first instance Alberta is divided into 12 watersheds under the province's Water for Life policy introduced in 2003 and renewed in 2008. These 12 watersheds are each overseen by their own Watershed Planning and Advisory Council (WPAC). WPACs are designated as non-profit organizations and have a mandate to assess watershed conditions, prepare plans to address watershed issues, and conduct education and stewardship activities within their respective watersheds (Government of Alberta 2011). WPACs have a mandate to write 'State of the Basin' reports which, as the name suggests, report on water quality and availability in the watershed. State of the Basin reports also include recommendations that can (but importantly, need not) be implemented by government with jurisdiction over the issue in question.

In a separate process, Alberta introduced the Land Use Planning Act in 2009. This legislation is intended to 'manage growth, not stop it, and to sustain [Alberta's] growing economy, but balance this with Albertans' social and environmental goals' (Government of Alberta 2008a: 2). To meet this goal, the Act divides the province into seven Land Use Planning regions, each governed by a Regional Advisory Council (RAC). The boundaries of these regions are 'based on the major watersheds, with boundaries aligned to best fit with existing municipal boundaries and natural regions' (Government of Alberta 2008a: 24). The RACs are responsible for the creation of land use plans within their regions; after cabinet approval, these regional plans are legislative instruments (Land Stewardship Act, s.13(1))[2] and can serve as umbrella regulations under which municipal plans and WPAC activities fall. In other words, land use RACs are legislatively superior to the WPACs: RAC recommendations have the weight of legislative authority, while WPACs remain classified as not-for-profit organizations and their authority remains limited.

As such, and as shown in Figure 2.1, there are now two sets of watershed boundaries in present-day Alberta: one drawn within a hydrologic and stewardship-based framework, and another drawn with explicit recognition of existing municipal boundaries with a legal mandate to carry out land use planning on social, economic and ecological bases. The Alberta case thus presents an example of conscious and deliberate delineation of natural boundaries, emphasizing Blomquist and Schlager's point (2005: 105) that boundary definition is 'a supremely political act' that leads to the inclusion or exclusion of particular actors or issues, and prioritizes some factors over others.

The different levels of authority conferred on these two different watershed-based spaces are important to understanding the politics of scale in this particular case. While WPAC mandates are specific to water and stewardship, RACs are legislatively empowered to make land use planning decisions on the basis of 'a healthy economy, healthy ecosystem and environment, and people-

---

2   Alberta Land Stewardship Act, SA 2009, c A-26.8.

Figure 2.1   Alberta's watershed boundaries

friendly communities' (Government of Alberta 2008a). Although it is too early to say how the two policies will play out in relation to one another, legislative structures associated with these spaces set the scene for potential prioritization of the economic over the environmental by imbuing the RACs (with their three-part mandate) with legislative authority and classifying the WPACs (with an environmental stewardship mandate) as not-for-profit organizations subordinate to the RACs. The different levels of authority at these two iterations of the watershed speak not only to the political implications of the legislative setup, but also to scalar scholarship. Specifically, the findings here reflect McCarthy's (2005) observation that the politics of scale is not only about the relationship *between* scales (although this is certainly important), but also about the power dynamics *within* them.

Moreover, and most relevant to the other chapters in this volume, this example shows how watershed delineation may begin as the construction of a spatial scale through the cordoning off of particular areas of land labelled as 'the watershed', but can evolve into a social scale through the assigning of particular governance structures and functions to these 'new' boundaries. In the Alberta example, new governance organizations with new responsibilities were created at each of the new spatial scales, thus also leading to the construction of new social and political scales associated with the watersheds' boundaries.

The creation of new social and spatial scales through the delineation of watersheds is not simply a point about semantics or the many and varied ways in which the watershed boundaries are difficult to define, both technically and socially. More than that, watershed boundaries are intensely political. They draw a line between who and what is 'in' or 'out', and the kinds of decision-making authorities and power assigned to social organizations affiliated with watershed boundaries further intensify the political ramifications of boundary-drawing.

Here, 'politics' refers not to the 'big P' politics of elections, parties and so on, but rather to the distribution patterns of costs and benefits of particular forms of social relationships. In this sense, all scalar constructions have political outcomes in that when a boundary is drawn, some actors and ecological features are located inside the boundary and others are outside it. Although this may seem overly simplistic, an example building on the Alberta case demonstrates the far-reaching implications of this kind of construction.

As discussed above, two different types of watershed boundaries have been constructed in Alberta: one set that divides the province into 12 water stewardship organizations and another that divides the province into seven land use planning units. The mandates for these two sets of boundaries are radically different: The former has a mandate that relates primarily to stewardship, while the latter has significant regulatory powers. As Cohen and Bakker argue, these two sets of re-territorialization have had the effect of creating power structures that prioritize the economic over the environmental. This is so for two interrelated reasons: RACs are legislatively superior to WPACs and RACs have a mandate to consider the economic, environmental and social, while WPAC mandates are restricted to water. These factors are further compounded by the way in which WPAC and RAC members are chosen, and the role of each organization:

> Compounding these factors is the issue that the provincial government handpicks RAC members. Citizens concerned with the negative environmental effects of heavy irrigation in the south or rapid energy development in the north can join a WPAC (which has no regulatory authority), or plead their case to their municipality, which is now under the umbrella of the legislatively powerful RAC. Interestingly, neither the RACs nor the WPACs are electorally accountable, as citizens do not vote along ecosystem boundaries. None of these points are to argue that there is anything normatively wrong with empowering one scale over another (indeed, it would be impossible not to), but we discuss them here in order to highlight some of the deeply political consequences of re-territorializing state spaces and redesigning power relationships accordingly. (Cohen and Bakker, 2014)

Another way in which the politics of scale matter to the way water governance is conceived of and carried out relates to the power and impact of discursive framings. Kaiser and Nikiforova (2008), for example, helpfully engage with debates about the utility and ontological status of the concept of scale in critical geography in the following way. They suggest that ongoing disagreement in the critical geography community over the reification, ontological status (Marston et al. 2005 and others) or investigative utility (Jessop 2009) of scales are perhaps misplaced. That is, they argue that the question of whether or not scales – whether ecological, social, legislative or any other type – exist in any real or material sense is perhaps less important than whether or not we behave as though they do.

Drawing on the case of the city of Narva, Estonia, on the Estonia–Russia political border, Kaiser and Nikiforova (2008: 545) show how citational practices such as map-drawing, city statues and public discourse have been used for centuries to inculcate, variously, 'Narvan-ness, Estonian-ness, Russian-ness, European-ness, Western-ness, and Eastern-ness'. From Swedish rule through the sixteenth–eighteenth centuries to the incorporation of Estonia (and Narva) into the USSR following World War II and the Soviet era, through to the establishment of Estonia as an independent state and its more recent incorporation into the European Union in 2004, Narva has been the site of ongoing changes in iterative and citational practices that define scale effects.

The construction of monuments, borders (and their associated infrastructure), texts and so on that depict Narva as being of one identity or another are examples of the kinds of practices that produce the *effect* of scale. That is, that while the city of Narva stayed more or less stationary, it was incorporated into various political identities through reiterative practices affirming its 'new' identity time and time again. Using this example, Kaiser and Nikiforova (2008: 543) argue that 'instead of treating scales as things in the world that (inter)act … performativity approaches scale as a naturalized way of seeing the world, and explores the enacted discourses that over time work to produce "scale effects". Their work informs the arguments made in this chapter (and volume) by moving beyond the question of whether or not watersheds exist in an ontological sense to looking at what *effects* their politicization – in the sense that what were once 'simple' topographical lines are now decision-making spaces – has had.

This approach – that is, looking at the *effects* of particular scales – sheds new light on the politics of scale, and of watersheds in particular. Recent work, for example, explores the practices through which the watershed scale is produced as 'natural' and pre-given, arguing that this has two effects. First, it establishes watershed governance as a technical exercise rather than a political one; and second, it serves to entrench a focus on 'nature' such that activities undertaken at a watershed scale are framed as primarily having to do with nature rather than with politics or human activity – the human/nature binary effect (Cohen and Harris 2014).

Cohen and Harris show how these claims are borne out by looking at the Alberta example, where both the effects of labelling watersheds as natural are evident. The 'technical' effect can be seen, for example, in the official mandate of the province's WPAC organizations, which are charged with crafting 'state of the watershed' reports, described as follows:

A state of the watershed report is the *scientific* interpretation of watershed information and data, leading to conclusions about watershed condition; an *objective tool* that uses available data and information to assess conditions and concerns within a watershed, as well as identify information gaps. (Government of Alberta 2008b: 3–4; emphasis added)

In the above quote it is suggested that watershed governance can be reduced to a largely technical exercise. Although it is true that many stakeholders are involved in crafting 'state of the basin' reports and identifying priority areas, the mandate to create scientific and objective reports articulates with watersheds' ongoing framing as natural and the associated assumption that nature can be objectively quantified and measured. The human/nature binary effect also plays out in Alberta, where watersheds' 'naturalness' plays into the roles of the two different types of watershed boundary. In the case of WPACs, these organizations are described as:

> important *stewards* of Alberta's major watersheds. They are independent, non-profit organizations that are designated by Alberta Environment to assess the condition of their watershed and prepare plans to address watershed issues. They also conduct *education and stewardship activities* throughout their watershed. (Government of Alberta 2011; emphasis added)

Yet the RACs, with a land use planning mandate, are charged with overseeing activities that have a decidedly more 'human' element. In other words, when watersheds are framed as natural it becomes easier to assign to their associated governance bodies responsibilities that focus on nature, such as stream cleanups or outreach and education, rather than on the messier – and arguably more effective – tasks relating to human activity such as zoning, resource development and so on (Cohen and Harris 2014).

Moreover, making discursive recourse to the naturalness of watershed boundaries can have the effect of both de- and re-politicizing environmental decision-making (Cohen and Bakker 2014). As Warner et al. (2008: 123–4) explain: 'by presenting [watersheds] as natural, they acquire a supernatural, untouchable, legitimacy. Current water policy, then, works to depoliticize important issues of scale and voice and may prematurely close very necessary debates on appropriate institutional arrangements for river basin management.' Indeed, as Cohen and Harris (2014) note, teasing apart the natural as the key characteristic of watersheds may be doing a disservice to governance initiated at this 'new' scale by silently and implicitly removing the more human elements of resource governance. These human elements, such as zoning bylaws, municipal water and wastewater infrastructure, transportation networks and so on can have an arguably greater impact on water quality and availability than efforts focused exclusively on 'stewardship', yet their conceptual situation outside of watershed planning and management precludes their inclusion in these 'water first' organizations.

Indeed, the bifurcation of the 'social' from the 'natural' is described by Cohen and Bakker (2014) as consistent with the two-pronged character of rescaled water governance: watershed scale governance is often promoted on the grounds that it is a scientific and apolitical move that makes good ecological sense, while the effects of this particular form of rescaling are often political in the sense that they create new winners and losers. Cohen and Bakker argue that although rescaling often seeks to de-politicize environmental governance, it may (often inadvertently) *re*-politicize environmental issues by shifting responsibility or authority to non-governmental actors, or by promoting environmental stewardship at the cost of de-emphasizing human–environment connections.

Watersheds as Distinct from Governance Tools

A third way in which watersheds demonstrate the connections between water governance and scale is their conflation with particular governance tools – namely, integration, participation and decentralization. Cohen and Davidson suggest that this conflation has occurred through the adoption of watersheds into the rubric of Integrated Water Resource Management (IWRM) in the following way:

> The adoption of international IWRM water dialogues by regional, national, and sub-national government agencies and water policy planners appear to have been fixated on watershed boundaries. Rather than as an arm of IWRM or a technical tool (as framed by IWRM's antecedents), watersheds were recast as frameworks; the watershed approach became an umbrella under which other features of IWRM, such as participation and integration, fell. (2011: 7)

This conflation between watershed boundaries, IWRM and other components of the water governance landscape is also discussed at length in the water governance literature. For example, Warner et al. (2008) discuss the 'holy trinity' of multi-stakeholder platforms, IWRM and the basin scale, and Molle (2008: 132) cites IWRM as a prime example of what he calls a 'nirvana concept': one that embodies an 'ideal image of what the world should tend to'. Here, Molle argues that IWRM acts as a 'photo negative' of the real world; as a concept that lives as the imagined opposite to the current problems plaguing water governance arrangements. In this view, rescaling to watersheds is very much a nirvana concept, particularly with respect to their putative ability to integrate, in a single physical space, the many and varied factors that have impacts on water-related decision-making.

Fragmented governance is a often a target of complaints: that water governance mandates are often split between various levels of government – as well as between ministries or departments *within* a level of government (Bakker and Cook 2011) – is frequently cited as a key barrier to effective environmental (and water) governance, especially in the Canadian case (Harrison 1996; Hill and Harrison 2006; Weibust 2009). Given the challenge that governance fragmentation poses to water governance, is it unsurprising that a framework promoting 'integration' is welcomed. The same might be argued for more normative perspectives on watersheds: they are often seen as 'more democratic' than their jurisdictional counterparts. Although the claim here is that more localized and participatory forms of decision-making are more democratic, the opposite assumption is that current jurisdictional scales and command-and-control styles of regulation are *less* democratic, although this latter point is rarely drawn out and made explicit.

Indeed, the local-ness with which watersheds are often imbued is another way in which watershed boundaries are political. Although watersheds are both a form of decentralization (i.e., a scaling down from national or provincial governments) and a form of centralization (a scaling up from municipal boundaries), they are most often framed as a form of decentralization and are frequently conflated with the local scale (however defined). Through the repeated citations reaffirming watersheds as local and decentralized, watersheds become imbued with those attributes typically associated with those scales – for example, participation, local 'buy in' and so on. One of the effects of the conflation is a coalescing of support around rescaling for political reasons. For example, previous work has shown how proponents of grassroots, bottom-up governance – as well as advocates of more neoliberal, 'small government' types of governance arrangements and members of the scientific community – have all rallied around the concept of watersheds, but for radically different reasons (see Cohen 2012).

This conflation of physical space with governance tools thus speaks directly to questions about the politics of scale. Especially in the case of rescaling to watersheds, where boundaries are often framed as 'natural' and therefore *a*political (Wester and Warner 2002), the fact that rescaling has political outcomes (Cohen and Bakker 2014) brings the politics of scale into greater relief. Going back to the Alberta example, the differential powers associated with the watershed boundaries under Water for Life as opposed to the Land Use Planning Framework exemplify the different kinds of governance tools that can be associated with the term 'watershed'. In this case, the former (i.e., WPACs) have organizational responsibility commensurate with their status as not-for-profit organizations, and the latter (RACs) have authority superior to the municipalities within their boundaries. This is not to say that one model is normatively 'better' than the other, but to point out that a given set of boundaries does not have an unquestioned set of governance structures associated with it. Nevertheless, the watershed (and its boundaries) continues to be touted as a scale with which certain governance characteristics – particularly those associated with putatively 'good governance', such as transparency, accountability, inclusivity and so on – are associated.

Conclusions

This chapter started by asking what insights can be gained by looking at water governance through a scalar lens, and by looking at scale through a water lens. In response, I propose three answers. First, by focusing on *construction* as a nexus between the two fields, I join others in suggesting that watersheds are social constructions. I emphasize here that I am not implying that hydrologic flows do not exist (of course they do), but rather that the boundaries that are chosen, the social groups and political powers created by the politicization of these boundaries, and the effects of producing 'insiders' and 'outsiders' are all a result of converting particular hydrologic features into decision-making boundaries. This theme runs through much of the scholarship in this volume (see Chapters 4 and 12) and informs the water governance community by making explicit the role that scale plays in decision-making structures and outcomes. Moreover, it also informs debates about scale in geography by providing an example of the ways in which particular boundaries (in this case hydrologic ones) can have different meanings over time.

Second, the water governance example from Alberta highlights the ways in which watersheds can be political: by reinforcing nature/society binaries and by being associated with decision-making groups with varying levels of legislative authority.

Third, discussion in this chapter (and elsewhere in this volume) shows that looking at scale through a 'water lens' lends a degree of materiality to concepts that are often abstract. Since the 'borderlessness' of water is one of the main drivers for governance at watershed scales (Cohen 2012) – i.e., since it can be difficult to manage water exclusively within the confines of political jurisdictions due to its physical properties of cyclical flow – water is arguably one of the most fruitful lenses through which we can explore the construction (and reconstruction) of scales and spaces. In other words, the physical realities of water have made the substance a primary vector through which various levels of government have introduced spatial innovations to governance structures and processes.

Watersheds, then, can serve as a conceptually useful bridge between scalar scholarship and the practicalities of water governance. Through efforts to conduct water governance in more effective ways at ecologically meaningful scales, watersheds have been promoted for decades as the 'natural' scale at which to carry out water governance initiatives. The remaining chapters in this section help to explore how these constructions have shaped environmental management practices, and vice versa.

References

Bakker, K. 2007. The 'commons' versus the 'commodity': Alter-globalization, anti-privatization and the human right to water in the global south. *Antipode* 39(3): 430–55.

Bakker, K. and C. Cook. 2011. Water governance in Canada: Innovation and fragmentation. *International Journal of Water Resources Development* 27(2): 275–89.

Biro, A. 2007. Water politics and the construction of scale. *Studies in Political Economy* 80: 9–30.

Blomquist, W. and E. Schlager. 2005. Political pitfalls of integrated watershed management. *Society and Natural Resources* 18(2): 101–17.

Cash, D. et al. 2006. Scale and cross-scale dynamics: Governance and information in a multilevel world. *Ecology and Society* 11(2): 8.

Cohen, A. 2012. Rescaling environmental governance: Watersheds as boundary objects at the intersection of science, neoliberalism, and participation. *Environment and Planning A* 44(9): 2207–24.

Cohen, A. 2011. From water to watershed: An analysis of rescaled water governance in Canada. PhD thesis, University of British Columbia.

Cohen, A. and K. Bakker. 2014. The eco-scalar fix: rescaling environmental governance and the politics of ecological boundaries in Alberta, Canada. *Environment and Planning D* 32(1): 128–46.

Cohen, A., and S. Davidson. 2011. The watershed approach: Challenges, antecedents, and the transition from technical tool to governance unit. *Water Alternatives* 4(1): 1–14.

Cohen, A. and L. Harris. 2014. Performing scale: Watersheds as 'natural' governance units in the Canadian context. In *Performativity, Politics, and the Production of Social Space*, eds M. Glass and R. Rose-Redwood. New York: Routledge.

Cox, K.R. 1996. The difference that scale makes. *Political Geography* 15(8): 667–9.

Delaney, D. and H. Leitner. 1997. The political construction of scale. *Political Geography* 16(2): 93–7.

Fall, J. 2002. Divide and rule: Constructing human boundaries in 'boundless nature'. *GeoJournal* 58(4): 243–51.

Government of Alberta. 2008a. *Land Use Framework*. https://landuse.alberta.ca/PlanforAlberta/LanduseFramework/Pages/default.aspx.

———. 2008b. *Handbook for State of the Watershed Reporting: A Guide for Developing State of the Watershed Reports in Alberta*. http://www.landstewardship.org/media/uploads/Handbook_for_State_of_the_Watershed_Reporting_Nov2008.pdf.

———. 2011. *Watershed Planning and Advisory Councils (WPACs): Water for Life*. http://www.waterforlife.alberta.ca/01261.html.

Griffin, C.B. 1999. Watershed councils: An emerging form of public participation in natural resource management. *Journal of the American Water Resources Association* 35(3): 505–18.

GWP and INBO. 2009. *A Handbook for Integrated Water Resources Management in Basins*. Stockholm/Paris: Global Water Partnership/International Network of Basin Organizations.

Harrison, K. 1996. *Passing the Buck: Federalism and Canadian Environmental Policy*. Vancouver: University of British Columbia Press.

Hill, C. and K. Harrison. 2006. Intergovernmental regulation and municipal drinking water. In *Rules, Rules, Rules, Rules: Multilevel Regulatory Governance*, eds G.B. Doern and R. Johnson. Toronto: University of Toronto Press.

Jaworski, N.A., R.W. Howarth and L.J. Hetling. 1997. Atmospheric deposition of nitrogen oxides onto the landscape contributes to coastal eutrophication in the northeast United States. *Environmental Science and Technology* 31(7): 1995–2004.

Jessop, B. 2009. Avoiding traps, rescaling states, governing Europe. In *Leviathan Undone? Towards a Political Economy of Scale*, eds R. Keil and R. Mahon, 87–104. Vancouver: University of British Columbia Press.

Kaiser, R. and E. Nikiforova. 2008. The performativity of scale: The social construction of scale effects in Narva, Estonia. *Environment and Planning D* 26(3): 537–62.

Linton, J. 2010. *What Is Water? The History of a Modern Abstraction*. Vancouver: University of British Columbia Press.

Marston, S.A., J.P. Jones and K. Woodward. 2005. Human geography without scale. *Transactions of the Institute of British Geographers* 30(4): 416–32.

McCarthy, J. 2005. Scale, sovereignty and strategy in environmental governance. *Antipode* 37(4): 327–41.

Meyer, J.L. and W.T. Swank. 1996. Ecosystem management challenges ecologists. *Ecological Applications* 6(3): 738–40.

Mitchell, B. 1990. *Integrated Water Management: International Experiences and Perspectives*. London: Belhaven.

Molle, F. 2008. Nirvana concepts, narratives and policy models: Insights from the water sector. *Water Alternatives* 1(1): 131–56.

Montgomery, D.R., G.E. Grant and K. Sullivan. 1995. Watershed analysis as a framework for implementing ecosystem management. *Journal of the American Water Resources Association* 31(3): 369–86.

Norman, E.S. and K. Bakker. 2009. Transgressing scales: Water governance across the Canada–U.S. borderland. *Annals of the Association of American Geographers* 99(1): 99–117.

Omernik, J.M. and R.G. Bailey. 1997. Distinguishing between watersheds and ecoregions. *Journal of the American Water Resources Association* 33(5): 935–49.

Paerl, H.W., R.L. Dennis and D.R. Whitall. 2002. Atmospheric deposition of nitrogen: Implications for nutrient over-enrichment of coastal waters. *Estuaries* 25(4): 677–93.

Parkes, M.W. et al. 2010. Towards integrated governance for water, health and social-ecological systems: The watershed governance prism. *Global Environmental Change* 20(4): 693–704.

Sabatier, P.A., W. Focht, M. Lubell, Z. Trachtenberg, A. Vedlitz and M. Matlock, eds 2005. *Swimming Upstream: Collaborative Approaches to Watershed Management*. Cambridge, MA: MIT Press.

Savenije, H.H.G. and P. van der Zaag. 2000. Conceptual framework for the management of shared river basins; with special reference to the SADC and EU. *Water Policy* 2(1): 9–45.

Smith, N. 2000. Scale. In *The Dictionary of Human Geography* (4th edn), eds R.J. Johnston, D. Gregory, G. Pratt and M. Watts. Oxford: Blackwell.

Smith, N. 1992. Geography, difference and the politics of scale. In *Postmodernism and the Social Sciences*, eds J. Doherty, E. Graham and M. Malek, 57–79. New York: St. Martin's.

Swyngedouw, E. 1997. Excluding the other: the production of scale and scaled politics. In *Geographies of Economies*, eds. R. Lee and Wills, 167–176. London: Arnold.

————. 1999. Modernity and Hybridity: Nature, Regeneracionismo, and the Production of the Spanish Waterscape, 1890–1930. *Annals of the Association of American Geographers* 89 (3): 443–65.

————. 2003. Modernity and the production of the Spanish waterscape, 1890–1930. In *Political Ecology: An Integrative Approach to Geography and Environment-Development Studies*, eds K.S. Zimmerer and T. Bassett, 94–112. New York: Guilford.

————. 2004. Scaled geographies: Nature, place, and the politics of scale. In *Scale and Geographic Inquiry: Nature, Society, and Method*, eds E. Sheppard and R. McMaster, 129–52. Malden, MA: Blackwell.

US EPA (United States Environmental Protection Agency). 2012. What is a watershed? http://water.epa.gov/type/watersheds/whatis.cfm.

USGS (United States Geological Survey). 2008. *Introduction to Watershed Boundaries*. http://wa.water.usgs.gov/projects/wria01/wb_intro.htm.

Vogel, E. 2012. Parcelling out the watershed: The recurring consequences of organising Columbia River management within a basin-based territory. *Water Alternatives* 5(1): 161–90.

Warner, J., P. Wester and A. Bolding. 2008. Going with the flow: River basins as the natural units for water management? *Water Policy* 10(S2): 121–38.

Weibust, I. 2009. *Green Leviathan: The Case for a Federal Role in Environmental Policy*. Farnham: Ashgate.

Wester, P. and J. Warner. 2002. River basin management reconsidered. In *Hydropolitics in the Developing World: A Southern African Perspective*, 61–71. Pretoria: International Water Law Project, African Water Issues Research Unit.

Whitehead, M., R. Jones and M. Jones. 2007. *The Nature of the State: Excavating the Political Ecologies of the Modern State*. Oxford: Oxford University Press.

Winter, T.C., D.O. Rosenberry and J.W. LaBaugh. 2003. Where does the ground water in small watersheds come from? *Ground Water* 41(7): 989–1000.

Chapter 3

A Genealogy of the Basin: Scalar Politics and Identity in the Mekong River Basin

Chris Sneddon and Coleen Fox

Introduction

This chapter explores the genealogy of two 'basin narratives' in the Mekong River system, from early interventions by water resource experts in the 1950s to more recent efforts by grassroots and regional advocacy networks to re-imagine a Mekong-based identity. The Mekong is a transboundary basin encompassing part of southwestern China (Yunnan province), Myanmar, nearly all of Laos, northeast Thailand, Cambodia and southern Vietnam. It has been the focus of intense developmental interest since the late 1950s, an interest that has led to the construction of a series of large dams in the upper basin (Yunnan) and on tributaries throughout the lower basin, and current plans to build a dozen massive hydropower projects on the river's main channel (see Figure 3.1). Since the early 1990s, these plans have been heavily criticized by a coalition of regional and international non-governmental organizations (NGOs) that argue that large-scale dams will irrevocably alter basin ecosystems and livelihoods. Conflicting narratives over damming the Mekong thus revolve around different accounts of the likely impacts on fisheries and fisheries-based livelihoods of the basin's millions of rural residents, in addition to the probability of severe social and environmental disruptions throughout the basin if the dams proceed as envisioned by riparian governments.

These basin narratives construct the river basin as a unique spatial entity (a singular scale) in ways that are both problematic and potentially liberating in terms of water governance and scalar politics. This chapter traces the genealogy of these narratives and their associated practices in two steps, both reflecting different moments in the construction of the basin as a privileged spatial scale. It draws on maps and other kinds of 'inscriptions' to show how the scalar configuration that eventually became the 'Mekong basin' was forged within a very specific set of geopolitical and developmental agendas – in often contradictory ways – that only partially reflect the complex socio-ecological networks encompassing livelihoods, biophysical dynamics and the interrelations between the two in large river systems.

Second, we consider the possibilities of a radical scalar politics in the basin that incorporates a 'Mekong identity' into the complex interactions among present-day geopolitics, development agendas and scalar representations of the basin. In the hopes of provoking further discussion of what we feel is a neglected dimension

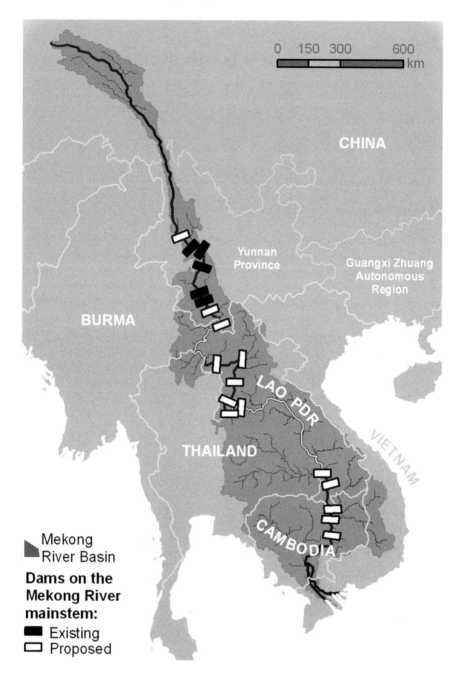

Figure 3.1   Mekong River basin showing existing and proposed dams

of the intriguing and growing work on water and scale, we question whether or not a scalar categorization originally defined by developmental agendas can be rescaled and rearticulated as an emancipatory political project. As our primary methodological approach, we use genealogy here in its most straightforward sense as an 'historical narrative that explains an aspect of human life by showing how it came into being' (Bevir 2008: 263).

Scale, Water, Region and Identity

Recent work in geography and related fields highlights how water governance is bound up with scalar politics (see Norman et al. 2012). For example, efforts by various governments to rescale transboundary water governance are ostensibly designed to confer greater decision-making powers over water management to local jurisdictions, yet such reforms do not necessarily result in the empowerment of local decision-makers (Norman and Bakker 2009); nor do they account for the complex interplay among scientific, political-economic and participatory discourses that shape water governance approaches founded on the basin or watershed unit (Cohen 2012). In the case of large basins, supposedly holistic governance and management has in many cases contributed to a fragmentation of administrative jurisdictions in an effort to disseminate the supposed benefits of water development, a process that Vogel (2012 and Chapter 4 this volume) calls the 'parcelling out' of the basin. In transnational contexts such as the Tigris/Euphrates and Jordan basins, states have effectively utilized narrative strategies – frequently underpinned by geopolitical imperatives – to 'perform' the scale of the river basin as an integral part of constructing national identity (Harris and Alatout 2010).

Molle (2006) shows conclusively that narratives of the river basin as a 'natural spatial unit' – particularly since the rise of a Western conceptualization of the river basin in the latter half of the eighteenth century (in France and other European settings) – are deeply intertwined with state-led narratives of modernization, industrialization and territorialization. Our intent is not to repeat this history here, but rather to point to the rise of what we have elsewhere called the 'modern' river basin (Sneddon and Fox 2011), which comes quite close to the values and perspectives attached to the early basin development efforts described by Molle. In its idealized form, the modern basin is a 'rational' planning unit that, if managed properly, can spur economic growth, promote the advancement of marginalized regions and even foster grassroots decision-making processes. This 'developmental' basin was the spatial scale constructed by engineers and development planners around the Mekong River in the late 1950s, a scale that would eventually become the focal point of a Mekong identity grounded in water resource expertise.

The Mekong identity, attached to the scale of a vast river basin, first emerged in the late 1950s during an era of high modernization that embraced economic development as a panacea for the ills of the third world. As evidenced by records and communiqués of the US Bureau of Reclamation, plans to transform the Mekong basin through hydropower and irrigation development were clearly a product of geopolitical machinations that sought to enrol Southeast Asia firmly in the orbit of US influence during the Cold War (see Sneddon 2012). Up to and including the 1990s, this identity resided almost exclusively within the practices of the extra-regional engineers, planners, government officials and development 'experts' and their Mekong national counterparts working to transform the basin through infrastructure development and social engineering. Within this view, it was the basin scale that became the object of devotion and intervention: not by virtue of the co-evolved hydrologic, ecological and livelihood processes it encompassed, but because of the developmental and geopolitical potential it represented. Only recently, we argue, has this identity been challenged by a novel kind of Mekong identity, one that transcends the human scale of the 'perceptible realm' (see below) and provides an organizing principle for a variety of social movements focused on sustainable livelihoods.

Recent work on regional and other place-based identities is also critical in helping to tease out the conceptual relations between 'river basin' and 'region' – two spatial categories that are often conflated in the Mekong case and elsewhere (see Dore and Lebel 2010; Sneddon and Fox 2012b) – and in exploring questions about the character of place-based identities, particularly those linked to the region. Indeed, there has been renewed interest in the re-emergence of the region – both in its transnational and subnational semblances – as a salient scalar unit, and with regard to its implications for economic revitalization and development, urbanization, environmental management and a host of other socio-ecological processes (Larner and Walters 2002; Allen and Cochrane 2007; Macleod and Jones 2007). A critical subset of this literature has begun to examine the connections between region and identity, in many cases building on the long history of geographical engagement with questions of place-based identity (see Paasi 2002, 2003, 2009; Taylor 2012).

Seen in this light, basins and watersheds do hold a different ontological status from other scalar and spatial constructions (e.g., 'national territory' or 'region'), but one that does not make them immune from interpretations as spatial categorizations. For example, there are multiple ecological and hydrologic relations that occur within a basin that are defined by that basin's spatial contours and topography (e.g., fish migrations, floodplain dynamics, sediment flows etc.). Yet (as we show below) the perception of the basin as a unitary object susceptible to human interventions hinges to a significant degree on a host of technologies, inscriptions and discourses in the service of a scalar categorization that is deeply political. This is in part what makes the construction of the Mekong and other large basins by planners, engineers and other experts so interesting; their epistemology of the basin is one of knowledge production in the service of what is essentially a political and economic end – a regulated river. Indeed, as the other chapters in this book make clear, the spatial scale at which water governance is directed and enacted is fundamentally 'one of the various ways actors deploy scale to further political projects' (Moore 2008: 217). An incisive example of this scalar politics is described by Budds's examination of how the mining industry in Peru shapes waterscapes through a complex interplay of institutional transformation, discursive strategies and material impacts (see Chapter 12).

While cognizant that there are numerous understandings and imaginings of what constitutes the 'Mekong region' and 'Mekong basin' (Dore and Lebel 2010; Sneddon and Fox 2012b), this discussion partially conflates them to emphasize the mutability of scalar narratives, which have become nearly synonymous in the discourses of advocates of Mekong development and their critics. Recent efforts to rethink our understanding of the region offer a fruitful means of capturing the two types of basin narratives and their associated scalar configurations, which we elaborate on in the next section. For example, Paasi draws distinctions between 'regional identity' and 'identity of a region'. We elaborate this distinction because it lies, we contend, at the heart of the divergent constructions of the Mekong basin that we are investigating. Broadly, interpretations of the relations between region and identity must focus on:

> the process through which a region becomes institutionalized, a process consisting of the production of territorial boundaries, symbolism and institutions. This process concomitantly gives rise to, and is conditioned by, the discourses/practices/rituals that draw on boundaries, symbols and institutional practices. (Paasi 2003: 478)

Within this broad understanding, the 'identity of a region' refers to 'those features of nature, culture and people that are *used* in the discourses and classifications of science, politics, cultural activism, regional marketing, governance and political or religious regionalization to distinguish one region from another' (Paasi 2003: 478). Such constructions of a region are typically directed from above with governance aims and state involvement, and are designed to define, designate and represent certain spaces and peoples. Conversely, 'regional identity' is more akin to regional consciousness, which 'points to the multiscalar identification of people [from below] with those institutional practices, discourses and symbolisms' characteristic of the aforementioned identification of a region (ibid.).

While a simplification, we can apply this framing to river basins and other scalar configurations of water governance to uncover how 'the basin' becomes institutionalized and is imbued with an identity much in the same way as a region: through top-down, highly institutionalized means that rely on territorialization, science and seemingly neutral symbolic representations (inscriptions). Moreover, an additional problematic of the identity of the Mekong region is that it has been deeply and irreparably constructed as a region by global geopolitical dynamics from its inception as a development unit (see Nguyen 1999; Sneddon and Fox

2012b).[1] But this framing of the Mekong basin also allows for an explication of alternative constructions of the basin/region that are more a hybrid of identification of a region and regional identity or regional consciousness (see below).

This brings us to a central point of the chapter: current conflicts surrounding the future of the Mekong basin – as a source of economic development, livelihoods, ecosystem services and biological diversity – are profoundly influenced by scalar politics and the ways in which different political actors infuse the basin with certain identities. Both 'pro-development' and 'alternative development' forces discuss the *basin* as the most critical scalar configuration for, respectively, rapidly transforming the basin and resisting those transformations. Yet these understandings of the basin rest on two divergent assumptions and sets of experiences. There is a quite vast disjuncture between the *scale* of basin or watershed planning typically constructed and adopted by development planners, state agencies and above all water resource experts over the course of the past century or so and the human scale through which most people who actually reside in a river basin experience their immediate surroundings and interact with material processes.

In contrast to the perspectives of planners and basin agencies, communities along the Mekong experience the river through fishing, flood recession agriculture, gathering of aquatic plants, pumped water for irrigation of rice fields, local transportation and as a water source, as well as – in numerous places targeted by state planners – a site of more intensive water development. It is this latter scale, which Gobster at al. (2007) refer to as the 'perceptible realm', that has been largely neglected in contemporary discussions within geography and related fields concerning the relationship between scale and water governance.[2] Importantly, the perceptible realm in the Mekong basin is bound up with ecosystem productivity and livelihoods, and this has become the basis for the recent efforts by civil society organizations within the region to 'scale up' their resistance and begin speaking about 'our' Mekong.

Inscripting the Mekong: The Construction of a Basin Identity

The early stages of constructing the Mekong as a river basin in need of alteration – a vision that has persisted to the present – is usefully explored through inscription

---

1   Ciută's examination of the Baltic Sea is an excellent example of how geopolitical conflicts (actual and potential) and perceptions of national security construct a region and imbue certain actors with its identity. The key point is that the 'region is not just a playing field for this conflict: the conflict itself defines the region, which becomes the subject of geopolitical engineering via the logic of security that in its turn defines the conflict' (Ciută 2008: 130).

2   However, there are increasing efforts to explore in more detail the prospects for a watershed- or basin-oriented notion of place-based identity (see Brunckhorst and Reeve 2006).

devices such as maps, graphics, tables and other representations of biophysical entities and processes. Latour (1990: 36–40) makes the point that representation devices like these are convincing; they are in many instances more effective than text in enlisting 'allies' to embrace a specific scientific assertion or position. They also serve as a universal language of science and scientific expertise, often called upon as the final word in conflicts over the veracity of a knowledge claim. For Latour, inscriptions are also important references of spatial scale.

We focus here on two significant representations that established the Mekong River basin as a region in the top-down, state-directed sense described by Paasi (2009). The scope of this chapter prevents a more comprehensive description of the thousands of maps, tables, design drawings, graphs and other representations of the Mekong River basin. But it is these inscriptions that exert such powerful influence in the Mekong context; they serve the role of immutable mobiles in that they link and stabilize particular renditions of the Mekong across space and time. The first inscription we examine is, to our knowledge, the first map of the *lower* basin to identify existing or potential dam projects on the river's main channel and significant tributaries (see Figure 3.2). The US Bureau of Reclamation was first enlisted to study the river basin's development potential in 1955, spurred primarily by officials in the U.S. State Department who perceived integrated river basin development as a means of promoting interstate cooperation and staving off Soviet political inroads in an increasingly conflict-ridden Southeast Asia (see Sneddon 2012).

This representation is significant for several reasons. First, it establishes the lower basin as the exclusive region of concern, effectively exorcising the upper basin (located in China's Yunnan province, where it is known as the Lancang River) from consideration. Second, it establishes the Mekong as exclusively a space and object of development. Nearly every cartographic representation produced by the state and governmental agencies created in the wake of the Bureau's report (a period spanning nearly four decades from 1956 until the mid-1990s) reproduced this vision of the lower Mekong basin as a dammed, improved river system. Finally, the sheer number of times this particular device was reproduced over the years, admittedly in a multitude of guises, established the Mekong's regional identity in a very specific and quite abstract way.

Figure 3.2 is taken from a draft copy of what would become the Bureau of Reclamation's official report in March 1956. The following excerpt, speaking of the critical need for further hydrologic investigations, is typical of the tone of the report, and gives a good sense of the textual narratives that accompany representations like the one shown in the image.

> Continuous records of the quantity of water carried in the river and its important tributaries are essential for planning substantial river developments regardless of type. They are needed for determining capacities of reservoirs, for river regulation, for spillway design, for estimating power capabilities and determining power plant design, for determining the water available for irrigation and other

Figure 3.2   Lower Mekong basin showing sites targeted for the construction of three major hydroelectric dams (Pa Mong, Tonlé Sap and Sambor)

Source: US Bureau of Reclamation (1956).

consumptive uses, for determining measures that should be taken to develop and
maintain adequate channels for navigation, and for a variety of other uses. The
need for such data is so basic to studies of all types of river development projects
that a start should be made immediately to collect these data, if such projects are
to be considered at all. (US Bureau of Reclamation 1956: 3)

This statement is notable in part for its sheer banality; of course any sort of human
manipulation of the river is contingent on accurate data. But note the impressive
array of things and processes brought into the orbit of human progress and water
development. The millions of cubic metres of water flowing through the Mekong's
channels will be asked to churn out thousands of megawatts of electricity; produce
untold tonnes of rice and other crops for both consumption and export; and bear
the weight of enormous barges laden with commodities. More than this, there is a
unity to the lower basin in the map and accompanying text; it is the Mekong and its
tributaries, envisioned as a unified and coordinated system that will be harnessed
for economic growth. This basic image of the transformed Mekong – whether
emphasizing future projects sites, agricultural research stations, geologic features,
potential transmission networks or any one of dozens of qualities deemed to a
part of the basin's development – was constantly repeated across the decades and
became, for all intents and purposes, *the* Mekong basin for the engineers, planners
and state officials committed to its improvement.

Our second inscription is also an expression of power relations: the power of
human ingenuity and labour to control water; the power derived from flowing water
and converted into electricity to serve the interests of economic development; and
the power to radically simplify and hence make comprehensible the transformation
of a river basin. Figure 3.3 shows the planned development of the Mekong River
as a cascade or stairway of dam projects that will exert utter control over the
unruly river and its seasonally defined flows.

The cascade image is an exemplar of how inscriptions literally 'draw things
together', in both the meanings intended by Latour (1990). The cascade brings
the massive dam projects closer together on the page, again emphasizing the
malleability of the river (if engineered properly) and the rational behaviour of
water as it flows methodically from one reservoir to another under the careful
guidance of dam operators. The most significant aspect of this inscription is how
it collapses space; dam projects separated by hundreds of kilometres crossing
national territories are envisioned within a single frame, with the reservoir of one
releasing water downstream to the next in the line. The assumption is that rational
water governance – coordinated across international boundaries – will guarantee
the maximum possible benefits of the basin in terms of hydroelectric power, flood
control and irrigation water.

Moreover, this particular vision of the Mekong basin, as a staircase of flowing
water, was reproduced in hundreds of planning documents running from the mid-
1960s through to the present era. It is worth noting this representation's other
characteristics and how these relate to spatial scale. The vision effectively erases

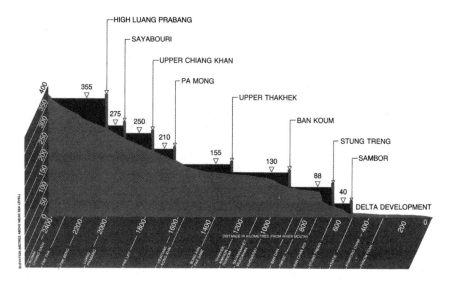

Figure 3.3   The Mekong cascade as conceptualized in 1987
Source: Interim Mekong Committee (1988: 12).

the broader network of financial and political actors necessary to build the dam projects it depicts. At the time of its production in the late 1980s, these actors were largely limited to the riparian governments of the lower basin and the cadre of international donors (without the United States, which had pulled out of all Mekong engagement in 1975) and international financial institutions (e.g., the World Bank and the Asian Development Bank). Moreover, the cascade inscription also eliminates the multiple ecohydrologic processes (e.g., floodplain dynamics, estuary processes) that drive the incredible productivity of this aquatic system, particularly in terms of fish production.[3] Relatedly, the Mekong-as-cascade sees the basin's value almost entirely linked to the production of electricity, reiterating that the basin's riparian states' central goal in altering the Mekong was bound up in cheap energy that would in theory drive industrialization.

These inscriptions (as immutable mobiles) *became* the Mekong basin and region for the multitude of engineers, planners, economists, physical scientists, government officials, politicians and numerous NGOs for most of the period from the inception of interest in Mekong development in the late 1950s and indeed until the present day. Within this narrative, the basin is conceived as a natural unit of water management and planning amenable to (and greatly in need of) human interventions to realize its full potential. Despite this overlay of technological specificity and scientific rationality, it is a radically simplified vision of the social,

3   Fisheries production in the Mekong amounts to nearly 2 million tonnes annually, and is an important food source – irreplaceable in many parts – for basin residents (see Sneddon and Fox 2012a).

ecological, hydrological and political dynamics that are experienced by the humans and nonhumans residing in the basin's territorial boundaries (see Sneddon and Fox 2006). The inscriptions examined in this section thus help us draw linkages between conceptualizations of the river basin as a privileged scale of water governance and the inscription devices that make that particular conceptualization possible. They help us answer McCarthy's critical questions of 'who produces scale, how, and for what purposes?' (2005: 733).

The Constructed Basin as Site of Resistance: An Empowered Mekong?

In sharp contrast to the scalar categorizations employed by state officials and international development experts in the Mekong, the recent activities of a range of grassroots organizations, region-oriented NGOs and global advocacy groups signal a different kind of Mekong. This more recent narrative still posits the basin scale as highly relevant, but insists that it is the deep connection between basin-level hydrologic processes and the livelihoods of the 70 million or so basin residents that give the basin scale its overarching importance. Dore documents different types of 'regionalist' movements engaged in Mekong governance, contrasting the traditional, top-down regionalism of the Mekong River Commission (MRC) and the riparian governments with more recent initiatives to ground the vision of the Mekong in civil society networks critical of mainstream development planning. While some of these initiatives are characterized by global epistemic communities of scholars and professionals, others are populated by 'localists' who champion rural livelihoods and are sceptical of 'government intent or capacity' given past abuses by elites (Dore 2003: 414). Localists tend to support activity at the regional scale in the following ways:

> solidarity lobbying to support other local groups who may have restricted national space; or to deal with genuine transboundary or region-wide issues where solidarity or a 'whole of region' perspective could help; or to take advantage of regional platforms, or to counter what are seen as illegitimate and inappropriate regional agendas. (Ibid.)

Yet to what extent are the recent activities of localists constitutive of a novel Mekong identity linked to the basin scale? In what ways are activists and communities within the region articulating a basin-scale identity – in the sense used by Li (2000);[4] and what are the political possibilities of redefining the Mekong and hence Mekong development in more progressive ways? Thinking carefully about

---

4   Li (2000) interprets the differential articulation of an indigenous identity by communities on the island of Sulawesi (Indonesia) as a part of a broader political strategy to oppose (or not) state-led development initiatives. While successful for one community, the articulation of indigeneity, or indeed any specific identity, carries with it the risk of undermining the capacity to build broader social coalitions and other dangers.

scalar politics and the role of identity in political struggles over water governance provides some useful direction for responding.

We start from the basic assumption that the 'success or effectiveness of social and political strategies for empowerment is related to the ways in which geographical scale is actively considered and mobilized in struggles for social, political, or economic resistance or change' (Swyngedouw 2004: 26–7). Both the idea and the materiality of the river basin have resulted in its becoming a key site of political struggle over water governance. Understanding the basin (and other territorial entities) as crucial kinds of 'scale-making projects' (Tsing 2005) leaves open the possibility for 'making' the basin in ways that encourage more transparent, participatory and ecologically mindful water governance decision-making.

Scholarship connecting water rights, identity and scalar politics is also carving out conceptual space for thinking through the possibilities of political and social movements that incorporate the type of regional- and/or basin-oriented identities we posit as (partially) emerging in the Mekong context. The notion of 'water territories' advanced by Boelens et al. – defined as a 'rooted and multilayered political water community' – articulates the kind of linking between space and identity that we wish to explore in the Mekong context. Water territories 'involve socionatural webs with landscapes and waterscapes in which people live and make livelihoods and identities', and foster a sense of moral engagement. Such territories stand in stark contrast to the 'placeless irrigation systems and watershed plans' characteristic of water bureaucracies and state officials (Boelens et al. 2010: 19). Most importantly, the ability of local water users to shape struggles over water to their advantage seems contingent on 'the power to compose or manipulate patterns of multiple scales' (ibid.: 20). This occurs through a variety of mechanisms and political strategies, including advocating for legal reforms at the state level and articulating with discourses and movements constructed around governance, class, gender and ethnicity (ibid.: 19–20).[5] The notion of water territories captures well the recent articulations of a shared Mekong identity.

Since the mid-1990s, when the newly re-formed Mekong River Commission helped reinvigorate large-scale hydropower development and basin-scale planning, oppositional politics have attempted to construct a counter-narrative based on the notion of 'watershed peoples' and of a transboundary basin identity, which was intended to be bound up with a common interest in an intact river ecosystem supporting livelihoods. An excellent example is offered by the early narratives propagated by the Thailand-based NGO Towards Ecological Recovery and Regional Alliance (TERRA). Created to focus on Thailand-based environment and development dilemmas in the 1980s, TERRA re-envisioned itself as a regional advocacy network in the early 1990s. This occurred in part because of efforts by the Thai government – effectively stymied from building large dam projects

5   We are aware of the dangers of a scalar politics that becomes, in Swyngedouw's words (2004: 43), a 'one-sided obsession with a politics of identity', to the detriment of building broad-based coalitions to confront the elite-controlled global order.

within Thailand – to enter into hydropower negotiations with Laos, Cambodia and Myanmar, where autocratic state apparatuses created little opportunity for democratic water governance (Hirsch 1998).

From TERRA's pioneering work on building coalitions of community-based organizations and allies within academic institutions, the media, student groups and an assortment of civil society organizations, a more or less coherent regional movement has coalesced around conflicts over Mekong development. Yet, in practice this regional movement has been largely focused on conflicts at the sub-basin scale, and has struggled to engage effectively in politics at the basin scale and fully realize its potential as a 'water territory'.

This situation may be changing. With the acceleration of mainstream dam construction in China (a cascade of eight dams – four of which are completed – is planned for Yunnan province), and with the impending US\$3.2 billion Xayaburi Dam on the mainstream in Laos, the actual material transformation of the river is poised to become more dramatic. Given this impending ecological 'tipping point' (Cronin and Hamlin 2012), we are possibly witnessing a concurrent intensification of the counter-narrative being put forward by communities affected by dams and development. We suggest that there may be new opportunities for a scalar politics that draws on a basin identity as a site of resistance. The Xayaburi Dam in particular has created the impetus for 'whole of region' solidarity (Dore 2003: 414). As the first dam on the mainstream in the Lower Mekong, it will have a host of regional ecological impacts. The dam will block the migrations of up to 100 fish species, reduce downstream flows, trap fertile silt and problematically affect fisheries and agriculture throughout the basin, with especially dramatic impacts on resource-dependent, impoverished communities in Cambodia (Fuller 2010). The dam also paves the way for up to 11 additional dams planned for the mainstream, which most scientific studies suggest would be ecologically (and likely socially) catastrophic for the lower basin and for tens of millions of residents (see ICEM 2010).

In response to this likelihood, opposition groups are moving beyond their local interests to put forward distinctly regional demands. For the first time, a coalition of 37 villages – which make up the Thai's People Network of Eight Mekong Provinces – is filing a lawsuit against the Electricity Generating Authority of Thailand (EGAT) over its plan to purchase power from the Xayaburi Dam in Laos. The regional nature of the action is evident as, according to Pianporn Deetes – campaign director for environmental group International Rivers in Thailand – 'this is the first regional legal case on a transboundary project involving overseas investment' (quoted in Win 2012).

Xayaburi has inspired transboundary regional activism, as evidenced by Cambodians travelling to Bangkok in September 2012 to demand that the Thai prime minister tear up the agreement to buy power from the dam. They joined with villages from northeast Thailand to deliver a petition with 8,000 signatures to the Thai government. This action represented an evolution of scalar politics in the region. A TERRA representative said that meeting with the upper echelons of the Thai government could be 'an important turning point for [the] Xayaburi campaign for the Mekong regional civil society networks and, even more important, for the Thai people who live along the Mekong River' (Worrell 2012). Regardless of the outcome of the anti-Xayaburi campaign, the Mekong basin has in recent years been re-imagined as a critical scale of political struggle and resistance by a networked coalition of NGOs and community groups operating largely within the region.

Conclusions

One of the most critical research questions in discussions of contemporary world politics concerns 'how regional distinctions and classifications are produced and reproduced and how they express relations of power', in part because it prompts the additional question of 'whose regional identity is in question and for what purpose it is articulated' (Paasi 2009: 146). In the Mekong case, the basin was originally constructed as a site of development largely under the aegis of a complex network of technological expertise, geopolitical objectives and aspirations to modernization, a network that for decades was bound together through a range of ideological and political-economic processes. Inscriptions of the basin – propagated through maps and other visual representations – played a key role in creating and maintaining this network and imbuing it with a developmental and technological identity.

More recently, the Mekong has been reconfigured as a site of resistance by agents who, by virtue of their experience of and dependence on the river's biophysical dynamics, privilege a basin scale to confront and critique the basin-wide plans of governments to transform an enormous river system in the name of development. Somewhat ironically, this latter construction hinges crucially on the realization that the human, localized scales through which most basin residents experience and identify with 'the Mekong' are acutely linked to political and material dynamics encompassing the entire basin. While the functional unity of the river system and promotion of 'basin thinking' is often perceived as a means of both conducting more sustainable water resource development and enhancing water governance decisions through more effective vehicles for engagement by basin residents, such common-sense assumptions about the basin scale and their underpinning narratives become increasingly untenable in the light of genealogical scrutiny.

Our invocation of a Mekong identity is certainly too simplistic. For example, the individuals, communities and organizations resisting government-led development plans may adopt the rhetoric of 'our Mekong', but these agents articulate with the basin's biophysical and political processes in a wide variety of ways. The consideration of a Mekong identity does, however, offer a useful frame – one that has been largely neglected in a good deal of the water governance and specifically Mekong-oriented literature – for exploring how certain constructions of a seemingly natural spatial unit (the basin) come into being and are maintained (and challenged) via human agency. We also realize that our use of theoretical discourses emphasizing inscriptions and regional identity are only some of the numerous conceptual reference points applicable to thinking through the scalar politics of water governance. Still, we see this chapter as a valuable contribution to the growing literature on scale and water because it brings together an important set of ideas – the construction of scales of water governance and the politics of water-based identities – for thinking about alternative water–society relations.

References

Allen, J. and Cochrane, A. 2007. Beyond the territorial fix: Regional assemblages, politics and power. *Regional Studies*, 41(9), 1161–75.

Barnes, T. 2002. Performing economic geography: Two men, two books, and a cast of thousands. *Environment and Planning A*, 34, 487–512.

Bevir, M. 2008. What is genealogy? *Journal of the Philosophy of History*, 2, 263–75.

Boelens, R., Getches, D. and Guevara-Gil, A. (eds). 2010. *Out of the Mainstream: Water Rights, Politics and Identity*. London: Earthscan.

Brunckhorst, D. and Reeve, I. 2006. A geography of place: Principles and application for defining 'eco-civic' resource governance regions. *Australian Geography*, 37(2), 147–66.

Ciută, F. 2008. Region? Why region? Security, hermeneutics, and the making of the Black Sea region. *Geopolitics*, 13, 120–47.

Cohen, A. 2012. Rescaling environmental governance: Watersheds as boundary objects at the intersection of science, neoliberalism, and participation. *Environment and Planning A*, 44(2), 2207–24.

Cronin, R. and Hamlin, T. 2012. Mekong turning point: Shared river for a shared future. Washington, DC: Stimson Center. Available at http://www.stimson.org/images/uploads/research-pdfs/SRSF_Web_2.pdf.

Dore, J. 2003. The governance of increasing Mekong regionalism. In Kaosa-ard, M. and J. Dore (eds), *Social Challenges for the Mekong Region*. Chiang Mai: Chiang Mai University, Social Research Institute, 405–40.

Dore, J. and Lebel, L. 2010. Deliberation and scale in Mekong region water governance. *Environmental Management*, 46(1), 60–80.

Fuller, T. 2010. Countries blame China, not nature, for water shortage, *New York Times*, 17 April.

Gobster, P., Nassauer, J., Daniel, T. and Fry, G. 2007. The shared landscape: What does aesthetics have to do with ecology? *Landscape Ecology*, 22, 959–72.

Harris, L. and Alatout, S. 2010. Negotiating hydro-scales, forging states: Comparison of the upper Tigris/Euphrates and Jordan River basins. *Political Geography* 29, 148–56.

Hirsch, P. 1998. Dams, resources and the politics of environment in mainland Southeast Asia. In Hirsch, P. and C. Warren (eds), *The Politics of Environment in Southeast Asia*. London: Routledge, 55–70.

ICEM (International Centre for Environmental Management). 2010. *MRC Strategic Environmental Assessment (SEA) of Hydropower on the Mekong Mainstream: Summary of the Final Report*. Hanoi, October. Available at: http://www.mrcmekong.org/ish/SEA/SEA_FR_summary_13oct.pdf (accessed 5 September 2011).

Larner, W. and Walters, W. 2002. The political rationality of 'new regionalism': Toward a genealogy of the region. *Theory and Society*, 31(3), 391–432.

Latour, B. 1990. Drawing things together. In Lynch, M. and S. Woolgar (eds), *Representation in Scientific Practice*. Cambridge, MA: MIT Press, 19–68.

Li, T.M. 2000. Articulating indigenous identity in Indonesia: Resource politics and the tribal slot. *Comparative Studies in Society and History*, 42(1), 149–79.

Macleod, G. and Jones, M. 2007. Territorial, scalar, networked, connected: In what sense a 'regional world'? *Regional Studies*, 41(9), 1177–91.

McCarthy, J. 2005. Scale, sovereignty, and strategy in environmental governance. *Antipode*, 37(4), 731–53.

Molle, F. 2006. *Planning and Managing Water Resources at the River-Basin Level: Emergence and Evolution of a Concept*. Colombo, Sri Lanka: International Water Management Institute.

Molle, F. 2009. River basin planning and management: The social life of a concept. *Geoforum*, 40(3), 84–94.

Moore, A. 2008. Rethinking scale as a geographical category: From analysis to practice. *Progress in Human Geography*, 32(2), 203–25.

Mustafa, D. 2007. Social construction of hydropolitics: The geographical scales of water and security in the Indus basin. *Geographical Review*, 97(4), 484–501.

Norman, E. and Bakker, K. 2009. Transgressing scales: Water governance across the Canada–U.S. borderland. *Annals of the Association of American Geographers*, 99(1), 99–117.

Norman, E., Bakker, K. and Cook, C. 2012. Introduction to the themed section: Water governance and the politics of scale. *Water Alternatives*, 5(1), 52–61.

Nguyen, T.D. 1999. *The Mekong River and the Struggle for Indochina: Water, War, and Peace*. Westport, CT: Praeger.

Paasi, A. 2002. Bounded spaces in the mobile world: Deconstructing 'regional identity'. *Tijdschrift voor Economische en Social Geografie*, 93(2), 137–48.

Paasi, A. 2003. Region and place: Regional identity in question. *Progress in Human Geography*, 27(4), 475–85.

Paasi, A. 2009. The resurgence of the 'region' and 'regional identity': Theoretical perspectives and empirical observations on regional dynamics in Europe. *Review of International Studies*, 35, 121–46.

Schiff, L., Van House, N. and Butler, M. 1997. Understanding complex information environments: A social analysis of watershed planning. *Proceedings of the Second ACM Digital Libraries Conference*, Philadelphia, 23–6 July 1997, 161–86.

Smith, L., Best, L., Stubbs, D.A., Johnston, J. and Bastiani Archibald, A. 2000. Scientific graphs and the hierarchy of the sciences: A Latourian survey of inscription practices. *Social Studies of Science*, 30(1), 73–94.

Sneddon, C. 2012. The 'sinew of development': Cold War geopolitics, technological expertise and river alteration in Southeast Asia, 1954–1975. *Social Studies of Science*, 42(4), 564–90.

Sneddon, C. and Fox, C. 2006. Rethinking transboundary waters: A critical hydropolitics of the Mekong River basin. *Political Geography*, 25(2), 181–202.

Sneddon, C. and Fox, C. 2011. The Cold War, the US Bureau of Reclamation and the technopolitics of river basin development, 1950–1970. *Political Geography*, 30(8), 450–60.

Sneddon, C. and Fox, C. 2012a. Inland capture fisheries and large river systems: A political economy of Mekong fisheries. *Journal of Agrarian Change*, 12(2/3), 279–99.

Sneddon, C. and Fox, C. 2012b. Water, geopolitics, and economic development in the conceptualization of a region. *Eurasian Geography and Economics*, 53(1), 143–60.

Swngedouw, E. 2004. Globalisation as 'glocalisation'? Networks, territories and rescaling. *Cambridge Review of International Affairs*, 17(1), 25–48.

Taylor, B. 2012. Regionalism as resistance: Governance and identity in Western Australia's wheatbelt. *Geoforum*, 43, 507–17.

Thorp, J., Thoms, M. and Delong, M. 2006. The riverine ecosystem synthesis: Biocomplexity in river networks across space and time. *River Research and Applications*, 22, 123–47.

Tsing, A. 2005. *Friction: An Ethnography of Global Connections*. Princeton, NJ: Princeton University Press.

US Bureau of Reclamation. 1956. *Lower Mekong River Basin: A Reconnaissance Report Prepared for the International Cooperation Administration*. Denver, CO: USBR, March.

Vogel, E. 2012. Parcelling out the watershed: The recurring consequences of organising Columbia River management within a basin-oriented territory. *Water Alternatives*, 5(1), 161–90.

Win, T.L. 2012. Thai villagers to fight Lao Mekong dam in court. Thomson Reuters Foundation, 25 July. Available at: http://www.trust.org/item/20120725103000-0lshu?view=print (accessed 12 October 2013).

Worrell, S. 2012. Cambodians protest Xayaburi in Bangkok. *Phnom Penh Post*, 18 September. Available at: http://www.phnompenhpost.com/national/cambodians-protest-xayaburi-bangkok (accessed 7 October 2013).

Chapter 4
River Basins versus Politics?
Interactions, Patterns and Consequences

Eve Vogel

Introduction

What difference *does* a river basin or watershed territory make? Do water management institutions organized within river basins and watersheds shape management policy and practice, and social and environmental outcomes in intended ways? How do they play out over time?

This chapter offers a preliminary set of answers to these questions, using three long-term case studies of river basin management to derive patterns in their evolution and impacts. The chapter begins with an outline of the often unexplained logic that justifies proponents' hopes that river basin management can transform water management in positive ways. Following this, I describe three patterns that have *actually* occurred following efforts to establish river basin management over the last 40–75 years:

1. unified authority and authoritarian unity
2. institutional narrowing, fragmentation and ad hoc coordination
3. parcelling out the watershed.

In the first pattern, a river basin territory largely overpowers the politics of conventional jurisdictional spaces. In the second, the opposite occurs: conventional jurisdictional spaces prevail against a river basin governance territory. In the third, a strong river basin management institution survives long term, but only by winning the support of the political and legal apparatuses of conventional jurisdictional spaces. Three US river basins are used to illustrate these patterns – the Tennessee, Connecticut and Columbia – with briefer comparisons to other river basins around the world. The conclusion emphasizes the need for a more interactive and longer-term political geographic model to explain what happens when water management is organized along river basin and watershed lines, and calls for broader comparative study.

The Ideal: River Basins and Watersheds as Holistic Management Spaces

Advocates of river basin and watershed management argue that organizing management along hydrologic lines can harness water resources more efficiently, achieve greater and wider human benefit, and also sustain renewable natural resources. What is their reasoning? Documents from development banks, non-governmental organizations (NGOs), government agencies and scientists suggest that the expected positive outcomes of river basin and watershed territories derive from their natural *holism* (see e.g. Doppelt et al. 1993; National Research Council 1999; McNally and Tognetti 2002; Millington et al. 2006). More specifically, the logic follows from natural boundaries to holistic spaces, to holistic management, to positive outcomes.

The starting premise is that river basins and watersheds have *natural boundaries*. 'Natural' is often contrasted with human political and governmental organization. Basin-delineated governance is seen to overcome or sidestep a host of legal, administrative, and geographic divisions endemic to conventional government and governmental spaces. Because of their natural boundaries, watersheds and river basins are believed to be *holistic spaces*, encompassing water flow, aquatic ecologies, and human communities. The logic continues: because of this geographic holism, basin-delineated governance is thought to produce *holistic management* that can integrate analyses of different goals, sectors, and geographical areas; balance management practice among different sectors and locations; and distribute management benefits across diverse peoples and places. Proponents conclude that river basin and watershed management can *produce positive outcomes*, providing significant environmental and social benefits, at lower long-term cost and with less ongoing conflict (Vogel 2012b; for examples from this literature see Doppelt et al. 1993; National Research Council 1999; McNally and Tognetti 2002; Millington et al. 2006).

Figure 4.1 and the left-hand column of Table 4.1 at the end of the chapter summarize the river basin management ideal – how management organized along river basin lines is thought by its enthusiasts to work. In the ideal (on the right of Figure 4.1), the river basin geography overcomes other political spaces: country or state borders disappear, and a balanced range of management practices and benefits are spread out across the region. Management is holistic, balanced and well distributed, shown by wide-ranging power lines, multiple sites of irrigation, numerous protected areas of forest and relatively limited numbers of dams, which allow fish still to reach and thrive in a large portion of the basin. The results are improved social and environmental benefits, greater efficiencies and less conflict.

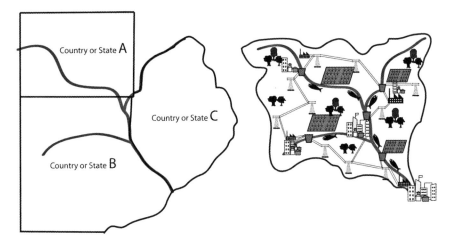

Figure 4.1 **The river basin management ideal (right), contrasted with a river that simply crosses three country or state territories (left)**

The Reality: Patterns from Empirical Histories

Are water management institutions organized within river basins and watersheds truly able to escape the fragmentations and conflicts of conventional political territories and their governments? Do they consequently build balanced and sustainable management, and spread benefits widely?

Long-term river basin management histories suggest that actual river basin management often cannot overcome the politics and authorities of more conventional political territories; rather, it is the *interaction* between governance within a river basin territory on the one hand, and continued governance and politics within more traditional political territories on the other that determine the outcomes of river basin management. This interaction has created at least three discernible river basin management practices and outcomes, all of which differ from the ideal.

Pattern 1: Unified Authority and Authoritarian Unity

Organizing water management along river basin lines *can* sometimes overcome the fragmentations, conflicts and bureaucracy of traditional political units and spaces. However, critical histories suggest this comes at extreme cost: unified authority too easily becomes authoritarian unity; and river basin institutions extract resources and profit for cities and political goals, at great cost to the basin's people and environments.

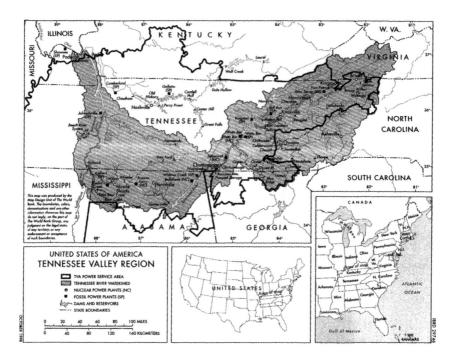

Figure 4.2   The Tennessee Valley Authority
Source: Miller and Reidinger (1998).

The classic case is the original institution of mid-twentieth century river basin development, the USA's Tennessee Valley Authority (TVA) (Figure 4.2). Created in 1933, the TVA was envisioned as a truly holistic river basin management effort. In its early years it aimed to build dams for power, navigation and flood control; help farmers conserve soils; reforest the hillsides; support farmers' cooperatives; build idyllic new communities; foster wide civic participation; and spread cheap electricity to ease life and to power economic development (Lilienthal 1944).

The TVA was authorized by the US federal government, whose territory – and therefore authority – encompassed the whole area (and beyond). TVA proponents argued that this basin-unifying authority provided tremendous benefits. The TVA could coordinate developments up and downriver, prioritize the hiring of trained professionals and overcome resistance from powerful interested parties (Lilienthal 1944).

However, critics rejoin that unified authority did *not* provide for holistic basin management. The TVA often advanced federal, that is, *national*, priorities rather than regional ones – a direct outcome of its identity as a *federal* agency

(Creese 1990; Hargrove 1994). It flooded huge areas of fertile valley bottom land, displacing over 50,000 people (McDonald and Muldowny 1981); often reinforced racial and landowning hierarchies (Selznick 1949; Grant 1990); and largely abandoned its agricultural and forestry missions and regional planning in order to provide electric power for the national war machine in World War II. By the 1950s and 1960s the agency became so fixated on power production – in part to provide for national military prowess in the Korean and the Cold War – that it undertook a huge build-up of coal and nuclear power, paying little attention to endangered species or other environmental concerns (Droze 1983; Hargrove 1994). TVA developments did not spread prosperity and small-scale industry to rural areas; rather, they enabled large-scale outmigration from rural areas and the growth of a few large urban centres (Friedmann 1955).

Literature on other major river basin efforts from the mid-twentieth century wave echoes both the praise and critique of the TVA, and no wonder, as most were explicitly modelled after the TVA. Initial reports glowed with excitement about institutions launched in the 1940s and 1950s in places as diverse as Iran, India, Latin America, Afghanistan and Southeast Asia (see e.g. Clapp 1957; TVA Technical Library 1961; Cole et al. 1984). Since then, however, critics have attacked many of these efforts. For example, Klingensmith (2007) argues that in India the Damodar Valley Corporation supported postcolonial nationalist ambitions, ignoring the vast dislocations its reservoirs caused. Wester et al. (2009) and Tortajada (2008) note that in Mexico a national system of river valley authorities established in the 1940s centralized control of river development and led to rampant overbuilding. In Iran a corporation modelled on the TVA in the Khuzestan region in the 1950s undermined millennia-old systems of indigenous local and regional water management (Molle et al. 2009); and in the Mekong in the 1960s the US supported river basin development in part to convince people to stay on the side of the US during the Vietnam War (Ekbladh 2002).

As Sneddon and Fox suggest, a river basin territory's key function in these cases may in fact be to allow and legitimize intervention by a national government or an international geopolitical regime over regional, state and local governments and citizens' resistance (see Chapter 3). All these examples suggest that a river basin territory may successfully overpower the fragmentation of smaller conventional political spaces, but often only at the backing of larger and more powerful ones.

Figure 4.3 and the second column of Table 4.1 summarize the pattern of unified authority and authoritarian unity. River basin geography overcomes smaller traditional political spaces. However, dark outer lines reveal the supremacy of a still larger scale political space, as the river basin is harnessed for nationalist or geopolitical aims under authoritarian decision making. The basin is overbuilt for narrow economic benefits which concentrate in overburdened cities and exports. Dams run from headwaters to mouth; there are vast irrigated areas (many watered via out-of-basin transfers); and manufacturing industries harness electricity at

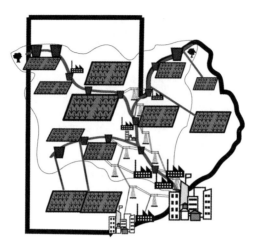

**Figure 4.3   River basin management under unified authority and
                authoritarian unity**

numerous dam sites and urban centres. Few remaining forested areas or wild fish
populations remain. Benefits are extracted to cities and exports. Rural people,
displaced or impoverished by agribusiness and reservoirs, move en masse to
booming, overburdened cities. The results include strong economic gains and
efficiencies, but also large social and environmental costs and externalities.
Conflict is reduced, but only because opposition is suppressed.

Pattern 2: Institutional Narrowing, Fragmentation and Ad Hoc Coordination

Though the stories of authoritarian river basin institutions are powerful, few of
these institutions seem to last more than a decade or two. Far more commonly,
institutions authorized to manage a river basin across existing territorial and
administrative lines appear either not to be set up or else to fail within 10–30 years.
In many river basins, coordination attempts are tried repeatedly in different forms,
but can become ad hoc over time as institutions come and go, and change their
focus, participants and range of responsibilities. If long term, they are often centred
on fairly narrowly defined institutions. I suggest that this frequent fragmentation
and narrowing is because most watershed and river basin authorities ultimately
rely on conventional jurisdictions for authority and funding. Powerful opponents,
organized around a host of geographical territories, can often persuade these
jurisdictions to deny funding to river basin authorities, reduce their mandate or
de-authorize them. In the end, the conventional jurisdictional spaces prevail
against a river basin governance territory.

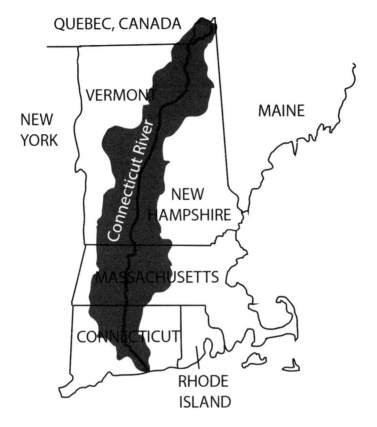

Figure 4.4 **The Connecticut River watershed**
Adapted from Connecticut River Watershed Council 2013

The Connecticut River Basin provides one example (Figure 4.4). During the 1930s, 1940s and 1950s the US federal government made repeated proposals for a comprehensive Connecticut River Basin Authority. However, leaders of other federal agencies saw such proposals as a threat and opposed them within the national administration. Activists and policy makers in the Connecticut basin also launched particularly vociferous and effective opposition. They lobbied their political representatives in Congress, who then either opposed federal comprehensive river basin development or were voted out of office. Local activists harassed surveyors with protests, while state and local governments cited engineers for trespass, denied them permits to buy explosives and threatened them with loss of gas rations. In the end the Connecticut River received only 13 as-small-as-possible flood-control only dams, and management remained fragmented among different states, parts of the river, management sectors and institutions. There have been recurring efforts to build basin-wide coordination, but they have been mainly advisory, advocacy or planning institutions without implementation authority (Leuchtenburg 1953; Vogel 2012a; Foster 1984).

The consequences of the failure of basin management on the Connecticut River are mixed. Because storage dams are smaller and coordination is very limited, the river produces less hydropower than it might (Leuchtenburg 1953; Vogel 2012a), and many tributaries can still swell to destructive proportions during high flow events (Pealer 2012). The restoration of diadromous fish (those that migrate between freshwater and saltwater) has a dismal record (Brown et al. 2013). It is virtually impossible to address in a comprehensive way the smaller-scale fragmentations caused by thousands of small mill dams from early New England development[1] or the complex daily and subdaily flow fluctuations from a host of dam owners (Zimmerman et al. 2008, 2010).

Surprisingly, however, there are also positive results. Much less land was permanently inundated, sparing numerous Vermont communities and valleys. Mainstream flood control is, with only 13 federal flood control dams in the tributaries, still effective (e.g. Samaris 2011). On an annual and seasonal basis, river flows are not overly altered by dams, and federal flood control dams often provide natural tributary flows to aid in fish restoration (Vogel 2012a). In short, failure to coordinate seems to have staved off the largest scale interventions that could have devastated the river and its human communities even further. Arguably, this un-holistic development is more balanced than fully coordinated development would have been. And importantly, it was successful – and legitimate – democratic challenge that resulted in fragmentation, re-elevating the spaces of traditional governments where challengers retained important political access.

In other rivers around the world, too, river basin and watershed management have often failed or remained weak, and traditional political spaces remain dominant (see Chapter 6). Indeed, with the insights from the Connecticut River in mind, other river basin institutions that *seem* to overcome the fragmentations of traditional political spaces begin to appear more partial or temporary. On the Mekong, despite grand geopolitical ambitions, the wars in Vietnam and Cambodia fragmented river policy and practice in the 1960s and 1970s; and today China refuses to participate in the current institutional incarnation, the Mekong River Commission (Ekbladh 2002; Sneddon and Fox 2006, Chapter 3 this volume). Iran's 1950s era river basin development effort was destroyed with the nationalist Iranian revolution in 1979 (Molle et al. 2009; Fisher 2011). The Mexican river valley authorities that had been launched in the 1940s were discontinued in the 1960s, undone by federal government budget reductions, opposition from Mexican states and broader governmental reform. In recent

---

1   B. Graber, Personal communication, Amherst, MA, 21 April 2011.

decades they have been re-formed in much more decentralized fashion (Tortajada 2008; Wester et al. 2009).

As a result of so many cases like these, a few brave commentators have begun to suggest that narrower and ad hoc approaches to river basin management may often be better. They can be more flexible and effective than large-scale comprehensive governance institutions. They can also gradually build trust, familiarity and relationships of cooperation without the burden of a comprehensive river basin agency (Merrey et al. 2007; Merrey 2008; Mollinga 2006; Molle et al. 2007; Molle 2009; Ashcraft 2011).

Figure 4.5 and the third column of Table 4.1 summarize river basin management under institutional narrowing, fragmentation and ad hoc coordination. Conventional political spaces, both larger and smaller than the basin, prevail over the river basin. Development and conservation are directed (or neglected) state by state or country by country, and often forestalled by conflict between them. The results are uneven, but ironically may sometimes be more balanced. Each country or state has developed its portion of the river, or enabled private developers to do so, and directs the benefits to its own priority areas. For both worse *and better*, many of the largest developments that might have been built have been blocked. In some places, fish still thrive and people still farm on a seasonally renewed floodplain. In others, there are disputes where the river has been dewatered or polluted near a border. There is no sense of a general regional benefit.

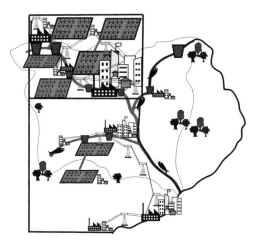

Figure 4.5   A river basin under institutional narrowing, fragmentation and ad hoc coordination

Pattern 3: Parcelling out the Watershed

In pattern 1, river basin geography successfully overcame the fragmentations of conventional political spaces, but at a significant cost to local and regional autonomy. In pattern 2, conventional political spaces won out over the river basin territory. In pattern 3, the two kinds of political geographical spaces, hydrological and conventional, engage in ongoing negotiation. In this pattern, the long-term survival of a river basin institution requires accommodation of people organized within a host of local, state or provincial, and federal jurisdictions, as well as other political and administrative spaces.

I term this pattern 'parcelling out the watershed'. The 'watershed' part of the pattern is that large-scale management is coordinated basin-wide. The 'parcelling out' is that some management functions are relinquished to other jurisdictions and agencies, while those aspects of river management that are coordinated basin-wide are used to produce spreadable benefits which are then distributed to the discrete territories of more conventional jurisdictional, administrative and political districts. Decision-making influence is also parcelled out, as the interests, agencies and institutions that can harness other territories' legal and political powers are brought into a variety of basin-wide decision-making processes (Vogel 2012b).

The history of the Columbia River (Figure 4.6) exemplifies this pattern (Vogel 2012b). As on the Connecticut River, ambitions for a valley authority on the US portion of the Columbia River in the 1930s to 1950s were curtailed in the face of hostility from the heads of other federal agencies, growing Congressional scepticism and opposition from leaders of the region's states and cities. However, in the 1930s the Columbia basin was still a comparatively undeveloped region. Regional leaders agreed on a compromise. The traditional federal dam-building agencies would build, own and operate new Columbia River federal dams, and a new regional federal agency, the Bonneville Power Administration (BPA), would transmit and sell the dams' power to encourage 'the widest possible use' within the region. Over time, the BPA – an agency outwardly unrecognizable as a river basin management agency – became the core of a tightly integrated river basin management system. It grew to coordinate river flows almost from headwaters to the river's mouth; delivered hydropower cheaply and reliably throughout the region; won private and federal investment in locations throughout the river system; and, in more recent decades, funded huge programmes of energy conservation and fish and wildlife mitigation (Bonneville Power Administration 1980; Vogel 2007, 2012b).

However, at almost every step of the way, the BPA also faced powerful critics who represented or leveraged the might of numerous more conventional jurisdictional, political and administrative spaces, including:

- the US federal government and states
- political representatives' districts

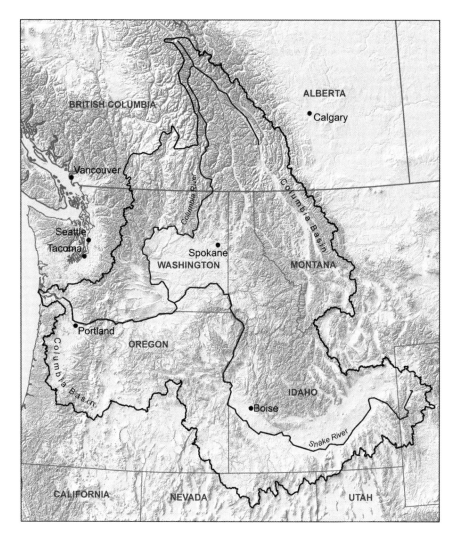

Figure 4.6   The Columbia River basin
Source: Map by Lynn Songer, Eve Vogel and Richard Turk. Reprinted from Vogel 2012b.

- local government territories
- Canada and British Columbia
- areas in which Native American tribes have recognized rights (reservations and ceded lands)
- electrical utility districts.

Political representatives from some of these spaces were at different times able to reduce the BPA's funding, block its initiatives and threaten to de-authorize it entirely. Sometimes they demanded a greater share of cheap federal hydropower for their favoured constituents, new dams in desired places or simply a share in the profits from hydropower that would be produced by their water storage. Native American tribes won a series of federal court cases, forcing the BPA and other river managers to provide protection and mitigation for Columbia River fish and wildlife. Advocates for energy conservation used their control of local public utilities to thwart BPA plans to invest in nuclear power, and to embrace energy conservation (Davis 1945; Lee et al. 1980; Blumm 1983; Cohen 1986; Pope 2008; Vogel 2007, 2012b).

Over the years, BPA officials repeatedly responded – sometimes happily, sometimes strategically and sometimes only when forced through legal or political compulsion – to placate these challengers. As a result, in each of the ways that watershed and river basin management are expected to be more holistic, the pattern on the Columbia has instead been parcelling out the watershed. The BPA's leaders distributed new or increased benefits to each era's next set of claimants and their territories: in the early years doling out dams and electric power industries to each political district; since the 1990s granting states and tribes funds for fish and wildlife programmes; and all along, distributing and selling cheap power to an array of industrial centres, cities, towns, rural areas and electrical utility districts. As time went on, the BPA also welcomed participants from many jurisdictions and territories into river management and electric-power decision making (or at least tolerated them). Over time, BPA-centred Columbia River management in many ways came closer to the river basin management ideal, providing for a wide array of people, places and issues (Vogel 2012b).

Nonetheless, management has not been particularly balanced. River management prioritizes hydropower production above all because that is what generates abundant cheap electricity, attracts investment and produces the receipts to fund burgeoning fish and wildlife programmes – in other words, it funds the benefits to appease an ever widening range of claimants. Unsurprisingly, this approach to river management is also very expensive: for example, the BPA spends over $400 million per year on fish and wildlife programmes. And conflict is ongoing – there has been continuing litigation for most of the last 20 years – though it is also continually being negotiated (Northwest Power and Conservation Council 2011; Vogel 2012b).

The Columbia River is an extreme case, but the pattern is not unique. On closer inspection, other long-established river basin institutions also look like examples of parcelling out the watershed. The TVA is still in operation after 80 years, but even in its early years it had to accommodate the interests of existing county-based agricultural institutions (Selznick 1949). It shed tasks like regional planning that were opposed by other state and federal agencies. Today, it retains support by distributing cheap power to the political districts of its Congressional delegation and helping local electrical utilities recruit investment for economic development

(Droze 1983; Gordon 1984; Hargrove 1994; Miller and Reidinger 1998; Daily 2013). Similarly, the Damodar River Commission survives, but like the Tennessee (in much reduced form), thanks to opposition from its constituent Indian federal states (Klingensmith 2007).

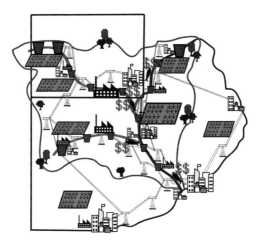

Figure 4.7   Parcelling out the watershed

Figure 4.7 and the right-hand column of Table 4.1 summarize parcelling out the watershed. River basin managers must negotiate with people from other political spaces; the result is additive decision making and distributive benefits sharing. As a result, the river is managed as a watershed unit to maximize lucrative, spreadable benefits. The figure shows:

- The river is heavily dammed to produce profitable, spreadable benefits.
- Transmission lines, factories and cities, conservation areas, and funding for fish and wildlife are dispersed so that benefits reach not only states but also towns, political districts, tribal areas, utility service areas and other territories with political and legal sway.
- Proceeds from hydropower have been used to fund hatchery fish production – shown by the dollar signs next to fish – and conservation of forested watershed areas in each country.

Conclusion: Practical Guides for Managing Political Geographical Interactions and Patterns

The three patterns discussed above are summarized in Table 4.1. Together, the patterns suggest that both scale and water scholars would do best to think of river basin management with an *interactive* political geographical model. In the river basin management ideal, the hope is that the river basin geography can overcome the fragmentations, conflicts and bureaucracy of traditional political units and spaces. Ironically, the first long-term pattern – unified authority and authoritarian unity – rests on having that hope realized. However, the weight of evidence, as described in patterns 2 and 3, suggests that most river basin management will not escape the fragmentation and fractiousness of traditional governmental and administrative spaces. Instead, a host of territorial spaces, both larger and smaller than river basins, linked to multiple jurisdictional levels inevitably continue to exist even as a river basin management institution does its work. Almost as inevitably, the leaders and constituents of these spaces pressure, cajole, challenge, obstruct and negotiate with managers of river basin territories. These interactions fundamentally shape river basin institutions' policies, management practice and evolution over time, producing discernible patterns of management and outcomes.

Further comparative work is needed to refine and elaborate these patterns to think through how they translate across time and space and what their consequences are in different contexts. Recognizing and understanding such interactions and patterns, we can develop more practical guides for river basin management; and, ultimately, we can better advance the social, environmental, economic and democratic outcomes we *hope* to achieve through the reorganization of water management and governance within river basin and watershed territories.

Table 4.1   Idealized versus realized patterns of river basin management

River basin and watershed ideal	Unified authority and authoritarian unity	Institutional narrowing, fragmentation and ad hoc coordination	Parcelling out the watershed
Political–geographical relationship between river basin and other political spaces			
River basin geography overcomes other political spaces	River basin geography overcomes other political spaces	Other political spaces overcome river basin geography	River basin geography negotiates with other political spaces
Management: Holistic versus fragmented			
Holistic decision making	Authoritarian decision making	Fragmented decision making	Decision making adds together many interests and spaces
Balanced and sustainable management	Overbuilding	Spatially uneven, piecemeal development	Overbuilding, evened out spatially
Holistic benefits distribution	Benefits extracted to cities and exports	Each political territory distributes its own benefits to its priority areas	Benefits parcelled out to each constituent political territory within the basin
Outcomes: Environmental and social benefits, efficiency, conflict			
Environmental and social benefits	Economic (GDP) gains; large social and environmental losses	Patchwork of benefits and costs; often high downstream costs	Large economic benefits, environmental impact and mitigation, all widely spread.
Greater efficiencies	Perhaps more efficient but costs externalized onto poor, rural people and environment	Inefficient, but total costs may be lower because less can be done	Inefficient; extremely high costs
Less conflict	Less conflict because opposition suppressed	Intractable conflict, resolved by fragmentation	Ongoing conflict, continually negotiated

References

Ashcraft, C.M. 2011. Adaptive governance of contested rivers: A political journey into the uncertain. PhD thesis, Massachusetts Institute of Technology.

Blumm, M.C. 1983. The Northwest's hydroelectric heritage: Prologue to the Pacific Northwest Electric Power and Conservation Act. *Washington Law Review* 58(2), 175–244.

Bonneville Power Administration. 1980. *Columbia River Power for the People: A History of the Policies of the Bonneville Power Administration*. Portland, OR: Bonneville Power Administration.

Bonneville Power Administration, US Army Corps of Engineers and Bureau of Reclamation. 2001. The Columbia River system: The inside story. In *Columbia River System Operation Review*. Portland, OR: Bonneville Power Administration, US Army Corps of Engineers and US Bureau of Reclamation.

Brown, J.J. et al. 2013. Fish and hydropower on the U.S. Atlantic coast: Failed fisheries policies from half-way technologies. *Conservation Letters* 6(4), 280–86.

Clapp, G.R. 1957. A TVA for the Khuzestan region. *Middle East Journal* 11(1), 1–11.

Cohen, F.G. 1986. *Treaties on Trial: The Continuing Controversy over Northwest Indian Fishing Rights*. Seattle: University of Washington Press.

Cole, W., Neuse, S.M. and Sanders, R. 1984. TVA: An international administrative example. *Public Administration Quarterly* 8(2), 166–83.

Creese, W.L. 1990. *TVA's Public Planning: The Vision, the Reality*. Knoxville: University of Tennessee Press.

Daily, M. 2013. Role reversal: Republicans blast Obama proposal to sell Tennessee Valley Authority. *Associated Press*, 16 April. [Online]. Available at: http://bigstory.ap.org/article/role-reversal-gop-blasts-obama-plan-sell-tva [accessed 12 June 2013].

Davis, L. 1945. *History of the Bonneville Power Administration, September 1939 to January 1942*. Portland, OR: Bonneville History Project (unpublished report).

Doppelt, B., Scurlock, M., Frissell, C. and Karr, J. 1993. *Entering the Watershed: A New Approach to Save America's River Ecosystems*. Washington, DC: Island Press.

Droze, W.H. 1983. The TVA, 1945–80: The power company. In *TVA: Fifty Years of Grass-Roots Bureaucracy*, ed. E.C. Hargrove and P.K. Conkin, 66–85. Urbana: University of Illinois Press.

Ekbladh, D. 2002. 'Mr. TVA': Grass-roots development, David Lilienthal, and the rise and fall of the Tennessee Valley Authority as a symbol for U.S. overseas development, 1933–1973. *Diplomatic History* 26(3), 335–74.

Fisher, C.T. 2011. 'Moral purpose is the important thing': David Lilienthal, Iran, and the meaning of development in the US, 1956–63. *International History Review* 33(3), 431–51.

Foster, C.H.W. 1984. *Experiments in Bioregionalism: The New England River Basins Story*. Hanover, NH: University Press of New England.

Friedmann, J.R.P. 1955. *The Spatial Structure of Economic Development in the Tennessee Valley: A Study in Regional Planning*. Chicago: University of Chicago.

Gordon, G.J. 1984. TVA and intergovernmental relations: Variations on a recurring theme. *Public Administration Quarterly* 8(2), 184–201.

Grant, N. 1990. *TVA and Black Americans*. Philadelphia: Temple University Press.

Hargrove, E.C. 1994. *Prisoners of Myth: The Leadership of the Tennessee Valley Authority, 1933–1990*. Princeton, NJ: Princeton University Press.

Klingensmith, D. 2007. *'One Valley and a Thousand': Dams, Nationalism, and Development*. New Delhi: Oxford University Press.

Lee, K.N., Klemka, D.L. and Marts, M.E. 1980. *Electric Power and the Future of the Pacific Northwest*. Seattle: University of Washington Press.

Leuchtenburg, W.E. 1953. *Flood Control Politics: The Connecticut River Valley Problem 1927–1950*. Cambridge, MA: Harvard University Press.

Lilienthal, D.E. 1944. *TVA: Democracy on the March*. New York: Harper.

McDonald, M.J. and Muldowny, J. 1981. *TVA and the Dispossessed: The Resettlement of Population in the Norris Dam Area*. Knoxville: University of Tennessee Press.

McNally, R. and Tognetti, S. 2002. *Tackling Poverty and Promoting Sustainable Development: Key Lessons for Integrated River Basin Management*. WWF Discussion Papers. Godalming: WWF-UK. [Online]. Available at: http://assets.panda.org/downloads/irbmtacklingpoverty2.pdf [accessed 24 October 2013].

Merrey, D.J. 2008. Is normative integrated water resources management implementable? Charting a practical course with lessons from Southern Africa. *Physics and Chemistry of the Earth, Parts A/B/C* 33(8–13), 899–905.

Merrey, D.J. et al. 2007. Policy and institutional reform: The art of the possible. In *Water for Food, Water for Life: A Comprehensive Assessment of Water Management in Agriculture*, edited by D. Molden. London: Earthscan, 193–231.

Miller, B.A. and Reidinger, R.B. (eds). 1998. *Comprehensive River Basin Development: The Tennessee Valley Authority*. Washington, DC: World Bank.

Millington, P., Olson, D. and McMillan, S. 2006. *Integrated River Basin Management: From Concepts to Good Practice*. Briefing note 1: An introduction to integrated river basin management. World Bank. [Online]. Available at: http://go.worldbank.org/NL3M26G260.

Molle, F. 2009. Water, politics and river basin governance: Repoliticizing approaches to river basin management. *Water International* 34(1), 62–70.

Molle, F. and Hoanh, C.T. 2011. Implementing integrated river basin management in the Red River basin, Vietnam: A solution looking for a problem? *Water Policy* 13(4), 518–34.

Molle, F., Ghazi, I. and Murray-Rust, H. 2009. Buying respite: Esfahan and the Zayandeh Rud River basin, Iran. In *River Basin Trajectories: Societies, Environments and Development*, edited by F. Molle and P. Wester. Wallingford and Cambridge, MA: CABI, 196–213.

Molle, F. et al. 2007. River basin development and management. In *Water for Food, Water for Life: A Comprehensive Assessment of Water Management in Agriculture*, edited by D. Molden. London: Earthscan, 585–625.

Mollinga, P.P. 2006. IWRM in South Asia: A concept looking for a constituency. In *Integrated Water Resources Management: Global Theory, Emerging Practice and Local Needs*, edited by P.P. Mollinga, A. Dixit and K. Athukorala. New Delhi: Sage, 21–37.

National Research Council. 1999. *New Strategies for America's Watersheds*. Washington, DC: National Academy Press.

Samaris, C.P. 2011. New England district well prepared for Hurricane Irene. *Yankee Engineer*, 45(11), 4–7. [Online]. Available at: http://www.nae.usace.army.mil/Portals/74/docs/YankeeEngineer/2011/September11.pdf.

Northwest Power and Conservation Council. 2011. *2010 Expenditures Report Columbia River Basin Fish and Wildlife Program*. Portland, OR: Northwest Power and Conservation Council, Document No. 2011–04.

Pealer, S. 2012. *Lessons from Irene: Building Resiliency as We Rebuild*. Waterbury: Vermont Agency of Natural Resources. [Online]. Available at: http://www.anr.state.vt.us/anr/climatechange/Pubs/Irene_Facts.pdf [accessed 4 June 2013].

Pope, D. 2008. *Nuclear Implosions: The Washington Public Power Supply System's Nuclear Plants*. Cambridge and New York: Cambridge University Press.

Selznick, P. 1949. *TVA and the Grass Roots: A Study in the Sociology of Formal Organization*. Berkeley: University of California Press.

Sneddon, C. and Fox, C. 2006. Rethinking transboundary waters: A critical hydropolitics of the Mekong basin. *Political Geography* 25(2), 181–202.

Tortajada, C. 2008. River basin management: Approaches in Mexico. *VertigO* Hors série 1. [Online]. Available at: http://vertigo.revues.org/1927?file=1 [accessed 23 October 2008].

TVA Technical Library. 1961. *TVA – Symbol of Valley Resource Development: A Digest and Selected Bibliography of Information*. Knoxville: Tennessee Valley Authority L.

Vogel, E. 2007. The Columbia River's region: Politics, place and environment in the Pacific Northwest, 1933–Present. PhD thesis, University of Oregon.

Vogel, E. 2012a. New deal vs. Yankee independence: The failure of comprehensive development on the Connecticut River, and its long-term consequences. *Northeastern Geographer* 4(2), 66–94.

Vogel, E. 2012b. Parcelling out the watershed: The recurring consequences of organising Columbia River management within a basin-based territory. *Water Alternatives* 5(1), 161–90.

Wester, P., Mollard, E., Silva-Ochoa, P. and Vargas-Velázquez, S. 2009. From half-full to half-empty: The hydraulic mission and water overexploitation in the Lerma-Chapala basin, Mexico. In *River Basin Trajectories: Societies, Environments and Development*, edited by F. Molle and P. Wester. Wallingford and Cambridge, MA: CABI, 75–98.

Zimmerman, J., Lester, A., Lutz, K., Gannon, C. and Nedeau, E.J. 2008. *Restoring Ecosystem Flows in the Connecticut River Watershed*. Northampton, MA: The Nature Conservancy, Connecticut River Program.

Zimmerman, J., Letcher, B.H., Nislow, K.H., Lutz, K.A. and Magilligan, F.J. 2010. Determining the effects of dams on subdaily variation in river flows at a whole-basin scale. *River Research and Applications* 26(10), 1246–60.

Chapter 5

The Politics of Scale Framing, Ambiguity and Uncertainty: Flood Interventions in the Netherlands

Jeroen Warner, Philippus Wester, Martinus Vink and Art Dewulf

Introduction

Safety from floods has significant discursive power in the low-lying, densely populated Netherlands. The combination of public concern and governmental awareness has led to a search for new and innovative flood interventions. These new interventions have, however, at times created temporal and spatial ambiguity, as the scale of social and technical interventions – and their costs and benefits – is far from settled. In these controversies, the framing of spatial and temporal scales has been an important strategy, linking water management to a changing climate as a looming crisis (Deltacommissie 2008; Verduijn et al. 2011; Vink et al. 2013; Boezeman et al. 2013; Dewulf 2013).

Scale frames can be understood as sense-making devices for understanding reality and organizing action (cf. Van Lieshout et al. 2011; Termeer et al. 2010). By framing, actors portray their understanding of what *is* at stake as well as a normative stance on what *ought to be* (Schön and Rein 1994). Through language, actors often interactively select or emphasize issues that point towards a certain problem definition or moral standpoint, implying certain solutions (Entman 1993; Dewulf et al. 2009). We will focus on the framing and counter-framing occurring in the context of controversial flood policies in the Netherlands. These policies are situated at the intersection of global climate change (and attendant sea-level rise), national government and local organization and infrastructure.

In this chapter we sketch how both proponents and opponents frame their arguments in terms of specific *scales* (after Kurtz 2003). The 'scalar frames' discussed here relate to an invoked sense of crisis and insecurity, lending urgency to the frames bringing particular 'solutions' into view. These solutions may value some scales (regional or national) or positions (urban or rural) over others, and are bound to yield winners and losers. In the flood domain, criteria that appear to be most technically and economically effective in facing floods may not tally with equ(al)ity and vulnerability considerations (Johnson et al. 2007).

Conceptual Framework

We conceive of scale as a cognitive construct representing a specific ordering of society and space, which through its 'deployment and social contestation' can have material consequences. Hence, we are interested in how scale is expressed in contending frames of reality. Through the process of framing, actors operating and situating themselves at different spatial scales strategically manipulate, negotiate and attempt to reshape power and authority (Delaney and Leitner 1997: 95). Kurtz (2003) defines the construction of scale frames and counter-scale frames as strategic discursive representations of a social grievance that do the work of naming, blaming and claiming, with meaningful reference to particular geographic scales. Scale framing – as a way of representing reality and dividing the world for specific *political* purposes (Marston 2000) – favours a particular analysis in order to justify (or exclude) certain solutions. Through framing, different scales are invoked to legitimize certain actors and strategies. Scales are constructed (framed) to favour a particular analysis, which may involve blame (e.g. 'water shortages are due to careless farmers'), or to justify (or exclude) certain solutions (Molle 2007).

Along with the range of actors involved and actors' level of engagement and responsibility in political debate, scale frames legitimize *knowledge* systems as well as the inclusion or exclusion of certain solutions and actions (Herod 1991; Lebel et al. 2005; van Lieshout et al. 2011). As a result scale frames may function as strategic processes of allocating responsibility, resources and decision-making (van Lieshout et al. 2011; Vink et al. 2013). In this chapter, we identify four different scales of water governance in the Netherlands, and argue that these scales have each been highlighted (or downplayed) at different times according to different national priorities. Indeed, we suggest that scale framing is the central mechanism through which certain scales are emphasized or *de*-emphasized, and show how this has been the case for over 100 years in Dutch water management.

Aware that intervention in people's backyards is prone to controversy, both authorities and activists may invoke a crisis narrative to open up space for change (Lebel et al. 2005). Such crisis stories are 'manufactured ... as a way of gaining public acceptance for what would otherwise be controversial reforms or projects' (ibid.: 13). The safety argument and crisis frame legitimizing scale is used by proponents to legitimize interventions, and by opponents to delegitimize them (Buzan et al. 1998; Warner 2011). A 'scalar fix' may be framed as a 'naturalized' solution to such a crisis; to provide stability and order as opposed to flux and fluidity; and to hold out the prospect of problem solving (McCann 2003) (Table 5.1).

Table 5.1   Spatial politics and strategic relations

	Spatial Politics		
Strategic Relations	**Scale**	**Position**	**Place**
Telling stories about	What are the arguments made for vesting authority to manage irrigation waters at different levels?	What are the narratives around upland watershed and lowland floodplain land-use policies?	How have stories about injustice around dam construction sites affected approaches to projects?
Building alliances with	How are actors based at a level able to interact effectively with other levels?	How can conflicts between upstream and downstream users be resolved?	How do alliances among stakeholders in different places arise?
Deliberating over	Which responsibilities and rights for water management should be held at what level, and by whom?	What is an acceptable impact from upstream infrastructure and uses, and how should it be compensated?	What priority should be given to state capitals and 'rice bowls' for dry-season water and flood protection measures?
Controlling technologies for	How do different ways of storing water affect the levels at which it can be controlled?	How are downstream impacts on ecosystems and people taken into account in decisions to build and operate dams?	How do place-based technologies empower certain groups over others?

Shifting Scale Frames and Scale Ambiguity in the Netherlands

Scale 1: Polders

Although Molle (2007) and Warner et al. (2008) have highlighted the role of the river basin as a dominant scale frame with national governments, the basin approach has never sat well with low-lying deltas such as in the Netherlands because the landscape in such deltas is defined by polders (reclaimed areas below sea level surrounded by embankments or dykes) rather than rivers. As such, water in the Netherlands has traditionally been managed on a polder-centric basis.

In recent decades, the Dutch water management domain has seen a broadening of its mandate: from an almost exclusive emphasis on protection (flood risk prevention, assuming flood risk can be reduced to zero) to risk management (assuming risk can never be zero). This change has had scalar implications. Previously, flood management between dykes was the exclusive domain of water managers, farmed out between the national water department (main rivers) and the regional water boards (secondary rivers). However, since the 1980s and the rise of integrated water management, river and coastal management became increasingly interwoven with land-use planning behind the dykes.

Scale 2: Spatial Planning at the Provincial Scale

The Netherlands is one of the most densely populated countries in the world, with 16.5 million people living in an area of 41,526 km^2. While the Dutch have sought to control water for centuries, the endeavour to organize and monitor water at a national scale was given a major push after the storm of 1 February 1953, when a coastal surge caused 1,800 deaths and displaced 1 million citizens. The resulting Delta Plan blueprint of the 1950s completed a process of national policymaking that started in 1798, when the Netherlands were under French occupation, and was maintained after independence.

In the highly fragmented Netherlands of the eighteenth century hundreds of polders were the central units of water management, even after the Dutch Republic was established in 1648. It was the occupying French forces (1798–1806) that started a state-making exercise by centralizing the Dutch water sector: pursuing the state's 'Promethean project' (Kaika 2005 cited in Sze et al. 2009) of state formation through infrastructure, leading to the establishment of the Dutch Public Works Department. The Dutch delta is criss-crossed by infrastructure designed to reclaim and protect land from water. The initial purpose of this infrastructure was to enclose all of the low-lying parts of the country with dykes, which were to be administered by a central authority working side by side with the thousands of local water boards, each responsible for its own polder. Today the Netherlands' water system is managed by 26 water boards.

After the storm surge of 1953, the Netherlands sought to close off some major estuaries from the sea and to reinforce the rest of the country's flood protection and correspondingly maintain the illusion of control over floodwaters. The country was carved up into three safety zones which were guaranteed equal protection from flooding:

- a 1 in 10,000-year return period (the probability that events such as floods will reoccur) for the coast;
- 1 in 1,250 for the main rivers cross-cutting the central Netherlands;
- 1 in 4,000 for the north Netherlands (cf. 1 in 1 million for an air crash).

Significantly, as we shall see, the province of Limburg, having the highest elevation, was not included as a protected zone (Figure 5.1).

Figure 5.1   Relief map of the Netherlands. The lighter the colour the higher the elevation

Source: Rijkswaterstaat

After the completion of this infrastructural megaproject of concrete, steel and stone, the 1980s and 1990s were characterized by the emergence of a 'blue-green coalition' bent on greening flood defence. This movement has become increasingly dominant in Dutch water management (see Disco 2002). An environmental consciousness movement originated in social protests against 'ugly' dykes and started to pervade the public works department responsible for flood safety and navigation, eventually leading to a coalition between civil and environmental engineers (van den Brink 2009). An attendant drive to 'make space' for rivers also propelled a shift toward greener engineering and non-structural interventions, such as river widening, building on stilts or mounds and embanking population concentrations. We will see later that these innovations were far from uncontroversial.

Scale 3: Climate Change and the Regional Risk-Based Approach

When the rivers Rhine and Meuse peaked in 1993 and 1995, Dutch climate research was still in its infancy. Since then, climate fears have seriously affected water policy dynamics, instilling a sense of 'crisis' and inciting a change of approach. After the two freak high-water events in the 1990s, scenarios of up to 24,000 m³/s flow in the Rhine were seriously considered (De Boer 2003); yet it is highly doubtful if flows greater than 16,000 m³/s could physically make it down the Rhine before the flows reach the Netherlands (Kolkman et al. 2007). While at the national level flood planning in the Netherlands involved minimal coordination with neighbouring countries (Becker et al. 2007), local actors such as provinces and water boards sought to coordinate with local partners on the other side of the border.[1]

The climate issue thus invoked a paradigm shift from a 'standards'-dominated approach, in which safety is expressed by the strength of the dykes and their protection standard, to a 'risk management' approach customary in other security domains and familiar in the Anglo-Saxon countries (Frerks et al. 2011). This shift meant that the blanket coverage implied by uniform safety standards per region were broken up into smaller units, and that cost-benefit standards became more localized than they used to be. Already in the 1960s after the major flood of 1953, the Dutch state applied different safety standards to three large territories: the coastal West, the centre-east riverine regions and the rural northeast. However, within these large territories safety norms were uniform. The current shift towards more specified norms legitimizes a risk differentiation at lower levels in which relatively small less-populated rural areas could be 'sacrificed' for the benefit of densely populated urban(izing) areas like major cities with greater economic assets and productivity. Unsurprisingly, it was the latter dimension of this shift that triggered protest in a number of locales.

Meanwhile, Hurricane Katrina in New Orleans in 2005 served to focus Dutch attention on risk in low-lying areas, and the Dutch government turned its efforts toward crisis management plans. As a result, the 2009 Dutch water plan introduced

---

1   While we did not extensively research the reasons underlying Dutch reluctance to coordinate with their neighbours, interviews suggest that one issue at the time was the level of representation. The Netherlands being the size of a German federal state (*Bundesland*), the Germans apparently did not see why they should be represented at the federal level when the Dutch had sent a national-level delegation.

the concept of multi-layer flood security connecting different institutional domains whose dynamics happen at different scales (Ministerie van Verkeer en Waterstaat 2009). Emerging, if hotly contested, thinking in much of the flood domain is to combine prevention, protection and preparedness into a more coherent 'multi-layer safety' approach to flooding.

Scale 4: The Re-Emergence of the 'Delta'

In recent years, a partial recentralization of water governance has taken place: The 2008 Second Dutch Delta Plan included, for example, the re-securitization of flood risk, which reflects elements of the original delta plan from the 1950s (Deltacommissie 2008). Moreover, this second Delta Plan introduced a new scale of water governance: the delta and its regions. This new scale gave a new role to Lake Ijssel (Ijsselmeer) – a former estuary which was disconnected from the sea in 1936 and turned into one of the largest freshwater lakes in western Europe – and made it a central feature of the Delta Plan's new focus on flood control, particularly as it pertained to freshwater availability and the prevention of salinization of 'the Delta' during future heatwaves (ibid.).

The addition, the Delta scale in contemporary Dutch water management is significant because it is essentially a socio-political invention. The Netherlands has four deltas in a hydrological sense, two of which are transboundary: the Scheldt shared with Belgium and the Ems shared with Germany. The Ijssel delta is fed by the River Ijssel, an offshoot of the Rhine, while the main branch of the Rhine joins with the Meuse to empty into the sea at Rotterdam. The extent of the 'delta' is thus never quite clear: in one sense, delta can be interpreted as encompassing the entire Netherlands – with the exception of the province of Limburg, which lies above sea level. Table 5.2 summarizes the four domains introduced above: their scale and unit numbers in the Netherlands.

Table 5.2   Scale disparity in Dutch flood risk management

Layer of Multilayer Safety	Scale	No. of Units in the Netherlands
Prevention: dyking	Polder	95
Protection: spatial planning	Provincial scale	12
Preparedness: crisis management	Safety region scale	25
Climate adaptation	Delta regions	7

Scale-Frame Conflicts

Four cases of scalar conflict highlight the politics of scale as it has played out in the Dutch framings of flood risk and mitigation. As Johnson and Penning-Rowsell (2007: 374) note, 'flooding is not fair *per se*: the inherent natural spatial inequality of flood frequency and extent, plus the legacy of differential system interventions, being the cause'. Competing interpretations of fairness appear to be central to each of the scale–frame conflicts discussed in this section.

Kampen–Ijssel Delta Bypass

The River Ijssel is an offshoot of the river Rhine, draining into Lake Ijssel (see scale case 4). Popular for its beauty, the Ijssel is prone to floods and ice floes. In

Figure 5.2   Bathtub cartoon: metaphor of Kampen as an island
Source: Werkgroep Zwartendijks (the opponents) leaflet. © Dik Hendriks

light of climate predictions, in the nationwide plan to make 'Space for the River' the national water authority proposed a relief channel at the town of Kampen, where the river encounters a bottleneck, and a ban on floodplain development as part of its measures to 'make space' for the Ijssel.

     Provincial and local authorities resisted this plan, which they associated with the national plan, and devised an alternative plan to prevent flooding. In opposing the bypass, conservationists stumbled upon an expert report showing that a dyke breach would have broader consequences than the national plan had predicted (HKV 2005). Based on this finding, conservations introduced a 'bathtub' metaphor showing Kampen as an island in a deep bathtub, effectively broadening the frame to include the town's vicinity (Figure 5.2). The metaphor invoked a terrifying vision of a flooded island from which there could be no escape, although the national water manager insisted that the land surface was large enough to ensure escape. Fatally, this different scale frame conveyed the impression that flooding was considered a valid option by planners. A mixed coalition of left- and right-wingers, farmers and environmentalists resisted the plan, resulting in continuing stalemate up to the present.

Ooij Polder: Controlled Flood Storage

In 2000, the Vice-Minister responsible for water management presented 'Space for the River' on Dutch national news. At the end of the broadcast, a map indicating tentative flood storage areas was shown. These so-called 'calamity polders' were to be designated for controlled flooding in the event of a peak flood in order to protect more densely populated areas. As in the Kampen case, many of the 15,000 residents of one of the planned calamity polders, the Ooij polder, were afraid that any designation of their backyard as a flood storage area would have a negative economic impact on the region, as no one would invest there. A national advisory commission was created to rethink the necessity and selection of the inundation polders.

Residents of the polder protested about the sacrifice they were expected to make to alleviate flood risks in downstream urban areas. Should upstream rural areas be flooded to save downstream cities? The scale frame thus linked upstream and downstream interests and assigned costs squarely to the upstream end. Protesters framed the intervention at the transboundary scale by including the adjoining German Düffel polder, which was indirectly at risk for calamity inundation should the Ooij be designated a controlled flood storage area.

The local protest successfully enrolled sympathetic academics. The most prominent among them, Delft Professor Emeritus Van Ellen, set about discrediting the climate projections on which the controlled flooding plans were based. He proposed a tried and trusted alternative technology: a channel to discharge excess flood peaks. While the authorities did not accept his proposal, the Van Ellen Channel was included in the Public Works Department's toolbox (*Blokkendoos*) for future determinations of costs and impacts of proposed 'Space for the River' policies (this case after Roth and Warner 2009).

Limburg: Maaswerken

While the river interventions under scrutiny here are, as a matter of course, 'sold' as climate change adaptation strategies, opponents claim that in fact the interventions make the Netherlands *less* adaptive. One example of such critique comes from the province of Limburg.

Identity is important to Limburg, the south-easternmost province of the Netherlands that joined the state later than other provinces. Residents of Maastricht, a city that has changed hands repeatedly during its turbulent history, are especially concerned with identity. Limburgers have long resented the 'Hollanders' who inhabit the prosperous and culturally dominant West Netherlands, feeling that the latter continue to colonize and dominate Limburg. Primary resources such as marlstone and gravel used for construction were ruthlessly mined, destroying the landscape and leaving large excavation holes in central Limburg which filled up with water.

Plans (*Maaswerken*) for a project to broaden and deepen the border Meuse River (in the south of Limburg) were presented as a way of finally phasing out gravel excavation in the region while restoring natural values. While it was widely applauded as daring leadership when struck, the deal was later tainted by corruption and thus came to be seen by local stakeholders as symptomatic of the corruptibility of Limburg politicians (Warner 2011). This history, and the absence of sufficient project funding, gave the river-widening project a legitimacy deficit right from the start.

The Meuse plan became the focus of a process of strategic scale framing and counter-framing. Despite the best efforts of the Limburg government at the time, the Meuse River had not been part of the national Delta Plan drawn up after the 1953 storm surge (Wesselink et al. 2012). Limburg's demand for protection under Delta's standards was greatly helped by the flooding events of 1993 and 1995, which badly affected the province. The Water and Transport Minister promised 'safety' by 2005 (later, by 2015), raising expectations in the province. In 1997 the national government upgraded the Maaswerken Project, extending it to the northern part of Limburg, where the Meuse is sandy rather than gravelly. In the absence of the option for remunerative gravel extraction, the cost of the project grew without an increase in attendant benefits. Further, the project also included the upgrading of a shipping channel to create the Maaswerken Project in the river valley, a channel alongside the Meuse. Navigation is the responsibility of the national government, thus the expanded project suggested to the regional authorities a national takeover. While reinforcing Limburger resentment of Hollanders, the expansion also created expectations of the original Grensmaas Project securing funding as a national safety project. Alas, the Public Works Department emphatically rejected the safety label for the Meuse and refused to pay up.

For different reasons, regional citizen platforms also rejected the 'security' label. Some noted that Limburgers had always coped with floods and did not need an external protection plan. Local citizen groups – especially a protest group in the project's testing ground, the parish of Lomm – professed that they did not want the Maaswerken in their backyard because dykes would obstruct views and unsightly piles of aggregate would despoil the landscape. With little affinity for the 'wild nature' proposed on the banks of the Meuse, the people of Lomm were angry that major cities in the region, such as Venlo, received protection before the smaller population centres; isolated farmsteads were even left unprotected.

The citizens gained some traction when the national commission overseeing Environmental Impact Assessment (EIA) rejected the Maaswerken EIA, and the project consortium seemed about to implode. Participating environmentalists believed that too much gravel was slated for extraction and that natural values were overly compromised. The provincial authority revised the EIA and invited local stakeholders to the table to contribute to an alternative within six months.

Parallel to negotiations, fighting continued. Small-scale local protests by local groups were upgraded in 2002 into a regional platform called *Bewoners Overleg Maaswerken* (BOM), an acronym which in Dutch connotes 'bomb', with a view to stopping the Maaswerken. Farmers supported BOM to express their resentment at facing the threat of expropriation under emergency legislation, the Delta Law of 1995, to make space for the river intervention ('eminent domain').

As part of their case, they noted that the interventions were only planned on the Dutch side of the river, and not coordinated with the Belgian river protection trajectory. Transboundary cooperation with neighbouring Belgium was meagre, so that a more integrated approach was not forthcoming until 2005. Unlike the project planners, the citizen groups sought strategic cooperation; to thwart the Maaswerken's progress; local opponents even struck a 'deal with the devil', allying with Belgian gravel magnates to seek a European ruling to defeat the Maaswerken. While ultimately unsuccessful, this move halted decision-making on the project for a full year. In 2005 construction of the Maaswerken finally started.

In the end, the province of Limburg won the battle: Limburg was included in the national flood plan. The whole province was guaranteed a 1 in 250-year protection standard, and the national government was made ultimately responsible for river protection on the Meuse (Wesselink et al. 2012). The provincial scale frame wherein regional flood protection was a security issue and a national concern eventually triumphed thanks to unexpected, and perhaps unintentional, 'support' from both national and local actors.

Lake Ijssel (Ijsselmeer)

Concern over climate predictions prompted the creation of a 2007 Advisory Commission to assess Dutch water management vulnerability to climate change. In September 2008 the commission's report was launched with great fanfare on Dutch television. Among various proposals for changing the country's water management institutions and reinforcing flood protection structures in view of a rising sea levels, the most controversial recommendation was to increase the storage capacity of Lake Ijssel by raising the lake's water level by 1.5 m. Framed by the commission as a project in the interests of national drinking water (i.e., risk mitigation), raising the level of Lake Ijssel would dramatically change waterfronts in picturesque old fishing towns, flood nature reserves and potentially alter groundwater levels around adjacent cities.

The northerly Ijsselmeer is connected with the southerly Markermeer, adjacent to Amsterdam and the rapidly expanding new town of Almere. The proposed 'decoupling' of the levels of Ijsselmeer (to be raised) and Markermeer (to remain at the old level) pitted north against south and rural against urban. Requested to accept interventions, the burden of national freshwater availability was put squarely on rural areas while urban zones such as Amsterdam remained largely unaffected (Van Buuren et al. forthcoming).

At a more abstract level we could interpret the process as follows: national public administration followed the political advisory committee in framing the issue at a national scale, making sense of the climate issue as a problem for the nation as a whole, employing national identity as a metaphor and implicitly reinforcing the need for a national Delta Programme as the solution. Operationalizing the national solution became a matter of involving the regional public and private players, which would not cause too much political conflict between urban and rural frames. This yielded a network governance approach in the Lake Ijssel region coordinated by an ad hoc administrative office to formulate a plausible strategy towards a national solution; hence, a regional network process to puzzle over possible strategies, embedded in a national administrative programme centring on a nationally framed problem.

Triggered by the committee's proposal, urgency among regional public and private players was high. To prevent a political conflict the administrative office started with a depoliticized puzzling process over technical possibilities and problems, yielding a variety of scenarios. These scenarios were framed rather technically as the corner points of a range of possible strategies. This technical framing minimized debate over societal concern. The ambiguity that came with the corner points gave little room for concrete negotiation over costs and benefits, but triggered highly complicated technical deliberations over water management possibilities, hypothetical win-win situations and a persistent national-interest framing. The lack of concreteness and the persistent national framing caused local authorities to shift their interest towards other venues for negotiation once the technical puzzle became concrete. At the time of publication, a nationwide cost benefit analysis questioned the national benefits of the Ijssel's 1.5 m rise on a mid-range time scale (CPB 2012; Van Buuren et al. forthcoming).

Discussion and Conclusions

Framing Winners and Losers

Spatial interventions legitimized by invoking the future 'crisis' of climate change have more often than not given rise to controversies in the Netherlands. The cases analysed here can be seen as examples of environmental activism or passive resistance (Lake Ijssel) to interventions, with a view to adapting to climate change scenarios. Environmental activism is all about scale (Towers 2000), but not everyone has the resources to mobilize.

The Dutch context does not provide a typical arena for environmental justice. The water scaling and water justice literature tends to foreground the poor, marginalized and vulnerable, with the countryside habitually portrayed as the underdog. Uniquely in the Dutch case, the areas under threat are neither necessarily poor nor marginalized. For example, the contestation between countryside/provincial interests and city/western conurbations in the Netherlands is not necessarily one of poor vs. rich. Moreover, the countryside is populated not only by farmers, but also by the landed rich and the new rich escaping the city. We find that the latter are most vocal in opposing infrastructural interventions in their 'backyards' and in expressing their equity concerns.

So, did scale frames exclude or benefit particular actors, solutions and knowledge? In each case, planners sought to enhance flood protection for a wider group, with the assumption that local stakeholders would be willing to accept a degree of sacrifice for the greater good. In so doing, however, they tended to overlook the interests of rural stakeholders, whether farmers or town dwellers in the region.

Identities and Position Frames

In two of the four cases discussed, a clear 'growth coalition' sought to combine flood safety with building houses, while in the other two cases significant actors resisted sacrificing their area for emergency planning that would benefit another region. Farmers and landscape conservationists, who felt victimized by urban gain, resisted urban development. Each case supports Lebel et al.'s (2005) *politics of position* (upstream vs. downstream):

- the sentiments of country people sacrificed for urbanites (Kampen, case 1);
- upstreamers for downstreamers (Ooij, case 2);
- periphery for core (Meuse, case 3);
- rural (or rather peri-urban) northerners for urban southerners (Ijssel, case 4).

It is also interesting that compensation as practised elsewhere (e.g. Pigeon 2012 for France) was not an obvious part of any of the plans.

In addition, identity might be as important as equity in the cases discussed here, which share an anti-urban bias/rhetoric. But identity may be a recent affectation: vocal protest often comes from urbanites who have migrated from the city in search of rural peace and quiet, and who are opposed to *any* intervention that may disturb them. For example, in the rural province of Limburg it is well known that second home owners and newcomers feel at risk of flooding, but first home owners and long-time residents are used to flooding.

Reframing and politicizing a project in terms of scale gave opponents a discursive advantage (see also Van Buuren and Warner, forthcoming). Proponents of the proposed flood relief channel on the Ijssel River at Kampen (case 1) branded the intervention with a label that focused on the water system. Opponents, however, reinterpreted it from the land-use angle, shifting attention away from the river discharge measure to the uncertain consequences on the local environment, with the effective 'bathtub' label. This brought the 'integrated spatial planning' focus chosen by project initiators in conflict with 'crisis management' and revealed a taboo (evacuation) with Kampen citizens.

Delta Frames and Scalar Politics

In the Ooij and Lake Ijssel cases, local stakeholders reinterpreted proposed interventions (defended by emphasizing their national relevance) by drawing on local scale frames and highlighting the inequitable consequences of intervention: a small region has to suffer for the benefit of other (larger) regions. Stakeholders concretized local effects, or insisted on their concretization, seeking to make the uncertain more certain. Policymakers, on the other hand, emphasizing the national importance of the proposed intervention, appeared to try to keep uncertainties uncertain in the Lake Ijssel case, even extending uncertainty to the bargaining procedure. When the scale and positioning of the Delta Programme for the lake were presented as a managerial decision, in the great tradition of Dutch engineering and fine-tuned water management, it was clear to stakeholders that this was a political decision differentially affecting stakeholders.

Conversely, in the Meuse case the provincial authorities used a *larger* scale frame, presenting the Maaswerken as crisis policy and as a consequence of national importance. They insisted on being included in the Delta flood safety system. Meanwhile locals scaled the intervention to local effects, but pragmatically upscaled their resistance and even made an alliance with the 'devil' next door (Belgium) to score victories.

It is notable that in all cases the Dutch government thought it politically inconvenient to venture outside Dutch territory in looking for solutions to heightened flood risk due to climate variability. This meant no agreement with upstream Germany on the Rhine or with Belgium on the River Meuse, and no international analysis of the climate scenarios underlying the Ijsselmeer plans. Yet the selection of a flood peak storage polder on the Rhine presented a transboundary problem: the physical connectivity between the Dutch Ooij polder and the German Düffel. The Germans were unhappy about the potential additional flood risk they would face if the Ooij was used as a flood storage reservoir. As a result, opposition commissioning counter-expertise was composed of Dutch and German local authorities (De Boer 2003).

Time

Both McCann (2003) and Loo (2007) have called attention to the temporal aspect in the politics of scale. The time scale is frequently linked to uncertainties in the future. In all cases studied here, local sacrifices are deemed to be required for climate-induced flood and drought management. In the Ooij polder case, Professor Van Ellen actively discredited the climate scenario legitimizing the tougher flood standards. In the Ijssel Lake case, the time frame was so long that it was hard to get a sense of urgency. Moreover, as one of the State Advisory Commission's prominent members said in an interview in Delft with one of the present authors in early 2009: 'We tried to look two centuries ahead, but [when presenting the report in early September 2008] we couldn't even foresee the economic crisis two months ahead' (M. Stive, pers. comm.).

On this note, we argue that in some contexts history matters more than in others. We noted the legitimacy deficit in Kampen and Limburg, where the past casts a long shadow (Sebastian 2008). In the Ooij polder, however, the idea of flooding the polder every year, which was common practice until some 50 years ago, was rejected by local stakeholders right from the start.

Knowledge and Uncertainty

Local knowledge is not necessarily decisive in territorial struggles. Opponents consciously mobilized external expertise to make their scalar point in exactly the same domain as the proponents did. It emerged from all cases that the evidence opponents relied on tended to come from the expert community rather than much-celebrated local knowledge. The counter-claims and frames therefore relied on knowledge generated within the same depoliticized, homogenizing tradition as the claims and frames launched by the policy initiators.

It was also noted that a more strategic aspect of scale framing might be the *labelling* effect of a scale frame in political negotiations between and over scales and locations. Water policy labels, which have strong scale connotations, may boomerang (Van Buuren and Warner, forthcoming) and may be contested with an evocative counter-label, such as the Kampen bathtub. This aspect could merit further research.

References

Apostolopoulou, E. and Paloniemi, R. (2012). Frames of scale challenges in Finnish and Greek biodiversity conservation. *Ecology and Society* 17(4): 9. Online: http://www.ecologyandsociety.org/vol17/iss4/art9 (accessed 10 November 2013).

Becker, G., Aerts, J. and Huitema, D. (2007). Transboundary flood management in the Rhine basin: Challenges for improved cooperation. *Water Science and Technology* 56(4): 125–35.

Beter Onderwijs Nederland (n.d.). Online: http://www.beteronderwijsnederland. nl/deltaplan (accessed 5 November 2013).

Boer, E. de (2003). *Het Noodoverloopgebied; airbag of luchtzak: Een kritiek op het rapport van de commissie-Luteijn.* Delft: Delft University of Technology. Available at: http://www.hoogwaterplatform.nl/dmdocuments/ noodoverloopgebied.pdf (accessed 10 November 2013).

Boezeman, D., Vink, M.J. and Leroy, P. (2013). The Dutch Delta Committee as a boundary organisation, *Environmental Science and Policy* 27(March): 162–71.

Brink, M.A. van den (2009). Rijkswaterstaat on the horns of a dilemma. PhD thesis. Radboud University Nijmegen.

Buuren, M.W. van and Warner, J. (2014, online first). From bypass to bathtub. Backfiring policy labels in Dutch water governance. *Environment and Planning C.* doi:10.1068/c12212

Buuren, M.W. van, Vink, M. and Warner, J. (forthcoming). Constructing authoritative answers to a latent crisis: Strategies of puzzling, powering and framing in Dutch climate adaptation practices compared. *Journal of Comparative Policy Analysis.*

Buzan, B., Waever, O. and de Wilde, J. (1998). *Security: A New Framework.* London: Harvester Wheatsheaf.

CPB. (2012). *Een snelle kosten-effectiviteitanalyse voor het Deltaprogramma IJsselmeergebied.* The Hague: Centraal Planbureau.

Delaney, D. and Leitner, H. (1997). The political construction of scale. *Political Geography* 16(2): 93–7.

Deltacommissie (2008). *Samen werken aan water: een land dat leeft, bouwt aan zijn toekomst.* The Hague: Deltacommissie.

Dewulf, A. (2013). Contrasting frames in policy debates on climate change adaptation. *WIREs Climate Change* 4(4): 321–30.

Dewulf, A., Gray, B., Putnam, L., Lewicki, R., Aarts, N., Bouwen, R. and van Woerkum, C. (2009). Disentangling approaches to framing: A meta-paradigmatic perspective. *Human Relations.* 62(2): 155–93.

Dewulf, A., Mancero, M., Cárdenas, G. and Sucozhañay, D. (2011). Fragmentation and connection of frames in collaborative water governance: A case study of river catchment management in Southern Ecuador. *International Review of Administrative Sciences* 77(1): 50–75.

Disco, C. (2002). Remaking 'nature': The ecological turn in Dutch water management. *Science, Technology and Human Values* 27(2): 206–35.

Dolfing, B. and Snellen, W.B. (1999). *Sustainability of Dutch Water Boards: Appropriate Design Characteristics for Self-Governing Water Management Organisations*. Wageningen: International Livestock Research Institute (ILRI).

Duncan, S. (2013). Personal life, pragmatism and bricolage. *Sociological Research Online* 16(4): 13.

Entman, R.M. (1993). Framing: Toward clarification of a fractured paradigm. *Journal of Communication* 43(4): 51–8.

Frerks, G., Warner, J. and Weijs, B. (2011). The politics of vulnerability and resilience. *Ambiente and Sociedade* 14(2): 105–22.

Grijzen, J. (2008). A whole village buried alive: The dramaturgy of participation in water projects. Freude am Fluss Final Conference, Nijmegen, October.

Herod, A. (1991). The production of scale in United States labor relations. *Area* 23: 82–8.

Hertsgaard, M. (2007). On the front lines of climate change, *Time*, 9 April.

HKV/Lijn in Water (2005). Aandachtspunten *Bypass Kampen*, report, May.

Immink, I. (2007). Established and recent policy arrangements for river management in the Netherlands: An analysis of discourses, PhD thesis, Wageningen University. Available online at http://library.wur.nl/ojs/index.php/frontis/article/viewFile/1134/705 (accessed 5 November 2013).

Johnson, C., Penning-Rowsell, E. and Parker, D. (2007). Natural and imposed injustices: The challenges in implementing 'fair' flood risk management policy in England. *Geographical Journal* 173(4): 374–90.

Kolkman, M.J., van der Veen, A. and Geurts, P. (2007). Controversies in water management: Frames and mental models. *Environmental Impact Assessment Review* 27(7): 685–706.

Kurtz, H.E. 2003. Scale frames and counter-scale frames: constructing the problem of environmental injustice. *Political Geography* 22(8): 887–916.

Lammersen, R. (2004). *Grensoverschrijdende effecten van extreem hoogwater op de Niederrhein: eindrapport*. Düsseldorf: Ministerium für Umwelt und Naturschutz, Landwirtschaft und Verbraucherschutz des Landes Nordrhein-Westfalen.

Lebel, L. (2006). The politics of scale in environmental assessments. In W.V. Reid et al. (eds), *Bridging Scales and Knowledge Systems: Concepts and Applications in Ecosystem Assessment*. Washington, DC: Island Press. Online: http://www.unep.org/maweb/documents/bridging/bridging.03.pdf (accessed 5 November 2013).

Lebel, L., Garden, P. and Imamura, M. (2005). The politics of scale, position, and place in the governance of water resources in the Mekong region. *Ecology and Society* 10(2): 18.

Loo, T. (2007). Disturbing the peace: Environmental change and the scales of justice on a northern river. *Environmental History* 12: 895–919.

Marston, S.A. (2000). The social construction of scale. *Progress in Human Geography* 24: 219–42.

McCann, E.J. (2003). Framing space and time in the city: Urban policy and the politics of spatial and temporal scale. *Journal of Urban Affairs* 25(2): 159–78.

Ministerie van Verkeer en Waterstaat (2009). *Nationaal Waterplan 2009–2015*. The Hague: Ministerie van Verkeer en Waterstaat.

Molle, F. (2007). Scales and power in river basin management: The Chao Phraya River in Thailand *Geographical Journal* 173(4): 358–73.

Molle, F. (2009). Water, politics, and river basin governance: Repoliticizing approaches to river basin management. *Water International* 34(1): 62–70.

Moore, A. (2008). Rethinking Scale as a geographical category: From analysis to practice. *Progress in Human Geography* 32(2): 203–25.

Pahl-Wostl, C. et al. (2005). *Transition to Adaptive Water Management: The NeWater Project*, NeWater Working Project 1, Institute of Environmental Systems Research, University of Osnabrück. Online: http://www.newater.info/index.php?pid=1020.

Pateete, A. (2012) Levels, scales, linkages, and other 'multiples' affecting natural resources. *International Journal of the Commons* 6(2): 134–50.

Pigeon, P. (2012). Flood risk and watershed management conflicts in France: Upper catchment management of the River Rhine. In J. Warner, M.W. van Buuren and J. Edelenbos (eds), *Making Space for the River*. London: International Water Association (IWA), 149–62.

Roth, D. and Warner, J.F. (2009). Rural solutions for threats to urban areas: the contest over calamity polders. *Built Environment* 35(4): 545–62.

Schön, D.A. and Rein, M. (1994). *Frame Reflection: Toward the Resolution of Intractable Policy Controversies*. New York: Basic Books.

Sebastian, A.G. (2008). *Transboundary Water Politics: Conflict, Cooperation, and Shadows of the Past in the Okavango and Orange River Basins of Southern Africa*. Ann Arbor, MI: ProQuest.

Sze, J., London, J., Shilling, F., Gambirazzio, G., Filan, T. and Cadenasso, M. (2009). Defining and contesting environmental justice: Socio-natures and the politics of scale in the delta. *Antipode* 41(4): 807–43.

Termeer, C.J.A.M., Dewulf, A. and van Lieshout, M. (2010). Disentangling scale approaches in governance research: Comparing monocentric, multilevel, and adaptive governance. *Ecology and Society* 15(4): 29.

Towers, G. (2000). Applying the political geography of scale: Grassroots strategies and environmental justice. *Professional Geographer* 52(1): 23–36.

Turton, A.R. (2000) Precipitation, people, pipelines and power in southern Africa: Towards a 'virtual water'-based political ecology discourse. In P.A. Stott and S. Sullivan (eds), *Political Ecology: Science, Myth and Power*. London: Arnold, 132–53.

van Lieshout, M., Dewulf, A., Aarts, N. and Termeer, C. (2011). Do scale frames matter? Scale frame mismatches in the decision making process of a 'mega farm' in a small Dutch village. *Ecology and Society* 16(1): 38.

Verduijn, S.H., Meijerink, S.V. and Leroy, P. (2012). How the Second Delta Committee set the agenda for climate adaptation policy: A Dutch case study on framing strategies for policy change. *Water Alternatives* 5(2): 469–84.

Verloo, M. (2005) Mainstreaming gender equality in Europe: A critical frame analysis approach. *Greek Review of Social Research* 117: 11–34.

Vink, M.J., Boezeman, D., Dewulf, A. and Termeer, C.J.A.M. (2013). Changing climate, changing frames: Dutch water policy frame developments in the context of a rise and fall of attention to climate change. *Environmental Science and Policy* 30: 90–101.

Warner, J. (2011). *Flood Planning: The Politics of Flood Insecurity*. London: Tauris.

Warner, J., Wester, P. and Bolding, A. (2008). Going with the flow: River basins as the natural units for water management? *Water Policy* 10(S2): 121–38.

Wegerich, K. (2007). A critical review of the concept of equity to support water allocation at various scales in the Amu Darya basin. *Irrigation and Drainage Systems* 21(3–4): 185–95.

Wesselink, A., Warner, J. and Kok, M. (2012). You gain some funding, you lose some freedom: Hegemony in flood protection in the Netherlands. *Environmental Science and Policy* 30: 113–25.

Chapter 6

Dynamics towards Domestic Territorialization of Water Governance in the EU: The Case of Southern Spain

Andreas Thiel[1]

Introduction

Finding the 'right' scale to govern water is probably impossible. Nevertheless, the European Water Framework Directive (WFD) provides strong advocacy in this regard. In its quest to find 'the right geographical scale' for water management the WFD advocates management within hydrographic regions while respecting national differences in the set-up of responsibilities (CEC 2007). As a legal requirement it asks all European member states to undertake water planning at the basin level (Thiel and Egerton 2011; Meyer and Thiel 2012). This chapter looks at the case of the southern Spanish Guadalquivir River basin. In contrast to the above advocacy of the basin level at the European level, in 2008 the Spanish national and subnational Andalusian governments decentralized water management to the regional level of Andalusia, abandoning River Basin Management (RBM) and thereby disempowering the central state administration.

Ample criticism challenges basins as the 'natural' unit for water management because they conceal the inherently political nature of choices that must be made (Molle 2008). Indeed, discrete river basins are often hard to define in biophysical terms, and potential institutional mismatches with other spatially organized political and administrative units almost inevitably emerge (Moss 2004; Mostert et al. 2008). Moreover, the physical reality of an integrated river basin system rarely requires an organization precisely coinciding with its boundaries (Mollinga et al. 2007). Instead, the 'politics of scale' illustrate that 'the appropriate scales for science, management, and decision making' in this domain are 'the joint product of social and biophysical processes' (Lebel et al. 2005). Studies contesting RBM argue that management functions and ecosystem processes are central and,

---

1 Research for this chapter benefited from the 'People' Specific Programme (Marie Curie Actions) of the European Union's Seventh Framework Programme; under REA agreement No. 289374 – 'ENTITLE', from a grant by the Einstein Foundation Berlin. Special thanks are due to Kerstin Lohr and Carmen Baake.

therefore, that cross-scale management is actually the relevant challenge that needs to be resolved in ecosystem and resource management.

In this chapter, I explain the conditions leading to the rescaling of water governance *away* from river basins (which are recommended in the WFD) and instead towards a more decentralized approach to water governance along territorial boundaries in Spain's Guadalquivir River. To do this, I develop a heuristic to help make sense of the strategic use of a window of opportunity that led Andalusia to move towards 'hydrological regionalism', understood by Lopez-Gunn (2009) as the reproduction of the hydrological paradigm entailing a symbolic, now 'regional', state–agriculture nexus. The chapter shows that the Spanish case is an example of a situation in which supranational frameworks (i.e., the WFD) and the dominant river basin model were secondary to regional concerns. As such, the chapter illustrates and further substantiates Falkner et al.'s (2007) arguments about the dominance of domestic politics in Spain, in contrast to dynamics in other countries. This finding stands in direct contrast to work positing the rise of a 'post-sovereign' environmental governance in Europe (e.g. Johnson, Chapter 11 this volume), and reaffirms the centrality of domestic politics not only to local issues (see Norman and Bakker 2009) but to international ones as well.

The Study of Negotiations over Scale

Scalar reorganization of governance implies a horizontal element (changes in the size of the area covered); a vertical element (the level within a vertically nested set of jurisdictions with which the respective institutions are associated); and a relational element (changes in the vertical and horizontal interconnections to other institutional arrangements). As detailed in the introduction to this volume, scale is socially constructed and constituted; it is not an ontologically given category, but is rather seen as being 'political', involving shifts in the relationships between state and society as part and parcel of changes in the scalar configuration of governance (Marston 2000). State actors thus play a central role in rescaling processes (Gualini 2006: 886), which have significant implications for resource management.

Providing an alternative perspective to critical geographers, scholars working on international environmental regimes and social-ecological systems analyse scale in the context of (mis)match between social and ecological systems (e.g. Cash et al. 2006). The underlying contention is that, where human responsibility does not match the spatial, temporal or functional scale of natural phenomena, unsustainable use of resources is likely and will persist until mismatch of scales is rectified (Lee 1993). In other words, rescaling redefines how resource management relates to the problems of 'fit', 'scale' and 'vertical and horizontal interplay' for resource management (Young 2002).

For the purposes of this chapter, I conceptualize the negotiations over the scalar reorganization of water governance as reliant on a set of categories that shape the positions of interdependent actors that interact in an action situation.

Indirect drivers concerning actors' positions are shaped by the properties of social-ecological transactions which shape actors' perceptions of the specific management problem at hand (such as rivalry, technological excludability and spatial distribution of transactions). I address them as contextual factors shaping the object of governance (Hagedorn 2008).

Following Knight (1992), Theesfeld (2005) and Schlüter (2001) I propose a heuristic of four categories that shape negotiations with respect to governance (cf. Thiel and Egerton 2011). In addition, the constitutionally defined structure of the negotiation process concerned with the allocation of responsibilities for resource management across jurisdictional levels needs to be considered. For example, in a 'de facto asymmetrical federal' state like Spain the reconfiguration of environmental governance needs to be agreed to by the province as well as at the federal level (Martinez-Herrera and Miley 2010: 6). The heuristic consists of the following four factors that directly shape the power resources of actors that negotiate the scalar reorganization of governance.

1. The credibility of a strategy increases an actor's bargaining power. Credibility is reinforced if an actor expects insignificant losses from failure of agreement; when an actor disposes of powers to impose sanctions on other actors; or when they dispose of positional power that gives easy access to certain resources (e.g. information) and therefore lowers the costs for taking a specific strategic choice (Knight 1992). A federal state constellation further implies that lower- and higher-level actors depend on the preferences of their constituents as well as on their institutionally determined ability to implement commitments. Also, ratification procedures or ways of tying the hands of negotiators may constrain their options and credibility. Further, significant scope for issue linkages and side payments emerges from this setting, which can enlarge the feasible space of agreement.

2. As dynamic considerations that affect actors' strategies I consider the temporal dimension of reaching an agreement as preferring a swift agreement, for example where a political window of opportunity opens up, as opposed to lack of preferences for the timing of an agreement (Theesfeld 2005). For example, in federal states the temporal dimension of potential changes in actors and preferences at different levels, for example through elections, needs to be considered.

3. Network membership in large advocacy groups can allow access to information and lower efforts necessary for persuasion, consequently lowering efforts to secure support for one's position (Knight 1992, in Theesfeld 2005).

4. Transaction and transition costs influence negotiations. Here, transaction costs are defined as the costs of actors informing themselves about options, negotiating, agreeing, monitoring, enforcing and adapting institutions (Dahlmann 1979), while transition costs are the costs of decision making for institutional change and the costs of implementing institutional reforms (Challen 2000). They depend on the political implications and organizational changes entailed in reforms. Transaction costs further depend on the characteristics of transactions that are the object of governance and how they change. Sometimes it is not characteristics

that actually change, but rather priorities concerning management, foregrounding specific characteristics of social-ecological transactions.

Case Study: The Setting for Change in Spanish Water Management

Continental Spain has a long tradition in RBM, with the Spanish Constitution stipulating that planning and management of river basins that cross several communities (*comunidades*) is a responsibility of the central state, and exercised by state-run hydrologic organizations known as *Confederaciónes Hidrográficas* (hereafter *Confederaciónes*). *Comunidades* can manage intracommunitarian river basins (see Figures 6.1 and 6.2). But, because intercommunitarian river management and transfers became mechanisms through which national unity could be reinforced, they are more frequently managed by *Confederaciónes*, which are part of the *Ministerio de Medio Ambiente y Medio Rural y Marino* (Ministry of the Environment and Rural and Maritime Affairs, MMARM). The ministry is responsible for policy guidelines and negotiations regarding European agricultural and environmental policies (Varela Ortega and Hernández-Mora 2010). During the 1990s, *comunidades* acquired responsibility for economic and agricultural policy as well as land use planning.

Figure 6.1   Borders of Spanish *comunidades*

Source: http://www.msssi.gob.es/organizacion/ccaa/img/spain.jpg (accessed 20 July 2013).
Reproduced with the kind permission of Ministerio de Sanidad, Servicios Sociales e Igualdad.

Figure 6.2   Spanish rivers: inter- and intracommunitarian

Source: http://www.prtr-es.es/Upload/2012/Demarcaciones_hidrogr%C3%A1ficas.png (accessed 4 July 2013). Reproduced and modified with the kind permission of Registro Estatal de Emisiones y Fuentes Contaminantes.

Confederaciónes have a high degree of organizational, functional and economic autonomy and bear most of the administrative weight. They were instruments of economic modernization driven by technology and surface water engineering (Swyngedouw 1999; Bukowski 2007). Engineers took the main operational decisions, adopting criteria often described as 'technical' as opposed to political. National, subnational and local administrations as well as water users with a legal title to use water were represented on operational decision-making bodies. Since legal titles were long term and inflexible, increasing numbers of groundwater users abstracted water illegally without title and without representation in operational decision making.

Since the mid-1990s, priorities for water management in Spain have been increasingly concerned with reserving water for maintenance of water-related ecosystems, aquifer management, water pollution and the formal recognition of new and 'illegal' uses. As a result, attempts were made to make water management more integrated and embed it into a multi-tiered participation and consultation structure alongside the central and regional administrations and users (Irujo 2010). Nevertheless, Spanish and Andalusian water management still face significant problems that also concern the Guadalquivir basin, such as pollution and degradation of wetland ecosystems. Continuously growing irrigation demand increasingly relied on the (over-)exploitation of groundwater (MMARM/ Confederación Hidrográfica del Guadalquivir 2010). Governance problems include fragmented legislation and competencies, and insufficient coordination and cooperation – specifically between water management, land use policies and agriculture. Transparent, integrated water planning is hampered by the absence of comprehensive inventories of existing uses. In addition, existing financial, technical and human resources to manage such complexities are considered insufficient (Irujo 2010).

Decentralization of Andalusian Water Management and the Guadalquivir

The Guadalquivir River is the fifth largest in Spain; 90 per cent of the surface of the basin, 97 per cent of the population of the basin and 99 per cent of the uses of the basin are situated in Andalusia (Consejería de Medio Ambiente de la Junta de Andalucía 2008). The basin accounts for 58 per cent of total water used in Andalusia. Its principal use is agriculture, with water consumption for irrigation more than doubling between the early 1960s and 2000 (Figure 6.3). Interviewees called the Guadalquivir the 'spine of Andalusia', referencing its outstanding role for Andalusia, and underlining the river's symbolic value. The fact that Andalusia is the dominant actor in the basin becomes the necessary condition enabling decentralization of water management to Andalusia, as other *comunidades* have no material reasons for opposition.

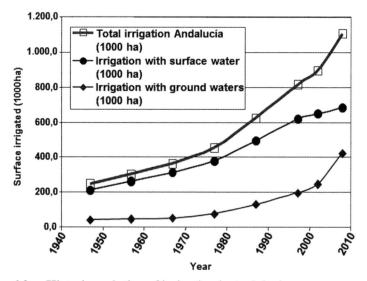

Figure 6.3 **Historic evolution of irrigation in Andalusia**
Source: Corominas Masip, unpublished. Reproduced with the kind permission of Joan Coriminas.

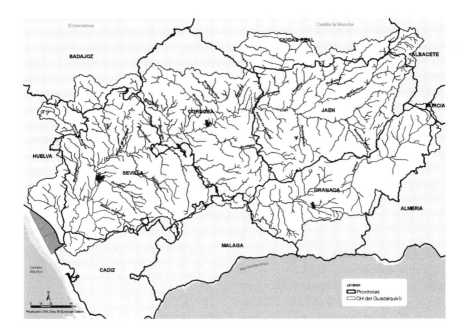

Figure 6.4   The Guadalquivir basin in Andalusia and its reach into neighbouring *comunidades*

Source: http://www.chguadalquivir.es/export/sites/default/portalchg/laDemarcacion/guadalquivir/descripcion/ambitoTerritorial/imagenes/AmbitoTerritorial.jpg (accessed 11 February 2013). Reproduced with kind permission of Gobierno de Espana, Ministerio de Agricultura, Alimentación y Medio Ambiente, Confederación Hidrográfica de Guadalquivir.

Tourism, construction and energy production sectors, as well as a growing local population, are driving demand for water in the basin that is expected to continue. The ecological flow regime requested by European Union directives is a further 'demand' on the basin requiring further reduction of use by other users (MMARM/Confederación Hidrográfica del Guadalquivir 2010).

In 2004, after the Spanish Socialist Party (PSOE) came to power, several *comunidades* began renegotiating their statutes, which regulate overall relations between the *comunidades* and the federal state. In particular, several renegotiations addressed decentralization of competencies for water management, reflecting regional efforts to pursue what Lopez-Gunn (2009) has called 'hydrological regionalism'. Interviewees for the present study argue that this effort emerged because *comunidades* wanted to prevent the type of initiatives previously launched by the Conservative government as part of the national water plan, which had aimed to redistribute water resources among *comunidades* and favoured coastal *comunidades* (Figure 6.4).

Between 1989 and 2004 Andalusian decentralization of water management had been dormant, but over that 15-year period the regional administration's profile in water management was gradually strengthened (Blomquist et al. 2005).

Then, on 1 January 2005 the new Socialist government transferred competencies for the intracommunitarian Mediterranean basin to the Andalusian administration. Two further transfers followed: the transfer of the Atlantic basin and the de facto transfer of the Andalusian part of the international Guadiana River. Below I explain, through reference to the specifically emblematic case of the intercommunitarian Guadalquivir, why this de facto transfer was possible.

The new Andalusian statutes that included the transfer of responsibilities for the Guadalquivir were agreed to by the Spanish Parliament in October 2006 and by the Senate in December 2006; they were ratified by a referendum supported by 88 per cent of the Andalusian population in February 2007 and entered into force in March 2007. These statutes stipulate that 'the Autonomous Community of Andalusia has exclusive competencies over the waters of the Guadalquivir which flow through its territories and do not affect another Autonomous Community' (Junta de Andalucía 2007). Thus, in 2009, for the first time in Spain management of an intercommunitarian river (except responsibility for water planning, which for constitutional reasons had to remain with the *Confederaciónes*) – the Andalusian part of the Guadalquivir – was transferred to the administration of the *Comunidad*. The socialist *Comunidad* Extremadura and the conservative Castilla-La Mancha – both of which in effect had little interest in the transfer – appealed the transfer, and in summer 2011 the court declared the transfer of the Guadalquivir to be unconstitutional (Europapress 2011).

Thus, in the four years from 2005 and 2009 Andalusia received responsibilities over management of all its waters, including planning for intracommunitarian basins. To manage these new responsibilities, the Andalusian Water Agency (*Agencía Andaluza del Agua*) was founded in 2005. Politically appointed office-holders in the provinces were put in charge of operational water management. In this new Andalusian water management structure users and stakeholders without concessions gained representation in participatory and decision-making bodies. In order to bring regional stakeholders together, a strategic document entitled 'Andalusian Water Vision' was developed after extensive consultation. Subsequently, the vision drove the adoption of an Andalusian water law that aimed to adapt management to regional conditions (Consejería de Medio Ambiente de la Junta de Andalucía 2008; Junta de Andalucía/Consejería de Medio Ambiente 2009; Junta de Andalucía 2010). The next section elaborates on the positions of the different actors vis-à-vis the transfer of responsibilities over the Guadalquivir before using the above described heuristic of actors' power resources to explore why far-reaching decentralization of water management was possible between 2005 and 2009.

Positions on the Decentralization of Management of the Guadalquivir

The socialist president of the Junta de Andalucía launched the renegotiation of the statutes regulating overall relations between the *comunidad* of Andalusia and the Spanish federal state in 2001. In 2004, politicians and experts in Andalusia voiced demands to also assume greater responsibilities in water management, with the nebulous aim of a 'new water culture' and better management integration (Agudo Zamora 2005). The possibility that the region could finally gain control over its entire water resource base, including the Guadalquivir, was also symbolically charged (Consejería de Obras Públicas y Transportes 2008). In 2005, the ongoing transfer of responsibilities from the Mediterranean basin to the regional administration already indicated that participatory and decision-making bodies would be opened up to broader societal concerns, which partially explains the positions of actors concerning the transfer of responsibilities for the Guadalquivir described below.

The Socialist Party, as well as the regional administration, supported the transfer of responsibilities for the Guadalquivir. One political reason for embracing it was to associate the overall statute with an issue that might translate into gains in votes. This expresses fears that, otherwise, the new statutes may have become politically irrelevant because they lacked saliency and were negotiated in a favourable political environment (see below). In addition, responsibility for water management of the Guadalquivir added significantly to the portfolio of the regional government, while also increasing resources of the bureaucrats involved. Regional and national conservative parties (*Partido Popular*) favoured a strong national state and did not support the transfer of responsibilities (ABC 2007).

Among stakeholders, the Andalusian Association of Entrepreneurs (*Confederacion de Empresarios de Andalucia*/CEA) and several private sector associations, the tourism sector and the renewable energies sector supported decentralization, hoping for flexible allocation of water titles. Public and private water companies did not make any pronouncements. The important association of irrigation farmers, which historically held water titles (*Feragua*), voiced significant concerns, fearing loss of influence through reconfiguration of management bodies and flexibilization of the water use titles. Later, however, they officially supported the transfer for reasons of overriding 'regional interests'. In contrast, a more recently founded association of irrigation farmers – representing farmers who did not hold use titles, and most of whom relied on groundwater – wholeheartedly supported the transfer as they expected flexibilization and legalization of illegal water use. Officially then, all sectoral regional actors supported the transfer in the end. Opposing decentralization were experts and environmental NGOs, the latter fearing the sidelining of the ecological dimension of water management and loss of influence, as their regional organizations were relatively weak.

At the national level, Guadalquivir's *Confederación Hidrográfica* opposed the transfer because it wanted to maintain its responsibilities; it distrusted the regional institutions to manage water; and it feared that decentralization of the intercommunitarian Guadalquivir basin would set a precedent for further decentralization all over Spain. Finally, all interviewees in the study confirmed that the transfer of responsibilities over water management of the Guadalquivir was a 'political decision', supposedly at the highest level, following negotiations between the Prime Minister and the president of the regional government. Even the Minister of the Environment and the Director of Water (an Andalusian) were opposed. Based on this analysis, the following description reduces the action situation to negotiations of the water-related content of the statutes between the national government of Spain (level I) and the Andalusian government (level II).

The Determinants of Negotiations

Against the background of the above-described constitutional setting of the Spanish asymmetric federal state, challenges of water management and positions of actors I use heuristics of power resources (introduced above) to explain the outcome of negotiations over the transfer of water management responsibilities of the Guadalquivir River to the regional level in the reform of the statute.

Credible Commitment

Throughout the negotiations the Andalusian regional government appeared to be highly credible in its commitment to the decentralization of water management, because of the homogeneous support of regional actors, while national government opposition would not have seemed credible. In fact, once in power, the socialist central government openly supported a renegotiation of statutes all over Spain. Thus, in possible cases of failure of such negotiations, the central level would have incurred great exit costs, as its promises would not have been delivered at the national or at the regional level.

The most credible commitment at the national level against transferring responsibilities for water management as part of reforms of statutes was the national constitution's stipulation guaranteeing the unity of management of intercommunitarian basins (Consejeria de Medio Ambiente 2008). Still, failure to include decentralization of water management in the Andalusian statutes could have had negative consequences within the Socialist Party and in elections, with Andalusia being one of its strongholds. By linking the new statutes to the decentralization of water management, the distributional outcome for both actors was increased, creating a win-win situation. Consequently, given this advantageous context from the perspective of the regional government, decentralization of management of the Guadalquivir became an integral demand of statute reform.

For the regional government, an important reason for including the transfer in the statute was to gain politically from the renegotiation of statutes that otherwise appealed little to the electorate. In contrast, under the previous government before 2004, the reigning national Conservative Party would have had low exit costs from non-agreement, as it opposed regionalization of responsibilities. Further, the Conservative Party would never have wanted to play into the hands of the Andalusian socialists.

The distribution of expected monetary benefits from the transfer of responsibilities for water management may have also influenced the credibility of commitments. Yet, analyses of savings to be had through regionalization have never been made. Nevertheless, little doubt exists that the regional level would gain politically from obtaining authority for water management, increasing the credibility of its commitment. Gaining responsibility for water management in its entire territory added a missing piece to the CA's responsibilities, which had been simultaneously decentralized (agriculture, regional economic development, land use planning), and provided control over a valuable factor of production. In contrast, the national level lost important influence over regional, environmental and economic policy, for which water policy was increasingly instrumentalized (del Moral 2007).

Dynamic considerations
Both levels of government negotiations aimed to achieve swift agreement because successful conclusion of the transfer of responsibilities was expected to depend upon the contingent majority of the socialists at national and regional level. Therefore, these temporal considerations played an important role in concluding the negotiations.

Network membership
The actors involved within the *comunidad* could hardly oppose a strengthening of the region. With emerging regionalism throughout the 1990s an issue network of unquestioned support for the decentralization of water management had been constructed in Andalusia which made it a 'quasi-ideology', bound up with a strong *comunidad* independent of party politics. Thus, to a certain degree the transfer became a hegemonic project for the Andalusian water sector. Such hegemonic projects can provide a degree of orientation and social cohesion in attempts to establish new modes of regulation and solve problems that threaten continuing economic prosperity. For Jessop, they can also serve to (re-)integrate strategically significant interests (Jessop 1990; cf. Thiel 2009). Linking the transfer of responsibilities for the Guadalquivir to the broader statutes further heightened the symbolic status of the statutes and also made questioning of the decentralization of water management by actors in Andalusia more difficult. Even if they had wanted to, national level actors could not feasibly build alternative alliances with regional actors seeking to break up the overall, homogenous coalition at the regional level. The regional government further avoided regional opposition by demanding control of water management, but without making explicit how it would subsequently restructure it.

Transaction and transition costs and their distribution
Transaction costs associated with the scalar reorganization of governance, including the costs of its transition, potentially reduced perceived gains from negotiations on both sides. In this regard, first it needs to be acknowledged that the cost effectiveness of different arrangements for managing water did not play a role in the transfer. At the same time, the constellation of negotiations was favourable to resolving such potential issues. Furthermore, by that time the Andalusian water administration had already been set up, thus reducing the transition costs

for decentralizing management of the Guadalquivir. Gradual decentralization of intracommunitarian rivers in 2005 had already resulted in a strategic rethinking of Andalusian water management by the regional administration. As one interviewee poignantly noted: 'After Andalusia had received all responsibilities for its waters, it became necessary to develop an idea of what to do with those responsibilities.'

In addition, changes in water management priorities – and the characteristics of the nature-related transactions whose governance was at stake – facilitated reorganization. As explained above, large investments and basin-wide responsibilities for realizing surface water infrastructure had become less important since the turn of the century, whereas groundwater management and integrated management of water demand and supply sectors (land and agricultural uses) had gained importance. Specifically, the regional level administration advocated changes in water management as a result of these changes in use patterns. Arguably, it increased relative cost effectiveness of territorially oriented management as opposed to basin-oriented management.

The above-mentioned changes in management priorities and desires to better coordinate between water management and other water use-related sectors also played a role in the structure Andalusia adopted for water management. Economies of scale and scope in governance were the aims of integrating water management into the overall administrative structure at the level of the sub-regional provinces, as well as reduced transition costs – i.e. the costs of shifting to a new governance structure. This put politically appointed provincial leaders in charge of water management decisions which had previously been made by technicians in charge of local hydrographic areas. Among experts, this shift caused significant doubts about the criteria underlying future management decisions.

Furthermore, allowing for recovery of costs of governance, water metering and monitoring techniques were gradually introduced, and water tariffs were increased and gradually expanded to groundwater. In this way, indirectly, transaction and transition costs of decentralized management were to be matched.

Conclusions

This chapter employed a framework to explain the outcomes of negotiations between interest-led actors over the scalar reorganization of water governance of the intercommunitarian Guadalquivir River in southern Spain. The analysis shows that Andalusia's dominance in the Guadalquivir basin was central to the success of the *comunidad* in gaining almost entire control over basin management. Factors further promoting the stance of regional actors in favour of decentralization were:

• changes in water management priorities;
• increased focus on groundwater-related transactions whose management followed a different territorial logic from surface water management;
• gains in responsibilities of the regional administration in interrelated areas;

- the symbolic value of decentralizing policymaking for one of the economically most significant natural resources; and
- failure to reform water management at the national level.

Particularly crucial for decentralization were the contingent constellation of party majorities at both levels and the relatively weak position of the Prime Minister. Furthermore, the credibility of the *comunidad* in the water management negotiations seems to have been increased by linking decentralization to the changing of national statutes and the subnational hegemonic project of strengthening the region. As a result, water management in Andalusia diverged from the hitherto reigning RBM set-up in Spain.

Although this chapter has focused on the Spanish case, it speaks to rescaled water governance elsewhere in its treatment of the contingent, national and subnational – rather than international – dynamics that shape water management. In fact, the most interesting and perhaps most controversial finding of the case is that the requirements of the European WFD to coordinate management across the basin and plan for the entire basin, and its strong advocacy of basin management, did not play any role in its implementation in southern Spain.

In contrast, the corresponding ideas that were now promoted at the supranational level and that had been realized in Spain for long did not withstand domestic dynamics, such as the regionalization tendencies and a shift from priority for surface water management to an increasing need to address groundwater management and a need to coordinate policies. This finding balances Corey Johnson in this volume, who suggests the need to introduce nature (in the form of ecologically prescribed boundaries of river basins) into discussions about the emergent post-sovereign territoriality of environmental governance in Europe (see Chapter 11). Johnson specifically argues that since introduction of the European WFD the analytical level of basins needs to be added to discussions. While he is probably right for most cases, the case of the Guadalquivir shows that the fundamental questions are what domestic economic and political interests control the processes of scalar reconfiguration, and whose technical, economic or political vision of natural resource governance prevails at a specific moment of reform.

Such an understanding allows us to paint a more differentiated picture of the role of European prescriptions such as water management on the basin scale. In Spain, where there exists a strong tradition of basin management, it was emphasized less than the role of existing jurisdictional scales. However, this focus does not mean that such a reorientation improves water management. The conclusion is that a more differentiated picture needs to be painted in order to understand why, for example, across all of Spain the basin scale was significantly downplayed in favour of administrative boundaries (Thiel et al. 2011), while in case of the German rivers Elbe or Rhine or in Portugal the opposite happened (Thiel 2012).

It is important to note that following the transfer of responsibilities for the Guadalquivir, decentralized water management may in fact have held the potential to better deliver on the WFD. The scalar reorganization of governance also has an important functional dimension to it, relating to the best way to address changes in water management priorities. In Spain, the institutional set-up of water management was traditionally tied to the development of surface waters. Yet this set-up seems to be strongly questioned in its ability to address current water management issues such as water pollution; requirements for cross-sector coordination; flexibility for meeting demands of new actors; ecological requirements and groundwater management. An overarching challenge is to steer demand and align water policy with the ecologically driven objectives of the WFD. In Spain, because of the constellation of divergent interests at stake at the national level and the fragmentation of relevant responsibilities across levels of jurisdiction, water management reform at the national level had failed in the last decade, leaving doubts over abilities of the national authorities to resolve these issues.

The restructuring of Andalusian water management according to the administrative boundaries of the provinces empowered provincial politicians. Whether they are 'better' or 'worse' decision makers on operational water management has never really been examined, as decentralization was reversed too quickly in 2012, when its unconstitutionality was confirmed, to come to any serious conclusions on that score. Potentially, politics is more transparent and accountable than technocratic decision making by engineers. To summarize, the Andalusian case presented here clearly illustrates that panaceas (Ostrom 2007) do not exist for water management, and that domestic politics continue to dominate policy.

References

ABC (2007). http://www.abcdesevilla.es/andalucia (accessed 19 March 2010). 6 October, p. 36; 6 March; 29 August, p. 28.

Agudo Zamora, M.J. (2005). *La reforma del Estatuto de Autonomia para Andalucia: Contexto e inicio*. Seville: Centro de Estudios Andaluces. (Actualidad, 03/05).

Blomquist, W.A., Giansante, C., Bhat, A. and Kemper, K. (2005). *Institutional and Policy Analysis of River Basin Management: The Guadalquivir River Basin, Spain*. Washington, DC: World Bank.

Bukowski, J. (2007). Spanish water policy and the national hydrological plan: An advocacy coalition approach to policy change. *South European Society and Politics* 12(1), pp. 39–57.

Cash, D.W. et al. (2006). Scale and cross-scale dynamics: Governance and information in a multilevel world. *Ecology and Society* 11(2), 8.

CEC (2007). *Towards Sustainable Water Management in the European Union: First Stage in the Implementation of the Water Framework Directive*. Working paper. Communication from the Commission to the European Parliament and the Council. Brussels: Commission of the European Communities.

Challen, R. (2000). *Institutions, Transaction Costs and Environmental Policy: Institutional Reform For Water Resources*. Cheltenham: Edward Elgar.

Consejeria de Medio Ambiente (2008). *Decreto de 7 de enero, por el que se aprueben los estatutos de la agencia andaluza del agua no. 1067/08-MA.* Seville: Consejeria de Medio Ambiente.

Consejería de Medio Ambiente de la Junta de Andalucía (2008). *Medio Ambiente en Andalucía Informe 2008.* Seville: Consejería de Medio Ambiente de la Junta de Andalucía.

Consejería de Obras Públicas y Transportes (2008). *El Rio Guadalquivir.* Seville: Consejería de Obras Públicas y Transportes.

Dahlmann, C.J. (1979). The problem of externality. *Journal of Law and Economics* 22, pp. 141–62.

Del Moral, L. (2007). Integración de políticas sectoriales: agua y territorio. Fundación Nueva Cultura del Agua. Panel Científico-Técnico de Seguimiento de la Política de Aguas. Vicerrectorado de Doctorado, Universidad de Sevilla, Pabellón de México (Avda. de la Palmera). Seville, 24 January.

Denzau, M. and North, D.C. (1994). Shared mental models: Ideologies and institutions. *Kyklos* 47(1), pp. 3–31.

Europapress (2011). 30.3.20122. http://www.europapress.es/noticiaprint (accessed 1 April 2011).

Falkner, G., Hartlapp, M. and Treib, O. (2007). Worlds of compliance: Why leading approaches to European Union implementation are only 'sometimes-true theories'. *European Journal of Political Research* 46(3), pp. 395–416.

Gualini, E. (2006). The rescaling of governance in Europe: New spatial and institutional rationales. *European Planning Studies* 14(7), pp. 882–904.

Hagedorn, K. (2008). Particular requirements for institutional analysis in nature-related sectors. *European Review of Agricultural Economics* 35(4), pp. 357–84.

Howitt, R. (2003). Scale. In J. Agnew, K. Mitchell and G. Toal (eds), *A Companion to Political Geography.* Malden, MA: Blackwell, pp. 138–57.

Irujo, E. (2010). The foundations and principles of modern water law. In A. Garrido (ed.), *Water Policy in Spain.* Leiden: CRC/Balkema.

Jessop B. (1990). *State Theory: Putting the Capitalist State in Its Place.* Cambridge: Polity.

Junta de Andalucía (2007). *Estatuto de Autonomía para Andalucía: Texto aprobado por el congreso de los diputados.* Seville: Junta de Andalucía.

Junta de Andalucía (2010). LEY 9/2010, de 30 de julio, de Aguas para Andalucía. *Boletín Oficial de la Junta de Andalucía (BOJA)* 155, pp. 6–40.

Junta de Andalucía/Consejería de Medio Ambiente (2009). *Acuerdo Andaluz por el agua.* Seville: Junta de Andalucía.

Knight, J. (1995). Models, interpretations, and theories: Constructing explanations of institutional emergence and change. In J. Knight and I. Sened (eds), *Explaining Social Institutions.* Ann Arbor: University of Michigan Press.

Knight, J. (1992). *Institutions and Social Conflict.* Cambridge: Cambridge University Press.

Lebel, L., Garden, P. and Imamura, M. (2005). The politics of scale, position, and place in the governance of water resources in the Mekong region. *Ecology and Society* 10(2), 18.

Lee, K.N. (1993). Greed, scale mismatch, and learning. *Ecological Applications* 3, pp. 560–64.

Liefferink, D., Wiering, M. and Uitenboogaart, Y. (2011). The EU Water Framework Directive: A multi-dimensional analysis of implementation and domestic impact. *Land Use Policy* 28(4), pp. 712–22.

Lopez-Gunn, E. (2009). Agua para todos: the new regionalist hydraulic paradigm in Spain. *Water Alternatives* 2(3), pp. 370–94.

Marston, S.A. (2000). The social construction of scale. *Progress in Human Geography* 24(2), pp. 219–42.

Martinez-Herrera, E. and Miley, T.J. (2010). The constitution and the politics of national identity in Spain. *Nations and Nationalism* 16(1), pp. 6–30.

Meyer, C. and Thiel A. (2012). Institutional change in water management collaboration: Implementing the European Water Framework Directive in the Eastern German Odra basin. *Water Policy* 14(4), pp. 625–46.

MMARM (Ministerio de Medio Ambiente y Medio Rural y Marino)/Confederación Hidrográfica del Gudalquivir (2010). *Esquema de Temas Importantes: Demarcación Hidrográfica del Guadalquivir.*

Molle, F. (2008). Nirvana concepts, narratives and policy models: Insights from the water sector. *Water Alternatives* 1(1), pp. 131–56.

Mollinga, P.P., Meinzen-Dick, R.S. and Merrey, D.J. (2007). Politics, plurality and problemsheds: A strategic approach for reform of agricultural water resources management. *Development Policy Review* 25(6), pp. 699–719.

Moss, T. (2004). The governance of land use in river basins: Prospects for overcoming problems of institutional interplay with the EU Water Framework Directive. *Land Use Policy* 21(1), pp. 85–94.

Mostert, E., Craps, M. and Pahl-Wostl, C. (2008): Social learning: The key to integrated water resources management? *Water International* 33(3), pp. 293–304.

Norman, E.S. and Bakker, K. (2009). Transgressing scales: Transboundary water governance across the Canada–U.S. borderland. *Annals of the Association of American Geographers* 99(1), pp. 99–117.

Ostrom, E. (2007). A diagnostic approach for going beyond panaceas. *Proceedings of the National Academy of Sciences of the United States of America* 104(39), pp. 15181–7.

Pahl-Wostl, C., Mostert, E. and Tàbara, D. (2008). The growing importance of social learning in water resources management and sustainability science. *Ecology and Society* 13(1), p. 24.

Sauri, D. and del Moral, L. (2001). Recent developments in Spanish water policy: Alternatives and conflicts at the end of the hydraulic age. *Geoforum* 32(3), pp. 351–62.

Schlüter, A. (2001). *Institutioneller Wandel und Transformation: Restitution, Transformation und Privatisierung in der tschechischen Landwirtschaft.* Aachen: Shaker.

Swyngedouw, E. (1999). Modernity and hybridity: Nature, regeneracionismo, and the production of the Spanish waterscape, 1890–1930. *Annals of the Association of American Geographers* 89(3), pp. 443–65.

Swyngedouw, E. (1997). Neither global or local: 'Glocalisation' and the politics of scale. In K. Cox (ed.), *Spaces of Globalization: Reasserting the Power of the Local.* New York: Guilford, pp. 137–66.

Theesfeld, I. (2005). *A Common Pool Resource in Transition: Determinants of Institutional Change for Bulgaria's Postsocialist Irrigation Sector.* Aachen: Shaker.

Thiel, A. (2009). Europeanisation and the rescaling of water services: Agency and state spatial strategies in the Algarve, Portugal. *Water Alternatives* 2(2), pp. 1–20. Available online at http://www.water-alternatives.org.

Thiel, A. (2012). The politics of problem solving: A co-evolutionary perspective on the recent scalar reorganisation of water governance in Germany. UFZ Discussion Paper 1436–140X (09). Available online at http://hdl.handle.net/10419/59595.

Thiel, A., Schröder, C. and Sampedro, D. (2011). Explaining re-scaling and differentiation of water management on the Iberian Peninsula. VII. *Congreso Iberico sobre gestión y planificación del agua. Facultad de Ciencias Sociales,* Talavera de la Reina, Spain, 16 February.

Thiel, A. and Egerton, C. (2011). Re-scaling of resource governance as institutional change: The case of water governance in Portugal. *Journal of Environmental Management and Planning* 54(3), pp. 383–402.

Varela Ortega, C. and Hernández-Mora, N. (2010). Institutions and institutional reform in the Spanish water sector: A historical perspective. In A. Garrido (ed.), *Water Policy in Spain.* Leiden: CRC/Balkema.

Young, O.R. (2002). *The Institutional Dimensions of Environmental Change: Fit, Interplay, and Scale.* Cambridge, MA: MIT Press.

PART II
Beyond the Watershed: Rescaling Decision-Making

Introduction to Part II

Tom Perreault

The chapters in Part II examine the production and framing of scale in water governance. As considered throughout this volume, the concept of 'scalar politics' focuses attention not on scale *per se*, but on institutionalized practices, processes and relationships, and the ways these become differentially scaled (MacKinnon 2011; McCarthy 2005). Attentive to recent scholarly work on scale and scalar politics in geography, the chapters in this section examine an array of processes and social relations involved in governing water. These include the 'strategic decentralization' of water governance in highly differentiated states (Furlong, Chapter 8); the role of hydraulic technology in defining water rights (Jepson and Brannstrom, Chapter 9); and the production of citizen subjectivities in relation to water resources (Perramond, Chapter 10). As the authors of these chapters suggest, scale is socially produced and reconfigured through the frictions of socionatural relations. Such scales are dynamic; and while scales of governance, once established, shape future possibilities for social action, they do not *determine* the possibilities (Sayre 2009).

The historically and spatially dynamic nature of scale and scalar politics is evident in the regulatory challenges posed by the EU's Water Framework Directive (see Johnson, Chapter 11), and water and wastewater provision in Ontario (Cook, Chapter 7). The chapters in this section, rooted in political economic and political ecological analyses, highlight the networked relations involved in water governance (Neumann 2009). These chapters, and this volume more generally, are fundamentally about the production and contestation of scale in water governance. As such, it is worthwhile considering in some detail the key terms: water, governance and scale.

Water

Among political ecologists and other critical human geographers it has become nearly axiomatic to consider water in terms of the 'hydrosocial'. Water, in this sense, is neither purely 'natural' nor purely 'social', but rather simultaneously and inseparably both: a hybrid 'socio-nature'. Water exists apart from human influence (as rainfall, in aquifers and oceans, as soil moisture and evaporation etc.), and is simultaneously produced and enacted through human labour and social action (as irrigation systems, fountains, water law, sewer systems, thirst, customary rights etc.). Water is given meaning through cultural beliefs, historical memory and social practice, and exists as much in discourse and symbol as it does as a physical, material thing (Bakker 2002). It is, as Erik Swyngedouw (2004) notes, a product of historically sedimented social actions, institutions, struggles and discourses, and in turn helps shape the social relations through which it is produced and enacted (see also Loftus 2009). And, unlike virtually all other natural resources, water is as universally necessary for individual bodies as it is for civilizations (Bakker 2003).

As the chapters in this section highlight, water is not politically neutral, but instead both reflects and reproduces relations of social power. Such is the case in Furlong's examination of alternative service delivery (ASD) arrangements in Ontario, Canada. In this case, ASD is both a result of and a condition for socio-spatial change. This has involved what Furlong, drawing on Soja (2009), refers to as the 'strategic decentralization' of water governance – a process that reflects but cannot be reduced to the goals of neoliberal state restructuring.

Water, then, is not an inert object of nature, but rather an 'actant' (in Latour's language) whose materiality and geo-ecological properties shape social relations, even as those social relations act on and transform water's materiality. As Swyngedouw (2004: 28) puts it: 'Water is a hybrid thing that captures and embodies processes that are simultaneously material, discursive, and symbolic.' For example, the processes by which people abstract water from a river, lake or aquifer, and channel it through hydraulic infrastructure, both transforms the water and its ecology (through processes of diversion, filtration, storage, delivery etc.) and transforms society (through socially differentiated processes of water provision, sanitation, class formation, luxury consumption etc.). Such is the case in northern New Mexico and south Texas, as demonstrated in the chapters by Perramond and by Jepson and Brannstrom, respectively. In both cases, water rights and hydraulic citizenship are structured through the articulation of law and technology. As Jepson and Brannstrom discuss, the form of water rights (riparian versus prior appropriations) and technology for accessing water (water jugs versus pumps and pipes) shape the scales and social relations through which some residents of south Texas access drinking water – or, alternatively, are excluded from such access. Similarly, in northern New Mexico scale is inscribed in law through the adjudication of water rights for *acequia* (traditional irrigation) systems. As Perramond shows, however, these scales are not fixed, but rather shift between the body, the acequia system and the regional water management association, and are mediated by state and federal water law.

The chapters in this section demonstrate that water cannot be understood apart from the social relations that produce it and give it meaning, and that those social relations are always historically constituted and exist within a context of uneven power. This view of the world is at once historical-materialist and cultural-political, attentive to the social relations of production and the capitalist production of nature *and* the symbolic meanings with which social relations and nature are imbued. This view of water – as social and natural and thoroughly *political* – matters for the forms of governance we establish or struggle against. If water is understood as *only* 'natural', if its social history and political character are ignored – as is commonly the case in public debates, policy discussions and environmental impact assessments (witness the current debates over hydrofracking in the USA) – then water governance is more easily represented as merely a techno-scientific problem, and the practices and institutions of decision-making may serve to veil the power relations inherent in water's production (Li 2007). This recognition draws attention to the concept of governance.

Governance and Scale

Just what do we mean by 'governance'? Like 'sustainable development' and 'social capital', the term 'environmental governance' has gained broad acceptance, and is often deployed in policy and academia, without the benefit of rigorous critique. Indeed, the vagueness and malleability of the term may serve to obscure politics and ideological positions, as in the World Bank's formulaic calls for 'good governance'. Who can argue with that? Who wants *bad* governance? But such calls help conceal the political and economic interests that lie behind the sorts of institutional arrangements, social relations, practices and spatial scales that are considered proper (as well as those considered improper). If we are to employ this concept, then it is imperative we do so critically, carefully elucidating the political nature inherent in the institutional arrangements and socio-environmental relationships to which it refers.

The concept of governance has emerged in recent decades to address the problematic of economic and political coordination in society, and refers to the ways that institutional stability is achieved through the establishment of rules, social order, rights and norms (Bridge and Perreault 2009). Karen Bakker (2010: 44) defines governance somewhat broadly, as 'a process of decision making that is structured by institutions (laws, rules, norms, and customs) and shaped by ideological preferences'. *Environmental* governance, then, has been deployed by geographers and others to analyse the institutional diversification of environmental management in the context of political-economic restructuring. This is denoted by the well-known shorthand 'govern*ment* to govern*ance*': what Bob Jessop (1990) has referred to as the 'hollowing out of the state', or what Erik

Swyngedouw (1997) has called 'glocalization'. Both terms refer fundamentally to the rescaling of state functions under neoliberal capitalism. The concept thus serves as a broad conceptual framework for analysing the interplay of institutional arrangements, spatial scales, organizational structures and social actors – state, non-state and quasi-state – involved in making decisions regarding nature and natural resources (Himley 2008).

Crucially, environmental governance is concerned with the production of particular social orders through the deployment of particular institutional arrangements. In other words, environmental governance is less about governing nature *per se* than it is about governing society *through* nature – and it is here that this understanding of governance most closely resembles Foucault's notion of governmentality (see also Agrawal 2005; Bridge and Perreault 2009). This is shown in the chapters in this section by Johnson and Cook, both of which address questions of rescaling in water governance. In his examination of the EU Water Framework Directive (WFD), Johnson considers the challenges of 'post-sovereign' water governance in Europe and the ways that environmental regulation has been re-territorialized and rescaled through the implementation of the WFD. Similarly, Cook's discussion of the historical evolution of water governance in Ontario demonstrates that rescaling is not unidirectional (i.e. it has not shifted progressively toward the local or toward the global), but instead changes as new scales (municipal, provincial, federal, transnational) emerge as relevant in particular historical moments. As both authors demonstrate, the scales of governance reflect social relations more than they do hydraulic imperatives; and in Ontario as in the EU, the institutional arrangements of water governance stem from a desire to achieve particular socio-spatial orders: governing *through* nature.

A central recognition of the chapters in this volume is that there is no prescribed, privileged scale at which governance should take place. The concept of water governance may be applied across a broad range of scalar arrangements: watershed-based forms of management, canal-based irrigators' associations, municipal service providers, global water forums etc. But if water governance is flexible as to the preferred scales of action, it is insistent as to the importance of hydro-social scales as spaces of policy implementation and political action. Water governance, in other words, is *all about scale*. Little wonder, then, that the watershed appears as the privileged scale for managing water. Watersheds are natural and tangible, and seemingly ideal for managing complex hydro-social relations. But as François Molle (2009) has pointed out, watershed management is shot through with problems, not the least of which is the spatial malleability of the concept itself. Which of the multiple nested watersheds forms the proper scale for governance? The concept seems to lose analytical purchase altogether when we consider the effects of trans-basin diversions, the drilling of deep wells, desalinization schemes etc. As MacKinnon (2011: 22) notes: 'the social construction of scale [is] a material expression of evolving power relations'. This includes the power to establish scales of governance as 'natural' and therefore privileged.

A comprehensive review of the literature on scale and scalar politics is far beyond the scope of this study (see Chapter 1). For our purposes, however, we may usefully borrow from Sayre (2009: 105), who characterizes geographical and ecological scale as (in part):

1. fundamentally concerned with process, rather than with fixed states;
2. simultaneously spatial and temporal;
3. indeterminate (i.e. there is no single, correct scale of analysis or politics);
4. produced through social and/or geo-ecological processes.

As a consequence of these defining features, Sayre argues, scale has both an 'ontological moment', as material manifestations of socio-natural processes, and an 'epistemological moment' determined by the scale at which one observes or comes to know a given process or relationship. Moreover, scale is a fundamentally relational concept which only has meaning relative to other scales. As James McCarthy (2005: 738) points out in parsing the politics of scale:

> It is impossible to separate out the delineation *of* any single scale from relationships *among* scales. More precisely, the establishment of scales as spatially organized and differentiated units of socio-spatial organization … unavoidably occurs in relationship to other scales: the delineation or elimination of any particular scale *as* an arena, locale, place, or so on is always done *relative to* other scales and the relationships among them, and necessarily introduces changes into their ordering and hierarchies …

In other words, the politics involved in the production and differentiation of scale (e.g. efforts to establish water users' associations within a city, or for rights to irrigation within a river basin) are inseparable from the relationships between scales established through processes of scale ordering (e.g. the delineation of use rights on the part of particular groups relative to the use rights of others). Once established, spatial scales have lasting effects that help shape (but do not determine) future spatial configurations and possibilities for social action. As such, scale is always temporal as well as spatial (see also MacKinnon 2011; Neumann 2009; Sayre 2009).

As struggles over watershed management have demonstrated, the choice of scale for water governance is not politically neutral. To the extent that particular scales for water governance are seen as 'natural' and immutable (e.g. watershed management, canal-scale irrigation), they run the risk of obscuring the politics that lie behind the production of such scales. This, then, is a scalar expression of Tania Murray Li's (2007) notion of 'rendering technical': scalar choice in this sense becomes a technique of government, a conceptual machine for manufacturing consent while treating political struggles and power relations as mere technical problems to be resolved through the right mix of administrative policy and hydraulic technology.

Here, the notion of 'waterscape' may serve as an analytical corrective to simplistic scalar assumptions inherent in much water governance policy. In the view of Budds and Hinojosa (2012), the waterscape is not an alternative scale to the 'watershed', but rather a co-produced socio-natural entity 'in which social power is embedded in, and shaped by, both water's material flow and its symbolic meanings, and which becomes embodied in, and manifested through, a wide array of physical objects and forms of representation' (ibid.: 124). Budds and Hinojosa define 'waterscape' as, 'the ways in which flows of water, power and capital [and here we might productively add labour] converge to produce uneven socioecological arrangements over space and time, the particular characteristics of which reflect the power relations that shaped their production' (ibid.; see also Perreault et al. 2012). The concept of waterscape, then, permits analysis of the relationship between water and society: not at a fixed, pre-given spatial scale – an analytical frame that both underpins and undermines watershed analyses (Cohen and Davidson 2011; Molle 2009) – but as a spatially indeterminate, networked assemblage of hydro-social relations.

Although he does not employ the concept of 'waterscape', Perramond makes a similar point. While the watershed plays a role in water management in northern New Mexico and southern Colorado, other factors – including the historical constitution of water rights, rural/urban tensions and federal Indian law – are at least as important in shaping forms of water governance and everyday practices of water access. This networked view of hydro-social relations highlights the place-based material effects of processes, relations and phenomena that may be spatially and/or temporally distant (Loftus 2007).

Another concern has to do with the growing scalar disjuncture between water governance and social reproduction. As Adrienne Roberts (2008: 546) argues, 'the primitive accumulation of water [through water grabbing or water service privatization] has led to a restructuring of the geography of water' in which conceptualizations of the right to water based on social citizenship have been eclipsed by the allocative principles of the market. Drawing on the work of Cindi Katz (2001) and Nina Laurie (2005), among others, she argues that whereas water governance decisions are increasingly made at national and transnational scales, the contradictions of market-based water governance continue to be experienced at the more localized scales of the city, community, neighbourhood or body, where the principles of the market run up against the immediate, material requirements of social reproduction. Such contradictions are demonstrated in the case of south Texas, as discussed by Jepson and Brannstrom. Here, the interface of law and property with different hydraulic technologies – even technologies as seemingly banal as water jugs, pumps and pipes – carries dramatic and highly differentiated implications for the ways residents access drinking water.

Conclusion

Scale matters. As a material manifestation of uneven relations of social power, scale and its contestation are inherent features of water governance. As the chapters in this section demonstrate, however, there is no preconceived, privileged scale for governing water – however much the proponents of watershed management may believe otherwise. Whether in Ontario, Europe, northern New Mexico or south Texas, the scales of water governance both reflect and help reproduce existing relations of power. They also shift historically, in response to emergent social and political constellations, population growth, economic interests and social conflict. The key to understanding scale in water governance, then, is to focus not on particular pre-given scales such as the watershed or the municipality, but rather to examine the ways that particular processes and social relations are differentially scaled; the ways certain scales come to be fixed or privileged at particular historical moments; and the socio-natural implications of these scalar arrangements. The chapters that follow provide examples of such a focus.

References

Agrawal, A. 2005. *Environmentality: Technologies of Government and the Making of Subjects*. Durham NC: Duke University Press.

Bakker, K. 2002. From state to market? Water mercantilización in Spain. *Environment and Planning A* 34: 767–90.

Bakker, K. 2003. *An Uncooperative Commodity: Privatizing Water in England and Wales*. Oxford: Oxford University Press.

Bakker, K. 2010. *Privatizing Water: Governance Failure and the World's Urban Water Crisis*. Ithaca: Cornell University Press.

Bridge, G. and T. Perreault 2009. Environmental governance. In N. Castree, D. Demeritt, D. Liverman and B. Rhoads (eds), *Companion to Environmental Geography*. Oxford: Blackwell, pp. 475–97.

Budds, J. and L. Hinojosa. 2012. Restructuring and rescaling water governance in mining contexts: The co-production of waterscapes in Peru. *Water Alternatives* 5(1): 119–37.

Cohen, A. and S. Davidson. 2011. The watershed approach: Challenges, antecedents, and the transition from technical tool to governance unit. *Water Alternatives* 4(1): 1–14.

Himley, M. 2008. Geographies of environmental governance: The nexus of nature and neoliberalism. *Geography Compass*, 2(2): 433–51.

Jessop, B. 1990. *State Theory: Capitalist States in Their Place*. Oxford: Blackwell.

Katz, C. 2001. Vagabond capitalism and the necessity of social reproduction. *Antipode*, 33(4): 709–28.

Laurie, N. 2005. Establishing development orthodoxy: Negotiating masculinities in the water sector. *Development and Change*, 36(3): 527–49.

Li, T.M. 2007. *The Will to Improve: Governmentality, Development and the Practice of Politics*. Durham, NC: Duke University Press.

Loftus, A. 2007. Working the socio-natural relations of the urban waterscape. *International Journal of Urban and Regional Research* 31(1): 41–59.

Loftus, A. 2009. Rethinking political ecologies of water. *Third World Quarterly*, 30(5): 953–68.

MacKinnon, D. 2011. Restructuring scale: Towards a new scalar politics. *Progress in Human Geography*, 35(1): 21–36.

McCarthy, J. 2005. Scale, sovereignty and strategy in environmental governance. *Antipode*, 37(4): 731–53.

Molle, F. 2009. River-basin planning and management: The social life of a concept. *Geoforum*, 40: 484–94.

Neumann, R.P. 2009. Political ecology: Theorizing scale. *Progress in Human Geography*, 33(3): 398–406.

Perreault, T., S. Wraight and M. Perreault 2012. Environmental justice in the Onondaga Lake waterscape, New York. *Water Alternatives*, 5(2): 485–506.

Roberts, A. 2008. Privatizing social reproduction: The primitive accumulation of water in an era of neoliberalism. *Antipode* 40(4): 535–60.

Sayre, N.F. 2009. Scale. In N. Castree, D. Demeritt, B. Rhoads and D. Liverman (eds), *A Companion to Environmental Geography*. Oxford: Blackwell, pp. 95–108.

Soja, E.W. 2009. Regional planning and development theories. In R. Kitchin and N.J. Thrift (eds), *International Encyclopedia of Human Geography*. Boston: Elsevier, pp. 259–70.

Swyngedouw, E. 1997. Neither global nor local: 'Glocalisaiton' and the politics of scale. In K. Cox (ed.), *Spaces of Globalization: Reasserting the Power of the Local*. New York: Guilford, pp. 137–66.

Swyngedouw, E. 2004. *Social Power and the Urbanization of Water: Flows of Power*. Oxford: Oxford University Press.

Chapter 7

Getting to Multi-Scalar:
An Historical Review of Water Governance
in Ontario, Canada

Christina Cook

Current discussions on water governance reflect broader trends in nation-state governance. Since the mid-1990s, scholars from multiple disciplines have remarked on changes in the traditional understanding of how nation-states are governed, especially in the Western democracies (Rhodes 1996; Stoker 1998; Pierre and Peters 2000; Jessop 2004). A broad and diffuse literature on governance discusses observed trends in societal decision-making. Much of the literature postulates a shift (of some degree) from government – where the state exerts control over society, economy and resources (Termeer et al. 2010) – to governance, where a variety of stakeholders, from the local to the global, are engaged in decision-making.

This chapter shows that multi-scalar water governance is not new: Ontario has practised it since the nineteenth century. Through an historical review of the multiple scales at which water has been governed in Ontario over the last 150 years, I show that although critical scalar scholarship has focused especially on rescaled environmental governance in light of neoliberalism and turns toward more participatory forms of environmental governance in the latter part of the twentieth century (McCarthy and Prudham 2004; McCarthy 2005; Lemos and Agrawal 2006; Bakker 2007; Cohen 2012), the rescaling of water governance is, in fact, a centuries-old phenomenon. Indeed, as is demonstrated in this chapter, in the ongoing challenge of managing water – a fugitive or flow resource – governance may invoke or move through multiple and various scales, including household, municipal, provincial, national and bi-national (Swyngedouw 1999).

Shifting and Multiple Scales: A Starting Point

In Canada, provinces have primary authority for water management (Hill et al. 2008). Provincial authority for water is derived from Section 109 of the Constitution Act, 1867,[1] which grants provinces jurisdiction over land and, by extension, proprietary rights in water (Gibson 1969; Kennett 1991). In addition to

---

1 Constitution Act, 1867 (U.K.), 30 & 31 Vict., c.3, reprinted in R.S.C. 1985, App. II, No. 5.

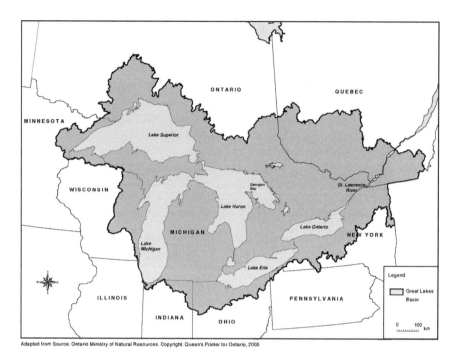

Adapted from Source: Ontario Ministry of Natural Resources. Copyright: Queen's Printer for Ontario, 2005

Figure 7.1   Map of the Great Lakes basin

Section 109, a number of provisions in Section 92 of the Constitution Act, 1867 supplement provincial legislative jurisdiction over freshwaters (Figure 7.1). These include authority over:

- the management and sale of the public lands belonging to the province;
- property and civil rights;
- generally all matters of a merely local or private nature in the province;
- local works and undertakings.

Constraints on provincial authority include specific federal heads of power (found primarily in Section 91 of the Constitution Act, 1867) for Indian land trusts; Aboriginal and treaty rights to water; public rights such as the right to fish in tidal waters; and extra-provincial rights (Kennett 1991). The federal government's trade and commerce power gives it authority for transboundary waters, but compared to the provincial government the federal government's domestic water jurisdiction is more limited and more specific. Over the years, the power over navigation and shipping has been invoked, and navigable waters have been broadly interpreted to permit the federal government to regulate aspects of some provincial projects such as dams and flood control projects (Kennett 1991). The sea coast and inland fisheries power has given the federal government some scope to address water quality, especially through the federal Fisheries Act.[2] Additional federal water-related legislative authority includes Indian lands administration; the concurrent agriculture jurisdiction (s.95); and the 'remainder basket clause' in which all classes of subjects which are expressly excepted in the constitutional enumeration, and are not assigned to the provinces, are assigned to the federal government, together with federal works and undertakings.

In sum, the provincial powers related to water are broad, making the provinces responsible for intra-provincial water management and for creating effective governance institutions to facilitate that management. Additionally, the Constitution grants provinces jurisdiction over a third level of government, municipalities. Shortly after Confederation, Ontario passed legislation giving municipalities the responsibility to provide local water and wastewater services.

Learning How to Shift Scales to Manage Water in Ontario (1840s–1960s)

Water Provisioning: Beyond the Individual (1840s–1910s)

In the early days of European settlement in Ontario, most people relied on riparian rights to water (or groundwater) that allowed them to withdraw drinking water for domestic needs. As Ontario's population grew, the provision of water was taken up by private companies. Eventually, because private provision proved insufficient, the municipality became (and remains) the scale of water provision in urban areas. With respect to wastewater facilities, the management shifted from the individual scale to the provincial scale and, despite provincial efforts, took time to settle at the municipal scale, while the province continued to manage public health.

By the midpoint of the nineteenth century, the growing and increasingly urban population of nearly 1 million in pre-Confederation Ontario needed networked water supply services (Jones and McCalla 1979). Many people in urban areas were not riparians (i.e., they did not own land that abutted a watercourse) and thus 'lacked direct access to natural water supplies' and instead relied on alternative water supplies including urban wells, 'communal pumps, commercial carters and water bearers, and rooftop rain-collection systems feeding cisterns' (Benidickson 2007: 57).

The fast-growing city of Toronto was in desperate need of waterworks by 1840. The city had considered providing waterworks itself, but financing proved a major constraint. Instead, a private concern – the Toronto Gas, Light and Water Company – distributed water through a small-scale system from the 1840s to the 1870s (Jones and McCalla 1979; City of Toronto 2013). After Confederation, the province passed legislation requiring municipalities to provide water supplies; gradually, private water supply services were supplanted by Ontario municipal services.

---

2 Fisheries Act, R.S.C. 1985, c. F-14.

In a pattern that would persist, wastewater treatment services lagged behind water provision. In 1882, a legislative committee determined that privies were polluting much of Ontario's water supply and causing widespread disease; in response, the province appointed a Provincial Board of Health (PBH) (Benidickson 2007). In the same year, Ontario enacted the Municipal Waterworks Act to give all municipalities the 'power to construct, build, purchase, improve, extend, hold, maintain, manage and conduct water-works'.[3] Such waterworks included early sewage treatment such as storage facilities for filtration (City of Toronto 2013). However, since the Act was permissive – meaning municipalities had the power, but were not compelled, to create water utilities – few municipalities immediately developed sewage treatment facilities (Strategic Alternatives 2001).

The PBH struggled to convince local councils to invest in sewage infrastructure. Finally, the province mandated municipal construction of water supply and sewage systems; the PBH would approve the plans (Bryant 1975). This meant the PBH, through public health legislation, managed water quality, in particular sources of water pollution (Berry 1959; Bryant 1975).

Treating the Symptoms: Finding a Scale (1910s–1930s)

Water provision was now firmly established at the municipal scale, but all was not well. At the end of the nineteenth century, Ontario sewage treatment was minimal, consisting 'mainly of dilution of the effluent from the outflow pipes'; it was assumed that any organic waste deposited into the lakes and rivers would be managed by aerobic bacteria (Davey 1985: 9). This inadequate treatment impacted public health: from 1903–13 in Ontario deaths from typhoid fever per 100,000 people was three times the rate of large European cities (Davey 1985). Overreliance on dilution as the solution to pollution and a failure to treat drinking water had catastrophic effects on public health throughout the Great Lakes basin. This new problem – pollution – confounded the municipal scale; to solve the typhoid fever problem would require engagement of the national and bi-national scales.

The Boundary Waters Treaty of 1909, made between Great Britain (on behalf of the Dominion of Canada) and the United States, set out a management framework for the boundary waters between the two countries, including the Great Lakes. The treaty included provisions relating to water quality and water quantity: neither country was to impair the other's use of the water. It created a bilateral organization, the International Joint Commission (IJC or the Commission), and empowered it to assist the parties in implementing the treaty. To this day, if the two federal governments agree, they may put a water-related question, known as a reference, to the IJC for guidance on resolution.

In 1912, Canada and the US put the first Great Lakes reference to the IJC. The reference asked the Commission to examine and report on pollution (its extent, causes and location) in the Great Lakes, and to recommend how to rehabilitate

---

3   Municipal Waterworks Act, S.O. 1882, c.25.

or prevent further damage (IJC 2013). In its 1914 interim report, the Commission found that the high prevalence of typhoid fever in the Great Lakes basin was 'due in greatest measure to sewage pollution of interstate and international waters used as a source of public water supplies [and that] such water [is] unfiltered or untreated or by faulty operation or poor efficiency of filter plants' (IJC 1914: 349). Consequently, cities began chlorinating their water supplies for distribution.

In its final report on the reference in 1918, the IJC concluded that pollution was highly intense in certain areas of the Lakes and, moreover, was so severe that 'conditions exist[ed] which imperil[ed] the health and welfare of the citizens of both countries in direct contravention of the Treaty' (IJC 1970: 1). According to the IJC, the source of pollution in the Great Lakes was 'the sewage and storm flows from the riparian cities and towns and the sewage from vessels' (IJC 1918: 51). Shore pollution was so bad in some places that municipalities issued ordinances prohibiting public bathing. To 'prevent or remedy pollution' of both 'boundary waters and waters crossing the boundary' the IJC made three recommendations that would not impose 'an unreasonable burden upon the offending communities' (IJC 1918: 52). First, city sewage should be addressed by 'installation of suitable collecting and treatment works'. Second, vessel sewage should be disinfected before discharge. Third, garbage and sawmill waste discharge should be prohibited and discharge of other industrial wastes 'causing appreciable injury' should be restricted as 'prescribed' (IJC 1918: 52).

The outcome of the IJC 1912 Pollution of Boundary Waters Reference – the drastic decrease in mortality from typhoid fever that resulted from a widespread increase in chlorination of municipal water supplies – must be seen as a success. Nonetheless, the reference shows that decision-makers were struggling with a classic water management issue: how to balance water uses. The IJC emphasized the primacy of 'sanitary considerations', while being sensitive to the need to balance, 'properly', a number of 'conflicting elements existing in the individual cases' (IJC 1918: 52). To demand sewage treatment was to risk overburdening an upstream polluter by potentially 'retard[ing] its progress both industrially and in respect to population' (IJC 1918: 38).

In the post-war era, restricting industrial growth was an unpopular option. In the end, each municipality chlorinated its drinking water and improved public health independently of other communities. With no coordinating mechanism to guarantee that other municipalities would invest in sewage treatment, there was no incentive for any municipality to invest in it. Thus, from 1912 to 1918 the issue of typhoid fever moved from the individual (those dying from typhoid fever) to the municipal scale to the national scale and, finally, to the binational scale – where a solution was found. When the straightforward solution to the immediate problem was found, the issue moved back to the municipal scale, where the fix was implemented. The underlying cause – pollution – remained without a scale.

Tackling the Cause: A Problem without Scale (1930s-1950s)

Chlorinating drinking water did nothing to address water quality in the Great Lakes, which continued to deteriorate. In 1946, the Canadian and US governments put another reference to the IJC. This time the Commission studied the pollution of boundary waters, focusing on the rivers connecting the Lakes – St. Marys, St. Clair, the Detroit and the Niagara – using the 1918 IJC report data as a baseline. In 1950, the IJC found water quality much diminished. Sewage treatment was not unheard of; it was simply insufficient. According to the IJC, since 1912 'the bacterial concentration in these waters [the Great Lakes] is in places three to four times greater, on the average, than it was in 1912' (IJC 1950: 5). In addition to domestic waste, the Commission found that industrial waste had become a major source of pollution. Not only were there numerous chemical pollutants, but the biological oxygen demand of the industrial waste was greater than 'the combined total of the domestic wastes of the area'. The combined pollution caused a 'serious health menace' (e.g. forced beach closures) as well as 'adverse economic effects' (e.g. reduced waterfront property values); treatment costs for domestic water were increasing, and some water tasted 'objectionable' (IJC 1950: 5).

In the 1950 report, the IJC made an environmental finding on the Great Lakes: 'fish and wildlife are destroyed by a number of industrial pollutants' (IJC 1950: 5). But again, the immediate concern was the impact on recreation and the economy, rather than the health of aquatic ecosystems. Nonetheless, the IJC did cast doubt on the limitless assimilative capacity of the Great Lakes, finding that 'the cumulative effect of uncontrolled waste disposal into these boundary waters seriously reduces the capacity of the waters to perform many beneficial and necessary functions vital to the health, recreation and economy of the people of the area' (IJC 1950: 5). This was a new finding: dilution might not be the solution to pollution after all.

As to whether pollution on one side of the boundary adversely affected the other side, the IJC was definitive: 'the interchange of waters across the boundary is such that any pollution on either side is a matter of concern to both countries' (IJC 1950: 6). It was becoming clear that the Great Lakes needed to be managed at multiple spatial scales, from the bi-national to the municipal, by multiple levels of government. The 1950 report detailed in 'Objectives for Boundary Waters Quality Control' a series of general and specific recommendations to address the pollution problem. The general objectives required that all waste (sanitary sewage, storm water and industrial effluents) should be treated sufficiently upon discharge to prevent it adversely effecting domestic or industrial water supplies, navigation, fish and wildlife, bathing, recreation, agriculture and other riparian activities. The specific objectives detailed limits of contamination for particular types of waste. With the 1950 report the problem of pollution by insufficiently treated wastewater was assigned a scale: bi-national. Although useful for drawing attention to an issue, the bi-national scale relies almost exclusively on national and sub-national scales to ensure action. The IJC urged the US and Canada to implement the objectives, but without regulatory authority it could not enforce them.

The 1950 report refocused attention on the problem of city sewage that had been largely unaddressed in the three decades since the 1918 report. The problem of industrial pollution would languish a little longer. The Commission recommended that all municipalities install primary treatment of sewage 'by sedimentation and disinfection of the effluent' and secondary treatment where required. The Commission invoked the principle of 'polluter pays' and also recommended that 'the costs of the necessary remedial measures should be borne by the municipalities, industries, vessel owners and others responsible for the pollution' (IJC 1950: 9). In Ontario, municipalities had no ability to raise sufficient funds to pay for sewage infrastructure; moreover, the polluter pays principle was not yet a feature of regulatory regimes. The problem of wastewater had a scale – municipal – but no solution.

Municipal financial constraints had long been a major reason for limited sewage treatment in Ontario. Amendments to the Municipal Act in 1943 had permitted municipalities to establish user rates for services, but the economic reality of the interwar period meant that water and wastewater infrastructure languished (Strategic Alternatives 2001). The infrastructure deficit in water and wastewater in Ontario in the post-war era was extreme, 'especially on the sewage side, following a 15-year disruption accompanied by substantial population increase and industrial growth' (Benidickson 2002: 56). Municipalities would need senior government to finance infrastructure upgrades: financing for sewage infrastructure would have to come from the federal or provincial government, or both.

In the immediate aftermath of the 1950 report, the US and Canada directed the IJC to create a permanent Technical Advisory Board (TAB) to supervise remedial measures to control boundary waters pollution. The TAB's powers were few, but it encouraged border municipalities to adopt the objectives of the 1950 report (Read 2000). As long as the federal and provincial governments refused to take responsibility for financing municipal sewage infrastructure, Ontario's sewage continued to flow into the Great Lakes. In southern Ontario, the post-war period had produced substantial industrial and population growth and a voracious need for good-quality water (Berry 1959). The IJC's 1950 report had been clear: the pollution problems reported in 1918 persisted, and were now coupled with a major problem of industrial waste. Ontario and Canada needed to take decisive and urgent action to reduce pollution in the Great Lakes. Notwithstanding the engagement of the bi-national scale and clear direction from the IJC, Ontario's pollution problem in the Great Lakes continued without a scale.

The Sewage Stalemate: Shirking Scales (1950s–1960s)

Despite a clear common goal to reduce Ontario's pollution contribution to the Great Lakes, there was no clarity regarding roles and responsibilities of different scales, no coordinating institution and no (government) scale financial responsibility. In 1953, the mayor of Sarnia – a city on the St. Clair River at the southern edge of Lake Huron – requested funding for municipal sewage infrastructure (Read

2000). Although municipalities had long struggled to finance water services infrastructure, Ontario Premier Frost's government was concerned that assistance for Sarnia might set a 'dangerous precedent', obliging the province to finance sewage facilities across the entire province and not merely those discharging into the Great Lakes (ibid.).

The federal government joined the fray in late 1954 as Prime Minister St. Laurent and Premier Frost exchanged a series of letters. St. Laurent's position was that 'abatement of pollution in boundary waters cannot usefully be considered within the context of federal/provincial fiscal arrangements' (Davey 1985: 88–9). Thus, despite the nation's embarrassment, the province and federal government could not find a solution to the pollution problem. Signalling that the negotiations had stalled, Frost was noncommittal in the spring of 1955, telling St. Laurent that Ontario 'would do what is feasible to bring about an abatement of this problem' (Read 2000: 346). Yet another year would pass before Ontario did much of anything about the sewage problem.

In the spring of 1955 an independent committee from the Waterloo region advised Premier Frost that water shortages in southwestern Ontario needed government action (Read 2000). By May 1955 the Ontario Water Resources Supply (OWRS) Committee was struck and charged with examining the state of the province's water resources, including supply and pollution issues (Mitchell and Shrubsole 1992). The Committee's mandate included two tasks that may have allowed it to contemplate the multi-level (or scalar) governance of water resources in Ontario. In the end, the OWRS Committee articulated a specific and narrow view of multi-level governance whereby the province kept control over water resources – especially those subject to 'international boundary water treaties and any other relevant statute' – and coordinated municipal and provincial activities.[4] Unfortunately, the Committee does not seem to have considered the relationship between the federal and Ontario governments in water management.

The OWRS Committee's report resulted in the Ontario Water Resources Commission Act (OWRCA) (see Berry 1959). Premier Frost did not understate his objectives for the Act. He introduced a bill to the legislature stating: '[I]ts implications are very great. It provides the method by which the problems of water and pollution may be dealt with on an area basis.'[5] Regarding finances, Premier Frost reiterated his government's firm position that municipalities had responsibility for addressing the problem of 'the contamination of our own lakes and streams with all of its undesirable effects upon the people of the areas and affecting great natural assets such as fish and wildlife'.[6] Frost had seized the spatial scale of water management[7] – it would be done on an area basis; the province

---

4   Ontario, Legislative Assembly, *Debates* (28 February 1956), at 556 (Mr. Frost).

5   Ontario, Legislative Assembly, *Debates* (23 February 1956), at 447 (Mr. Frost).

6   Ontario, Legislative Assembly, *Debates* (28 February 1956), at 558 (Mr. Frost).

7   In 1946 Ontario passed legislation permitting municipalities to form conservation authorities, in essence watershed management agencies. However, they were not mandatory

would decide what area – but sewage remained a municipal responsibility. Frost acknowledged that the stalemate on pollution reduction was 'also causing increasing embarrassment in our relationships with neighbouring provinces and states'.[8] Evidently, the embarrassment was insufficient to prompt the province to find a definitive solution to financing sewage infrastructure.

The provincial stance on municipal responsibility for water distribution and sewage treatment remained unequivocal: '[T]he distribution of water and the elimination of pollution is essentially a municipal problem. Both are very clearly duties and responsibilities of municipal governments.'[9] Here it is worth recalling that the municipal mandate is set exclusively by the provincial government. Other than lobbying the provincial and federal governments for money, municipalities could do little to raise financing for sewage infrastructure. During the second reading of the bill, Frost stated:

> The financing problem, however, is so formidable that many of [the municipalities] are simply unable to obtain the money, with the result that there are places which feel that, in the matter of sewage and pollution, there is nothing to be gained by them doing anything when others cannot or will not.[10]

The province recognized that municipalities – which relied mainly on taxes with minimal user rates to raise funds for water infrastructure – had struggled to provide water services to growing populations, an arrangement under which municipalities were incapable of improving water management outcomes. Plus, Frost's statement acknowledged the multi-scalar and multi-jurisdictional nature of the sewage problem, and the need for a coordinating institution. The IJC had found that every municipality on either side of the Great Lakes was contributing to the pollution problem. Therefore, to begin to reduce pollution, governments at all levels needed to implement the 1950 objectives. Unsure of whether its neighbours were also investing in sewage infrastructure, a municipality had no incentive to do so itself.

The OWRCA created a new institution, the Ontario Water Resources Committee to coordinate municipal action in water services provision. Frost explained that the Committee was necessary as 'an auxiliary to municipal government which can provide for the form of partnership required under which municipalities can work'.[11] The Committee was given the Department of Public Health's (the successor to the PBH) powers regarding municipal sewage plants and the ability to arrange financing for municipalities. Together the Act and the Committee allowed the province 'more effective control' of water supply and pollution (Berry 1959: 290), but even with the Committee coordinating, the sewage stalemate dragged on.

---

and their initial mandates were narrower than they are today.
  8   Ontario, Legislative Assembly, Debates (28 February 1956), at 558 (Mr. Frost).
  9   Ontario, Legislative Assembly, Debates (28 February 1956), at 556 (Mr. Frost).
  10   Ontario, Legislative Assembly, Debates (28 February 1956), at 558 (Mr. Frost).
  11   Ontario, Legislative Assembly, Debates (28 February 1956), at 555 (Mr. Frost).

By 1958 the Committee was, reportedly, a 'water management agency concerned with all aspects of the "water part" of the natural environment' (Bryant 1975: 164).[12] The creation of the Committee signalled that Ontario had 'adopted a program of pollution abatement and the full protection of all watercourses in the Province' (Berry 1959: 293). Reflecting on the Committee's progress on its mandate, its general manager and chief engineer stated:

> It is not possible to predict with accuracy the length of time needed to deal with all sources of pollution now reaching the streams, but the work is proceeding at a rapid pace, and there has been real cooperation received from municipalities and from industry ... Cooperation of all concerned, which is the basis of this program, cannot fail to achieve the desired results. (Berry 1959: 294)

Berry's favourable outlook on his agency's work glossed over the fact that not all municipalities were cooperating with the Committee. The province's high regard for the Committee was not shared by Ontario's larger municipalities. Some, including Sarnia, found the Committee and its financing arrangements for sewage infrastructure heavy-handed. The Committee controlled the details of municipal water and sewage projects and 'forc[ed] the community to pay for them' (Read 2000: 350). In addition, the Committee's financing programme fell foul of the Ontario Municipal Board (OMB), the provincial agency charged with overseeing municipal expenditures. The OMB vigilantly enforced 'fiscal responsibility' and opposed Committee projects where the municipality's debt would exceed the set threshold of 15 per cent of the municipality's total assessment (ibid.: 348). Even with the Committee, the sewage stalemate was not immediately resolved; it was a coordinating institution, but municipalities disagreed with the Committee's outline of roles and responsibilities.

Throughout the 1950s, the federal and Ontario governments were under considerable political pressure from municipalities, American states and the IJC to address boundary waters pollution. Although Canadian governments in the Great Lakes basin shared common goals of improving sewage treatment and reducing pollution, they were slow to agree on who had the responsibility to finance it.

Finally, in 1960 the federal government, under Prime Minister Diefenbaker, took definitive action on sewage. Amendments to the National Housing Act[13] allowed the Central Mortgage and Housing Corporation (CMHC, now known as the Canada Mortgage and Housing Corporation) to assist municipalities in the construction of sewage treatment facilities (Quinn 1985; Read 2000). Sarnia was among the first cities to participate in the CMHC programme (Read 2000). The federal government offered an additional impetus for municipalities to begin work

---

12   The Committee's mandate was distinct from the mandate, at the time, of conservation authorities, Ontario's regional agencies which remained concerned with managing water resources on a watershed basis.

13   R.S.C. 1985, c. N-11.

immediately: up to one quarter of the total loan would be forgiven. Forthwith, municipalities installed sewage facilities, and Canada slowly began to address its pollution contribution to the Great Lakes. Ontario continued through the 1960s to fund the Committee to facilitate the construction of municipal water and sewage works (de Loë 1991).

By 1960 the sewage stalemate – in essence, a standoff in the politics of scale of sewage – had been resolved, as 'all three levels of government had finally accepted their respective responsibility for sewage treatment' (Read 2000: 354). Arguably, the shirking of financial responsibilities that characterized the stalemate may have been fuelled in part by partisan interests (a Liberal Prime Minister and Conservative Premier from the start of the stalemate until 1957), as well as by dynamic federalism in a young Canada. Importantly, resolution of the sewage stalemate was not achieved chiefly by an inter-jurisdictional coordinating institution, but came instead from two different funding programmes: one led by the federal government, the other by the province. The story of sewage in 1950s Ontario illustrates how, in the absence of constitutional guidance and pressure from constituents, governments can refuse to take financial responsibility for a management issue, leaving it without a scale.

Managing Complexity: A Commitment to Multiple Scales (1960s–1970s)

After more than 100 years of a mostly ad hoc approach to water-quality management, in which problems were moved through scales in an attempt to find a solution, the governments of Ontario and Canada began to take an active approach to management that included a commitment to multiple scales.

Unfortunately, however, the resolution of the sewage stalemate did not stop the continuing deterioration of water quality in the Great Lakes basin, which by 1966 had a population of 30 million people (IJC 1970). In 1964, Canada and the US put yet another reference to the IJC, entitled 'Pollution of Lake Erie, Lake Ontario, and the International Section of the St. Lawrence River'. This reference examined pollution in what are known as the Lower Great Lakes – the downstream water bodies located closest to the St. Lawrence River and the ocean.[14] Even though Ontario and the eight states bordering on the Great Lakes (Illinois, Indiana, Michigan, Minnesota, New York, Ohio, Pennsylvania and Wisconsin) were not formally involved in the IJC, this reference required significant resources from them, in addition to the requesting federal governments. The IJC reached beyond the bi-national and national scales to the sub-national (state or provincial) scale in preparing its report.

14　The reference asked about pollution of the waters – Lake Erie, Lake Ontario and the international section of the St. Lawrence River – as well as the potential for oil pollution in Lake Erie. 'The International section of the St. Lawrence River extends from Lake Ontario to Cornwall, a distance of 112 miles' (IJC 1970: 12).

The final report on the reference was delivered in 1970. The IJC noted that the use of Great Lakes basin waters for 'municipal and industrial water supplies, cooling purposes, recreating, navigation, commercial fisheries and wildlife ... [and] for domestic and industrial waste water disposal' had rendered them gravely polluted (IJC 1970: 13). For the third time, the IJC reported deteriorating water quality in the Great Lakes. The study conducted by the two IJC advisory boards for the reference (the International Lake Erie Water Pollution Board and the International Lake Ontario-St. Lawrence River Water Pollution Board) was, at the time, 'the most extensive water pollution study to be undertaken anywhere' and included a series of public hearings, held in a variety of border municipalities (IJC 1970: 15–17).

The public hearings were spurred in part by a growing citizen movement on environmental issues that had emerged in response to a handful of environmental crises around the Great Lakes, including heaps of algae piled up on Lake Ontario beaches; a massive die-off of alewife[15] in Lake Michigan; the burning of the Cuyahoga River; the eutrophication of Lake Erie; and the discovery of high levels of mercury in Lake St Clair and Lake Erie (Botts and Muldoon 2005). The study found that insufficiently treated wastes had 'destroyed much of the general satisfaction and enjoyment that we refer to as the Lakes' contribution to the quality of life' (IJC 1970: 21).

Especially grave was the eutrophication of Lakes Erie and Ontario caused by reduced dissolved oxygen and attributed to 'increased population, industrialization, intensified agricultural practices and the use of phosphorus-based detergents since the late 1940s' (IJC 1970: 22). According to the same report, other concerns included bacterial and viral contamination, accumulation of solids, organic contaminants, oil, radioactivity, calefaction and toxic substances. Against this list of concerns the Commission recommended 'adoption and adherence' to its 'General and Specific Objectives as a matter of urgency', and, more particularly, urged the 'immediate reduction of the phosphorus, chiefly by removal from detergent' (IJC 1970: 81–2).

On the heels of the 1970 IJC report, the US and Canadian governments began negotiations for a bi-national agreement to clean up the Great Lakes. Canada's newly created Department of the Environment commenced negotiations with the US Environmental Protection Agency. In 1972 – 60 years after putting the first reference to the IJC on water quality in the Great Lakes – the two countries signed the Canada–US Great Lakes Water Quality Agreement (GLWQA), which was a major innovation to coordinate Great Lakes basin water quality governance (Botts and Muldoon 2005). The 1972 GLWQA was established as a standing reference under the Boundary Waters Treaty that in its amended form (the 2012 Protocol to the GLWQA) animates the treaty's anti-pollution provision (see Botts and Muldoon 2005).

Although the Canadian government is responsible for international negotiations, it cannot implement international agreements pertaining to issues of

15   *Clupea serrata*, a species of fish resembling herring.

provincial authority. The federal and provincial governments made an agreement in 1971 – the first Canada-Ontario Agreement Respecting the Great Lakes Basin Ecosystem (COA) – to implement the GLWQA. Also, the 1971 COA showed that Ontario and Canada were together committed 'to stemming the tide of environmental degradation within the Basin and to restoring the Ecosystem's health' (COA 2002: 3). In its multi-scalar construction (that would expand even further later) the GLWQA offered the potential to coordinate bi-national as well as federal and provincial efforts in Great Lakes basin management, and it also offered Canada and Ontario a chance to recover from the embarrassment of the sewage stalemate. Perhaps most importantly, the 1972 GLWQA signalled a commitment to multi-scalar governance in the Great Lakes. After years of shifting scales, it became obvious that multiple scales would need to be engaged to manage water.

Conclusions

From the early days of private provision of drinking water and little concern for sewage and wastewater, through to the 1972 bi-national agreement on water quality, water governance in Ontario shifted scales. Where jurisdictional responsibilities were less clear, scales shifted until a resolution (of some degree) could be found. In the late nineteenth century the provincial government, through its delegated authority to municipalities, resolved the problem of water provisioning with legislation. Addressing typhoid fever, a problem without clear constitutional responsibility that was affecting two nations, shifted scales to the provincial, national and bi-national in the quest to find a solution. Once a solution to the symptoms was found, the issue returned to the municipal scale, where water was easily chlorinated. The problems of sewage and industrial pollution were left without a scale for many years: the former until sewage infrastructure funding started in Ontario in the late 1950s, the latter until the 1972 bi-national agreement on water quality was signed.

In early water governance in Ontario shifting scales may have been, in part, the outcome of learning how to govern water. Riparian rights were fine in sparsely populated, well-watered areas (see Rose 1994: 163–96). However, larger populations in urban areas required provisioning of water and increased industrial activity required learning to balance water uses; and both required learning about pollution and wastewater. Private companies were inadequate providers, thus government stepped in to develop networked supplies.

Shifting scales in mid-twentieth century water management may be attributed in part to the fact that no authority had responsibility for 'environment', because in Canada environment is a 'constitutionally abstruse matter'.[16] The sewage stalemate

16   Per Justice La Forest, *Friends of the Oldman River Society v. Canada (Minister of Transport)*, [1992] 1 S.C.R. 3 at 64.

was ultimately about environmental protection; without constitutional clarity, even though the solution was known (install infrastructure), governments shirked responsibility, not wanting to set a precedent for further financial commitments.

Ultimately, these experiences of shifting scales may have helped the governments of Canada and Ontario to understand the utility of a governance approach that engaged multiple scales to solve water management challenges – a critical point for contemporary water governance in the Canadian context. The 1972 GLWQA and the COA marked a commitment to multi-scalar water governance. Today, multi-scalar governance has become a standard feature in Canadian water governance, from the 2012 Protocol to the Great Lakes Water Quality Agreement of 1978 to the ever-increasing engagement of the watershed scale (see Cohen 2012).

References

Bakker, K. 2007. The 'commons' versus the 'commodity': Alter-globalization, anti-privatization and the human right to water in the global south. *Antipode*, 39(3), 430–55.

Benidickson, J. 2002. Water Supply and Sewage Infrastructure in Ontario, 1880s-1990s Legal and Institutional Aspects of Public Health and Environmental History. Toronto: Ontario Ministry of the Attorney General.

———. 2007. *The Culture of Flushing: A Social and Legal History of Sewage*. Vancouver: University of British Columbia Press.

Berry, A.E. 1959. The Ontario water resources program. *Sewage and Industrial Wastes*, 31(3), 288–94.

Botts, L., and Muldoon, P.R. 2005. *Evolution of the Great Lakes Water Quality Agreement*. East Lansing: Michigan State University Press.

Bryant, A.W. 1975. An analysis of the Ontario Water Resources Act, in *Environmental Management and Public Participation*, edited by P.S. Elder. Toronto: Canadian Environmental Law Research Foundation/Canadian Environmental Law Association, 162–81.

City of Toronto. 2013. *Water Treatment: Past and Present*. [Online]. Available at: http://www.toronto.ca/water/supply/filtration.htm [accessed: 18 February 2013].

COA. 2002. *The Canada-Ontario Agreement Respecting the Great Lakes Basin Ecosystem*. [Online]. Available at: http://www.ec.gc.ca/grandslacs-greatlakes/default.asp?lang=En&n=B903EE0D-1.

Cohen, A. 2012. Rescaling environmental governance: Watersheds as boundary objects at the intersection of science, neoliberalism, and participation. *Environment and Planning A*, 44(9), 2207.

Davey, T. 1985. *Recollections of Water Pollution Control in Ontario*. Aurora: Pollution Control Association of Ontario.

de Loë, R.C. 1991. The institutional pattern for water quality management in Ontario. *Canadian Water Resources Journal*, 16(1), 23–43.

Gibson, D. 1969. The constitutional context of Canadian water planning. *Alberta Law Review*, 7, 71–71.

Hill, C., Furlong, K., Bakker, K., and Cohen, A. 2008. Harmonization versus subsidiarity in water governance: A review of water governance and legislation in the canadian provinces and territories. *Canadian Water Resources Journal*, 33(4), 315–32.

IJC. 1914. *Progress Report of the International Joint Commission on the Reference by the United States and Canada in Re the Pollution of Boundary Waters, Whether or Not Such Pollution Extends across the Boundary in Contravention of the Treaty of January 11, 1909, and If So, in What Manner or by What Means It Is Possible to Prevent the Same, Including Report of the Sanitary Experts*. International Joint Commission.

———. 1918. *Final Report on the Pollution of Boundary Waters Reference*. International Joint Commission.

———. 1950. *Pollution of Boundary Waters Reference: Great Lakes Channels Final Reports*. International Joint Commission.

———. 1970. *Pollution of Lake Erie, Lake Ontario and the International Section of the St. Lawrence River*. International Joint Commission.

———. 2013. *Docket 4R*. [Online]. Available at: http://www.ijc.org/en_/Dockets?docket=4 [accessed: 3 March 2013].

Jessop, B. 2004. Hollowing out the 'nation-state' and multi-level governance, in *A Handbook of Comparative Social Policy*, edited by P. Kennett. Cheltenham: Edward Elgar, 11–25.

Jones, E., and McCalla, D. 1979. Toronto waterworks, 1840–77: Continuity and change in nineteenth-century Toronto politics. *Canadian Historical Review*, 60(3), 300–23.

Kennett, S. 1991. *Managing Interjurisdictional Waters in Canada: A Constitutional Analysis*. Calgary: Canadian Institute of Resources Law.

Lemos, M.C., and Agrawal, A. 2006. Environmental governance. *Annual Review of Environment and Resources*, 31, 297–325.

McCarthy, J., and Prudham, S. 2004. Neoliberal nature and the nature of neoliberalism. *Geoforum*, 35(3), 275–83.

McCarthy, J. 2005. Devolution in the woods: Community forestry as hybrid neoliberalism. *Environment and Planning A*, 37(6), 995–1014.

Mitchell, B., and Shrubsole, D. 1992. *Ontario Conservation Authorities: Myth and Reality*. Waterloo, Ont: Dept. of Geography, University of Waterloo.

Pierre, J., and Peters, B.G. 2000. *Governance, Politics, and the State*. New York: St. Martin's.

Quinn, F. 1985. The evolution of federal water policy. *Canadian Water Resources Journal*, 10(4), 21–33.

Read, J. 2000. Managing water quality in the Great Lakes Basin: Sewage pollution control, 1951–1960, in *Ontario since Confederation: A Reader*, edited by E.-A. Montigny and A.L. Chambers. Toronto: University of Toronto Press.

Rhodes, R.A.W. 1996. The new governance: Governing without government. *Political Studies*, 44(4), 652–67.

Rose, C.M. 1994. *Property and Persuasion: Essays on the History, Theory, and Rhetoric of Ownership*. Boulder, CO: Westview.

Stoker, G. 1998. Governance as theory: Five propositions. *International Social Science Journal*, 50(1), 17–28.

Strategic Alternatives. 2001. *Drinking Water Management in Ontario*. Ontario Sewer and Watermain Construction Association. Prepared for the O'Connor Inquiry.

Swyngedouw, E. 1999. Modernity and hybridity: Nature, Regeneracionismo, and the production of the Spanish waterscape, 1890–1930. *Annals of the Association of American Geographers*, 89(3), 443–65.

Termeer, C.J.A.M., Dewulf, A., and van Lieshout, M. 2010. Disentangling scale approaches in governance research: Comparing monocentric, multilevel, and adaptive governance. *Ecology and Society*, 15(4), 1–29.

Chapter 8

Beyond the Local State as 'Container': Scale, Positionality and Water Supply Reform

Kathryn Furlong

Introduction

Water supply has undergone significant institutional and organizational change across a variety of jurisdictions in both the North and South since the 1980s. Examples include: the introduction of private sector principles into public sector management; the involvement of new actors in governance; the extension of private property rights; liberalization; new tariff structures; the creation of water markets; a greater focus on the environment and conservation; and decentralization (Bakker 2007; Furlong 2010).

Such policy shifts have encouraged the adoption of a diversity of alternative service delivery (ASD) models for water supply. ASD comprises a range of 'alternatives' to the traditional direct delivery model. Examples include stand-alone bodies, publically owned corporations, cooperatives and, at the limit, private sector participation (PSP) and privatization (Furlong 2012). As such, ASD is typically thought to entail organizational restructuring of water utilities along a continuum from lesser to greater independence from local government (see Figure 8.1).

This chapter explores the contestation of ASD reform in Canada's most populous province, Ontario, which underwent sweeping neoliberal reforms under a government led by the Progressive Conservative Party of Ontario from 1995 to 2004.[1] During that period the provincial government sought to drive organizational change for local service delivery through regulatory change, cuts to municipal funding and rescaling, which involved the devolution of additional responsibilities to the municipal scale. While several municipalities adopted new business models for water supply in response (Furlong and Bakker 2010), the reforms also met with widespread contestation within and between governments as well as between governments and a variety of constituents. As a result, the scope and degree of reform was limited.

---

1 The leader of the reform was Premier Mike Harris who resigned in 2002. The blueprint for his reform program was called the Common Sense Revolution (CSR).

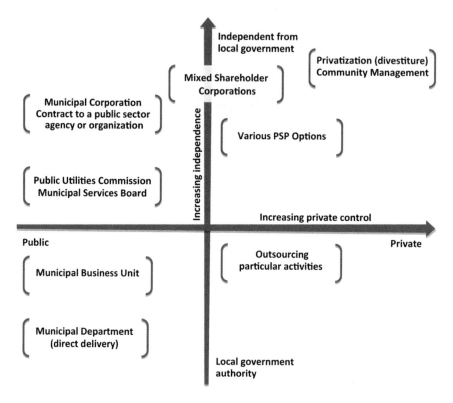

Figure 8.1   Schematic of alternative service delivery (ASD) options for water supply

What is novel about the Ontario case is that checks on efforts to promote ASD reveal important interactions between 'positionality' and the 'politics of scale'. In addition to scale, changes in service delivery models through ASD influence and are influenced by the positionality of actors at the local scale, that is their relative relationship to the issues in question (see Sheppard 2002). The effects of rescaling and ASD on local positionalities demonstrate two things. First, local government is not a homogenous policy unit, but one in which different positionalities result in contested policy positions. Second, these divergent positionalities within local government mean that activists contesting water supply reform have potential allies within local government, which often go unrecognized.[2]

2   The research on which this paper is based was conducted between 2004 and 2006 as part of a study on water supply reform in the province of Ontario.

Background: Ontario and ASD

In Ontario, interest in ASD for water supply was driven by a series of issues.[3] First, a legacy of underinvestment in water and sanitation infrastructure culminated in an infrastructure deficit crisis across Canada (CWWA 1997; Mirza and Haider 2003). For many water managers, this was the direct result of the 'politicization' of water supply such that elected officials kept prices low and shifted reserve funds from water supply to pay for other, more visible, municipal projects (Furlong 2012).

In the mid-1990s these issues were exacerbated by legislative changes as well as devolution combined with cuts to municipal and infrastructure funding, or what Soja calls 'strategic decentralization' (Soja 2009: 265). These changes were largely driven by a neoliberal ideology in which municipal government could be forced to become more 'efficient', where efficiency is evaluated on dollars spent as opposed to service quality (cf. Gross Stein 2001). First, legislative reforms under the Electricity Competition Act and changes to the Municipal Act forced the restructuring of municipal service provision (Furlong 2012). Second, 'strategic decentralization' served to increase the competition between water providers and municipal politicians for funds. Such budgetary conflicts served to increase ASD's appeal among water managers because ASD is associated with increasing independence from local government, and thus the ability to protect water revenues from use on other municipal projects. Seven new ASD models for services delivery were adopted in various municipalities across Ontario (Furlong and Bakker 2010).

This chapter is concerned with instances in which ASD reform was either unsuccessful or reversed, as it is in these cases that the complexities of inter- and intra-scalar positionalities become most obvious. Three cases are examined: Toronto, Hamilton and the provincial promotion of municipal services boards (MSBs). Briefly, Toronto's water managers initially sought a municipal corporation and then a municipal services board. Due to the limits of provincial legislation, internal conflicts and public protest, they eventually settled on an 'improved status quo' direct delivery model, which also proved difficult to implement. In Hamilton, direct delivery was re-adopted at the conclusion of a 10-year PSP contract, that is, water services were 'contracted back in' (cf. Hefetz and Warner 2004). Finally, despite provincial legislation in favour of the MSBs, municipalities circumvented the legislation in favour of the traditional direct delivery model.

These experiences raise several questions about 'the politics of scale'. First, as widely argued elsewhere, while the state matters, it does not determine policy at the local scale (e.g. Brenner and Theodore 2002; Jessop 2002). Second, the local state – i.e. municipal government – is not homogenous but diverse, and this influences the outcomes of rescaling and policy reform. These issues suggest, as many argue, that one needs to look beyond scale to broader sociospatial relations

---

3   For further detail, see Furlong (2012); Furlong and Bakker (2010, 2011).

in order to analyse phenomena affected by shifting scalar relations (Jessop et al. 2008). These issues are theorized in the next section.

The Local State beyond Scale

State rescaling and the concomitant transition from government to governance have had widespread effects on water management. Broadly, the transfer of responsibility to both sub- and supranational scales of governance has influenced organizational models for:

- service delivery (Furlong and Bakker 2010);
- who is included in decision-making (Page and Kaïka 2003; Sabatier et al. 2005);
- how problems are studied and defined (Cohen and Davidson 2011);
- perceptions of and strategies for dealing with scarcity (Bakker 2000);
- the nature of regulation (Bakker 2004).

In short, the topic of scale has been central to debates on water governance over the past decade (Norman et al. 2012), and, as explored in the introduction to this volume, has been the focus of many debates in critical geography. For the purposes of this chapter, Sheppard's emphasis on positionality as a means of interpreting roles in the production of scale and networks is useful. He argues that individuals have differing positionalities that 'var[y] through space/time' and that 'can be mapped by depicting the relationships between different agents in different places, and at different scales' (Sheppard 2002: 322–3).

Geographic focus on scale has been central in drawing analytic attention to municipalities, especially cities. In response to globalization, theorists across a range of disciplines began to recognize the importance of the local scale and to theorize it as more than subordinate to the nation-state (Keil 2003). Theorists argued that globalization and associated reductions in financial transfers from higher scales served to drive 'local initiatives to attract the private sector', leading to inter-municipal competition (Soja 2009: 266) or the 'entrepreneurial city' (Harvey 1989).

The focus on the entrepreneurial city, however, may be too narrow for the case of water supply. While municipalities may use water as a tool of inter-municipal competition (e.g. by keeping prices low to attract industry), many important issues are masked by this focus. The focus on capitalist accumulation in scalar analysis is limiting when thinking about water because it ignores 'social reproduction and consumption' (Marston 2000), which are central issues in the control of water supply. Research on the municipal scale recognizes that it comprises a variety of actors in governance. Yet, it generally does not differentiate between different groups within the governing body itself. Keil, for example, notes that 'urban politics' is more than 'municipal politics (as represented by local governments)' (Keil 2003: 286).

The public administration literature also has something to contribute to an analysis that recognizes the importance of the diverse positionalities within the local state. In the public administration field, research often considers the specificities of local government operations (e.g. taxing and revenue arrangements, bureaucratic structures, alternative services delivery), as opposed to broader processes such as rescaling and neoliberalization. An examination of the public policy literature in the context of geographical concerns with neoliberalization can generate a more nuanced picture of how and where these processes occur at the local scale.

There is specificity to municipal functions, such that how policy reform is experienced is relative to the municipal responsibility in question. The public administration literature and municipal governments themselves commonly distinguish between physical services (e.g. transportation, water and sewage) and social services (e.g. welfare, cultural activities) on the one hand, and between revenue and non-revenue generating services on the other hand. In large municipalities, water supply tends to be revenue-generating and self-funding. This creates a push–pull effect which is exacerbated by the constrained financial situations of municipalities. Municipal governments and corporate staff have incentives to retain revenue-generating services to mobilize opportunities to shift funds from those that are non- (or less) revenue generating. In order to retain control over the same needed funds, those engaged in utility governance seek to limit the influence of municipal governments and corporate staff, specifically through ASD reform.

Ontario: Provincial Pressure for ASD Reform

Most drivers of utility reorganization in Ontario were indirect, involving responses to provincial devolution and cuts to municipal funding. For example, the Savings and Restructuring Act (1996)[4] and the Services Improvement Act (1997) transferred a variety of responsibilities to municipalities and were accompanied by an announcement that funding to municipalities would be cut by 40 per cent within two years (see Furlong 2012). This amounted to a 16 per cent decrease in municipal budgets (Siegel 1997: 147). Such legislation served to exacerbate budgetary difficulties for municipalities, making water rates an increasingly attractive source of additional funds.

A more direct impact was felt through the Electricity Act (1998), which required the separation of electricity utilities from any multi-utility service provider. This made maintaining local Public Utilities Commissions (PUCs) unattractive in

---

4   This Act is also more lengthily referred to as 'An Act to Achieve Fiscal Savings and to Promote Economic Prosperity through Public Sector Restructuring, Streamlining and Efficiency and to Implement other aspects of the Government's Agenda' (1996).

several cases because of the negative effect on economies of scale (Furlong and Bakker 2010). In one instance, the province did directly target organizational models for water supply. Under revisions to the Ontario Municipal Act (2001) – which took effect on 1 January 2003 – much of the Public Utilities Commissions Act was repealed and the MSB model was defined to replace the PUC model. In the stipulations regarding the MSB under the amendments to the Municipal Act (2001), all existing PUCs 'shall be deemed to be municipal service boards established under this section'. These pressures, as well as the legislative and funding changes described above, resulted in a dramatic decline in the number of PUCs in the province: from 124 to just eight between 1990 and 2002 (SuperBuild 2002).

However, the MSBs did not become an important option for service delivery in the province. The municipal response to the provincial legislation signalling the end of the PUC was varied and, in many respects, counter to provincial goals. The Electricity Competition Act, the Municipal Water and Sewerage Transfer Act and revisions to the PUC under the Municipal Act all contributed to the decline of the PUC. Yet, the result was that many municipalities took their water services back in-house, i.e. through direct delivery, either from delegated management to the Ontario Clean Water Agency (OCWA) – a provincial crown corporation – or from a PUC.

Experiences in the city of Peterborough in central Ontario help to illustrate the limitations faced by the provincial government in achieving municipal compliance, and thus of hierarchical approaches to scale. In order to retain its PUC for water while complying with the new legislation, Peterborough adopted a two-tiered structure. Specifically, the city formed Peterborough Holdings Inc., which includes the municipal corporation Peterborough Utilities Services Inc. (PUSI). PUSI contracts the operation and maintenance of the city's water and wastewater to the Peterborough Utilities Commission, a separate entity. Effectively, Peterborough today has a corporate-commission hybrid (see Bakker and Cameron 2005), but not an MSB. In most cases, the municipal department, direct-delivery model was adopted. So what were the challenges to ASD at the local scale?

Challenges to Reform: Local Government 'Positionalities'

Within the debate on ASD for water supply there are at least three sets of differing positionalities within local government. These pertain to water management, city corporate management and municipal councils and will be discussed in turn below. Recognizing the overlapping and competing challenges faced by different branches of local government opens possibilities for more nuanced discussions on scale and sociospatial change with respect to water supply. In general, the tendency is for water management to support ASD (with the exceptions of PSP and privatization), and for city corporate staff to have reservations with respect to all forms of ASD. For municipal councils, incentives and constraints are often mixed – leading to diverging positionalities.

The positionality of water management staff results from the pressure they face to meet the cost of water provision with income generated through water sales. This means controlling the costs of service provision and being vigilant about what is defined as a water cost (and therefore funded through water rates). Accepted costs of water supply include such things as infrastructure expansion and refurbishment; water treatment and distribution; water quality testing; equipment; personnel; certification and training; related administration; and – in the case of Ontario – a contribution to the budget of the local conservation authority.

Long-term underinvestment in infrastructure, new perceptions of how water supply costs should be accounted for, and a host of new regulatory measures and standards after 2002 have meant that the costs of service provision increased steadily from the mid-1990s, and dramatically after 2002.[5] The combination of rising costs and insecure or limited revenue tends to bolster support for ASD among water management staff who, in general, are seeking greater control over the utility and its finances: they want to wrest that control from municipal officials and politicians, but do not want to turn it over to the private sector. Reforms advocated by water managers typically involve arm's-length entities that retain public management while discouraging PSP or privatization. For example, although water management staff and councillors in Toronto agreed that there was pressure from the private sector to contract out operations, for water management this was something to be resisted. From their perspective, converting to an MSB would enable them to protect the water division from PSP by making the utility more competitive according to dominant business management criteria such as cost efficiency.

The positionality of city corporate staff differs from that of water management because they face different challenges stemming from provincial rescaling. These officials are charged with managing the municipal corporation as a whole. Following the neoliberal reforms outlined above, this has meant delivering increasing numbers of key services under greater fiscal constraint. This situation creates certain incentives for retaining water supply as a municipal department. First, to access additional sources of revenue, the impetus is to expand the definition of what is considered to be a water-related service, and thus what can be funded through water rates. This means retaining budgetary control over water departments as opposed to adopting arm's length ASD models.

A second disincentive for converting to ASD on the part of city corporate staff is the increased importance of ensuring that the water division continues to purchase corporate services from the municipality. A city must provide corporate services, regardless of how many departments use them. These include, for example, printing, human resources, finance and purchasing. It is through the

---

5   In May 2000, seven people died and thousands more made ill by E. coli contamination of the water supply in the town of Walkerton, Ontario. The Walkerton Public Inquiry was then held to examine the disaster. Four new pieces of legislation to improve water quality, testing and training standards as well as source water protection ensued.

collective use of corporate services that the services become more cost-effective; there is a collective mentality to government that is missed when each department seeks the lowest possible costs for itself (Slack 1996). One respondent gave the example of printing services. The City of Toronto must operate printing services to meet the rapid turnaround time required by city clerks. Demand for printing is such that the service must remain on standby and, as such, must experience periods of excess capacity.

> The rest of the city staff must use that service in order to make it cost effective. These are sunk costs. We've already paid for the equipment. We've paid for the staff to sit there whether they do work or not. So if everybody else just contracts it out, even though it would be cheaper or they can get it more timely somewhere else, we're wasting money by having our capital tied up and staff sitting there doing little ... So water is so narrowly focused, they don't see that concept ... What they are not seeing is that it's going to cost the whole corporation that much more when they don't use the services that are there.[6]

From the positionality of water management staff, however, corporate staff can use these services to generate extra revenue by overcharging. For example, in 2002 Toronto Water and Wastewater Services (TWWS) paid $78.4 million (23.2 per cent of its budget) for various internal services. Toronto's Chief Administrative Officer (CAO) noted that the 'rationale for determining the allocation of $23.1 million for corporate overhead costs has been lost to history', and that TWWS could exert little control over the scheduling of these services even though it was dependent on them for the completion of work (Chief Administrative Officer 2002: 13–14). On the other hand, the same report found that TWWS was being accurately billed overall. Thus, for water management, ASD has the advantage of enabling them to purchase external support services or hire their own in-house staff. This, they argue, would save money, guarantee a higher level of service quality and responsiveness, and enable them to tailor services to their needs.

A third incentive for retaining the department model for city corporate staff is the importance of water supply as a public service to ensure a healthy and safe community, and the profile this gives the city in the eyes of the public. As a senior corporate staff member from Toronto stated, the purpose of municipal government is:

> to protect the public, provide services at reasonable cost and low-risk to the public. So, if you think of all of the services that the city provides, which are the ones that you would say pose the biggest threat to the community if not done properly. And water's probably it. That is the most essential service that we provide. Well, if we don't do that directly, what the hell are we here for?[7]

---

6   Interview (May 2006).
7   Interview with a member of senior corporate staff in Toronto (May 2006).

The desire of city corporate staff to retain operational control was also considered key in 'contracting back in' in Hamilton in 2004. In 1994 the city signed a 10-year PSP contract with a local company, Philip Utilities Management Corporation (PUMC). Ten years later, in 2004, Hamilton tendered a request for proposals (RFP) on a second 10-year PSP contract. In the end, however, water was brought back in-house under a direct delivery model. The primary reason given was that the RFP did not yield any satisfactory proposals.[8] Yet, several respondents argued that the RFP was made purposely onerous, making a successful bid unlikely and thus inherently favouring the return of operations to a municipal department: 'City staff was driving the process and they had a lot of political support [from the council] for doing what they wanted to do, which was to bring the operation back into the city department.'[9]

To explain the push to contract back in, respondents cited strong public sentiment against the first contract; the job security associated with being responsible for a major mandate of the city; and the division of liability in the first contract that disadvantaged the city.[10] The degree to which public sentiment and city staff preference for contracting back in had an influence over the process cannot be concretely determined. According to the respondent quoted above, however, city corporate staff were also against contracting out in 1994. At that time, however, both city staff and the public were excluded from the process.

In Toronto, city corporate staff played a role in ensuring that the municipal department model was retained and that ASD was avoided. This is evidenced in the city's choice of Water Advocate, whose job it was to follow the decision-making process and to make recommendations. The selection of Councillor Irene Jones as Toronto's first Water Advocate, in February 2002, is indicative of an early uneasiness with ASD reform: Councillor Jones had been active in many left-leaning initiatives, and had been an early critic of the sitting mayor's government. In her role as Water Advocate she would find little substance to the city's MSB proposal, and much in common with advocacy groups who were against the plan (cf. Jones 2002).

The MSB option was defeated. All parties settled on an 'improved status quo', yet the modifications to the status quo were not fully implemented. The reasons for this also reflect the diverse positionalities within municipal government. The improved status quo, adopted in November 2002, included three changes. First, the TWWS would be classified as a business unit within, rather than a division of, the Department of Works and Emergency Services. Second, a special committee of council dedicated to water and wastewater would oversee the new unit. Third, service level agreements (SLAs) between the new business unit and

---

8   Interview with utility management in Hamilton (June 2005).

9   Interview with a representative of the Hamilton Utilities Corporation (June 2005).

10   Interviews with utility management (June 2005) and a union representative (February 2006) in Hamilton; and with a representative of the Canadian Council for Public Private Partnerships (February 2006).

the city departments from which it purchased services would be required (Chief Administrative Officer 2003).

Neither the special committee nor the SLAs materialized. The SLAs were meant to guarantee levels of service quality and responsiveness. They were designed as contractual commitments between TWWS and the departments from which it purchased corporate services. If the agreed levels of services under a given SLA were not met, TWWS would have had the option of contracting out these services two years after having notified the department in question. However, city staff did not enforce the signing of the SLAs. As a result, only two were signed. According to water management, this did little to improve their situation:[11] the CAO faced pressure from the departments responsible for corporate services because the SLAs inherently threatened the potential of outsourcing; as such, these departments were reluctant to commit to such agreements.

The third positionality identified within the local state is that of local councils. Their incentives, however, tend to be more mixed. Councils are faced with budgetary stress and political pressure to keep costs, and thus local taxes and service charges, down. In this way, although pressured by budget constraints, councillors also have strong incentives to avoid raising water rates and property taxes. The shorter municipal political cycle also means that the added relevance of a councillor's position (and thus security) that is associated with retaining the responsibility for water competes with an incentive for the political security that might be achieved by distancing themself from a service that can involve controversial political decisions. Councillors thus tend to have a wider range of positionalities vis-à-vis water supply reorganization than is common among water management or city corporate staff.

In sum, rescaling and underfunded infrastructure for water supply strengthen the case for ASD among water management staff in an effort to distance water services from city council and corporate staff. Under a situation of increasing responsibilities and funding constraints, water supply revenues and reserves become more attractive to corporate staff and councils as an additional source of funds, and thus in need of greater protection from the perspective of water management. As such, it is not ideology, but rather conflicting mandates under budgetary stress that drive ASD for water management. Understanding municipal government as unitary obfuscates the real substance of the restructuring debate. Rather than a debate about ideology, it is about how, under the challenges of neoliberalization, to define what activities fall under the umbrella of water supply; what activities should be funded with water rates; who should participate in these decisions; and in what manner their interests and concerns should be incorporated.

---

11 Interview with a member of TWWS management (2006).

Challenges to Reform: Local 'Water Watchers'

The above conflicts within local government were compounded by public protests against the reforms. Water Watch Alliances formed to contest PSP in Hamilton in 2004 and MSB reform in Toronto in 2002.[12] In both cities, the extensive public support garnered by the groups was deemed important in retaining and returning to direct delivery. A comparison of the two campaigns, however, reveals certain differences. In the Toronto campaign, environmental groups – and therefore the impact of ASD on environmental issues – were of much greater importance, as environmentalists' issues are best promoted via access to councils. However, if a council's influence on water supply is curtailed through ASD, so too is that of environmentalists. As such, the water watch campaigns had common concerns with those of city corporate staff regarding ASD. That is, they had unknown allies in municipal government.

Yet, distrust of municipal council and staff was salient in the minds of Torontonians involved in public meetings and in protesting the MSB (Chief Administrative Officer 2002). For Toronto Water Watch, the municipal department model was the least of evils rather than a satisfactory solution to the challenges faced in terms of water supply, source water protection and effluent water quality. This dissatisfaction with municipal-led management is associated with the lack of attention given to environmental issues under the model: environmentalists must continuously lobby councils for improvements to water resource protection and conservation. As such, the challenges that environmentalists face in having their concerns met are not remedied through ASD because it limits council influence over water supply – and the influence of environmentalists as a result. The TWW literature, for example, argues for direct delivery by attributing environmental successes (and associated cost savings) with respect to water supply in Toronto to the fact that the public is in a position to influence the council. The service delivery model must be retained so that the public can watch over councils; under pressure from the public, councils will ensure that water management acts appropriately.

In Hamilton there was a similar dissatisfaction with the city council. Although Hamilton Water Watch (HWW) concentrated on the limitations of PSP, the many critical newspaper articles were indicative of a local dissatisfaction with the council. These argued that the council operated as a closed shop in cooperation with private interests, and that it was ineffective in ensuring quality services during the first PSP contract (see e.g. McGuinness 1999; Whittle 1999; Yemen 1999). In contrast to TWW, however, HWW was not as concerned with environmental issues.[13]

---

12   The data used below include the documents generated by the Water Watch groups, minutes of public and council meetings, city reports, media articles and interviews.

13   The Hamilton Water Watch Alliance expressed concerns with the environmental implications of contracting operations to a private operator, but did not address the issue of advancing an environmental agenda for water supply.

Still, in both Toronto and Hamilton the alliances saw local government as a single actor, expressing a like ideology for policy reform. The reality that emerges, however, is that the diverse positionalities of environmental and labour groups coincide with those of municipal corporate staff on the issue of ASD. Avoiding the trap of mistaking local government as a homogeneous unit and adopting a more nuanced perspective might be of benefit in engaging with a range of water governance issues in addition to ASD.

Conclusions

This chapter underscores four issues. First, municipal government should be understood as comprising multiple and competing interests, rather than as a unitary actor. Second, challenging neoliberal reforms need not be the sole purview of non-governmental actors and agencies; contestation also comes from within local government. Third, privatization and PSP, although they command the most attention, are less desirable among water managers than other types of ASD reforms. Finally, while the status quo may not present a satisfactory solution for all parties, it is often upheld, given the complex positionalities of various actors faced with 'doing more with less' under neoliberalism.

The efforts of those who oppose ASD reorganization demonstrate that while the municipal department model limits the achievement of their policy goals, advancing alternatives is difficult. This issue is most acute for environmental advocates, whose work involves the continuous lobbying of municipal government. City corporate staff favour direct delivery for a somewhat similar reason: the ability to engage directly with decision-making processes.

Contestation within municipal government and between scales of government is important in mollifying the outcomes of organizational reform at the local scale. Governments do not necessarily act in concert toward the achievement of neoliberal goals. Conflicts arise between the branches of municipal government and between scales of government over reforms that challenge the role of government. Understanding the local state in its diverse positionalities is fruitful for the analysis of water supply. Such an approach can generate alternative and more nuanced governance solutions that need not be antagonistic to the local state. In misreading the municipal scale as homogenous, potential avenues for political engagement and alternative governance approaches risk being overlooked.

References

Bakker, Karen. 2000. Privatizing water, producing scarcity: The Yorkshire drought of 1995. *Economic Geography*, 76(1), 4–27.

———. 2004. *An Uncooperative Commodity: Privatizing Water in England and Wales*. Oxford: Oxford University Press.

———. 2007. The 'commons' versus the 'commodity': Alter-globalization, anti-privatization and the human right to water in the global south. *Antipode*, 39(3), 430–55.

Bakker, Karen, and David Cameron. 2005. Governance, business models and restructuring water supply utilities: Recent developments in Ontario, Canada. *Water Policy*, 7(5), 485–508.

Brenner, Neil, and Nik Theodore. 2002. Cities and the geographies of 'actually existing neoliberalism'. *Antipode*, 34(3), 349–79.

Chief Administrative Officer. 2002. Re: Recommended Governance Structure for Water and Wastewater Services. Toronto: City of Toronto.

———. 2003. Re: Designating Water and Wastewater Services as a 'Business Unit'. Toronto: City of Toronto.

Cohen, Alice, and Seanna Davidson. 2011. The watershed approach: Challenges, antecedents, and the transition from technical tool to governance unit. *Water Alternatives*, 4(1), 1–14.

CWWA. 1997. Municipal Water and Wastewater Infrastructure: Estimated Investment Needs 1997–2012. Ottawa: Canadian Water and Wastewater Association.

Furlong, Kathryn. 2010. Neoliberal water management: trends, limitations, reformulations. *Environment and Society: Advances in Research*, 1(1), 46–75.

———. 2012. Good water governance without good urban governance? Regulation, service delivery models, and local government. *Environment and Planning A*, 44(11), 2721–41.

Furlong, Kathryn, and Karen Bakker. 2010. The contradictions of 'alternative' service delivery: Governance, business models, and sustainability in municipal water supply. *Environment and Planning C*, 28(2), 349–68.

———. 2011. Governance and sustainability at a municipal scale: The challenge of water conservation. *Canadian Public Policy/Analyse de Politiques*, 37(2), 219–37.

Gross Stein, Janice. 2001. *The Cult of Efficiency*. Toronto: Anansi.

Harvey, David. 1989. From managerialism to entrepreneurialism: The transformation in urban governance in late capitalism. *Geografiska Annaler Series B: Human Geography*, 71(1), 3–17.

Hefetz, Amir, and Mildred E. Warner. 2004. Privatization and its reverse: Explaining the dynamics of the government contracting process. *Journal of Public Administration Research and Theory*, 14(2), 171–90.

Jessop, Bob. 2002. Liberalism, neoliberalism, and urban governance: A state theoretical perspective. *Antipode*, 34(3), 452–73.

Jessop, Bob, Neil Brenner, and Martin Jones. 2008. Theorizing sociospatial relations. *Environment and Planning D*, 26, 389–401.

Jones, Irene. 2002. Safe Clean Accountable: Water Advocate's Solution to the Current Debate on Water Governance. Toronto: City of Toronto.

Keil, Roger. 2003. Globalization makes states: Perspectives on local governance in the age of the world city, in *State/Space: A Reader*, edited by N. Brenner, B. Jessop, M. Jones and G. Macleod. Oxford: Blackwell, 278–95.

Marston, Sallie A. 2000. The social construction of scale. *Progress in Human Geography*, 24(2), 219–42.

McGuinness, Eric. 1999. Philip utilities president denies bad-faith bargaining. *Hamilton Spectator*, 16 July.

Mirza, Saeed M., and Murtaza Haider. 2003. The State of Infrastructure in Canada: Implications for Infrastructure Planning and Policy. Ottawa: Infrastructure Canada.

Norman, Emma S., Karen Bakker, and Christina Cook. 2012. Introduction to the themed section: Water governance and the politics of scale. *Water Alternatives*, 5(1), 52–61.

Page, Ben, and Maria Kaïka. 2003. The EU water framework directive: Part 2. Policy innovation and the shifting choreography of governance. *European Environment*, 13, 328–43.

Sabatier, Paul A., Will Focht, Mark Lubell, Zev Trachtenberg, Arnold Vedlitz, and Marty Matlock, eds. 2005. *Swimming Upstream: Collaborative Approaches to Watershed Management.* Cambridge, MA: MIT Press.

Sheppard, Eric. 2002. The spaces and times of globalization: Place, scale, networks, and positionality. *Economic Geography*, 78(3), 307–30.

Siegel, David. 1997. Local government in Ontario, in *The Government and Politics of Ontario*, edited by G. White. Toronto: University of Toronto Press, 126–57.

Slack, Enid. 1996. Finance and governance: The case of the Greater Toronto area, in *Urban Governance and Finance: A Question of Who Does What*, edited by P.A.R. Hobson and F. St-Hilaire. Montreal: Institute for Research on Public Policy, 81–111.

Soja, E.W. 2009. Regional planning and development theories, in *International Encyclopedia of Human Geography*, edited by R. Kitchin and N.J. Thrift. Boston: Elsevier, 259–70.

SuperBuild. 2002. Organization of Municipal Water and Wastewater Systems in Ontario. Toronto: Ontario SuperBuild Corporation.

Whittle, Mark Alan. 1999. Council failed on PUMC issue. *Hamilton Spectator*, 25 May.

Yemen, Peter. 1999. Water plant deal is not in the public's best interest. *Hamilton Spectator*, 12 June.

Chapter 9

Techno-Nature and Scaling Water Governance in South Texas

Wendy Jepson and Christian Brannstrom

Introduction

Technology circulates within society and reconfigures foundational social relations. As Marx wrote, technology 'lays bare the process of the production of social relations of his life, and of the mental conceptions that from flow those relations' (Marx 1867: 493–4). Technology – a system of knowledge, skills, practices and discourses arranged in order to make some change the world (Barry 2001) – is neither static nor separated from human capacity; rather, it is emergent and shifting in relation to social life. Science and technology scholars detail the complex, political dimensions that technologies, devices and practices bear on social life (Barry 2001; White and Wilbert 2009) and how rending problems 'technical' is a political practice and exercise of power (Ferguson 1990; Li 2007; Robertson 2010).

Technical devices and technical practices physically divert the flow of water and reconfigure the assembled waterscape materially and discursively. Groups and individuals choose specific technologies, devices and practices to govern the flow of water to create a 'metabolic circulation' that materializes 'socio-natural and socio-technical relations organized through socially articulated networks and conduits' (Swyngedouw 2009: 73). Technical devices and practices are central points of negotiation in changing water–society interactions because they determine how to physically move water, what kind of water, to whom and by whom. As such, they are central to the politics of water governance, not merely instrumental in water management.

Geographers have examined the interaction between technology and water resources using several case study settings. Critical analyses of large hydro-engineering projects reveal how waterscapes are socio-natures, 'techno-natural assemblages' that act as both medium and expression of shifting power regimes (Swyngedouw 1999; Kaika and Swyngedouw 2000; Gandy 2004; Loftus 2006b). Contested environmental knowledge reveals the highly interdependent relationship between state and state subjects around water technical devices (Birkenholtz 2009). In addition to a water supply, stand-alone technical devices such as tube-wells for agriculture and domestic consumption play symbolic and cultural roles in everyday life (Birkenholtz 2010; Sultana 2013). Other researchers have explored how 'mediating technologies' modify existing waterscapes and destabilize the otherwise obdurate urban water infrastructure (Furlong 2011). Mediating technologies leave the core water system intact, but they can 'lead to important shifts [in] urban metabolism and who can influence it' (Furlong 2011: 466). In sum, technical devices introduce flexibility and new options for water conveyance that cascade into contested social relations, subjectivities and institutional form.

This chapter seeks to delineate the relationship between technology and water with an eye toward identifying how technologies influence water governance and what that reveals about scalar politics and power. Technology systems and devices are more than *exogenous innovations* for creating profits; they enable or constrain individuals or groups to *claim* authority over water, and this claim is either explicitly or implicitly scalar. Indeed, the scale of water governance is a fundamental factor in the creation of techno-nature assemblages. Therefore, the selection of technical devices and subsequent conflicts can be interpreted as a form of scalar politics in water governance.

To advance this thesis we examine two disputes over water technology. We ask: what are the specific ways conflicts over technical devices and practice intersect with and shape scalar politics of water governance? We examine key moments in the historical and geographical development of governance over Rio Grande water in south Texas. Our approach juxtaposes historical events in order to convey a second point about scalar politics which is present throughout the volume: scale is emergent and contingent, always undergoing processes of becoming through social practice, yet always confronting an already partitioned geography (MacKinnon 2011: 28). Brenner calls this durability 'scalar structuration', which involves 'relations of hierarchization and rehierarchization among vertically differentiated spatial units' (Brenner 2001: 605). Our point is that technology and technical devices contribute to process and, therefore, conflicts over these devices are a type of scalar politics.

The chapter examines two twentieth-century moments in which the contest over water governance intersected with debates over water technologies. In each moment we show how elites tried to exercise social power over water through a political strategy (electoral and legal) that pivoted on technical devices related to irrigation (pumps or gravity) or domestic water conveyance (pumps or jugs). The first moment covers a ferocious political contest between Anglo[1] land developers and farmers over whether to convey irrigation water to fields by pump or gravity technology. The second moment relates to the material consequences of the water adjudication process for Mexican-American claims on Rio Grande water for domestic purposes, and the central role water conveyance technical devices (jugs or pumps) played in the outcome.

---

1   The term 'Anglo' here refers to non-Hispanic, English-speaking people of European descent.

Governing the Flow of Water: Scale and Technology

We bring together debates over scale and environmental governance in conversation with current analysis of technology and nature to argue that conflicts over technical devices offer new perspectives on scalar politics of water governance. Although water policymakers have embraced the biophysical watershed as a physical hydrological unit that offers an optimum scale of governance, scholars have drawn on broader debates in human geography to challenge this position (Norman and Bakker 2009; Cohen and Davidson 2011; Norman et al. 2012).

Technical devices that operate within water systems are contested, but the scale of the devices does not predetermine scalar outcomes. This should not be surprising, as scalar politics and geometries of power articulate differently through water networks and because water itself is redefined through technological interventions. Efficient pumping technologies, for example, catalysed new efforts to redefine water access rights to groundwater (Roberts and Emel 1992). Technical devices and technologies that alter, fragment or rework water conveyance systems redefine water, and thus change social relations, subjectivities and institutions (Linton 2010; Sultana 2013).

Furlong (2011) looks to science and technology studies and the model of a network to complement how geographers may theorize technology in relation to scale. As Furlong argues, small devices can equate 'to big change'. This chapter builds on Furlong's approach but reorients the analysis to examine the politics and social relations of technical devices as central to the socio-spatial configuration of authority over water. It is clear that technical devices offer new sources of relative surplus value. But more than exogenous innovations for creating profits, we argue that technical devices enable or constrain individuals or groups to *claim* authority over water, and this claim is either explicitly or implicitly scalar. Therefore, contests over the meaning, implementation and use of technical devices can be interpreted as a form of scalar politics in water governance.

Water Resources in South Texas

South Texas water politics confirm Swyngedouw's observation that 'the mechanisms of exclusion from and access to water manifest power relationships' through which the geographies of places are transformed (2004: 30). Water governance in south Texas favours irrigation, so-called 'water users', over domestic water provision. Changes to water governance need to be understood within the political economy defined by a constant reworking of capitalist accumulation strategies and local politics of ethnicity and poverty.

Water, Power and Poverty

Water flows towards social and economic power in the Lower Rio Grande Valley. Farmer-controlled irrigation districts manage water allocations and hold a monopoly on the conveyance of water from the Rio Grande to water suppliers, including municipal utility districts, non-profit water supply corporations and special water districts. Starting in the 1910s, Anglo elites who had migrated from Midwestern US states seized on a new rail connection to the valley and unclaimed water rights. They rapidly implemented a pump-based irrigation technology coupled with locally controlled irrigation-district institutions that territorialized water-delivery rules. Farmers paid fees to private irrigation companies or taxes to semi-public irrigation districts in exchange for the right to obtain water supplied by pumping and canal infrastructure (Schoolmaster 1991; Stubbs et al. 2003), creating a nationally important centre for irrigated fruit and vegetables.

As Anglo farmers controlled water flow, they also subordinated Mexican-Americans and Mexican immigrants as a poorly paid farm labouring class marginalized by segregationist laws (Montejano 1987). During the 1940s, for example, critical observers noted how cities had lived up to the 'Magic Valley' promotional literature (Brannstrom and Neuman 2009), but informal or irregular rural subdivisions ('colonias') that lacked domestic water and adequate sanitation grew in their shadow (Ward 1999). Mexican-born and Mexican-American farmworkers in adjacent rural neighbourhoods lived with 'rutted roads, without sidewalks or sewers', and in 'small shacks or huts, usually of crude construction' (Warburton et al. 1943: 7). Outsiders arriving in the region during January would see 'a modern version of the Garden of Eden' above a much larger 'base of toiling, brown-skinned Mexican laborers' who lived 'on the verge of actual starvation' (Stilwell 1947: 17).

Poverty and inadequate housing and water infrastructure still characterize the region. In the 1980s, 20–25 per cent of the colonia population lacked domestic water; up to 50 per cent lacked adequate plumbing; and many relied on cesspools and poorly built septic tanks (TDHS 1988). Today, the region also has the largest concentration of colonias in the US – approximately 1,400 – which are home to around 240,000 residents, or roughly 25 per cent of the region's population (Ward 1999; USGS 2007; Parcher and Humberson 2009). Despite millions of dollars spent on infrastructure investment, upwards of 40 per cent of colonia residents live with substandard water access or sanitation (Ward 1999; USGS 2007).

Water Governance

Water law and water districts are institutional pillars of water governance in south Texas. The foundation of Texas water law is the establishment of proprietary and usufruct water rights. Texas is a 'dual-doctrine' state, as legislators and courts have adopted a riparian water rights system and prior-appropriation system over the past century and a half (Dobkins 1959; Caroom and Elliot 1981; Hamilton 1984: 576). The common law riparian rights system gives usufruct rights to the owner of land adjacent to the watercourse. The doctrine of appropriation recognizes state ownership of water and licenses water use of a specific volume, location, time frame and purpose. Thus, water rights are tied to a state permit, not to land ownership. An important exception to the prior appropriation rule in the Texas Water Code is that any appropriation made after 17 May 1931 is subordinate to municipal claims for water, *except* those cities living along a transboundary river (Rio Grande).

The water district is thus a territorial political unit, created by the state legislature to convey and govern water allocation and use. Texas created irrigation districts (IDs), water control and improvement districts (WCIDs), special utility districts (SUDs) and municipal utility districts (MUDs) to manage water resources. WCIDs and IDs have the power to levy taxes, build infrastructure, allocate water according to water rights permits, and to contract with water-supply networks to move water from the river to the tap.

In the mid-twentieth century severe drought and volatile social and political change challenged the institutional framework for water governance. The drought, which lasted from 1950 until 1957, revealed that Texan rivers, including the Rio Grande, were over appropriated when stored water could not fulfil all water claims for irrigators and municipalities. Incompatibility between the two legal systems caused considerable conflict as the state failed to develop a method to adjudicate the rights of water users. A 13-year legal case, *State of Texas v. Hidalgo County Water Control and Improvement District No. 18* (1956–69), known as the 'Valley Water Suit', adjudicated competing claims for water (Smith 1977; Templar 1981). This case led the state to pass the Water Rights Adjudication Act (1967) to merge riparian irrigation rights into the prior appropriation system. In political terms, the adjudicated regime of water governance reaffirmed the Anglo farmer-controlled WCIDs as the primary scale for water governance because they had prior-appropriation water rights (Smith 1977) and dispossessed many riparian claimants, primarily Mexican-Americans, to domestic and irrigated water (Hamilton 1984).

Other groups also challenged Anglo power over water and water districts. During the 1960s Civil Rights Movement and following the passage of the US Voting Rights Act (1965), Chicano-led colonia organizations and advocates began to campaign for a treated water service, and looked to the WCID as the political mechanism to attain domestic water service for their low-income communities.[2] The WCIDs, concerned about the potential impact of colonia residents' voting behaviour, initiated a process to undermine legitimate political participation of low-income Mexican-American communities in water governance. They supported the passage of a new statute – Article 8280–3.23 (1971) – allowing water district boards to unilaterally exclude unplatted 'urban land' (e.g. colonias) from district territory. After a four-year legal battle, the court ruled in favour of water districts and determined that the exclusion of colonias from the district was legal, and thus consolidated the state-sanctioned landowners' power over water (Jepson 2012).

---

2 'Chicano' refers to politically engaged Mexican-Americans who participated in civil and political rights activism.

Contesting Technology, Negotiating Scale

We revisit water governance through the optic of water conveyance technology in two 'moments'. Technical devices, in their capacity to enable or constrain individuals or groups, offer new avenues to *claim* authority over water, and this claim is either explicitly or implicitly scalar. Therefore, contest over pumps, pipes, jugs and buckets can be understood as a form of scalar politics in water governance. South Texas elites tried to exercise social power over water through political strategies (electoral and legal) that relied on technical devices related to irrigation or water conveyance. Both cases illustrate that techno-scalar politics follow larger capital accumulation strategies to relegate responsibility for water necessary for social reproduction to the household (scale) and ultimately deepen processes of uneven water development that prioritize agricultural production.

Pumps or Gravity Irrigation

In the 1920s, as irrigated agriculture for Anglo accumulation seemed to reach its 'Magic Valley' promotional ideals, the privately controlled pump-district system faced challenges from supporters of an entirely different system: a proposed federally controlled gravity system that would bypass pumps and send impounded water directly to farmland. The current irrigation district pump-based conveyance system, therefore, was built on an early private system. This technology – pumps and, initially, earthen canals – captured a 'free' resource that farmers could not obtain on their own. The scalar dimension is visible in the business model and territories that land developers implemented. Land developers profited from sales of irrigated parcels of farmland that relied upon irrigation districts or firms for water. The private irrigation firms or districts, in turn, relied on land developers to keep promoting the farming economy, which generated water-use fees and taxes necessary to fund irrigation improvements. However, the private system was not inevitable; rather, it resulted from contested ideas about the desired locus of capital accumulation: agricultural production or land development. The proposed gravity system would re-territorialize and rescale water governance by implementing a new conveyance system for irrigation.

Tension between two prominent individuals representing competing techno-political visions of irrigation invoked different scalar arguments. In the 1910s, John Shary (1872–1945), a land developer, created 'Sharyland' from thousands of acres of shrubland near Mission, Texas (Figures 9.1 and 9.2). He then bought a bankrupt irrigation company that became the basis for his United Irrigation Company (IUC). Shary became an irrigation manager by accident after realizing that profits from land sales hinged on the ability to supply irrigation water. Shary's United Irrigation District (UID) was one of the last in the valley to remain in private ownership.

King and Queen of Rio Grande Valley Grapefruit. His Majesty, John the First, and Her Highness, Queen Lena, seated on their throne in the ball room of Shary mansion. In civilian life, Mr. John H. Shary, of Sharyland, and Mrs. A. Y. Baker, of Edinburg.

Figure 9.1   John Shary as king of Rio Grande Valley Grapefruit
Source: Monty's Monthly, December 1923, p. 16.

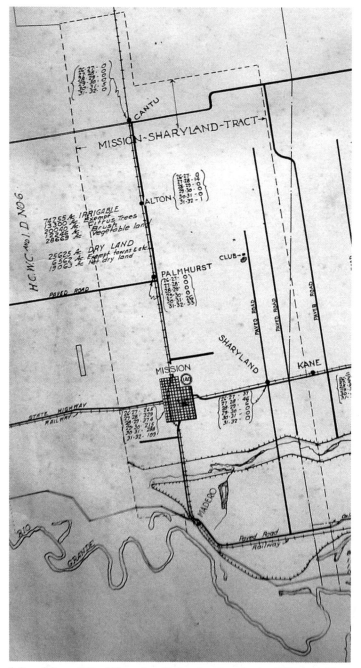

Figure 9.2   Map of the 'Sharyland' development near Mission, Texas, 1932

Source: Southern Pacific Lines Map of Rio Grande Valley (1932), Maps, LM002, John H. Shary Collection, Library Archives, University of Texas-Pan American, Edinburg.

The other protagonist was Charles Pease (1873–1933), who arrived in the valley shortly after Shary began purchasing land there. Pease established a bank at Raymondville but then moved into lobbying and politics, becoming the valley's most prominent advocate for gravity irrigation (Brannstrom 2012).

Shary's irrigation company nearly failed in the late 1910s, when he confronted the fact that irrigation water did not behave the way his promotional pamphlets had promised – as if from a tap. In fact, pumps had to lift the water out of the river; the water then flowed through earthen canals, where large volumes seeped underground – never to reach the intended fields. Shary borrowed heavily to finance a new pump, and then levied a new fee of $4 per acre, known as a flat rate, so that farmers could purchase irrigation water from his company. He intended the flat rate as a full-cost recovery of water infrastructure, which also created use value for land he wanted to develop further away from the river.

However, when the pump broke down angry farmers revolted, seeking 'fair, equitable, and economical distribution of water'. Farmers described Shary's irrigation infrastructure as 'insufficient' and 'inadequate' because of high seepage rates. They also argued that Shary was selling land that he could not hope to supply adequately with water unless he reduced the service to already established farmers (JHSC 1918a). Shary denied that concern for profits influenced his decisions, and presented his choice in stark terms to his supporters: he could abandon the irrigation system – which would have brought 'ruin to this great community' – or increase income to the UIC (JHSC 1918b).

The pump-canal infrastructure relied on contradictory imperatives. Shary's accumulation strategy was based on selling dear what he had purchased for little – his cheap land, now irrigated. For his business model to work, Shary had to increase the charges for irrigation water to maintain and upgrade his pumping system. If the water system failed, then crops would wither and Shary would have miserable harvests to show off to prospective land purchasers. Poor irrigation infrastructure would reduce the use value of a piece of land, which in turn would destroy the exchange value of other land in Shary's control. Therefore, Shary had to extract rents from landowners to support pump irrigation lest irrigation costs sap capital from his land-sales business. In this scalar strategy, control over territory overlapped with control of irrigation water by a single organization controlled by one person. The potential contradiction was that the water business could not extend enough water to match the land business, at least without extracting rents from water users that would cause political unrest among farmers.

By the mid-1920s many land developers had resolved this contradiction by selling their irrigation infrastructure to farmers, organized in IDs or WCIDs. Shary was a holdout in the valley, and for this reason he became the target of an opposing model for irrigation, articulated best by Charles Pease – who had formed an association of water users – with a weekly newspaper dedicated to promoting gravity irrigation in the valley. Gravity irrigation, modelled on the work of the US Bureau of Reclamation in the arid western states, would require major state investment for dam and canal construction that would establish means for cross-subsidization.

Central to Pease's argument for gravity irrigation was the use of scale to challenge the pump-canal infrastructure that supported Shary's locus of accumulation. Pumps were small-scale interventions, watering relatively small areas controlled by elites (e.g. Shary) at the expense of farmers. Gravity, on the other hand, would rescale governance to include the federal government and water technicians, while also benefitting more farmers. A dam across the Rio Grande was needed to capture more water than the individual pumps ever could, but a dam would require the US government to negotiate a treaty with Mexico and to finance the impoundment and federal resources to impound the Rio Grande water (NHC 1921; JHSC 1925). Therefore, Pease saw no useful role for private firms like Shary's in the economic development in the valley.

Disagreement between Shary and Pease came to a head in early 1924. In his newspaper, Pease argued that he was duty-bound in 'tearing down the unsightly structure which clutters the Valley and which constitutes a menace to the peace and prosperity of the people who are attracted here'; the pumping systems 'must be torn away'. Pease argued that it was 'repugnant to the very spirit of democracy to make a whole community to be dependent on one single man', John Shary, who 'lives like a feudal baron' and 'control[s] the water, holds at his mercy the owner of the land' (Pease 1924). He also argued for the need to break the relationship between land development and private irrigation firms: 'the ownership of water independently of the land makes the owner of the water virtually a dictator to the owner of the land unless his power is curbed either by law or in some other way' (Pease 1925).

In summary, gravity irrigation would shift the locus of accumulation and social power away from small groups of land–water developers such as Shary and towards a centralized entity that would represent the interests of the thousands of Anglo farmers attracted to the Magic Valley. Pease saw himself as a promoter of the 'common man at the end of the lateral' in confrontation with the local 'water dictator', a discourse that borrowed heavily from the social engineering and agrarianism of proponents of federal reclamation (Conkin 1960; Pisani 1983).

Neither Pease's gravity system nor Shary's pumping system was fully implemented on the US side of the Grande/Bravo. In the 1930s, after Pease died of a water-borne illness, the Bureau of Reclamation proposed a new gravity irrigation scheme. Pump-dependent irrigation districts mobilized to oppose the plan, but in the 1950s and 1960s they faced a significant new challenge in the form of the Valley Water Suit because Texas had over-appropriated water to the pump-based system, as Pease had long suspected. The complicated legal process created two classes of pump-based irrigators and helped initiate the steady decline in irrigated areas (Schoolmaster 1991; Smith 1977). Moreover, in the late 1920s Shary began converting his firm into an irrigation district that purchased some of his pumps and infrastructure, so that the 'water dictator' became a group of elites who controlled irrigation districts, which in turn taxed farmers to pay debts for upgrading the declining infrastructure (Brannstrom 2012).

Mexican officials viewed gravity irrigation as appropriate to state goals for mobilizing water and people. In the 1930s the Cárdenas administration built the Retamal gravity irrigation project. This supported the settlement of thousands of repatriated Mexicans on the other side of the Grande/Bravo, prompting the valley elites to renew calls for a treaty with Mexico that would cover water allocation (Hundley 1966: 93–5; Walsh 2008: 123–34).

Pipes or Jugs?

Later in the twentieth century scalar politics of water technology emerged between agricultural production and domestic water access. In 1964 rural Mexican-Americans formed the non-profit Union Water Supply Corporation (UWSC) to provide clean domestic water for 260 low-income families in the many colonias in Starr County, near the Rio Grande. That year, the Texas Water Rights Commission (TWRC) granted the UWSC a temporary water permit for 52 acre-feet per annum. In 1966, with a loan from the federal government, the corporation constructed infrastructure – including a river pump, storage tank and booster station.

The Valley Water Suit ended in 1971, and the TWRC, following the new institutional structure for the Lower Rio Grande, revoked the UWSC's temporary water permit. The Commission advised the UWSC to purchase water through the new water rights system and ordered the Rio Grande Watermaster, the administrator of water rights in the region, to turn off the pumps supplying the communities. In response, colonias residents and the UWSC filed a lawsuit against state officials (Rio Grande Watermaster and Texas Water Rights Commission), claiming that the loss of domestic water violated their rights. The plaintiffs' attorney made several arguments in federal court to support their claim to water and to restore household access to Rio Grande water without being 'forced to buy water rights' (MALDEF 1972b: 2).

First, the plaintiffs complained that the state had dispossessed individuals of long-standing riparian rights without following due process under the law. The plaintiffs insisted that their claim to Rio Grande water was to obtain 'the right to draw water for domestic and livestock use through the services of their agent, the Union Water Supply Corporation, which has a water distribution system that treats water after it is drawn from the river' (MALDEF 1972c). Such a claim for non-irrigation water use was explicitly left out of the valley water rights adjudication process. Therefore, the justification to turn off the water pumps, based on the Valley Water Suit, did not apply to them.

Second, they argued that their constitutional right of equal protection was violated by the Wagstaff Act (1931), which states that municipal water users have preference over irrigation water users, *except* those communities living along the Rio Grande. They argued that the geographical exclusion in the water code created 'an irrational and invidious discrimination in the distribution of State water for domestic and municipal uses between persons who live along the Rio Grande and persons living along other Texas Rivers' (MALDEF 1972d: 2).

The State's attorney and water-district attorneys wanted to keep the case out of the federal court and dismiss the colonias residents' claim for what they called 'free water'. They argued that federal courts did not have jurisdiction since water rights are under the authority of individual states (MALDEF 1972e). Therefore, the State's attorneys challenged each argument on the basis of *res judicata*: that is, they argued that consideration of the matter should be denied because of prior court rulings on water rights adjudication. Moreover, the State argued that the community members had a clear remedy for lack of water: they could buy water rights on the market.

Technical devices played a key role in litigation over water governance, the nature of water and scale. In the first instance, the plaintiffs demonstrated their claim to riparian rights by citing a long-standing conveyance of river water: residents historically 'used cans, buckets, barrels, and other containers to carry the water to their homes' until they organized to form the water supply corporation (MALDEF 1972a: 5). The State's attorney seized on this, and agreed that the plaintiffs had the right to exercise their 'domestic and livestock' riparian rights. But the State vigorously contested the use of pumps and pipes to convey water from the river to homes, arguing that these devices effectively changed the relationship between the individuals and the river, and thus their claim to Rio Grande water. Using pumps to convey water allowed a larger volume of water use than jugs, and thus exceeded the volume of the plaintiffs' usufruct right to water. Indeed, the debate came down to pipes versus jugs.

Debate over the technical devices used to convey water can be understood as a scale-specific political strategy to claim water and control water governance. The State of Texas sought to retain its authority over water conveyance and allocation. By defining water rights in terms of conveyance device (e.g., jugs, barrels and buckets), the state argued that its officials did not deny livestock and domestic water to residents (MALDEF 1972f: 2, 5), since community members could still walk to the river and haul water. Since physical access to the river's edge was not blocked, the plaintiffs had no claim under the US Constitution. Indeed, the state's attorney reiterated that there was no substantial question of federal law, and that the plaintiffs 'want to get some water under the guise of getting it for free instead of paying for it like everyone else' (MALDEF 1972g: 11).

Further, the state argued that the technical device, not user intention, defined the type of water (domestic, municipal or irrigation). For example, the state argued that for water to be defined as 'domestic and livestock' it could only be conveyed by physical labour: any other type of water conveyance, such as a pump, changed the nature of water because an increase in the *capacity for distribution* thus made it potentially open for 'municipal use' (MALDEF 1972g: 75–6). Moreover, the state's attorneys argued that the technical device used to convey the water also determined the claim to water because pumps and pipes potentially increased the *volume* of water and could result in a commercial enterprise (MALDEF 1972g).

In terms of water governance, different use designations would mean water would be governed differently. The state maintained that residents were welcome to continue pulling water in jugs, but the use of pumps and pipes changed water into a resource governable by the Texas Water Code. According to the state's attorney, as a pump moves water through pipes and networks, the nature of water is transformed in the eyes of the law: the technical device, by its ability to distribute high volumes of water, creates a commodity and, therefore, the state – not the federal government – possessed authority over its governance. In summary, a technical device (jug or pump-pipe) used to convey water not only determined who could claim water rights, but also transformed a riparian right into a property right and, thus, shifted the scale of authority over water.

In response, the plaintiffs' attorneys argued that the purpose of the statute giving priority to domestic users was to guarantee individuals their inherent civil rights to domestic water (MALDEF 1972d: 8). Moreover, they argued, this right to domestic water existed regardless of the technical device:

> to limit their ability to make use of modern methods to purify and distribute the water which they have a right to use is to diminish and actually effect a taking of an important function of their right without due process and in violation of equal protection. (MALDEF 1972d: 17)

Indeed, according to the plaintiffs' attorneys, denial of a technical device would also be an effective denial of the residents' right to domestic water: technical devices enable or enhance the intention of the user rather than transform water's nature. The plaintiffs' attorney commented:

> It seems to me that the position they are taking does not make any sense. If the water goes into a pipe to come to your house it is in a different nature than if it is taken out of a jug. I just don't understand the distinction they are making. (MALDEF 1972g: 40–42)

While the court found this claim was not a matter of federal interest and dismissed the case, a close examination of the legal contest over water conveyance demonstrates how technological devices are more than material systems to move water. The negotiation over technology is about the scale of water governance. As in similar cases (Jepson 2012), the federal judge accepted the state's case and considered the market as a viable fix to the region's water conflicts. After the litigation, an increasing number of colonias communities continued to live unconnected to the water network until the late 1980s, when political pressure and fears of a public health crisis forced the Texas state legislature to address the colonias water supply and sanitation problems. Water was not 'free'; the water supply corporations that ultimately built water and sanitation infrastructure first purchased the necessary water rights on the open market.

Conclusion

What are the specific ways technology systems and technical devices shape negotiations over the scale of water governance? Our analysis of two moments in Rio Grande water governance demonstrates that long-term competition over water was about capital accumulation, which determined the parameters of water governance. In each case, elites tried to exercise social power over water through legal means and political strategy that relied on technology – whether a type of irrigation system (pumps or gravity) or water conveyance devices (pumps or jugs).

Technologies deployed in the struggle over water reconfigure social power and simultaneously co-produce new meanings of water. This chapter has demonstrated that technical devices and water governance intersected because the various water conveyance systems, and thus competing uses of water (modes of accumulation and social reproduction), empowered different institutions, actors and organizations in water governance. In the first case, gravity irrigation (which relied on federal investment), changed the regime of accumulation and water governance structure – replacing one elite group (land developers) with another (Anglo farmers). The gravity system required the restructuring of water governance and the enrolment of new authorities (water districts) and actors (federal government). Competition over technology systems implied a changed scale of water governance.

In the second case, arguments in favour of certain rules for water governance hinged on the type of technical device employed to convey water from the river to the home. How the court answered 'Was water defined by device or intent?' determined the scale of governance and, thus, the regime of rights in play, the role of state law and markets. Attorneys for state agencies and water districts reinforced the line between capital accumulation (irrigation) and social reproduction (domestic water): riparian rights were inherently limited by manual water conveyance, and once technical devices could move the flow of water, rather than capture it in buckets or jugs, water became property. The court found, then, that the nature of water was transformed: pumps and pipes, by their ability to move high volumes of water, created a commodity; therefore, the State, not the federal government, possessed authority over its governance.

Analysis of water technologies and devices advances how we understand the negotiation of scale in water governance. Attention to the material demands of different technology systems or devices, how these different systems restructure accumulation strategies, and the contests over these technologies opens avenues for critical analysis of water politics.

References

Barry, A. 2001. *Political Machines: Governing a Technological Society*. New York: Continuum.

Birkenholtz, T. 2009.Groundwater governmentality: Hegemony and technologies of resistance in Rajasthan's (India) groundwater governance. *Geographical Journal* 175(3), 208–20.

Birkenholtz, T. 2010. Full-cost recovery: Producing differentiated water collection practices and responses to centralized water networks in Jaipur, India. *Environment and Planning A* 42(9), 2238–53.

Brannstrom, C. 2012. John Shary, Charles Pease, and contested irrigation landscapes in early-twentieth-century South Texas. *Journal of Historical Geography* 38(3), 234–46.

Brannstrom, C. and M. Neuman 2009. Inventing the 'Magic Valley' of South Texas, 1900–1935. *Geographical Review* 99(2), 123–45.

Brenner, N. 2001. The limits to scale? Methodological reflections on scalar structuration. *Progress in Human Geography* 25(1), 591–614.

Caroom, D. and Elliot, P. 1981. Water rights adjudication: Texas style. *Texas Bar Journal* (November), 1183–90.

Cohen, A. and S. Davidson.2011. The watershed approach: Challenges, antecedents, and the transition from technical tool to governance unit. *Water Alternatives* 4(1), 1–14.

Conkin, P.K. 1960. The vision of Elwood Mead. *Agricultural History* 34(2), 88–97.

Day, J.C. 1970. *Managing the Lower Rio Grande: An Experience in International River Development*. Chicago: University of Chicago, Department of Geography.

Dobkins, B.E. 1959. *The Spanish Element in Texas Water Law*. Austin: University of Texas Press.

Ferguson, J. 1990. *The Anti-Politics Machine: 'Development', Depoliticization and Bureaucratic Power in Lesotho*. Cambridge: Cambridge University Press.

Furlong, K. 2011. Small technologies, big change: Rethinking infrastructure through STS and geography. *Progress in Human Geography* 35(4), 460–82.

Gandy, M. 2004. Rethinking urban metabolism: Water, space and the modern city. *City* 8(3), 363–79.

Hamilton, A. 1984. Plight of the riparian under Texas water law. *Houston Law Review* 21, 577.

Harvey, D. 2009. On the deep relevance of a certain footnote in Marx's Capital. *Human Geography* 1(2), 26–32.

Hundley Jr, N. 1966. *Dividing the Water: A Century of Controversy between the United States and Mexico*. Berkeley: University of California Press.

Jepson, W. 2012. Claiming space, claiming water: Contested legal geographies of water in south Texas. *Annals of the Association of American Geographers* 102(3), 614–31.

Kaika, M. and Swyngedouw, E. 2000. Fetishizing the modern city: The phantasmagoria of urban technological networks. *International Journal of Urban and Regional Research* 24(1), 120–38.

Kerbey, M. 1939. The Texas delta of an American Nile: Orchards and gardens replace thorny jungle in the southmost tip of the Lone Star State. *National Geographic Magazine* 74, 51–96.

Li, T.M. 2007. *The Will to Improve: Governmentality, Development, and the Practice of Politics*. Durham, NC: Duke University Press.

Linton, J. 2010. *What is Water? The History of a Modern Abstraction*. Vancouver: University of British Columbia Press.

Loftus, A. 2006a. Reification and the dictatorship of the water meter. *Antipode* 38(5), 1023–45.

Loftus, A. 2006b. The metabolic processes of capital accumulation in Durban's waterscape. In *In The Nature of Cities: Urban Political Ecology and the Politics of Urban Metabolism*, edited by N. Heynan, M. Kaika and E. Swyngedouw. New York: Routledge, 173–90.

MacKinnon, D. 2011. Reconstructing scale: towards a new scalar politics. *Progress in Human Geography* 35(1), 21–36.

Marx, K. 1867. *Capital*. New York: Vintage.

Molle, F., Mollinga, P.P. and Wester, P. 2009. Hydraulic bureaucracies and the hydraulic mission: Flows of water, flows of power. *Water Alternatives* 2(3), 328–49.

Montejano, D. 1987. *Anglos and Mexicans in the Making of Texas, 1836–1986*. Austin: University of Texas Press.

Norman, E.S. and Bakker, K. 2009. Transgressing scales: Water governance across the Canada–U.S. borderland. *Annals of the Association of American Geographers* 99(1), 99–117.

Norman, E.S., Bakker, K. and Cook, C. 2012. Water governance and the politics of scale. *Water Alternatives* 5(1), 52–61.

Neumann, R.P. 2009. Political ecology: Theorizing scale. *Progress in Human Geography* 33(3), 398–406.

Parcher, J.W. and Humberson, D.G. 2009. Using GIS to assess priorities of infrastructure and health needs of *colonias* along the United States-Mexico border. *Journal of Latin American Geography* 8(1), 129–48.

Pease, C.H. 1924. Constructive destruction, *Gravity Irrigation News*, 5 February.

Pease, C.H. 1925. The irrigation district vs. private ownership, *Gravity Irrigation News*, 21 January.

Pisani, D.J. 1983. Reclamation and social engineering in the progressive era. *Agricultural History* 57(1), 46–63.

Roberts, R.S. and Emel, J. 1992. Uneven development and the tragedy of the commons: Competing images for nature-society analysis. *Economic Geography* 68(3) 249–71.

Robertson, M. 2010. Performing environmental governance. *Geoforum* 41(1), 7–10.

Schoolmaster, F.A. 1991.Water marketing and water rights transfers in the Lower Rio Grande Valley, Texas. *Professional Geographer* 43(3), 292–304.

Smith, G.F. 1977. Valley water suit and its impact on Texas water policy: Some practical advice for the future, *Texas Tech Law Review* 8, 577–634.

Stilwell, H. 1947. Portrait of the Magic Valley. *New Republic* 116, 14–17.

Stubbs, M.J. et al. 2003. *Evolution of Irrigation Districts and Operating Institutions: Texas, Lower Rio Grande Valley*. College Station: Texas Water Resources Institute/Texas A&M University.

Sultana, F. 2013. Water, technology, and development: Transformations of development technonatures in changing waterscapes. *Environment and Planning D* 31(2), 337–53.

Swyngedouw, E. 1999. Modernity and hybridity: nature, *Regeneracionismo*, and the production of the Spanish waterscape, 1890–1930. *Annals of the Association of American Geographers* 89(3), 443–65.

Swyngedouw, E. 2004. *Social Power and the Urbanization of Water: Flows of Power*. New York: Oxford University Press.

Swyngedouw, E. 2007. Technonatural revolutions: The scalar politics of Franco's hydro-social dream for Spain, 1939–1975. *Transactions of the Institute of British Geographers* 32(1), 9–28.

Swyngedouw, E. 2009. Circulations and metabolisms: (Hybrid) natures and (cyborg) cities. In *Technonatures: Environments, Technologies, Spaces, and Places in the Twenty-First Century*, edited by D.F. White and C. Wilbert. Waterloo, Ont: Wilfrid Laurier University Press, 61–84.

TDHS. 1988. *The Colonias Factbook: A Survey of Living Conditions in Rural Areas of South and West Texas Border Counties*.: Austin: Texas Department of Human Services.

Templer, O.W. 1981. The evolution of Texas water law and the impact of adjudication. *Water Resources Bulletin* 17(5), 789–98.

USGS (United States Geological Survey). 2007. Colonia Health, Infrastructure, and Platting Status Tool (CHIPS) Available at: http://borderhealth.cr.usgs.gov/datalayers.html (accessed 22 September 2009).

Walsh, C. 2008. *Building the Borderlands: A Transnational History of Irrigated Cotton along the Mexico–Texas Border*. College Station: Texas A&M University Press.

Warburton, A.A., Wood, H. and Crane, M.M. 1943. *The Work and Welfare of Children of Agricultural Laborers in Hidalgo County, Texas*. Washington, DC: Government Printing Office.

Ward, P.M. 1999. *Colonias and Public Policy in Texas and Mexico: Urbanization by Stealth*. Austin: University of Texas Press.

White, D.F. and Wilbert, C. (eds). 2009. *Technonatures: Environments, Technologies, Spaces, and Places in the Twenty-First Century*. Waterloo, Ont: Wilfrid Laurier University Press.

Archival Sources

John H. Shary Collection, Library Archives, University of Texas-Pan American, Edinburg (JHSC)

n.d. Lower Rio Grande Valley Water Users Association, Memorandum.

1914. *The Treasure Land of the Lower Rio Grande: Where Nature's Smiles are Brightest*, Omaha, p. 1, Advertisements, Folder 22, Box 85.

1918a. Water Users' Association, [untitled document] UIC Sharyland, Box 10 Folder 516.

1918b. Shary, untitled speech, ca. 1918, Other Irrigation Sub-collection, Old Irrigation County Files, A8D2, Water Troubles.

1925. Review of activities of Water Users' Association since its organization, *Gravity Irrigation News*, 30 December 1925.

Nola Harding Collection, Raymondville Public Library, Raymondville, Texas (NHC)

1921. Lower Rio Grande Valley Water Users Association, Memorandum of facts concerning the Lower Rio Grande Gravity Irrigation Project of Texas, McAllen, ca. 192.

Mexican American Legal Defense and Education Fund, Special Collections, Stanford University Library, Stanford, California (MALDEF)

(Manuscript Collection, Record Group, Box, Folder)

1972a. Fact Statement for the Union Water Supply Corporation, M063 RG5 B484 F4.

1972b. Letter Cisneros to Obledo, 7 March 1972, M063 RG5 B484 F6.

1972c. Letter, Idar to Olveda, 23 June 1972, M0673 RG5 B484 F6.

1972d. Supplemental Brief in Support of Federal Jurisdiction, M0673 RG5 B482 F1.

1972e. Letter, Cisneros and Ching, 22 April 1972, M0673 RG5 B484 F6.

1972f. Reply to Plaintiffs' Supplemental Brief in Support of Federal Jurisdiction, M0673 RG5 B486 F4.

1972g. Court Transcript, 1 May 1972. M0673 RG5 B482 F8.

1973. Memo, Korbel to Rosen, M0673 B485 F7.

Chapter 10

The Creation of Scaled Water Rights in New Mexico, USA

Eric P. Perramond[1]

Introduction

Fluid water respects no particular governance scale. However, scale is actively used in the politics, conceptualization and management of water. Here, I argue that scale is also fundamental in differentiating water users and water use rights in New Mexico, USA. More specifically, it is the *legal* politics of scale derived from adjudicating water rights which sort and scale water rights holders by identity (Indian and non-Indian) and the governance scale of jurisdiction (federal versus state oversight). Water rights adjudications are legal processes undertaken by individual states to map, quantify and certify the location, beneficial use and quantity of water. However, although the law attempts to treat all water users equally, the scales of legal water politics treat water users differently, often based on identity under the varying institutions of water governance (Whiteley et al. 2008).

Following the insights of Moore (2008) and MacKinnon, it is the dynamic aspects of scalar arguments and politics that matter here in that 'scale is primarily a category of practice' (MacKinnon 2011: 27). Different agents, actors and institutions 'practise' scale differently, although their actions are not necessarily apparent to water users and water agencies (cf. Cox 1998). Water as a resource is therefore a useful lens for analysing the interconnections between politics, scale and governance (Swyngedouw 1999). Additionally, the different scales of water management and use may conflict with one another. For example, inter-state river water compacts (agreements) in the southwest often ignore state-level and identity-level norms of water governance, as states share bodies of water. Furthermore, although water adjudications focus on individual rights, at the same

1 I am grateful to all the water rights users, managers, lawyers and personnel from the Office of the State Engineer (New Mexico). This work was funded by Colorado College through the Dean's office, Social Science Executive Committee and the Hulbert Center for Southwest Studies Jackson Fellowships, between 2007 and 2013. The final version was greatly improved by the editors of this volume. None of them are responsible for any remaining errors or shortcomings. A longer version of this contribution appeared in *Water Alternatives* (2012).

time many New Mexican communities still retain strong customs of water-sharing (Rodriguez 2006).

This chapter draws on the ethnographic and political-ecological insights gained over five years of field visits and interviews to analyse how scale and law actively reshape the identities and rights of water users. Adjudication offers a way to frame how scale is both conceptual and actively political and ecological in its shaping of water management and politics in New Mexico. Water managers and users in New Mexico face new and old challenges in the twenty-first century (Wilder et al. 2010; deBuys 2011). In this arid to semi-arid region, residents have long depended on meagre surface streams and have increasingly tapped groundwater resources. The state of New Mexico's Office of the State Engineer (OSE) has purview over adjudication, mandated as of 1907 and expected to continue for decades. The glacial pace of adjudicatory progress is frustrating to most water users, since the state may be certifying new uses or permits for water without knowing the full balance sheet of older, cumulative, historic uses of water or the possible new climate regime in the southwest.

My focus is on how adjudications especially affect local irrigation ditches (acequias; see Figure 10.1), inter-ditch relations and the larger concerns regarding regional water governance (see also Levine 1990; Rodriguez 1990). The analysis illustrates the various levels of scalar politics, and finishes with a discussion of why water users and managers mobilize scale on a daily basis. Using legal scalar politics as a lens also holds promise for understanding water governance challenges and the notion of property regimes (Conca 2006; Bakker 2010).

For the purposes of this chapter, I focus on the analytical level at which decisions are made, and how individuals become embedded in a particular spatial framework of decision-making. I also suggest that water adjudication has heightened citizen awareness of how legal scale is perceived, used and debated in New Mexico. I employ the notions of state legibility (Scott 1998), bodily politics and regional watersheds to illustrate how and why scale is mobilized by various actors concerned with water in New Mexico.

Adjudication, (Legal) Scale and Water Rights in New Mexico

The legal and administrative process of any general stream adjudication is monstrously complex. Briefly, adjudication entails a lawsuit – triggered by either water users (as in Colorado) or by a central state authority (as in New Mexico) – to document the number, type and locations of water rights owners in a watershed. For example, at the time of writing, in New Mexico nearly 72,000 defendants (water rights holders) were involved in active adjudications, yet less than 40 per cent of the state's area has been adjudicated. Adjudication touches on several scalar aspects of (legal) water governance: individuals have their water rights quantified, based on beneficial use. This process specifies the location, quantity of use, current ownership and other details unique to the property that is being watered. Once

Figure 10.1   An acequia running close to a house, Gallinas Valley, New Mexico

individuals agree to the offer of judgment, typically a quantity of water expressed in acre-feet per year, state or federal courts pass decrees (final or partial) on these procedures by watershed. Ultimately, the state engineer is responsible for administering rights. This individuated property procedure directly scales legal water users, starting at the individual level (Boelens 2009). But it also partitions individual water rights holders by identity, in that federal courts have jurisdiction over native water rights, while state courts handle all 'non-Indians' in this process.

Adjudications in New Mexico become known by the alphabetically first surname among a group of defendants (as in 'Aamodt' or 'Abeyta'), forming a personalized toponymy of water cases and becoming shorthand references to particularly long and difficult legal cases. Adjudications are also a vivid example of a technology of governance, a kind of 'hydromentality' (to paraphrase Agrawal 2005) – one in which the state engineer and attorney general (as legal appellants') attempt to quantify water use (through water rights) on a legal basis for managing state resources.

New Mexicans do not own the water, from the state's perspective; they own rights. The state is responsible for quantifying, monitoring and certifying those claims to rights. But adjudication is not just about property rights. The process fundamentally challenges community notions of water, of who has rights to manage the water and how water is apportioned. Today, adjudicating by watershed has become the spatial-legal terrain for quantifying state and individual water rights. But using watershed boundaries – seemingly more attractive than using political boundaries (Worster 2003) – has its own challenges (see Cohen and Davidson 2011).

New Mexico water law relies on the doctrine of prior appropriation, common in most of the western states of the US. Prior appropriation codifies the 'first in time, first in right' nature of water rights in the state. This creates a system of senior (older) and junior (more recent) water rights, based on the first date of beneficial use. The Pueblo Indians had their own customary norms of water management, and still retain customary norms, although details of these practices are scant.[2] Spanish and Mexican Indian colonists brought water management institutions shaped by the Moorish customs embedded in the Iberian Peninsula (Wescoat 1995). Common in semi-arid parts of the Americas, these customary legal irrigation assumptions dominated local understandings of water use in New Mexico between roughly 1600 and the early 1900s (Meyer 1984; Clark 1987; Rivera 1998; Perreault 2008).

Although individuals may have a 'water right' in the western US, as mentioned earlier, this does not mean ownership of the water itself. Rather, water rights were established historically by diverting surface waters to a land parcel for beneficial use (such as agriculture or industry). Water users are then given private property rights to the use of that water. These rights can be bought, leased and sold, and are valid as long as the property owner uses the water for beneficial use. Irrigators who sell their water rights to a distant third party (e.g. a farmer or a city) are thus a concern for an overall ditch community. If enforced, the loss of that water in the ditch can affect the hydraulic flow for the entire community. This privatization of a water right is a rather recent legal development in the southwest, where land and water were long considered to be linked rather than separate property regimes that could be severed.

---

2   The Pueblo Indians is the name given to the tribes along the Rio Grande.

Private property rights to natural resources were less explicit in native and Spanish practices, even when they were codified in Spanish law (Meyer 1984). When what is now the southwest US was lost by Mexico to the US through the Treaty of Guadalupe Hidalgo (1848), the protection of land and water rights was paramount to most residents of the region, even if they were only vaguely aware of the details at the time of nation-state transfer. Vast tracts of land were given to communities between the 1770s and early 1840s by both the Spanish and later the Mexican administrative governments. However, through a process of political and judicial manipulation, the vast majority of communal land grants were transferred to private hands or are now part of the public domain in New Mexico (Dunbar-Ortiz 2007). The change in the legal sovereignty, from Mexico to the US, resulted in hidden legal violence disguised as a simple national boundary move (Blomley 2003).

The United States never recognized many of the pre-existing Spanish and Mexican land grants given to communities (Nostrand 1992; Ebright 1994; Montoya 2002; Correia 2013). For the Hispano and Pueblo people, the ties connecting land and water remain vital, even if modern US law makes little room for this cultural conception of water and land (Quintana 1990). These land-based cultures both view land and water as inseparable,[3] and in many villages the deep cultural wounds left by such acts of dispossession remain a part of everyday conversation.

Many New Mexicans remain deeply suspicious of water adjudications, although the process is couched in terms of confirming their rights to water use. What appears to be an *equalizing* judicial process (from the state's perspective) can impact the social dynamics of water use, ownership and access in the state (see Boelens 2009). From a legal perspective, adjudication is a way of formalizing what state experts view as the informal way that water has long been managed at the community level, even if water expertise was slow to form (Lane 2011). The US rarely considered 'communal' as a meaningful land or water tenure arrangement. Just as the US did not accept the legal basis for communal land grants in the nineteenth and twentieth centuries, so too the notion of community or collective water remains largely unrecognized in courts and American law.

The scale of the individual, of the body, has shaped water governance: US and state legal norms provide written documentation for individuals, not communities, as the water rights holders. The atomization of community into individual rights can be seen clearly in the adjudication process. State agents, judges and the court system parse and produce notions of water rights based on identity construction

---

3   While unfortunate in the sense that categorization of peoples in New Mexico leads to the language of ethnicity, 'Hispano' here means anyone of Latino, Mexicano, Chicano or Indo-Hispano descent. Although there are other groups of Indians in New Mexico, here I limit discussion to the Pueblo peoples because of the study area involved and the peculiarities of Pueblo water law as compared to those of other North American Indian groups. Anglo-American is a grossly inadequate term to refer to all people who are not indigenous and not of Hispano descent in the state, but is also used here for simplicity and convention.

and framed by water governance boundaries (see also Espeland 1998 and Jepson 2012). Thus, the recognition of individual or community water rights is dependent upon which government has jurisdiction. Since the federal government has purview over recognizing native identity, Indian water rights are recognized as a *collective* resource for the entire group, not as individual water rights. Therefore a Native group can, in fact, get *de facto* (but not *de jure*) communal recognition of water rights – rights that are prior and paramount to all other claims for water rights (Colby et al. 2005). For non-Indians, in contrast, the assumption and treatment by the New Mexico government is always predicated on *individual*, not collective, water rights. This produces legal dissonance experienced by both indigenous peoples and by Hispanos. Since Hispano communities are land-based social organizations, water now serves as one of the last expressions of communal identity in a globalizing world (McCarthy 2005).

The adjudication process continues in courts and along streams across the western US (see Figure 10.2). At the same time, actual access to ditch water in New Mexico and how water is allocated and shared are a community enterprise not tied to individual ownership, at least along acequias and Pueblo ditches. This is also the case across many Latin American countries that share roots in Spanish water law (Rivera 1998; Rodriguez 2006; Perreault 2008; Boelens et al. 2010).[4]

Land without water in these communities is considered not only useless, but also senseless. The concept in Spanish of *querencia* echoes what humanist geographers and anthropologists consider the 'sense of place' created by a desire to remain close to home, in a village, next to a canal that sustains crops and life. Residents cannot imagine their village, town or even suburban neighbourhood without the sound of rushing water in the canals during the irrigation season. To many New Mexicans, notions of individual rights atomize the commons or community that is fundamental to the integrity of local ditches.

Since 1848, the system of American water jurisprudence has incrementally evolved to impose this third system of water law based on individual water rights as property, on top of Native and Hispano legal conceptions of water. Politicians in New Mexico knew that a full accounting of natural resources would be necessary, as water resources were of vital concern. Yet the scales of community, state and federal recognitions bound to water governance complicated any neat transition to organize access to these rights.

---

4   The distinction between a 'water right' and a 'ditch right' to access water is a subtle one. For example, even if the state of New Mexico recognizes someone's individual water right, that same person may not be able to get ditch rights along an acequia unless they have paid dues to the acequia or community ditch association. Thus, the water access is scaled (also), first at the individual scale and then at a community one.

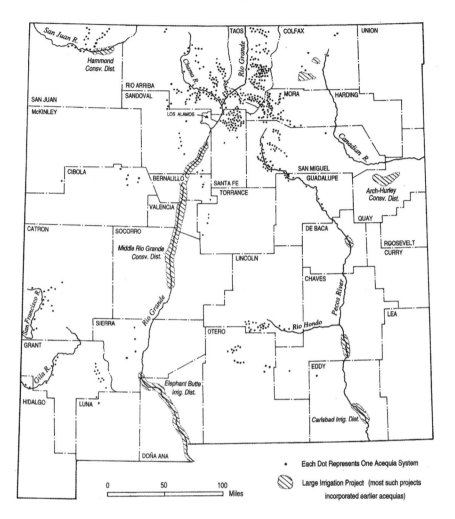

Figure 10.2   Locations of acequias throughout the state of New Mexico as of 2009

Source: Courtesy of Jerold Widdison and the Utton Center, University of New Mexico.

The Bodily Politics of Water Rights

To illustrate the bodily politics of water governance scale, I draw on an example from the earliest Spanish settlement in New Mexico. When the Spanish entered New Mexico in 1598 with colonists from Mexico, one of their first priorities was finding or building reliable water sources. Within three years at a settlement near the juncture of the Chama and Rio Grande rivers, a shared acequia had been built and put to use for agricultural purposes. An acequia is more than just a canal or ditch: the term acequia also refers to the institution which is governed by three elected commissioners and a mayordomo, water boss (see Crawford 1988). Commissioners serve basic governance needs for members of the ditch (*parciantes*), oversee the acequia's budget and work with the mayordomo to ensure that water rights and acequia maintenance proceed in an organized fashion. The mayordomo position pre-dates that of commissioner, and has traditionally been a powerful local figure charged with allocating water fairly and ensuring that the ditch remains functional and clean.

Where the Chama River joins the Rio Grande, the bodily politics of water governance and management are complicated. My treatment here is a partial perspective on relations between Hispano acequia institutions and Pueblo representatives.[5] Because of shared canals running between Ohkay Owingeh Pueblo and the village of Chamita, cooperation has been necessary for hundreds of years. Here, the biological is about cultural identity categories, compounded by the 'blood quantum' (percentage of Native descent) understandings of tribal membership, as constructed and reinforced by the US government over a century of indigenous policy (Kauanui 2008). Typically, the commissioners and the mayordomos in Chamita struggled, but found ways to communicate and resolve problems with the Pueblo's representatives. Below, I turn to the case of two brothers to illustrate the legal complexity of these bodily politics.

Juan Pacheco is a member of a Chamita acequia and has been active in its oversight and governance for decades. He considers himself Nuevomexicano, of joint Indian and Hispano descent, and actively participates in local affairs. However, his brother Miguel self-identifies as a member of Ohkay Owingeh Pueblo, and has also been prominent in local and regional Pueblo affairs. The two brothers – from the same father and mother, with completely different allegiances – are also partitioned into two different categorizations for water adjudications. Juan, a non-Indian (as the courts call all non-indigenous peoples), falls under state jurisdiction and the rather rigid terms of prior appropriation. Miguel, however, gets federal recognition as Indian. These categorizations ('Indian' and 'non-Indian') cleave their legal treatment into federal and state courts, and their bodies are also treated as biopolitically distinct.

These two brothers fall into different legal categories because of (blood) identity politics and preferred affinities. Juan and Miguel are aware they are caught within different state-scales of governance because of the state–federal divide. Many Pueblos, and certainly individual Pueblo members, do not recognize the state's laws in managing, much less designating, water uses on Indian lands.

---

    5   There is a long and rich history of how New Mexicans refer to themselves, especially for Nuevomexicanos, alternately labelling themselves as Spanish-Americans, Hispanos and now more recently Indo-Hispanos. This latest discursive move is intriguing for several reasons, but seems to still fit into Wilmsen's (2007) conceptualization of how Latino residents of the state have occasionally been caught between the category of Indian on one hand and the Anglo-American population on the other.

Thus, Juan and Miguel exist at the same level of scaled space but are entrapped in different boundaries of water governance and identity. At the same time, blood, like water, is also shared across the Indo-Hispano communities even if identity is not (see Brooks 2002; Wilmsen 2007).

Ditch Governance Dynamics under Adjudication

For state officials in New Mexico, trying to map and certify water rights was and largely remains a completely rational act. As one technician from the OSE working on water rights put it: 'How can you manage and regulate a limited resource when you do not understand who has rights to that water?'[6] There are 11 active adjudications, with another two now in settlement, backed by substantial federal resources. Settlements are a process, and negotiations are ongoing regarding the finer points of satisfying the Pueblo water rights by building further water infrastructure. Both settlements and adjudications are done on a regional watershed basis. In response, many non-Pueblo (Hispano and Anglo-Americans) water rights holders have organized themselves into regional acequia associations and coalitions to provide legal and financial resources for individual claimants. Simply put, the small ditches were forced to 'scale up' their form of institution to a regional level in response to adjudication.

The vast majority of acequias are in northern New Mexico (see Figure 10.2). Rural depopulation does threaten the human and social capital base that sustains acequias and contributes to a decline in agriculture that impacts water use (Ortiz et al. 2007). Participation rates in acequia governance, even with stable rural demography, vary dramatically by area. Small acequias might have only four to five members, but the state statute requires three commissioners and a separate mayordomo for each one (NMSA 2008). This can mean a lifetime commitment to local water governance.

On larger ditches, the sheer number of demands can make the formal positions of commissioner and mayordomo less attractive because of more complex ditch politics. Thus, the challenges of water governance at the ditch scale have intensified in modern New Mexico. Namely, acequias have had to formalize their political process and activism; they are now required to maintain open records, record all minutes, release meeting agendas and advertise meetings well in advance. This forced (local) transparency by state statute challenges smaller ditch organizations (Crawford 2003). On budgetary matters, the OSE has attempted to facilitate a centralized process for financial support, but even this assumes spreadsheet skills. As ditch communities struggle with the OSE, they must also pay attention to neighbouring ditches.

Senior water rights are the most valuable, since these rights holders can demand their full allocation of water based on their individual priority date,

6   A. Thompson, interview with the author, 12 October 2010, Santa Fe, NM.

regardless of stream conditions or the effects on junior water rights holders. This can create discord between villages or families if there is disagreement about dates. Most acequia communities, therefore, have pushed for ditch-wide priority dates (internally) and tried to create written agreements between ditches to retain their usual customary agreements.

The demands of water adjudications have intensified for acequia users. As one *parciante* from the Jemez River basin put it, referring to this blurring of scales and demands for governance: 'It's like we're caught in a telescope, and we're either pulled back to our acequia or the regional organization wants something bigger, something totally different, and our time gets sucked out of the village again.'[7] Thus, even the basin approach has not solved all problems (Molle 2009). However, the upside to this rescaling of ditch politics is that acequias communicate more, sharing information with other *parciantes* and mayordomos.

Elite Watershed-Scale Politics?

New Mexico has made regional water governance more democratic and transparent with the creation of watershed groups: regional assemblies put together a 'regional water plan' that brings interested stakeholders to comment, draft and amend water plans for their particular area of interest. They are laudable efforts for transparent water planning. Like all notions of participatory democracy, however, they are also subject to the potential of elite capture or at least co-option (see Larson and Lach 2010).

The New Mexico Interstate Stream Commission (ISC), a branch within the OSE, is charged with describing criteria for these regional plans and for their acceptance (both technical and public scrutiny). The ISC provides a template for suggested content and aspects to be considered by all regional water planning participants. However, the regional plan boundaries do not correspond with the watersheds being used by the state for other purposes; this creates jurisdictional fragmentation, obscured governance and overlapping political authorities.

The regional plans allow for public participation, even for persons not directly managing water. Attorneys, activist groups, new residents, policy enthusiasts and interested members of the public all attend. One such citizen group organizes an annual New Mexico Water Dialogue to discuss broader sets of watershed region concerns. Few Native individuals or Hispano members of acequias attend these events, which tend to be heady but populist discussions about climate change, urbanization and moving water to the 'highest use for the resource'. This is organized every year to discuss broader sets of regional watershed concerns, but while it is open to the public, only those who can afford the entry fee get to hear and be heard. This reinforces both the perception of limited participation by

---

7   F.J. Trujillo, interview with the author, 6 February 2010, San Ysidro, NM.

certain water rights holders and the notion that only those who can afford to 'pay to play' will have a voice in watershed planning.

Conclusions, with No End

At the local scale, water managers of all types are concerned about the implications of adjudication for their own purposes, but rural users are also rightfully worried that any 'senior water right' is at risk in a state where urbanized watersheds are still unaccounted for in adjudication. In other words, if the 'space of engagement' for legal scalar claims to water comes too late will rural users have recourse to any kind of politics? Individual water users in New Mexico have been increasingly disciplined by the state and tied to its adjudicatory spatial understanding of the legal process.

State agencies and individuals working in adjudications increasingly recognize the problematic scalar politics of embodied water rights. In many of the adjudications, state attorneys for New Mexico attempted to accommodate local-level negotiations by being more flexible about how water is managed. Although lawyers and state engineer personnel argue that parcel-specific priority management of water 'would be impossible', they realize that declaring individuated dates for every watershed, to manage prior appropriation, is biopolitically charged. In contrast, some federal attorneys representing tribes in New Mexico argue that parcel-level dates are a necessity because of state statute for prior appropriation.

At the regional scale, acequia defenders are worried that the spatial mismatch of jurisdictional boundaries with natural boundaries will create incommensurate water disputes between (or within) watersheds. Ditches cross county boundaries and 'regional water plan' area boundaries. The incompatibility of county, city, regional water planning boundaries and OSE service office boundaries complicates any sense of the unit for water governance. Finally, the macro-scale state drive to organize water users by watersheds creates unintended consequences. The legal basis for administering water law – prior appropriation – seems socially and ecologically inflexible and unadaptive. Distinguishing between 'state' and federal politics is important. These legal scalar politics are actively mobilized for the differential identity bound to water governance.

Of course, the adjudication process is not the only factor or concern that shapes water governance in New Mexico. First, individuals can sell their water right after it has been registered with the state of New Mexico, before adjudication is complete (Shiveley 2001; Pease 2010). Quite apart from concerns over legal treatment or due process in adjudications, water transfers concern locals more than any other facet when it comes to water rights because the loss of even minor flows impacts rural irrigators. Second, New Mexico has increasingly begun to make provision for 'environmental flows' as mandated by federal laws for species protection. In other words, human bodies and their politics are not the only party to account for in governance. Third, the State Engineer of New Mexico can appoint water masters, thereby inserting a new level of middle management into water governance and affecting the scale of governance and local access to water. Scale is thus mobile in water politics, and remains dynamic – much like the water itself. These are concerns that have to be considered by adjudicators as they seek to map, quantify and certify water rights for these newly scaled users. In summary, they need to understand that documenting water rights is not (viewed as) an innocent project. Adjudication has side effects.

Usual appeals by engineers and politicians for a rational approach, such as integrated water resources management (IWRM), are also not without problems (Blomquist and Schlager 2005). This has certainly been the case for New Mexico in its own version of IWRM, the active water resource management effort described above, and there has been strong local reaction regarding this new initiative. Attempting to extend rights to nature in a form of ecological governance is also not without problems. When residents feel short-changed about their *own* loss of access to land, forest or water they are unlikely to feel sympathetic to owls, fish or nature in general (Kosek 2006). Political and legal challenges remain for a rights-based approach towards non-human nature (Glennon 2006; Groenfeldt 2010).

The law, markets and the state all hope to treat all water rights holders equally, even if their end-games are putatively different (Boelens 2009). The states (federal and the state of New Mexico) have also encoded identity in the same locality in different (but related) bodies, as described above in the example of Juan and Miguel. In those cases, then, scale confounds and results in quite different 'rights' to water, whether communal (federal) or individual (state). Still, states and citizens continue to use and conceive of scale in different ways.

Adjudication can be viewed as a state's efforts to 'see' individual owners, to identify targets for free-market buyers and markets in general (Scott 1998; Perramond 2013). As I have briefly detailed above, that sight and recognition by the state is partial: scaled to the governance of identity (Indian/non-Indian) and to notions of resource governance as regards water (federal/state). In urban areas it may make clearer sense to price water (and water use) rates in an aggressive, progressive fashion. This has been the recent working model for municipal versions of water utilities, whether public or privately owned (Bakker 2010). Markets do have the ability to change individual behaviours (Matthews 2003; Bauer 2004). In rural areas, however, the capital heft that cities carry in offering lease rates to farmers, or when farmers retire and decide to sell their water rights, is worrisome to agricultural producers.

Water governance, legal politics, the bodily politics of identity and local–regional democratic water planning decisions intertwine in water adjudication in New Mexico. Scale as a lens for water governance offers a middle ground between the more fixed dimensions of land tenure regimes and the anarchic, larger resource commons like climate and oceans that are even more mobile than water. If actors and policy-makers can get water governance right – balancing the ecological, human and infrastructure needs of water users – perhaps there is reason for some optimism for pernicious open-commons problems like atmospheric use tied to climate change justice concerns. But the record of balancing competing water needs is mixed at best (Worster 1985; White 1990), and there are no simple, universal prescriptions for carrying out good water policy and governance (Ingram 2012). Like its older conceptual sibling, the region, scale is a geographic construct meant to aid in communication and visualization. Furthermore, it is clear that understandings of water – like markets, as Polanyi (1944) argued long ago, or scale, as I have argued here – remain embedded in particular societies. This explains why water rights, politics and scale still have resonance in many western US states (Agnew 2011). It also underscores why a dynamic understanding of how scale works in water remains important.

References

Agnew, J. 2011. Waterpower: politics and the geography of water provision. *Annals of the Association of American Geographers* 101(3), 463–76.

Agrawal, A. 2005. *Environmentality: Technologies of Government and the Making of Subjects*. Durham, NC: Duke University Press.

Bakker, K. 2010. *Privatizing Water: Governance Failure and the World's Urban Water Crisis*. Ithaca: Cornell University Press.

Bauer, C. 2004. *Siren Song: Chilean Water Law as a Model for International Reform*. Washington, DC: Resources for the Future.

Blomley, N. 2003. Law, property, and the geography of violence: the frontier, the survey, and the grid. *Annals of the Association of American Geographers* 93(1), 121–41.

Blomquist, W. and Schlager, E. 2005. Political pitfalls of integrated watershed management. *Society and Natural Resources* 18(2), 101–17.

Boelens, R. 2009. The politics of disciplining water rights. *Development and Change* 40(2), 307–31.

Boelens, R., Getches, D., and Guevara-Gil, A. (eds). 2010. *Out of the Mainstream: Water Rights, Politics and Identity*. London: Earthscan.

Brooks, J.F. 2002. *Captives and Cousins: Slavery, Kinship, and Community in the Southwest Borderlands*. Chapel Hill: University of North Carolina Press.

Clark, I. 1987. *Water in New Mexico: A History of Its Management and Use*. Albuquerque: University of New Mexico.

Cohen, A. and Davidson, S. 2011. The watershed approach: challenges, antecedents, and the transition from technical tool to governance unit. *Water Alternatives* 4(1), 1–14.

Colby, B.G., Thorson, J.E., and Britton, S. (eds) 2005. *Negotiating Tribal Water Rights: Fulfilling Promises in the Arid West*. Tucson: University of Arizona Press.

Conca, K. 2006. *Governing Water: Contentious Transnational Politics and Global Institution Building*. Cambridge: MIT Press.

Correia, D. 2013. *Properties of Violence: Law and Land Grant Struggle in Northern New Mexico*. Athens: University of Georgia Press.

Cox, K. 1998. Scales of dependence, spaces of engagement and the politics of scale, or: looking for local politics. *Political Geography* 17, 1–23.

Crawford, S. 1988. *Mayordomo: Chronicle of an Acequia in Northern New Mexico*. Albuquerque: University of New Mexico Press.

Crawford, S. 1990. Dancing for water. *Journal of the Southwest* 32(3), 265–7.

Crawford, S. 2003. *The River in Winter: New and Selected Essays*. Albuquerque: University of New Mexico Press.

deBuys, W. 2011. *A Great Aridness: Climate Change and the Future of the American Southwest*. Oxford: Oxford University Press.

Dumars, C., O'Leary, M., and Utton, A.E. 1984. *Pueblo Indian Water Rights: Struggle for a Precious Resource*. Tucson: University of Arizona Press.

Dunbar-Ortiz, R. 2007. *Roots of Resistance: A History of Land Tenure in New Mexico*. Norman: University of Oklahoma Press.

Ebright, M. 1994. *Land Grants and Lawsuits in Northern New Mexico*. Albuquerque: University of New Mexico Press.

Espeland, W.N. 1998. *The Struggle for Water: Politics, Rationality, and Identity in the American Southwest*. Chicago: University of Chicago Press.

Glennon, R. 2006. General stream adjudications and the environment. *Journal of Contemporary Water Research and Education* 133(1), 26–8.

Groenfeldt, D. 2010. The next nexus: environmental ethics, water management and climate change. *Water Alternatives* 3(3), 575–86.

Ingram, H. 1990. *Water Politics: Continuity and Change*. Albuquerque: University of New Mexico Press.

Ingram, H. 2012. No universal remedies: design for contexts. *Water International* 38(1), 1–6.

Jepson, W. 2012. Claiming space, claiming water: contested legal geographies of water in south Texas. *Annals of the Association of American Geographers* 102(3), 614–31.

Kauanui, J.K. 2008. *Hawaiian Blood: Colonialism and the Politics of Sovereignty and Indigeneity*. Durham, NC: Duke University Press.

Kosek, J. 2006. *Understories: The Political Life of Forests in Northern New Mexico*. Durham, NC: Duke University Press.

Lane, M. 2011. Water, technology, and the courtroom: negotiating reclamation policy in territorial New Mexico. *Journal of Historical Geography* 37, 300–311.

Larson, K.L. and Lach, D. 2010. Equity in urban water governance through participatory, place-based approaches. *Natural Resources Journal* 50, 407–30.

Levine, F. 1990. Dividing the water: the impact of water rights adjudication on New Mexican communities. *Journal of the Southwest* 32(3), 268–77.

MacKinnon, D. 2011. Reconstructing scale: towards a new scalar politics. *Progress in Human Geography* 35(1), 21–36.

Matthews, P.O. 2003. Simplifying western water rights to facilitate water marketing. *Water Resources Update* 126(1), 40–44.

McCarthy, J. 2005. Commons as counterhegemonic projects. *Capitalism Nature Socialism* 16(1), 9–24.

Meyer, M. 1984. *Water in the Hispanic Southwest*. Tucson: University of Arizona Press.

Molle, F. 2009. River-basin planning and management: the social life of a concept. *Geoforum* 40(3), 484–94.

Montoya, M. 2002. *Translating Property: The Maxwell Land Grant and the Conflict over Land in the American West, 1840–1900*. Berkeley: University of California Press.

Moore, A. 2008. Rethinking scale as a geographical category: from analysis to practice. *Progress in Human Geography* 32, 203–25.

Nieto-Phillips, J.M. 2008. *The Language of Blood: The Making of Spanish-American Identity in New Mexico, 1850–1940*. Albuquerque: University of New Mexico Press.

NMSA (New Mexico Statutes Annotated). 2008. *Michie's Annotated Statutes of New Mexico: Chapter 72 and Chapter 73*. Issued by the New Mexico Acequia Association. Charlottesville, VA: LexisNexis.

Norman, E. and Bakker, K. 2009. Transgressing scales: transboundary water governance across the Canada–U.S. borderland. *Annals of the Association of American Geographers*. 99(1), 99–117.

Norman, E., Bakker, K., and Cook, C. 2012. Introduction to the themed section: water governance and the politics of scale. *Water Alternatives* 5(1), 52–61.

Nostrand, R.L. 1992. *The Hispano Homeland*. Norman: University of Oklahoma Press.

Office of the State Engineer, New Mexico. n.d. The status of adjudication, figure. http://www.ose.state.nm.us/water_info_maps.html (accessed 8 September 2008).

Ortiz, M., Brown, C., Fernald, A., Baker, T.T., Creel, B., and Guldan, S. 2007. Land use change impacts on acequia water resources in northern New Mexico. *Journal of Contemporary Water Research and Education* 137(1), 47–54.

Pease, M. 2010. Constraints to water transfers in unadjudicated basins: the middle Rio Grande as a case study. *Journal of Contemporary Water Research and Education* 144(1), 37–43.

Perramond, E. 2013. Water governance in New Mexico: adjudication, law, and geography. *Geoforum* 45(2), 83–93.

Perreault, T. 2005. State restructuring and the scale politics of rural water governance in Bolivia. *Environment and Planning A* 37(2), 263–84.

Perreault, T. 2008. Custom and contradiction: rural water governance and the politics of 'usos y costumbres' in Bolivia's irrigators' movement. *Annals of the Association of American Geographers* 98(4), 835–54.

Polanyi, K. 1944. *The Great Transformation: The Political and Economic Origins of Our Time*. Boston, MA: Beacon.

Quintana, F.L. 1990. Land, water, and Pueblo-Hispanic relations in northern New Mexico. *Journal of the Southwest* 32(3), 288–99.

Rivera, J. 1998. *Acequia Culture*. Albuquerque: University of New Mexico Press.

Rodriguez, S. 1990. Applied research on land and water in New Mexico: a critique. *Journal of the Southwest* 32(3), 300–315.

Rodriguez, S. 2006. *Acequia: Water-Sharing, Sanctity and Place*. Santa Fe: School for Advanced Research.

Scott, J. 1998. *Seeing Like a State: How Certain Schemes to Improve the Human Condition Have Failed*. New Haven: Yale University Press.

Shiveley, D. 2001. Water right reallocation in New Mexico's Rio Grande basin, 1975–1995. *Water Resources Development* 17(3), 445–60.

Swyngedouw, E. 1999. Modernity and hybridity: nature, regeneracionismo, and the production of the Spanish waterscape, 1890–1930. *Annals of the Association of American Geographers* 89(3), 443–65.

Utton Center. 2009. *Water Matters*. Albuquerque: Utton Law Center.

Water Resources Research Institute (WRRI). n.d. New Mexico water planning regions figure. http://river.nmsu.edu/isc (accessed 7 July 2011).

Wescoat, Jr., J.L. 1995. The 'right of thirst' for animals in Islamic law: a comparative approach. *Environment and Planning D* 13(6), 637–54.

White, R. 1990. *The Organic Machine: The Remaking of the Columbia River*. New York: Hill and Wang.

Whiteley, J., Ingram, H., and Perry, R. (eds). 2008. *Water, Place, and Equity*. Cambridge: MIT Press.

Wilder, M., Scott C., Pablos N.P., Varady, R., Garfin, G., and McEvoy, J. 2010. Adapting across boundaries: climate change, social learning, and resilience in the US–Mexico border region. *Annals of the Association of American Geographers* 100(4), 917–28.

Wilmsen, C. 2007. Maintaining the environmental-racial order in northern New Mexico. *Environment and Planning D* 25(2), 236–57.

Worster, D. 1985. *Rivers of Empire: Water, Aridity, and the Growth of the American West*. New York: Pantheon.

Worster, D. 2003. Watershed democracy: recovering the lost vision of John Wesley Powell. *Journal of Land, Resources, and Environmental Law* 23, 57–66.

Chapter 11

Politics, Scale and the EU Water Framework Directive

Corey Johnson

Introduction

This chapter examines the European Union Water Framework Directive (EUWFD) as a hybrid form of territoriality (Sidaway 2006) and a largely unnoticed politics of scale that is changing the political geography of the European Union (Moss and Newig 2010). It argues that intellectual debates about the rescaling of governance in the EU have appropriately focused on monetary policy, social issues, migration and citizenship, but have neglected what may amount to the most far-reaching redrawing of political-administrative boundaries according to environmental criteria: transboundary river basin districts created under the EUWFD. The management of water resources in the EU provides an example of scalar politics that at least suggests a nascent form of 'post-sovereign environmental governance' (Karkkainen 2004).

To support my argument that analyses of environmental policy in the EU tend to privilege the nation-state as an ontological starting point, I first consider literature on territoriality of the state and the changing regulation of nature. In the second part I explore the EUWFD as an environmental governance regime. I then consider the relationship between the de- and re-territorialization of environmental governance on the one hand, and the changing character of sovereignty in the EU on the other. This case illustrates that a richer understanding of the scalar politics of the EU requires moving beyond nested 'multi-level governance' hierarchies to include territorially overlapping and transboundary political geographies.

This argument has implications for how we understand questions of sovereignty, territoriality and scale in the EU context. Murphy's (2008) call for a more geographical – as opposed to international relations (IR) – understanding of multilevel governance is applicable to the case of the EUWFD, which weds a shared governance regime to the materiality of transboundary nature. Given its recent existential crisis, it is worth examining the EU as a heterogeneous, multi-faceted, multi-level political-territorial construct and not just as a sum of intergovernmental arrangements. Any analysis that considers Europe institutionally and intergovernmentally, but fails to take into account how these arrangements manifest themselves geographically across European space, is bound to be a partial rendering (Johnson 2008).

Although the EUWFD represents a step toward a type of post-sovereign environmental governance, it has not negated the importance of the individual member states of the EU to water policy. Member states ultimately are responsible for implementing the EUWFD, and the instruments the European Commission has to punish member states' noncompliance are relatively weak. Moreover, the provisions of the EUWFD are not uniquely European, but rather they reflect the rescaling of state authority through the institutions of the EU. Moreover, the imprint of powerful member states such as Germany, France and the Netherlands is evident in EU water policy. Also, even within the EU traditional, state-centred international relations can stymie transboundary cooperation. For example, flood management along the Elbe in Saxony, Germany, and in the Czech Republic continues to be a source of conflict as these two EU member states debate appropriate ways to manage the river for economic benefit. Indeed, economic arguments often assume the traditional state-to-state roles. As climate change debates illustrate, states remain critical of environmental governance. Here I argue not that the state is no longer important, but rather that the reflexive nod to the state as the appropriate and natural place where decisions are made is being challenged and that lessons from the EUWFD may be instructive elsewhere. Transboundary water regimes such as the EUWFD need to be critically examined as attempts at social or political engineering (e.g. Sneddon and Fox 2012).

Why Water? On Natural Borders as Regulatory Spatial Scales

Political geography includes a rich history of examining human relations with the environment (Elden 2009). Increasingly, political geography and geopolitics are informed by examinations of ecology and politics (Neumann 2010); the 'environmental dimensions of geopolitics' and the nexus of security and environment (Dalby 2009, 2010); nature as a means of addressing ethno-territorial conflict (Cohen and Frank 2009); and nature's role in questioning the ontological status of nation-states (Harris and Alatout 2010). Geographers have been exhorted to use studies of water to bridge the gap between political ecology and political geography 'because of the way in which it challenges human political boundaries' (Robbins 2003: 642)

Recent work by Fall offers a critique of natural political borders, which are 'based on the assumption that political scenarios are inscribed in the material physicality of the world by God, Providence, Fate, or Nature'. Further she argues that it is 'profoundly questionable to claim there is such a thing as an uncontroversial materiality to nature to begin with' (Fall 2010: 6).

The EUWFD is based on the premise that the natural boundaries of watersheds or river basins *are* in fact there waiting to be discovered.[1] This does not mean

---

1   In the EU context and in British English 'watershed' refers to the topographical line separating drainage basins, where water on either side of the line flows in opposite

that all of nature is somehow materially manifest, waiting to be identified so that we can move on to the important stuff of governance. Clearly, the choice of natural boundaries is inherently political (Blomquist and Schlager 2005; Cohen and Davidson 2011). The delimitation of river basin boundaries in the EUWFD might suggest that certain elements of the natural world lend themselves better to the inscription of politics on territory than others. Equally, it is likely the case that delimitating European space into river basins by means of identifying watersheds was the least controversial of the negotiations comprising water policy, in part because such a geographical scale was assumed to be 'best practice' and in part because a clear-cut methodology for identifying such spaces existed.

While Fall (2010: 146) would ask us to '(re)think boundaries through the triad of reification, naturalisation, and fetishisation', there are limitations to this as an ontological position or an operational guide. If, for example, environmental managers were instructed to assume that nature is borderless – i.e. humans are not in a position to 'discover' natural boundaries – seemingly nothing else would remain except the existing map of sovereign states as the de facto political geography of environmental management. The EUWFD example suggests that the picture needs to be complicated; critiquing the notion of *les limites naturelles* should not blind us to environmental management practices that have shaped progressive new political geographies out of the environment in Europe and elsewhere (ibid.; see also Pounds 1951, 1954).

Of course, Europe is not the only place where transboundary river basin management is occurring. Recent work has examined the role of transboundary river basins in Southeast Asia, particularly the Mekong (Bakker 1999; Sneddon and Fox 2012). In the context of North America, Norman and Bakker (2009) examine regimes of river basin scale governance along the Canada–US border to show that smaller scale governance does not necessarily equate to empowerment for local actors. The novel character of the EU (i.e. a suprastate with extensive policy competencies) makes the reorganization of governance along watersheds more immediately possible than in some other political contexts because of the presence of established institutions and norms for rule-making that are absent in traditional international relations. Indeed, the EUWFD underscores that the EU cannot simply be viewed as a collection of independently acting nation-states. While there are examples of transboundary water governance in sub-Saharan Africa – such as the Senegal River Charter and the Lake Victoria Basin Commission (LVBC) – elsewhere on the continent where resource scarcity and live armed conflicts vastly complicate environmental cooperation, cross-border cooperation along these lines would appear unlikely in the near term (e.g. Gleditsch et al. 2006). While natural borders are not a panacea, the EUWFD offers possibilities for political action that escape the 'territorial trap' of European political borders (Agnew 1994; cf. Furlong 2006).

---

directions, and not to the area draining to a common body of water as it is used in North America. The word 'shed' connotes high ground or a ridge of land separating two areas, and not the areas themselves.

Territoriality, the EU and the Persistence of Nation-States

The concept of state sovereignty, or the notion that the ultimate authority for internal order and external relations rests in the hands of the state, too often is treated as the beginning and endpoint for all serious consideration of political – and indeed economic, social and environmental – affairs. A vast literature in international relations and political geography has considered the effects of European integration on the distribution of governance among different levels of state actors (Hooghe and Marks 2003; Gualini 2004; Schott 2007; Menon 2009; Bulkeley 2012). During the 1990s a series of foundational works began to break down the ingrained territorial assumptions that shaped social science inquiry, and indeed broader understandings of the nature of political space. Our Western 'spatial imaginations', argued Murphy, had been co-opted by the territorial state, which had become (and arguably still is) 'the privileged unit for analyzing most phenomena', while at the same time such a privileging seemed to prevent any serious 'consideration of the nature of the territorial state itself' (Murphy 1996: 103). Thus, our understanding of nearly any issue in which the state played a role was seriously impoverished (see also Agnew 1994; Taylor 1994).

Scholarly treatment of the EU has shown the bias of this 'territorial trap' (Agnew 1994): the a priori assumption is that sovereign states are handing certain aspects of sovereignty to another political entity that itself is still entirely subject to the whims of its sovereign state masters. This problematic assumption has been extensively revisited during the past two decades in a growing body of literature on multilevel governance (Hooghe and Marks 2003; Murphy 2008). Nevertheless, as is perhaps best illustrated by recent debates over the rescaling of state power under conditions of neoliberalization, the case for the continuing primacy of the sovereign state as a mode of analysis and locus of power is still powerful – even if its power is articulated in different forms than in the past (see, e.g., Heynen 2007).

The EU is different in many respects from traditional sovereign states but, somewhat paradoxically, state container-space thinking continues to play a dominant role in many readings of European integration. However, while the 'nature of political space' has received thorough treatment in the EU context, the 'political space of nature' is still not well understood. When one considers the many scales and shapes of environmental space (macro- and microclimates, oceans, biosphere etc.), the need to address the environment as political space becomes obvious, and the applications extend well beyond river basins in Europe.

Environmental Governance in the EU

At their zenith, European nation-states were arguably most effective in shaping social affinities and containing economic activity. In light of this, it comes as little surprise that the dismantling of some elements of state-centrism through the project of European integration would focus primarily on two projects: the encouragement of transboundary social relations and new scales of economic development beyond the state. Environmental degradation was not a central concern of the European Commission at its inception in 1957, a reflection no doubt of broader societal trends in Europe and elsewhere (Jordan 2005). Beginning in the 1970s, however, environmental issues became more important to the process of European integration (McGlade 2002) as awareness of the fundamental tension between the dominant regulatory-political spatial scale at which environmental rules are made (i.e. the state) on the one hand and the non-conformance of nearly all natural/environmental phenomena to state borders on the other became institutionalized (Shafer and Murphy 1998).

The past decades have witnessed a remarkable Europeanization of environmental policies within the EU (Thiel 2009; Bukowski 2011). Sustainable development and environmental protection are enshrined in the 1997 Treaty of Amsterdam (a major treaty clarifying the roles of the European Commission), along with economic growth and social cohesion, as the bases of the financial instruments of the EU (Moss and Fichter 2003). Disbursement of structural funds through the EU's regional policy is contingent upon the applicants showing they are meeting the objectives of creating jobs, stimulating development and combating social exclusion, all while respecting the environment (Moss and Fichter 2003). Meanwhile the text of the Lisbon Treaty (2007) indicates in general terms the current codification of environmental protection (such as the 'precautionary principle') in the EU (EU 2010).

In the last four decades, the EU has adopted more than 200 environmental directives and regulations (Beunen et al. 2009). These include directives on bathing water, drinking water, urban wastewater, nitrates and sewage sludge (EC 2008). Directives require that member state parliaments enact national laws compliant with general guidelines and within a specified timeline (McGlade 2002).[2] The Habitats Directive, which establishes protected sites and lists of protected species, is perhaps the best-known example (Diaz 2001). Natura 2000, an important component of the Habitats Directive, seeks to protect regional biodiversity by establishing a network of protected habitat sites (EC 2014). Member states have implemented networks of environmental monitoring systems that aim to harmonize fragmented approaches to measuring environmental indicators. Examples include the Eurowaternet (similar to the US Geological Survey's flow monitoring stations) and comprehensive remote sensing of landcover changes, forest types etc. across Europe (Vogt et al. 2004).

The EUWFD was preceded by several ad hoc transboundary water initiatives in Europe. For example, Germany, France and Switzerland undertook projects in the highly developed Upper Rhine region to clean up the river and coordinate hydroelectric projects. At Lake Constance, Germany, Switzerland and Austria

---

2   The example of directives, which must be implemented by national parliaments, helps illustrate to what degree European states are still active players in this, and that their power is rearticulated, or reterritorialized.

developed a cross-border water conservation programme, and the Umweltrat Bodensee (Environmental Council of Lake Constance) wields substantial power in the trilateral administration of the lake (Blatter 2004). In fact, prior to 2000 most international river basins in Europe had some sort of bilateral or multilateral treaty in place, but these varied widely in their effectiveness and depth. More recently, and under the auspices of the United Nations Economic Commission for Europe (UNECE), the 1992 Convention on the Protection and Use of Transboundary Watercourses and International Lakes (also known as the Water Convention) has made headway in shaping the discussion in Europe and beyond on a variety of transboundary water issues, including the impacts of climate change on shared resources (UNECE 2012).

EUWFD as a form of De- and Re-Territorialization

During the 1990s the European Union embarked upon a project to create uniform standards for water quality among member states. This resulted in the EU Water Framework Directive of 2000, which requires that all member states 'protect, enhance and restore' rivers to attain good surface water status by 2015 (Mance et al. 2002). The first task was for all member states to identify all surface water bodies that intersected with their jurisdictions: more than 70,000 surface water bodies were inventoried, and of those some 80 per cent are rivers, 15 per cent are lakes and 5 per cent are coastal or transitional water bodies (EC 2008). Through the same process, states were required to assess qualitatively the status of their water bodies – high, good, moderate, poor or bad – and categorize them as being 'at risk' of not achieving a 'good status' by 2015 (ibid.). Water quality was assessed using three types of monitoring: *surveillance* (tracking changes over time to the health of water bodies); *operational* (for unhealthy water bodies, assessing progress in remediation efforts); and *investigative* (collecting other types of data not available through regular surveillance) (EC 2008). The goal of these monitoring procedures was to gauge human impacts on the hydromorphology of European river systems. Once rivers were identified and assessed, river basin management plans (RBMPs) were required for each major river basin district (England, for example, has eight river basins according to EUWFD methodology), which were to include various assessments of the current status of the water, targets for improving the environmental conditions and operational plans (EC 2008).

The passage of the EUWFD marked a major step for European water policy, notable for its new approach to environmental protection that established the environment as a consumer of water alongside human economic uses (White and Howe 2003). The EUWFD called on member states to incorporate an economic analysis of water resources into their policy, and on consumers to pay the full costs of the water they use, while at the same time recognizing that water is not a commercial commodity in the same sense of other resources (EC 2008; Boscheck 2006). The World Wildlife Fund (WWF) announced that the EUWFD, if enacted as proposed, had the potential to be the EU's first 'sustainable development' directive (cited in Carter 2007).

Most interesting for geographers was the EUWFD's approach to rivers as complex systems that require multiscalar approaches (cf. Whitehead et al. 2007). Whereas previously rivers in most European contexts were treated as stable channel forms, based on engineering and hydrological principles, the EUWFD integrates geomorphology and is, at least in principle, more sensitive to 'the inherent dynamism of fluvial systems' (Clarke et al. 2003). This shift means that small-scale local contexts of sediment transport and deposition, which can create 'chaotic, unpredictable dynamics', are considered alongside the larger-scale systems view of a river basin (Newson 2002; see also Church 1996). The goal of integrating scale-sensitive geomorphological principles into the EUWFD was to avoid unintended consequences and environmental damage brought about by engineered responses to floods and droughts that fail to consider ecosystem and fluvial processes (Mance et al. 2002).

Yet the reviews since implementation of the EUWFD have not been uniformly positive. Boscheck (2006: 268) argues that the EUWFD, for all its promise, is 'built on vague objectives and unclear monitoring criteria, it is a compromise that risks diluting pre-existing regulatory norms, invokes national discretion to close EU legislative gaps, and for all practical purposes may be unenforceable'. Despite its lofty goal of replacing piecemeal water regulations with one act that commits member states to implementing in a timely manner uniform policies at the scale of the river basin, the EUWFD's effectiveness suffers under appeals to voluntarism and various opt-out clauses that make some aspects of water-quality assurance even weaker in some instances than what preceded it (Boscheck 2006). Brian Moss (2008) noted its 'ground-breaking' potential as a 'red hot and revolutionary' new approach to water management through informed science, but concluded that the EUWFD amounted to only a 'small revolution' because it lacked precise definitions of what constitutes the status categories and the difficulties of enforcement (see also Rettman 2007). Moreover, as previously mentioned, states still retain considerable power in the monitoring and implementation of the directive, as they do in all EU legislation.

The micropolitics of implementation poses additional challenges to the rescaling of water governance along river basin lines. On the Iberian Peninsula, for example, conflicts over transboundary river basins arise due to the overlapping scales of water governance giving rise to what Del Moral and Do Ó (2014) describe as 'not a pyramid but rather a constellation' of governance scales. Another issue is that of spatial fit. In Germany, where the subnational *Länder* have the primary responsibility for water resources management, numerous examples exist of ineffective or non-functioning collaboration and implementation between the different agencies that have jurisdiction over water-related issues (Moss 2012). In Sweden it is the municipalities that have substantial competencies for water and land use planning, and there is some evidence of emerging conflicts between local governments and supra-regional structures over implementation of the EUWFD (Andersson et al. 2012).

   The lacklustre response to the progress made in implementing the EUWFD is certainly warranted. The slow progress is partly a reflection of the directive's 'revolutionary' ambition in how waters in Europe should be managed in light of the realities of such things as resource limitations, EU and national parliamentary compromises and weak enforcement mechanisms. None of these, incidentally, is unique to environmental policies in the EU, but rather extend to all policy areas where the EU attempts to effect change. Moreover, some of the shortcomings can be addressed through aggressive use of the EU courts, which have more

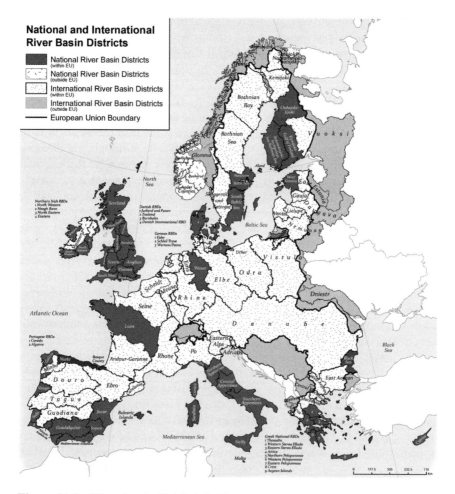

Figure 11.1   River basin districts in Europe

Source: EC (2008). Water Note 1: *Joining Forces for Europe's Shared Waters: Coordination in International River Basin Districts.*

enforcement powers than the Commission and its Environment Directorate. Despite its shortcomings, the attempt to 'introduce an integrated approach to water resource management at the river basin level' (Medd and Marvin 2008) is a significant step in water management and offers lessons to policymakers elsewhere on the melding of science and policy, and the often conflicting policy goals of ecological protection and economic progress.

To followers of the European integration process, moreover, the EUWFD marks an achievement that should be considered alongside other barrier-breaking events in recent decades – such as the introduction of a common currency and the dissolution of internal border controls. The EUWFD mandates that member states divide themselves into watershed basins, even if those districts cross international boundaries (see Figure 11.1). In fact, of the 4.4 million square kilometres of river basin area located within the European Union as of 2010, about 67 per cent of land area lies in transboundary river basins (author's calculations). In such international cases, neighbouring states are responsible for developing a common vision for implementing EUWFD directives in the river basin. Early empirical work on the level of cooperation in international river basin districts suggested that the greatest level was found in the larger river basin districts of Western and Central Europe where EU integration in other realms was most advanced (Nilsson et al. 2004).

Nested Subsidiarity or a New Scale of Environmental Governance?

On the surface, the EUWFD represents a transition in decision-making about environmental governance from strong, centralistic, Keynesian states to more 'fragmented decision-making clusters' (Kaika 2003). The mechanics of this rescaling of transboundary water management (Norman and Bakker 2009) carries with it consequences for how we understand European politics beyond environmental governance. This section examines some of the implications of European environmental governance for the modern system of territorial rule in Europe. Specifically, I propose that the EUWFD provides evidence of a new, non-nested scalar politics of governance in Europe. River basins cut across the well-established jurisdictional spaces of the EU – national, regional or local – and exist alongside existing hierarchies rather than being planted firmly within them.

The change in analytic scale of a problem is a major step forward since it considers the hydromorphological condition of rivers and other bodies of water, and therefore avoids some of the pitfalls of engineered responses to the inherent dynamism of fluvial systems as mentioned above (Mance et al. 2002; Clarke et al. 2003). Previously, states, because of their hegemonic position in the political organization of space, were the basic unit of analysis for framing governance responses to large-scale challenges or issues. Thus, first the EUWFD challenges the pervasiveness of the nation-state-centric view of environmental phenomena. Second, even when the state was not recognized as the appropriate scale of analysis, one of its nested units typically was. In the EU the Matryoshka doll-like logic of the Nomenclature of Territorial Units for Statistics (NUTS) divided European states into neat packages well suited to their purpose of collecting statistics. However, it also reflected a rigid nation-centric view of EU space, in that none of these territorial units crossed international borders. The division of Europe along geomorphological watershed lines fundamentally challenges this previous order by adhering to nature. Perhaps illustrative of the novelty of this form of rescaling is that, unlike other aspects of transboundary regionalism in the EU that have purposefully, and illogically, excluded non-member state neighbours from new regional constructs (Scott and van Houtum 2009), the EUWFD has attempted to incorporate non-members wherever one of the international river basins lies partly in EU territory (e.g. the Danube basin).

At this point, it is instructive to consider the normative roles of 'subsidiarity' and 'proportionality' as defining principles of EU governance and ask how they relate to the EUWFD. Subsidiarity is the general principle of governance that problems should be addressed at the lowest level possible to successfully resolve them. Proportionality is the general principle of governance that any action by the EU should not exceed what is necessary to accomplish the task at hand, i.e. it should be a proportional response (Craig 2012). In the EU context, subsidiarity generally suggests a set of 'nested' spatial scales, with the member states representing the most important point of reference at the appropriate level (i.e. all else being equal, the scale of the state is de facto the level appropriate to address a problem). The nested spaces of EU governance are typically non-overlapping and exclusive.

While it is true, as Jupille (1998) argues, that political authority under this principle may be geographically overlapping, in practice in the EU subsidiarity organizes political power in a territorially nested manner. Increasingly, the Union is seen as the most appropriate scale at which to address certain environmental issues, such as water quality, and this is suggested in the Lisbon Treaty itself in so far as Union policy should '[promote] measures at international level to deal with regional or worldwide environmental problems, and in particular combating climate change' (EU 2010: Title XX, Article 191.1).

The important point, however, is that the previously available political geographies were woefully inadequate to implement comprehensive policies on water quality, due to nation-state boundaries being the common frame of reference. So, while the power of member states is being rearticulated at a different spatial scale, what is new is that river basins are not simply nested within the existing EU → member state → subnational unit framework. It is rather an environmental scale of river basins that ignores extant political geographical lines. River basins as political geographical scales 'attempt to achieve an appropriate spatial fit between institutional boundaries and resource management' (Medd and Marvin 2008: 285), and in so doing they challenge conventional understanding of spaces of governance.

Towards a New Cosmopolitics of Nature?

In the 1990s John Gerard Ruggie summarized the modern system of territorial rule as being mainly about 'the consolidation of all parcelized and personalized authority into one public realm' wherein the exercise of rule proceeds in 'territorially defined, fixed, and mutually exclusive enclaves of legitimate dominion' (Ruggie 1993: 151). Ruggie also described the (then) European Community as 'the first "multiperspectival polity"' to have emerged in the modern era, in that the process of differentiation between member states that resulted in 'separate, single, fixed viewpoints' – which had previously been the basis for the exercise of international relations – was giving way to a system in which each member state increasingly takes into account the perspective of the other members. At that time Ruggie was vague (perhaps necessarily) about how this manifested itself in practice, but he alluded to the 'transformative potential' of new ways of scalar thinking in ecology (what he called 'global ecology') that are relevant here.

He singled out 'international custodianship' for additional examination, which I liken to the experiences with the EUWFD and river basins:

> Under [international custodianship] no other agency competes with or attempts to substitute for the state, but the state itself acts in a manner that expresses not merely its own interests and preferences but also its role as the embodiment and enforcer of community norms – a multiperspectival role, in short, somewhat in the manner of medieval rulers vis-à-vis cosmopolitan bodies of religion and law. (Ruggie 1993: 173)

Ruggie was sketching out the possibilities for an emergent cosmopolitan territoriality, and did not specifically bring natural spaces such as river basins into his discussion – but he well could have. The somewhat abstract 'unbundling' of state territoriality that Ruggie and others (e.g. Anderson 1996) have described is resulting in 'new and hybrid' forms of territoriality (Sidaway 2006). It is time to add nature into this mix, where a post-sovereign spillage of the EU across international boundaries – and the carving out of new administrative spaces – constitutes a partial realization of the new 'social episteme' Ruggie described in the 1990s. Indeed, Ruggie foreshadowed this possibility, when he spoke of 'the transformative potential of global ecology' into 'an episteme ... [based on] holism and the mutual dependence of parts' (Ruggie 1993: 173).

Conclusion: Possibilities for Post-Sovereign Environmental Governance

The implementation of the EUWFD marks an important milestone in how environmental governance is operationalized; and it has implications for how we understand questions of sovereignty, territoriality and subsidiarity in the EU and beyond. Processes of European integration afford new opportunities for challenging the theoretical and regulatory scales that we lay over nature (e.g. Natter and Zierhofer 2002). If this indeed is the case, as this chapter argues, what lessons can we learn from this reterritorialization of environmental policy?

First, nature warrants the attention of scholars seeking to understand the de- and reterritorialization of the state in Europe. To date, much research on deterritorialization and reterritorialization in Europe has been dominated by an econocentric thread, which focuses on new forms of economic interaction not contained by national boundaries, and a sociocentric thread, which seeks to analyse emergent social formations that transgress state boundaries. Water governance promises avenues for an 'envirocentric' way of understanding how state power is being rearticulated in Europe.

Second, post-sovereign environmental governance is possible, though it is by no means already fully realized. At this point in time, such governance will necessarily be messy, the cultural politics complicated and the power of states will continue to be seen and felt. But the possibility of a reconceived sovereignty as proposed more than a decade ago by Shafer and Murphy (1998) – one that prioritizes environmental rights and concerns above parochial state concerns such as economic growth or social welfare – is at least in part realized in the EUWFD. This is again not to suggest that this environmental regime has rendered states irrelevant; implementation, data gathering and monitoring are largely still enacted by the member states.

Third, there are lessons here for other environmental governance regimes. One such lesson is that scale matters in carving out possibilities for sustainable environmental governance (Reed and Bruyneel 2010). The regional scale of river basins – a territorialization that is readily observable and logical to political participants – is far more practical and palatable than, for example, the global scale that debates over climate change so often appeal to (Benson 2010).

Perhaps the greatest step forward in the EUWFD is that it does challenge the underlying geographical assumptions of how environmental regulation is achieved. Better aligning of the scale of analysis of a problem to the regulatory scale at which decisions are made is a major step forward (see, generally, Cash et al. 2006). The emergence of a transboundary politics of scale around water in the EU challenges earlier assumptions that states should be the basic unit of analysis for almost any large-scale issue for which intervention of the state was necessary. Even when the state was not viewed as the appropriate scale for policy action, the subsidiarity principle generally assured that one of its nested units was. Such a conventional wisdom of governance is seriously called into question by using watersheds.

Even though environmental quality is a realm that reveals most acutely the illogic of the sovereign territorial state system (Lipschutz 2000), scholars have not interrogated the consequences of new forms of environmental governance on notions of sovereignty. In this chapter I have argued that scholars and practitioners alike should consider the scalar politics of water governance as a key constitutive element of an increasingly post-sovereign Europe.

References

Agnew, J.A. 1994. The territorial trap: The geographical assumptions of international relations theory. *Review of International Political Economy* 1(1): 53–80.

Anderson, J. 1996. The shifting stage of politics: New medieval and postmodern territorialities? *Environment and Planning D: Society and Space* 14(2): 133–53.

Andersson, I., Petersson, M. and Jarsjö, J. 2012. Impact of the European Water Framework Directive on local-level water management: Case study Oxunda Catchment, Sweden. *Land Use Policy* 29(1): 73–82.

Bakker, K. 1999. The politics of hydropower: Developing the Mekong. *Political Geography* 18(2): 209–32.

Benson, M.H. 2010. Regional initiatives: Scaling the climate response and responding to conceptions of scale. *Annals of the Association of American Geographers* 100(4): 1025–35.

Beunen, R., van der Knaap, W.G.M. and Biesbroek, G.R. 2009. Implementation and integration of EU environmental directives. Experiences from the Netherlands. *Environmental Policy and Governance* 19(1): 57–69.

Blatter, J.K. 2004. From 'spaces of place' to 'spaces of flows'? Territorial and functional governance in cross-border regions in Europe and North America. *International Journal of Urban and Regional Research* 28(3): 530–49.

Blomquist, W. and Schlager, E. 2005. Political pitfalls of integrated watershed management. *Society and Natural Resources* 18(2): 101–17.

Boscheck, R. 2006. The EU Water Framework Directive: Meeting the global call for regulatory guidance? *Intereconomics* 41(5): 268–71.

Bukowski, J. 2011. Sharing water on the Iberian peninsula: A Europeanisation approach to explaining transboundary cooperation. *Water Alternatives* 4(2): 171–96.

Bulkeley, H. 2005. Reconfiguring environmental governance: Towards a politics of scales and networks. *Political Geography* 24(8): 875–902.

Bulkeley, H. 2012. Governance and the geography of authority: modalities of authorisation and the transnational governing of climate change. *Environment and Planning A* 44(10): 2428–44.

Carter, J.G. 2007. Spatial planning, water and the Water Framework Directive: Insights from theory and practice. *Geographical Journal* 173(4): 330–42.

Cash, D.W. et al. 2006. Scale and cross-scale dynamics: Governance and information in a multilevel world. *Ecology and Society* 11(2): 181–92.

Church, M. 1996. Space, time and the mountain – how do we order what we see? In Rhoads, B. and Thorn, C. (eds), *The Scientific Nature of Geomorphology*, pp. 147–70. New York: Wiley.

Clarke, S.J., Bruce-Burgess, L. and Wharton, G. 2003. Linking form and function: Towards an eco-hydromorphic approach to sustainable river restoration. *Aquatic Conservation: Marine and Freshwater Ecosysems* 13(5): 439–50.

Cohen, A. and Davidson, S. 2011. The watershed approach: Challenges, antecedents, and the transition from technical tool to governance unit. *Water Alternatives* 4(1): 1–14.

Cohen, S. and Frank, D. 2009. Innovative approaches to territorial disputes: Using principles of riparian conflict management. *Annals of the Association of American Geographers* 99(5): 948–55.

Craig, P. 2012. Subsidiarity: A Political and Legal Analysis. *JCMS: Journal of Common Market Studies* 50(S1): 72–87.

Dalby, S. 2009. *Security and environmental change.* Cambridge: Polity.

Dably, S. 2010. Recontextualising violence, power and nature: The next twenty years of critical geopolitics? *Political Geography* 29(5): 280–88.

Del Moral, L. and Do Ó, A. 2014. Water governance and scalar politics across multiple-boundary river basins: States, catchments and regional powers in the Iberian Peninsula. *Water International* 39(3), DOI: 10.1080/02508060.2013.878816.

Diaz, C.L. 2001. The EC habitats directive approaches its tenth anniversary: An overview. *Review of European Community and International Environmental Law* 10(3): 287–95.

EC (European Commission). 2008. *Waternotes.* http://ec.europa.eu/environment/water/participation/notes_en.htm (accessed 13 January 2012).

EC. 2014. *Natura 2000 Network.* http://ec.europa.eu/environment/nature/natura2000/index_en.htm (accessed 20 July 2014).

Elden, S. 2009. Reassessing Kant's geography. *Journal of Historical Geography* 35(1): 3–25.

EU (European Union). 2010. Consolidated versions of the treaty on the European Union and the treaty on the functioning of the European Union. *Official Journal of the European Union C* 83(53): 1–388.

Fall, J.J. 2010. Artificial states? On the enduring geographical myth of natural borders. *Political Geography* 29(3): 140–47.

Furlong, K. 2006. Hidden theories, troubled waters: International relations, the 'territorial trap', and the Southern African Development Community's transboundary waters. *Political Geography* 25(4): 438–58.

Gleditsch, N.P., Furlong, K., Hegre, H., Lacina, B. and Owen, T. 2006. Conflicts over shared rivers: Resource scarcity or fuzzy boundaries? *Political Geography* 25(4): 361–82.

Gualini, E. 2004. Integration, diversity, plurality: Territorial governance and the reconstruction of legitimacy in a European 'postnational' state. *Geopolitics* 9(3): 542–63.

Harris, L.M. and Alatout, S. 2010. Negotiating hydro-scales, forging states: Comparison of the upper Tigris/Euphrates and Jordan River basins. *Political Geography* 29(3): 148–56.

Heynen, N. 2007. *Neoliberal Environments: False Promises and Unnatural Consequences.* London: Routledge.

Hooghe, L. and Marks, G. 2003. Unraveling the central state, but how? Types of multi-level governance. *American Political Science Review* 97(2): 233–43.

Johnson, C.M. 2008. Euro-politics of scale: competing visions of the region in eastern Germany. *GeoJournal* 72: 75–89.

Jordan, A. 2005. *Environmental Policy in the European Union*. London: Earthscan.

Jupille, J.H. 1998. Sovereignty, environment, and subsidiarity in the European Union. In Litfin, K. (ed.), *The Greening of Sovereignty in World Politics*, pp. 223–54. Cambridge, MA: MIT Press.

Kaika, M. 2003. The water framework directive: A new directive for a changing social, political and economic European framework. *European Planning Studies* 11(3): 299–316.

Karkkainen, B.C. 2004. Post-sovereign environmental governance. *Global Environmental Politics* 4(1): 72–96.

Lipschutz, R.D. 2000. Crossing borders: Global civil society and the reconfiguration of transnational political space. *GeoJournal* 52(1): 17–23.

Mance, G., Raven, P.J. and Bramley, M.E. 2002. Integrated river basin management in England and Wales: A policy perspective. *Aquatic Conservation: Marine and Freshwater Ecosyyems* 12(4): 339–46.

McGlade, J.M. 2002. Governance of transboundary pollution in the Danube River. *Aquatic Ecosystem Health and Management* 5(1): 95–110.

Medd, W. and Marvin, S. 2008. Making water work: Intermediating between regional strategy and local practice. *Environment and Planning D: Society and Space* 26(2): 280–99.

Menon, A. 2009. Empowering paradise? The ESDP at ten. *International Affairs* 85(2): 227–46.

Moss, B. 2008. The Water Framework Directive: Total environment or political compromise? *Science of the Total Environment* 400(1–3): 32–41.

Moss, T. 2012. Spatial fit, from panacea to practice: Implementing the EU Water Framework Directive. *Ecology and Society* 17 (3): article 2.

Moss, T. and Fichter, H. 2003. Lessons in promoting sustainable development in EU structural funds programmes. *Sustainable Development* 11(1): 56–65.

Moss, T. and Newig, J. 2010. Multilevel water governance and problems of scale: Setting the stage for a broader debate. *Environmental Management* 46(1): 1–6.

Murphy, A.B. 1996. The sovereign state system as political-territorial ideal: Historical and contemporary considerations. In Biersteker, T.J. and Weber, C. (eds), *State Sovereignty As Social Construct*, pp. 81–210. Cambridge: Cambridge University Press.

Murphy, A.B. 2008. Rethinking multi-level governance in a changing European Union: Why metageography and territoriality matter. *GeoJournal* 72(1): 7–18.

Natter, W. and Zierhofer, W. 2002. Political ecology, territoriality and scale. *GeoJournal* 58(4): 225–31.

Neumann, R.P. 2010. Political ecology II: Theorizing region. *Progress in Human Geography* 34(3): 368–74.

Newson, M.D. 2002. Geomorphological concepts and tools for sustainable river ecosystem management. *Aquatic Conservation: Marine and Freshwater Ecosysyems* 12(4): 365–79.

Nilsson, S., Langaas, S. and Hannerz, F. 2004. International river basin districts under the EU Water Framework Directive: Identification and planned cooperation. *European Water Management Online*: 1–19.

Norman, E.S. and Bakker, K. 2009. Transgressing scales: Water governance across the Canada–U.S. borderland. *Annals of the Association of American Geographers* 99(1): 99–117.

Pounds, N.J.G. 1951. The origin of the idea of natural frontiers in France. *Annals of the Association of American Geographers* 41(2): 146–57.

Pounds, N.J.G. 1954. France and 'les limites naturelles' from the seventeenth to the twentieth centuries. *Annals of the Association of American Geographers* 44(1): 51–62.

Reed, M.G. and Bruyneel, S. 2010. Rescaling environmental governance, rethinking the state: A three-dimensional review. *Progress in Human Geography* 34(5): 646–53.

Rettman, A. 2007. Brussels names and shames EU water laggards. *EU Observer*, 22 March 2007.

Robbins, P. 2003. Political ecology in political geography. *Political Geography* 22(6): 641–5.

Ruggie, J.G. 1993. Territoriality and beyond: Problematizing modernity in international relations. *International Organization* 47(1): 139–74.

Schott, M. 2007. Geopolitical imaginations about the European Union in recent political discussions. *Tijdschrift voor Economische en Sociale Geografie* 98(2): 284–95.

Scott, J.W. and van Houtum, H. 2009. Reflections on EU territoriality and the 'bordering' of Europe. *Political Geography* 28(5): 271–3.

Shafer, S.L. and Murphy, A.B. 1998. The territorial strategies of IGOs: Implications for environment and development. *Global Governance* 4(3): 257–74.

Sidaway, J.D. 2006. On the nature of the beast: Re-charting political geographies of the European Union. *Geografiska Annaler, Series B* 88(1): 1–14.

Sneddon, C. and Fox, C. 2012. Water, Geopolitics, and Economic Development in the Conceptualization of a Region. *Eurasian Geography and Economics* 53(1): 143–60.

Taylor, P.J. 1994. The state as container: Territoriality in the modern world-system. *Progress in Human Geography* 18(2): 151–62.

Thiel, A. 2009. Europeanisation and the rescaling of water services: Agency and state spatial strategies in the Algarve, Portugal. *Water Alternatives* 2(2): 225-44.

UNECE. 2012. *Sixth Session of the Meeting of the Parties to the UNECE Convention on the Protection and Use of Transboundary Watercourses and International Lakes*. Available at: http://www.unece.org/env/water/mop6.html (accessed 18 February 2013).

Vogt, J., Puumalainen, J., Kennedy, P. and Folving, S. 2004. Integrating information on river networks, catchments and major forest types: Towards the characterisation and analysis of European landscapes. *Landscape and Urban Planning* 67(1–4): 27–41.

White, I. and Howe, J. 2003. Policy and practice: Planning and the European Union Water Framework Directive. *Journal of Environmental Planning and Management* 46(4): 621–31.

Whitehead, M., Jones, R. and Jones, M. 2007. *The Nature of the State: Excavating the Political Ecologies of the Modern State*. Oxford: Oxford University Press.

PART III
Scalar Politics, Networks and Power in Water Governance

Introduction to Part III

Leila M. Harris

In order to appreciate the contributions of this volume, and this section, we must become comfortable theoretically and empirically with complex entanglements. We cannot easily disassociate water governance realities from energy or food issues and we cannot discern where one scale ends and the other begins; nor can we proceed while failing to understand the ways that natural and social worlds are inevitably interconnected. Here, the focus is on the complex entanglements between scale, water governance and politics. The chapters in this section consider renegotiations of scalar politics and water governance regimes, revealing dynamic realities of changing biophysical and socio-political worlds. While many issues could be highlighted as part of this discussion, the focus here is on three primary concerns:

1. What does attention to the politics of scale, and of rescaling, offer for contemporary understandings of water governance?
2. What does attention to scalar politics in the water governance realm reveal in terms of dynamic changes across socio-political, economic and biophysical realms?
3. How does politics of scale in the water realm help us attend to socio-political inequities and power dynamics?

Each of these issues is highlighted in turn, drawing from and speaking to the specific case studies that follow in Section III.

Even as the body of literature on politics of scale is nuanced and speaks to complex politics and interactions, at the core of such examination is often a simple point: there are politics behind the invocation of a particular scale, and there are often certain politics and realities that are made possible by validating or sedimenting certain scales. Biophysically, the privileging of certain scales can have important consequences, e.g. setting up biodiversity conservation areas in ways that are more attentive to human administrative units or temporal requirements than for species needs and life courses (see Hazen and Harris 2007).

For social science evaluations, we might assume that a particular scale is more valid or relevant; for instance, we may privilege 'state' scales in ways that will force us to miss a range of processes and issues of importance at other scales (e.g. transboundary scales or local dynamics). There are also likely to be particular politics behind preferring the 'watershed' scale for decision-making, for instance, notions of effectiveness or commitment to broad engagement and political participation of communities (Cohen 2012). However, a crucial point to bear in mind is that while all the chapters that follow interrogate politics of scale, only the contribution by Norman makes an argument about those politics as an explicit choice or strategy. In the other chapters politics are linked to scalar renegotiations, yet most often it is not a deliberate choice or strategy. Nonetheless, both implicit and explicit manoeuvres of scale in relation to water governance must be understood as 'politics'.

In terms of *effects*, a shared interest of this section is to understand the political consequences of particular (re)scaling processes. One example relates to how particular administrative units (e.g. the state) or types of knowledge (e.g. engineering knowledge of irrigation) may be validated and consolidated, affirming that these scales of knowledge and management are valid or legitimate (see Chapters 14 and 15). In these senses politics is often the key to determining scales of analysis or of management, as well as determining how and why rescaling may occur. Increasingly, we also understand that governance 'failures' may result from inattention to the multiscalar dimensions of complex issues – as with the frequent failures in the sanitation realm (Chapter 13) – or indeed 'scalar mismatches', for example, between scale of process and decision-making entities (see Chapter 1 and Cumming et al. 2006) and examples of 'green water' scalar mismatches in Clarke-Sather (Chapter 14).

Several other general considerations in the following chapters are also worth bearing in mind. Among them, even if we sometimes refer to scales as if they are fixed and knowable (e.g. *the* watershed or *the* state scale), more likely, there is an *appearance* of fixity. This draws attention to yet another political dimension of scale: how is it that a certain scale appears to be fixed, and knowable, even if a particular territory or extent is not characteristic of the 'thing' itself? Alternatively, how do we begin to unpack and analyse the very political achievement of the naturalness or apparent fixity of a particular scale (Chapter 14; Harris and Alatout 2010)? For instance, the 'watershed' scale is frequently referred to as if it were knowable and natural, but it is useful to recognize (and even decipher) how this stability or 'scale' was and is consolidated over time, through specific practices (see Kaiser and Nikiforova 2008; Harris and Alatout 2010 and Cohen and Harris 2014 for examples of scalar performativity approaches).

Along these lines, it becomes imperative to understand that a 'state' scale invokes a particular historiography associated with state administrative and political forms, perhaps also validating the range of practices and efforts (including violent campaigns) to naturalize territories and power associated with those state forms – despite frequent and repeated challenges to such in many contexts (e.g. witness Basque or Catalan resistance in Spain, Tibetan resistance in China etc...). While this is a complex suite of issues, a key question to bear in mind is how and why certain scales 'appear' to be fixed and natural, and how water governance processes may rely on and even reinforce such notions.

What Does Attention to Scale and Rescaling Bring to Water Governance?

Speaking to these types of concerns, three themes have been selected to reflect on the contributions of this section. First, what does attention to scale and rescaling lend to key concerns for water governance? In a very basic sense, it is often precisely in an attempt to rearrange scales, or to overcome scalar mismatches, that we endeavour to manage water at all. Historically and contemporarily, attempts to dam, impound and divert rivers are often to overcome or rearrange temporal and geographical scales of water availability and use. We store water in reservoirs for use when we need it, particularly during hot and dry months when it may be most needed for agriculture (altering temporal scales of water availability and use). Spatially as well we often seek to alter the extent of areas served by particular watercourses. Historically, agriculture near rivers such as the Tigris or the Nile would be served by the natural flood regimes of those rivers. Water management and engineering increasingly served to divert that water over longer distances and to minimize the flood patterns that increasingly came to represent threats to human settlements. Thus, at an elemental level we can see a politics of scale inherent to any water governance effort.

Attention to scale also helps to foreground the political, social or ecological consequences of efforts that reconfigure, or privilege, particular governance units (e.g. local management, centralized institutions etc.). Consider that irrigation efforts in China or in Nepal help to consolidate state power as well as the authority and voice of engineers and others who can provide 'data' that speaks to broad scale issues of river management (Chapters 14 and 15). In the example of Peru provided by Budds in Chapter 12, rescaling potentially enables access to critical water resources for mining interests. In particular, this author argues that the establishment of new local-scale river basin councils may serve mining companies, particularly if mining interests are able to play a role in those new 'local' governance institutions, given that those institutions are often disconnected from regional and national scale decision-making processes.

In terms of other ways the chapter of this section respond to this general question, several case studies in this section deploy scalar analytics to enable us to think through what types of actors or information are involved in decision-making over water. For instance, one of the key shifts of the past several decades in water governance has been specifically to counter centralized control and authority with respect to water information, management and decision-making. Not only were top-down approaches of concern for equity reasons, but often these approaches resulted in 'failure' due to inability to gain traction 'locally', related to the difficulties in translating these interests across scales (Scott 1998; see the discussion of the state hydraulic paradigm by Vogel in Chapter 4). Mehta (Chapter 13) provides us with an example from the sanitation realm that is emblematic in this regard. With a history of failure in top-down sanitation efforts, community-led total sanitation (CLTS) represents a sort of scalar 'response': rescaling governance to gain input, traction and buy-in at individual and community scales (see also O'Reilly 2010). As Mehta explains through the case of CLTS in India, it is only when you have 'ignition' at the local community level – i.e. commitment and buy-in that is thought to trigger more large scale change – that government subsidies will kick in to create a coordinated response that is synchronized across household, community and state government scales.

Attention to scale helps to highlight these types of shifts in environmental governance, and their consequences. This also highlights the importance of reading the insights from these case studies in relation to other investigations, for instance studies that have looked at the effects of participatory and devolved governance for environmental resources, community dynamics or individual subjectivities (Cooke and Kothari 2001; Hickey and Mohan 2004; Agrawal 2005).

However, the accounts offered here also invite us to recognize that scalar reconfigurations are not simply about a shift from state to local, or vice versa. Instead, governance often occurs across these scales simultaneously. An explicit emphasis on scale helps focus attention on these complex realities and entanglements. Consider again the Peru example provided by Budds. Here, highlighting water and scale foregrounds the ways that villages are affected by mining, even if not proximate to those operations. Instead, it is the complex hydrologic linkages that forge interdependencies across sites and scales, connecting hydrologic or livelihood realities. Understanding these types of interdependences is difficult conceptually, but is a feature common to all the cases in this section.

Similarly, while the chapters by Clarke-Sather and Zwarteveen and Liebrand both document a consolidation of state scales and expertise 'from above', they do not suggest that this represents a clean shift or rescaling – far from it. Instead, there are complex and interconnected pathways of change and reconsolidation. Clarke-Sather suggests, for instance, that a series of interventions increasingly brought national institutions to bear on water management in China's Zuli valley, but in so doing also expanded decision-making opportunities for farmers in terms of how to manage their water at the household level. Consider as well Norman's example of rescaling in the North American Salish sea basin. In this example, scaling up and insisting on a basin-wide transboundary Salish identity serves in part to resituate and affirm local livelihoods and identities among the more than 70 diverse bands throughout the region.

The relative importance of different scales may change with these rescaling processes, but this does not suggest that any scale exists in isolation from other scales, or that governance processes are distinct from a range of biophysical or socio-political processes that also operate across scales – whether climate change; state-led poverty alleviation with the introduction of new crops in the case from China; or biophysical elements that are central to the health of salmon populations in the Pacific Northwest.

The idea of interconnection and entanglement refers both to connections across scales and also precisely the socio-natural linkages that connect processes. Budds offers an example that highlights these interconnections. In this case, mining companies gain access to water by creating new types of technologies and access points (e.g. drilling wells elsewhere or using desalinization technology near the coast). A key point then is to highlight these hydrologic reconfigurations, situating the impact of mining for rescaled hydrogeographies beyond any immediate and direct impacts (e.g. contamination). Note too that this problem of interconnection and interdependence has been one of the primary points of debate and contention in broader debates about scale – often with considerable discussion about what sorts of metaphors are most useful to move away from a strict hierarchical or embedded/ nested conceptualization. Wrinkles in these discussions have included invitations to retheorize nature–society linkages: consider for instance arguments for flat ontology offered by Marston et al. (2005); or the idea of rhizomes offered by Rocheleau and Roth (2007) as a metaphor for nature-society and interspecies relations.

All told, while we might continue to debate how to best convey these multiple linkages and interconnections, it is apparent that attention to scale is one way to investigate and lend nuance to our understanding. One response to the general query would be to say that attention to scale helps us to think through the fact that water governance is never solely about water. Indeed, the analytic of blue-green water engaged by Clarke-Sather foregrounds this point: crop choice, food security or subsidization schema are also about 'water governance', even if they do not track neatly along the lines of 'blue water' that we typically associate with the term (managing rivers or irrigation delivery). From the Budds case study it is also clear that mining governance is also at once also 'water governance', even if mining permits or other decisions may be made by non-water focused institutions or government agents. All told, the contributions of this section offer invaluable entry points to understanding and analysing these types of linkages and connections – tracing across scales and between socio-natural worlds.

Speaking to Dynamic Changes across Socio-Political, Economic and Biophysical Realms

Another element that is striking in the chapters in Section III is the extent to which a focus on scale usefully calls attention to the *dynamism* of key processes. Again, the cases speak to linkages across social and biophysical worlds, as well as how they change in complex relation. Clarke-Sather's example stands out for characterizing scalar dynamics in ways that foreground interdependencies between water, energy and food. He does so by highlighting issues of interest for both 'blue' and 'green' water, offering a rich treatment of work at the forefront of recent calls to more adequately analyse the water–energy–food nexus.

While attention to these issues is possible without explicit attention to scale, I would argue that work on scale productively brings these interconnections into view. This occurs not only by forcing attention to the local manifestations of particular broad scale processes, but also by 'scaling out' to consider broader regional or global dynamics and shifts that might occur concurrently with local manifestations or patterns that are being observed. Indeed, this argument has been foundational to claims of political ecology, as this multiscalar approach has often been promoted as offering a key corrective to earlier studies that appeared to isolate 'local' (indeed often 'village') patterns or processes in ways that ignored broader level processes and understandings (Robbins 2004). Consider as well recent debates related to neoliberal natures, where the argument has been made that we need to more usefully connect multiple case studies. It is clear that the cases in this volume provide rich detail and compelling analysis; but also do so in a way that responds to calls to better understand linkages or regional-global processes that might impinge on and inform diverse local articulations (Castree 2008; Bakker 2010).

Scale, Water and Linkages to Socio-Political Inequities and Power Dynamics

As a final way to think through the linkages between scale, politics and water governance, I would also like to emphasize what these readings provide analytically in terms of issues of inequity and power – both strongly implied by the interest in 'politics'. In many of the cases, we see that scalar politics and negotiations are consequential not only for water conditions (e.g. determining where and when water flows), but also in that they directly impinge on questions of gender, class, poverty or indigeneity. Indeed, just as I suggest that water governance perhaps is inherently about scale (since it is often about changing temporalities and spatialities of water), we might also say that politics of scale approaches are necessarily about social difference and inequality, whether about gender, race, impoverishment or other operations of difference.

We can also look to feminist interventions of the past several decades and see that a core contribution has been to highlight 'other' scales as meaningful for analysis and interpretation, including several scales that had often not been considered in mainstream approaches: scales of the body, the household or politics within communities (Marston 2000; Staeheli et al. 2004). These themes are borne out well in the analysis by Zwarteveen and Liebrand as they highlight gender issues related to particular types of knowledge about irrigation. These authors suggest that there are certain rituals of scientific knowledge production and sharing that validate and call into being masculinist knowledges and modes of representation. These enactments have the effect of validating particular types of knowledge, marginalizing others and also authorizing the continuing need for particular institutional forms (such as the state irrigation agency).

Notions of difference and inequality in relation to indigeneity are also key themes worked through by both Budds and Norman. For the analysis by Budds, the rescaling of water governance leads to changing access regimes and, ultimately, changes the conditions of water in ways that affect its traditional uses for indigenous agriculture. Norman traces the development and discourses of rescaling associated with the transboundary communities that inhabit different spaces around the Salish Sea. While clearly different in traditions, identities and lifeways, Salish communities have an interest in rescaling governance and identity around the entire sea – motivated by concern for the social and cultural implications of a degraded physical environment – and in resisting the imposition of scales, geographies and borders associated with colonialism. Here, the politics of scale and of identities is deployed purposefully and strategically to 'counter-map' different visions and understandings of the Salish Sea, of the salmon therein and of the diverse communities that rely on these resources.

In sum, the contributions of this volume (and of this section) highlight all of these issues, helping to begin to answer the questions of what a scalar approach offers for understanding water governance and what water governance offers to an analytics of scale – a worthy project and undoubtedly one that will spur continued thinking along these lines.

References

Agrawal, A. 2005. *Environmentality: Technologies of Government and the Making of Subjects*. Durham, NC: Duke University Press.

Bakker, K. 2010. The limits of 'neoliberal natures': debating green neoliberalism. *Progress in Human Geography* 34, 715–35.

Castree, N. 2008. Neoliberalising nature: processes, effects, and evaluations. *Environment and Planning A* 40(1), 153–73.

Cohen, A. 2012. Watersheds as boundary objects: scale at the intersection of science, neoliberalism, and participation. *Environment and Planning A* 44(9), 2207–24.

Cohen, A. and Harris, L. 2014. Performing scale: watersheds as 'natural' governance units in the Canadian context. In *Performativity, Politics, and the Production of Social Space*, edited by M. Glass and R. Rose-Redwood. New York: Routledge.

Cooke, B. and Kothari, U. 2001. *Participation: The New Tyranny*. London: Zed Books.

Cumming, G.S. et al. (2006). Scale mismatches in social-ecological systems: causes, consequences, and solutions. *Ecology and Society* 11(1), 14. Available at: http://www.ecologyandsociety.org/vol11/iss1/art14.

Harris, L. and Alatout, S. 2010. Negotiating scales, forging states: comparison of the upper Tigris/Euphrates and Jordan River basins. *Political Geography* (29), 148–56.

Hazen, H. and Harris, L. 2007. The limits of territorially based conservation: a critical assessment based on cartographic and geographic approaches. *Environmental Conservation* 35(1), 1–11.

Hickey, S. and Mohan, G. 2004. *Participation: From Tyranny to Transformation? Exploring New Approaches to Participation in Development*. London: Zed Books.

Marston, S.A. 2000. The social construction of scale. *Progress in Human Geography* 24(2), 219–42.

Marston, S., Jones III, J.P. and Woodward, K. 2005. Human geography without scale. *Transactions of the Institute of British Geographers* 30(4), 416–32.

Kaiser, R. and Nikiforova, E. 2008. The performativity of scale: the social construction of scale effects in Narva, Estonia. *Environment and Planning D* 26(3), 537–62.

O'Reilly, K. 2010. Combining sanitation and women's participation in water supply: An example from Rajasthan. *Development in Practice* 20(1), 45–56.

Robbins, P. 2004. *Political Ecology*. Oxford: Blackwell.

Rocheleau, D. and Roth, R. 2007. Rooted networks, relational webs and powers of connection: rethinking human and political ecologies. *Geoforum* 38(2), 433–7.

Scott, J.C. 1998. *Seeing Like a State*. New Haven: Yale University Press.

Staeheli, L.A., Kofman, E. and Peake, L. 2004. *Mapping Women, Making Politics: Feminist Perspectives on Political Geography*. New York and London: Routledge.

Chapter 12

The Expansion of Mining and Changing Waterscapes in the Southern Peruvian Andes

Jessica Budds

In July 2011, I was travelling in the Andes of southern Peru. My journey started in Moquegua, an inland provincial town in the Andean foothills, at about 1,300 metres above sea level. Accompanied by one of my local research assistants, Lilia, we left at dawn and drove up mainly unpaved roads in our hired four-wheel-drive vehicle, observing the changing scenery during the bumpy ride. As we ascended, the landscape around us was hilly and completely arid; the slopes consisted of dry dirt speckled with large cacti. By the time we reached our first field site – the village of Borogueña at about 2,700 metres above sea level – the parched surroundings were punctuated with steeply sloped and bright green agricultural terraces (Figure 12.1), where the local Aymara people grow maize and potatoes, as well as alfalfa for their livestock. The village itself had a brand new town square, courtesy of the municipality's share of the taxes that mining companies now have to pay to the Peruvian state. Here, we spoke to the community leader, who lamented not only the increasingly short supply of water entering the village's irrigation channels, which had recently been lined with concrete to avoid water loss (also paid for with the new mining revenue), but also the increasing number of villagers – particularly women – who had stopped tending their terraces in order to take up paid work for the newly enriched municipality.

Continuing our drive uphill, we reached the small rural highland town of Candarave, at about 3,800 metres above sea level, where we spent the night. The next morning we set out early for Huaytire, a village on the high Andean plateau (*altiplano*) at an altitude of approximately 4,500 metres. The landscape had now changed dramatically from that of the previous day, having become flat with mountain peaks and volcanoes in the distance, and the barren dirt having given way to wetlands bearing short waxy grasses (Figure 12.2). Here, my other local research assistant, Honorio, arrived with a village elder who took us to a lake, Laguna Suches, whose parched shores indicated that the water body had once been much bigger. Speaking in Aymara, which Honorio translated into Spanish, the elder angrily indicated dead patches of wetlands and dry holes where springs had once flowed. Bitterly, he described the decline in alpaca herds that the extensive wetland vegetation had sustained, and the subsequent outmigration of herders from his village. In the middle of the lake, the water pumping station that has supplied two large open-cast copper mines in the area for around the last half

Figure 12.1   Agricultural terraces in Borogueña, Moquegua, Peru (Jessica Budds)

Figure 12.2   Landscape near Huaytire, Tacna, Peru (Jessica Budds)

century was plain to see. Aside from a few tokenistic donations from the company that owns the mines, such as exercise books for the handful of children remaining in the village, Huaytire receives little in the way of benefits from mining, because it lies beyond the boundaries of the districts that are closest to the mine site, whose villages are those deemed the most affected by mining and thus are allocated the lion's share of the mining tax revenue.[1]

Villages like Boroguena and Huaytire are only two examples of many where lives, livelihoods and landscapes are changing, not necessarily because of the close proximity of the growing number of large mines in the region, but rather due to the increased demand for water that these generate. In the Andes of Peru and neighbouring countries, especially Bolivia, mineral extraction has increased rapidly since the 1990s due to a combination of rising global demand and mineral commodity prices, as well as the liberalization of Andean economies to attract foreign investment in extractive industries (Bebbington 2009; Bridge 2004). While much attention has been given to the dynamics and impacts of this increase in mining, something that is often underrepresented is the sheer amount of freshwater that mines require (Bebbington and Williams 2008). In the Andes of southern Peru, this scale of demand is complicated by the scarcity of water in the places where mineral deposits are located: because of arid conditions in the northern Atacama Desert; due to the location of minerals in basin headwaters; and/or given that existing water sources are used by local indigenous peasant highland communities. Indeed, communities originally settled precisely around highland water sources, and these are strongly connected with their cultural heritage and identity.

Although the effects of mining on water, and therefore on ecosystems and people, are very localized in this case study region, many of the ways in which water is regarded, used and governed happen beyond the local scale. It is already clear how water extraction can affect villages that have no other real connection with mining. Yet, while these concerns are significant, it is also the case that the very means by which mining companies can come to acquire access to water resources in places like these, with these kinds of social and ecological outcomes, depend upon power structures and relations that largely take place elsewhere. The effects of this growing access and use are not unidirectional, however. These struggles over water resources – which is what, in effect, many situations like this have become – have also influenced wider debates about mining and development in Peru, and have forced mining companies to modify their practices and discourses, especially in their efforts to expand operations.

The aim of this chapter is thus not to deploy a conventional analysis of how mining affects water at different scales, but to show how the particular case of mining configures water flows and issues in ways that transcend conventional spatial containers and administrative structures. It will not just look at where

---

1 The cases of Boroguena and Huaytire were featured in a BBC Radio 4 edition of *Costing the Earth*, entitled 'Gold of the Conquistadors', October 2011 (http://www.bbc.co.uk/programmes/b015p871).

material water flows, but will also examine how water becomes produced through processes related to mineral extraction, both material and discursive, and which lead to the formation of *waterscapes* with particular characteristics. An examination of the waterscape requires attention to a range of 'instances' of water, such as physical flows, patterns of access, technologies, institutions, practices, legislative reforms, governance frameworks and discourses around water. However, in analysing changing waterscapes through mineral extraction in the Andes, I also aim to show how these same processes of the production of water also counter-shape the nature of mining, and present challenges for the expansion of the industry.

The chapter is structured into four sections. Following this introduction, I briefly review debates over scale and scalar politics in relation to water, and put forward the case for thinking about the co-production of water and waterscapes. I then analyse the scalar dimensions of water in relation to mining in Peru, and demonstrate the ways in which the mining industry is producing new hydrosocial arrangements, which in turn shift debates and practices around mining. I conclude by arguing that thinking in terms of waterscapes rather than scales better captures the ways through which mining and water shape each other to produce new geographies in the Andes.

Rethinking Water Politics and Scale: Towards the Waterscape

Scale has long been a central tenet of geographical research and analysis, including that related to water. For instance, physical geographers could not approach water without referring to the multiple scales at which the hydrological cycle operates, from the micro-watershed to the globe. Equally, no human geographer could neglect the local, national and international institutions that structure water governance, or, increasingly, the importance of historical and wider political economic processes in shaping water flows and issues.

In practice, however, water has a complex and often uneasy relationship with scale. In physical terms, it is increasingly recognized that hydrological processes are extremely heterogeneous, dynamic and multi-scalar, often compounding efforts to identify and measure them over space and/or time or to isolate them from other ecosystem functions (e.g., Jakeman et al. 1993). In relation to policy, the 'traditional' mode of managing water resources in accordance with political-administrative boundaries is now widely considered to be ineffective, because it resulted in water resources that were physically connected being subjected to different forms of use, management and regulation, with little or no coordination across regional or international boundaries. This complexity was addressed by proposing the watershed as the ideal unit of water management and decision-making as part of a shift towards integrated water resources management (e.g., Molle 2009; Moss and Newig 2010), which also implied proposing stronger roles for local water users. In relation to governance, the increasing role of diverse social actors in decision-making processes around water mean that such functions are no longer confined to state institutions operating at hierarchical scales, but rather embody wider connections and dynamics. It is also increasingly recognized that these relations are influenced by the material and symbolic nature of water itself (Bakker 2003, 2012; Bear and Bull 2011; Perreault 2006; Strang 2004).

Recognizing the *politics* of scale prompts us to think about the ways in which these traditional 'containers' of space are not pre-given but socially constructed, politically mobilized and able to rework hydrosocial relations on the ground (e.g., Swyngedouw 1997). This draws attention to how scales or boundaries have been defined by people (e.g., Fall 2005); how scale is framed and mobilized in line with vested interests (e.g., Delaney and Leitner 1997); and how categories of space are not necessarily hierarchical, separate or ordered (e.g., Perreault 2005). However, we are also increasingly aware that scale is not simply a human construction, but is also shaped by the resource or environment that is being scaled – including forests (McCarthy 2005), water and natural gas (Perreault 2006) and urban environments (Swyngedouw and Heynen 2003).

In relation to water, analyses of the politics of scale have focused on the watershed as a unit of governance, the rescaling of governance under neoliberalism and the production of scale through water. The idea that the watershed is a 'natural' hydrological scale, and should thus form the basis of water governance (as above), is increasingly questioned (see Molle's introduction to Section I of this volume; Warner et al. 2008; Cohen and Davidson 2011). The main points raised include the fact that watershed boundaries are defined (and redefined) by people (Blomquist and Schlager 2005); that watersheds can be modified by humans, such as through hydraulic infrastructure, economic development and water policies (e.g., Turton et al. 2006); and that the adoption of the watershed as the scale for governance is not neutral, but political, since it can privilege hydrological expertise (Swyngedouw 1999) or reconfigure power relations within the watershed (Blomquist and Schlager 2005; Budds and Hinojosa 2012).

Other work has explored how neoliberal reforms have reconfigured scales of water governance. For instance, Norman and Bakker (2009) found that decentralization of Canadian-US transboundary water bodies had neither resulted in the delegation of decision-making power to lower levels of government nor the empowerment of local groups, while Perreault (2005) shows how Bolivian peasant irrigators mobilized arguments around local customary water usage at a national level in order to contest neoliberal reforms for water. Finally, Swyngedouw (2007) demonstrates that constructing hydraulic infrastructure to connect Spain's river basins and transfer water from the humid north-west to the arid south-east in an effort to foster national integration constituted a means by which water produced scale.

In order to move beyond the problematic hierarchies of scale – in terms of both spatial unit and administrative structure – and to examine how water flows and issues are politicized in relation to mining in Peru, I adopt the concept of waterscape to analyse changing hydrosocial relations. The waterscape reflects how various aspects of water become co-produced through power relations at any given moment and in any given context (Budds and Hinojosa 2012). Waterscapes comprise a 'panorama' of water flows, technologies, issues, institutions, discourses and meanings, all of which become constituted in particular ways as a result of the intersection of power relations and water, such that their constitution reflects how power has shaped water and how water has shaped power. As such, a waterscape is not just the context within which water is contained, but also 'a produced socio-natural entity' (Loftus 2007: 49). A waterscape does not have a predefined scale, but can be as extensive or as restricted as the analysis demands. It is thus not an alternative or additional spatial scale, but 'a socio-spatial configuration that is constituted by social and ecological processes, which become manifest through the particular nature of flows, artefacts, institutions and imaginaries that characterize a particular context' (Budds and Hinojosa 2012: 125).

The remainder of this chapter will show how the increased demand for water by the mining sector in Peru does not just have an impact in the localities where the mines are situated, but also influences a wider range of water connections in other places and between other social actors, which transcend spatial divisions and governance structures. It is precisely these connections through which the mining industry is reworking the social relations of control over water and reshaping waterscapes in the Andes, and also through which it is increasingly challenged due to its practices and discourses around water.

Mineral Extraction and the Reshaping of Waterscapes in Southern Peru

This section presents a case study from the southern Peruvian Andes to show what the particular water issues raised by the expansion of mining mean for an analysis of scalar politics and water governance. It starts by outlining water governance arrangements in Peru, considers the relationship between mining and water, and finishes by analysing how mineral extraction and changing waterscapes co-produce each other.

Governing Water in Peru

Until 2009, like in most Latin American countries, Peru's water governance framework split responsibility for water among different water-related sectors and adopted a vertical administrative hierarchy for its management and governance. The former 1969 General Water Law (*Ley General de Aguas*) was passed alongside agrarian reform, which reflected the importance of agriculture, Peru's primary water user. Under this framework, different ministries were charged with different aspects of water at the national level.

- The Ministry of Agriculture managed water for irrigation.
- The Ministry of Housing administered drinking water and wastewater.
- The Ministry of Health oversaw water quality.

• The Ministry of Energy and Mines regulated water contamination from mining.

At the local level, allocation of water rights (*licencias*) and water resource management were organized by irrigation district (*distrito de riego*), a relatively small administrative area with minimal overlap with watershed boundaries. Each irrigation district was managed by a technical administrator (*administrador técnico*) responsible for allocating and administering mainly surface water across all uses within their jurisdiction, although irrigation was usually the principal use. Due to the limited nature of their districts, their training and their resources, more complex issues – such as groundwater allocation, in which they lacked expertise – were forwarded to the national level to be addressed by the former National Institute of Natural Resources (*Instituto Nacional de Recursos Naturales*) in Lima.[2]

Under this framework, water was also managed and governed on the ground by various user-based water organizations, comprising water user associations (*juntas de usuarios*), irrigation committees (*comités de regantes*) and highland community water systems. The latter are the traditional water systems pertaining to largely indigenous Quechua and Aymara peasant communities in the Andes, which are predominantly organized on a communal basis and according to customary rules and practices, and are multiple, diverse and dispersed (e.g., Boelens 2008; Gelles 2000). All these water user organizations are predominantly agricultural, with little, if any, participation from other sectors, and with relatively weak representation at the national level and no formal role in water allocation, management or regulation under the 1969 law.

In 2009 a new Water Resources Law (*Ley de Recursos Hídricos*) was passed, based on integrated water resources management. The 1969 law had become outdated due to state restructuring and decentralization to the regions, provinces and districts in the late 1980s, and because the scale and nature of water use in Peru had changed significantly from the 1990s following growth in water-related industries: including export agriculture, urban development and drinking water expansion, extractive industries and hydroelectric power. A revised governance framework was needed to accommodate the increased demand for water from agriculture and other sectors, the increasing exploitation of groundwater and the development of new infrastructure and hydraulic works.[3] The legal and institutional principles to underpin the new law were proposed in 2004 and developed into the new legislation by a National Water Commission (*Comisión Nacional del Agua*) that comprised representatives of relevant government agencies and prominent independent institutes, and which received input and feedback from a panel of key sectoral stakeholders, including the National Mining, Petroleum and Energy Association (*Sociedad Nacional de Minería, Petróleo e Energía*).

---

2   Technical administrator, personal communication, Tacna, 2006.

3   Laureano del Castillo, Peruvian Centre for Social Studies, personal communication, Lima, 2010.

Alongside the new law, in 2008 an autonomous, cross-sectoral and decentralized state water institution, the National Water Authority (*Autoridad Nacional del Agua*), was created. In Lima, the National Water Authority assumed the previous water-related functions of the various ministries and the former National Institute of Natural Resources. A new regional level was established through the creation of 14 regional offices, known as Administrative Water Authorities (*Autoridades Administrativas del Agua*). At the local level, new Local Water Authorities (*Autoridades Locales del Agua*) were set up in each major river basin to replace the former irrigation districts and their technical administrators. As part of the shift from a centralized structure organized around political-administrative boundaries to an integrated framework based on the watershed, the new law also prescribed the establishment of river basin councils (*consejos de cuenca*). These were envisaged to incorporate all water user organizations and to be invested with significant decision-making powers in order to integrate water sources and users through coordination within the basin.

Expanding Mining, Producing Water

Mineral extraction has, of course, very material effects on water resources, as the situations in Borogueña and Huaytire showed. In this regard, however, I want to move away from the idea that mining simply impacts material flows of water, and stress how water is produced before, during and following its enrolment into mineral extraction in southern Peru.

The two most contentious effects on water arising from mining in the regions of Moquegua and Tacna have been contamination and depletion of water sources. Contamination occurs through blasting (to separate ore from rock), leaching (infiltration of chemicals used for ore separation) and disposal of tailings (finely ground rock from which ore has been extracted) (Balvín 1995; Urteaga 2011). Contamination has been associated with one company that has been operating copper mines in the region for around 50 years, primarily due to its dumping of tailings in natural watercourses – a practice that was banned in the 1990s following a campaign led by the Peruvian civil society organization, Labor (Balvín 1995). Nevertheless, this company continues to be strongly associated with contamination, not only through this ingrained historical association but also due to the lack of state monitoring to assess and potentially control water quality (the standards for which, in principle, are now much higher). In this way, regardless of whether contamination is actually present, it continues to be strongly associated with any mining activity, especially by Aymara villages and anti-mining groups, evidenced by claims of contaminated water in villages that are actually upstream of mines. This negative reputation has also affected new entrants to the area, including a new multinational mining company that presents itself as modern and responsible but which has been unable to overcome the association with contamination.

Depletion is the main issue faced by villages in the highlands near to and/or reliant upon the sources of surface and groundwater used by the mines, as in the cases of Boroguéña and Huaytire. Aymara communities located on the altiplano – such as Huaytire – allege that the extraction of water to supply mines has reduced the extent of high Andean wetlands (*bofedales*) – at about 4,000–5,000 metres above sea level – which they rely upon for grazing their alpaca (the principal livelihood in the highest Andean villages). In the lower Andean valleys, indigenous peasant communities such as Boroguéña practising terraced agriculture (at approximately 2,000–3,500 metres above sea level) claim that increasingly less water flows into their community irrigation systems as a result of mining, restricting their ability to maintain (or expand) their terraces.

A key implication of these connections is that communities can be affected by mining only through water. Importantly, not all sources of water used by existing mines are in the same political-administrative jurisdiction as the mines themselves, or even in the same watershed, meaning that the changes that these communities allege to have occurred to their water are not even being recognized, let alone compensated. This situation is exacerbated by the fact that no research has been conducted to see whether there is a cause–effect relationship between the extraction of water by mines and these alleged reductions in flows, which weakens the communities' claims of effects on water and enables the mining companies to suggest other, less plausible, causes, such as poor traditional agricultural practices or the effects of climate change. In southern Peru, the scarcity of water, both natural and produced, has caused mining companies to employ various strategies to acquire water. On the one hand, these illustrate how water allocation can take place in parallel with formal structures and procedures. On the other hand, the way in which these strategies have enabled mining companies to gain access to a large share of the region's fresh water resources help explain why water has become such a conflictive issue between mining companies and the Aymara communities.

One strategy has entailed buying land from Aymara landholders in settlements that are not legally constituted as 'communities': that is, in which resources are held individually rather than in common, and thus can be alienated. The sales have often been at a price that seems generous to rural landholders, but is often far below the market price.[4] The reason for buying land is to acquire the surface water rights that are allocated to it or the water sources held within it (such as springs or wetlands). The transfer of water rights is a grey area because in theory water rights are state concessions and cannot be bought or sold; if land is sold, the water rights should return to the state. However, it appears that – at least in practice under the 1969 law when technical administrators were in charge of water rights – these were simply reallocated to the new owner with minimal bureaucracy, effectively constituting the sale of water with land.

Another strategy has entailed direct negotiations between mining companies and government agencies and communities. For instance, a technical administrator based in Tacna reported that representatives from a particular mining company

---

4   Representative of labour civil society association 1, personal communication, Moquegua, 2006.

offered to commission studies and/or to provide the logistics for field inspections in order to facilitate an assessment of water availability.[5] Similarly, an official from the former National Institute of Natural Resources in Lima explained how a consultant representing a company seeking to open a new mine in Moquegua came to negotiate the acquisition of the necessary water rights, again offering to contribute to the necessary studies and infrastructure.[6]

A third strategy used by representatives of mines is the revision of existing water allocation in order to identify any unassigned resources that could be granted to the mine. For example, a multinational mining company seeking to develop a new copper mine in the region argued that the infiltration of water from a reservoir floor into the aquifer had not been taken into account and was thus available, and requested the rights to this water be granted.[7]

In the face of scarcity, as well as multiple tensions around water allocation between mining companies, the state and Aymara communities, an important means of acquiring the necessary flows of water for the mines – which must be secured for the planned term of the mining operation – is to construct hydraulic infrastructure to produce additional water. In southern Peru such infrastructure has included deep boreholes to extract groundwater; large-scale hydraulic works to enable inter-basin transfers; dams and reservoirs to both store water and generate energy; and desalination plants whereby desalinated water would either be pumped to mines or supplied on the coast in return for the use of highland water at source (thereby saving the energy costs of pumping) from the coast to the highlands. The construction of particular types of infrastructure to produce new supplies of water that enable the development of mining constitutes one of the clearest ways in which the mining industry is modifying hydrological regimes, and thus reconfiguring patterns of access in southern Peru.

Although at first sight infrastructure solutions are the most obvious and easiest means of supplying the water that the mines need, they are complicated by the fact that they are seldom cost-effective for the operational life of one mine. Thus, one mining company aiming to open a mine near Moquegua sought partial investment for a new dam and reservoir from the state, arguing that the infrastructure would also provide water and energy to other sectors (agriculture, urban centres) and would outlast the life of the mine.[8] In another case, a mining company sought to access water from a state irrigation project, proposing to draw water from the irrigation system in the highlands and replace it with desalinated water on the coast.[9] This proposal proved highly controversial, as agricultural organizations and anti-mining

---

5   Technical administrator, personal communication, Tacna, 2006.

6   National Institute of Natural Resources representative, personal communication, Lima, 2006.

7   Representative of labour civil society association 2, personal communication, Moquegua, 2011.

8   Mining company representative 1, personal communication, Lima, 2006.

9   State irrigation project representative, personal communication, Moquegua, 2010.

groups accused the company not only of trying to divert water from agriculture to mining, but also of taking unfair advantage of a state-funded irrigation project.

The principles according to which water is managed and governed in southern Peru are established by the 2009 law, which was influenced by those stakeholders who contributed to its formulation. Of particular interest here is the active participation of the National Mining, Petroleum and Energy Association in this process, which shaped the final outcome.[10] One contentious issue during the formulation of the law was whether development should be permitted in the headwaters of basins. The agriculture sector strongly opposed development in headwaters, on the basis that the effects were not known but with the real agenda of attempting to curtail the rapidly expanding mining industry and its demand for water, since the vast majority of mines are located in headwaters. Needless to say, the mining sector vigorously supported development in headwaters, using the counter-argument that negative effects were not proven; otherwise the majority of its industry would have become illegal.

One change that the new law introduced was an increase in state control over water user organizations. As the state has historically had little or no presence in the highlands, the particular nature and situation of highland community water systems –isolated, community-specific and organized in accordance with Andean indigenous customary norms and rules – were barely taken into account in the new law. The new provisions that these systems should formalize unregistered water rights (an estimated 25 per cent of the total in the highlands),[11] join local water user associations and become incorporated into river basin councils are thus unrealistic and, at least to date, have been ignored.

The situation in southern Peru also shows that it is not just material changes to water that are at stake as mineral extraction expands, but also the ways in which water becomes reframed in relation to mining. These are reflected in changing discourses around water efficiency and equity of access, which were specifically promoted by the mining sector during the debates to reform the water law. While at face value these principles appear positive and logical, they reflect a deeper tension between mining and agriculture in their roles as Peru's dominant industries and its most significant water users. The agriculture sector, the longest established and largest water user, feels threatened by increased competition over water from mining, while the mining sector resents the existing allocation of water to farmers that has forced it to develop alternative strategies to access water. The mining sector thus mobilizes the notion of efficiency to justify its role as a legitimate water user. Thus, it frequently contrasts its own extremely outdated and probably grossly underestimated *national* water use (2 per cent) with that of the agriculture sector (approximately 80 per cent) to both trivialize its own water use (despite

---

10   Laureano del Castillo, Peruvian Centre for Social Studies, personal communication, Lima, 2010.

11   Laureano del Castillo, Peruvian Centre for Social Studies, personal communication, Lima, 2006.

being significant at the *local* level) and frame the agricultural sector as inherently inefficient. This discourse is also often reproduced at the local level in the highlands; some mining company representatives have framed peasant irrigation as inefficient both technically (i.e. water consumption) and economically (i.e. value of produce).[12] While at face value the principle of equity appears to be positive and logical, it is used as a rhetorical device to signal that new water users (i.e. mining) should enjoy the same opportunities to access water as existing users (i.e. agriculture) and that historic water entitlements should be reformed.

Rescaling Water, Reworking Waterscapes

The ways in which mining influences the different aspects of water illustrated above shows how these 'instances' of water become produced in particular ways, in different places, at different moments and through various connections. What is also evident is that many of these instances are at odds not only with the spatial containers and administrative structures through which formal water governance is organized, but also with the wider political-economic processes that influence water – such as administrative decentralization, distribution of the mining tax, allocation of mineral concessions and livelihood strategies. This implies that hydrosocial relations cut across watersheds, administrative structures and the wider political economy rather than being organized within them.

This case study raises two important scalar implications. First, the watershed has little significance as a unit for organizing water governance in relation to mineral extraction because hydraulic works can transport water across watershed boundaries or even bring new water from the sea into the watershed. Second, the watershed is proposed as the most appropriate unit for water governance because the water resources within it are connected, but not much else is. The watershed that I have described in southern Peru is extensive and heterogeneous in almost every way imaginable: physically (topographically, ecologically, hydrologically), economically and culturally. While in terms of water resources it is presented as a coherent space, in terms of water use it is quite the opposite, as social groups located at different altitudes of the basin extract water from different sources; use water in different ways; commonly attribute water shortages to those further upstream; and fail to coordinate or jointly mobilize, even though the issues they claim affect them are similar.

Moreover, the rescaling of water governance to the watershed level has the potential to significantly reconfigure power relations in favour of the mining sector. While the mining sector has been less prominent in water governance than agriculture, the establishment of the new river basin councils will not only allow the mining sector – which has almost never participated in existing water user associations – to become involved in local water governance, but could also enable

---

12   Mining company representative 2, personal communication, Tacna, 2006; mining company representative 3, personal communication, Moquegua, 2011.

it to gain significant power within this new local-level institution, depending on how voting rights are weighted. This eventuality is exacerbated by the fact that the river basin councils are disconnected from the regional governments and from the wider political-economic processes, such as economic development, investment of the mining tax and land-use planning, which affect both water and mining.

Conclusion

This chapter has sought to demonstrate how power structures and relations in the context of the expanding mining industry shape the formation of waterscapes – water flows, social relations, hydraulic works, governance arrangements, practices and discourses – in southern Peru. These processes transcend conventional containers of space and institutional structures. In this region, the growth of mining has increasingly resulted in the transfer of water occupied by Aymara communities to mines, which both changes traditional livelihoods and landscapes, and enables the mining industry to expand and develop. This only comes to pass, however, as a result of mining companies bypassing formal governance mechanisms to negotiate water solutions directly with communities or government agencies; the mining sector influencing the new legal and administrative framework for water governance; or mining companies constructing and mobilizing framings around water efficiency to justify the diversion of water to the mining sector. In order to understand the multiple ways in which mining reworks waterscapes in southern Peru and elsewhere we must attend to these multiple practices, connections and discourses, and their interrelationship with power, rather than structure our analysis along existing spatial scales and administrative frameworks.

Through my analysis of changing waterscapes in southern Peru I have endeavoured to show that mining does not simply 'impact' water in a material sense or leave a 'water footprint' (Allan 2011), but that it produces particular instances of water, which in turn configure waterscapes in distinct ways. Moreover, it is not just the ways in which water is produced in the context of the mining industry that are important here, but how these instances of produced water have also shaped practices and debates around mining at both local and national level. Water scarcity, administrative rules and framings of water have all challenged mining companies' access to water, and its strategies to address these challenges have, in turn, changed the nature of the sector: in terms of the practice and discourses the sector employs; the ways in which it is governed and regulated; the nature of protests made against it; civil society's perception of it; and its ability to expand its operations.

Examining the ways in which mining changes waterscapes is thus not only a more productive way of understanding the effects of mining on water as inherently related to power structures and relations, but also of considering how water also influences the nature of mining. Moreover, it has not been my intention to present mining simply as the context within which these particular water issues arise and waterscapes become formed in my case study location. Rather, I contend that mineral extraction – at least in the context of physical and produced scarcity in southern Peru – presents particularly wide and varied dynamics around scale, and thus is especially appropriate to being analysed through the concept of waterscape. This, in turn, prompts me to add to existing critiques around the idea of the watershed as the ideal unit for water governance, by stressing that it is particularly problematic in relation to the specific issues and challenges posed by the expansion of natural resource industries with a high demand for water.

Due to the extent of mines' area of influence and their high demand for water, as well as the particular physical and cultural context of southern Peru, the rationale for basing water governance on the watershed is seriously undermined. Indeed, the case study shows how the construction of hydraulic works to capture water for mining pays little or no heed to watershed limits – many of the other political economic and governance processes that affect both water and mining occur beyond the watershed – and that one key challenge in relation to mining is to regulate upstream and downstream users and impacts, which would not be addressed by watershed-based governance. A shift to the watershed as the unit of water governance would, however, have the potential to significantly reconfigure decision-making at the local level through river basin councils, which would benefit greatly, and, more importantly, empower the mining sector.

References

Allan, J.A. 2011. *Virtual Water: Tackling the Threat to our Planet's Most Precious Resource*. London: Taurus.

Bakker, K. 2012. Water: Political, biopolitical, material. *Social Studies of Science*, 42, 616–23.

Bakker, K. 2003. *An Uncooperative Commodity: Privatizing Water in England and Wales*. Oxford: Oxford University Press.

Balvín, D. 1995. *Agua, Minería y Contaminación: El Caso Southern Peru*. Lima: Ediciones Labor.

Bear, C. and Bull, J. 2011. Water matters: agency, flows and frictions. *Environment and Planning A*, 43, 2261–6.

Bebbington, A. 2009. Latin America: Contesting extraction, producing geographies. *Singapore Journal of Tropical Geography*, 30(1), 7–12.

Bebbington, A. and Williams, M. 2008. Water and mining conflicts in Peru. *Mountain Research and Development*, 28(3/4), 190–95.

Blomquist, W. and Schlager, E. 2005. Political pitfalls of integrated watershed management. *Society and Natural Resources*, 18(2), 101–17.

Boelens, R. 2008. *The Rules of the Game and the Game of the Rules: Normalization and Resistance in Andean Water Control*. Wageningen: Wageningen University.

Bridge, G. 2004. Contested terrain: Mining and the environment. *Annual Review of Environment and Resources*, 29, 205–59.

Bryant, R. and Bailey, S. 1997. *Third World Political Ecology*. London: Routledge.

Budds, J. and Hinojosa, L. 2012. Restructuring and rescaling water governance in mining contexts: The co-production of waterscapes in Peru. *Water Alternatives*, 5(1), 119–37.

Cohen, A. and Davidson, S. 2011. The watershed approach: Challenges, antecedents, and the transition from technical tool to governance unit. *Water Alternatives*, 4(1), 1–14.

Delaney, D. and Leitner, H. 1997. The political construction of scale. *Political Geography*, 16(2), 93–7.

Fall, J. 2005. *Drawing the Line: Nature, Hybridity and Politics in Transboundary Spaces*. Aldershot: Ashgate.

Gelles, P. 2000. *Water and Power in Highland Peru: The Cultural Politics of Irrigation and Development*. New Brunswick: Rutgers University Press.

Jakeman, A., Beck, M. and McAleer, M. (eds) 1993. *Modelling Change in Environmental Systems*. Chichester: Wiley.

Loftus, A. 2007. Working the socio-natural relations of the urban waterscape. *International Journal of Urban and Regional Research*, 31(1), 41–59.

McCarthy, J. 2005. Scale, sovereignty, and strategy in environmental governance. *Antipode*, 37(4), 731–53.

Molle, F. 2009. River basin planning and management: The social life of a concept. *Geoforum*, 40(3), 484–94.

Moss, T. and Newig, J. 2010. Multilevel water governance and problems of scale: Setting the stage for a broader debate. *Environmental Management*, 46, 1–6.

Norman, E. and Bakker, K. 2009. Transgressing scales: Transboundary water governance across the Canada–U.S. borderland. *Annals of the Association of American Geographers*, 99(1), 99–117.

Perreault, T. 2005. State restructuring and the scale politics of rural water governance in Bolivia. *Environment and Planning A*, 37, 263–84.

Perreault, T. 2006. From the guerra del agua to the guerra del gas: Resource governance, neoliberalism and popular protest in Bolivia. *Antipode*, 38(1), 150–72.

Strang, V. 2004. *The Meaning of Water*. Oxford: Berg.

Swyngedouw, E. 1997. Neither global nor local: 'Glocalization' and the politics of scale. In *Spaces of Globalization: Reasserting the Power of the Local*, edited by K. Cox. New York: Guilford, 137–66.

Swyngedouw, E. 1999. Modernity and hybridity: Nature, regeneracionismo, and the production of the Spanish waterscape, 1890–1930. *Annals of the Association of American Geographers*, 89(3), 443–65.

Swyngedouw, E. 2007. Technonatural revolutions: The scalar politics of Franco's hydro-social dream for Spain, 1939–1975. *Transactions of the Institute of British Geographers*, 32(1), 9–28.

Swyngedouw, E. and Heynen, N. 2003. Urban political ecology, justice and the politics of scale. *Antipode*, 35(5), 898–918.

Turton, A., Schultz, C., Buckle, H., Kgomongoe, M., Malungani, T. and Drackner, M. 2006. Gold, scorched earth and water: The hydropolitics of Johannesburg. *Water Resources Development*, 22(2), 313–35.

Urteaga, P. (ed.) 2011. *Agua e Industrias Extractivas: Cambios y Continuidades en los Andes*. Lima: Instituto de Estudios Peruanos.

Warner, J., Wester, P. and Bolding, A. 2008. Going with the flow: River basins as the natural units for water management? *Water Policy*, 10(S2), 121–38.

Chapter 13

Community-Led Total Sanitation and the Politics of Scaling Up

Lyla Mehta[1]

Introduction

Despite its pivotal importance to human health and well-being, sanitation has been at the bottom of the pile of international development concerns. This is despite the fact that around 4,000 people, mostly babies, die daily due to complications related to poor sanitation, hygiene and unsafe water. About 40 per cent of the population in the global South live without access to 'improved' sanitation – that is about 2.5 billion people around the world.[2] Still, sanitation is considered a highly difficult to reach Millennium Development Goal (MDG): it is today the most off-track of all the MDGs, and sub-Saharan Africa is the most off-track region. Water continues to grab more attention globally and nationally; and, historically, sanitation and hygiene have rarely been separated from water.[3] Politicians and policymakers are reluctant to prioritize sanitation and to make the link to wider health, development and poverty reduction concerns. In addition, the 'sanitation issue' has remained strangely outside many water governance conversations. Governing sanitation, though, sits at the intersection between environmental governance and the politics

---

1   This chapter draws on Mehta (2011), and I am very grateful to the editors for their patience and useful comments.

2   This is according to the WHO/UNICEF Joint Monitoring Programme (JMP) for Water Supply and Sanitation, the official United Nations organ responsible for monitoring progress towards the water and sanitation Millennium Development Goal (see http://www.wssinfo.org). The JMP considers the following as improved sanitation: connection to a public sewer; connection to a septic system; pour-flush latrine; simple pit latrine; ventilated improved pit latrine. Public or shared latrines, open pit latrines and bucket latrines do not qualify as improved. However, it must be stated that these official definitions are contested and controversial, and may not take into account local people's own cultural perceptions and standards of what does or does not work for them (see Mehta and Movik 2014).

3   Sanitation is included under MDG 7 – Environment, Water and Sanitation – which sets the target of 'halving by 2015, the proportion of people without sustainable access to safe drinking water and basic sanitation' (http://www.un.org/millenniumgoals/environ.shtml, accessed July 2014). It was not even explicitly mentioned as an MDG in 2000, and was added to the water MDG at the 2002 Earth Summit in Johannesburg as a result of intense political pressure.

of scale, where one of the most personal and individual acts – defecation – moves beyond the governance of one's own body and practice. In recent years sanitation has moved from being 'the last taboo' (Black and Fawcett 2008) and into the discourse of larger political arenas. For example, the United Nations declared 2008 the International Year of Sanitation and the *British Medical Journal* voted sanitation as the greatest medical advance in the last 166 years (BBC 2007).

The focus on sanitation at higher scales of governance has prompted the global application of community-based initiatives such as Community-Led Total Sanitation (CLTS). CLTS has led to thousands of low-cost latrines and toilets springing up all around the global South, from South-East Asia to Africa and beyond.[4] Usually built by villagers and barefoot innovators out of local materials such as bamboo, tin and jute, the resulting 'open defecation free' (ODF) villages have led to a decrease in waterborne diseases associated with open defecation practices. These new installations have been accompanied by a changed discourse in societal perceptions of open defecation. Talking about 'shit' and building ODF villages has produced a noticeably increased sense of pride about toilet possession, self-confidence through newly gained dignity, health benefits and freedom from the shame caused by the lack of privacy, especially for women. Additionally, it has also led to women and girls feeling more secure and not having to face the risks of gender violence during trips to the fields at night (Kar and Pasteur 2005; Mehta and Movik 2011). CLTS has been a breakthrough in sanitation governance; it differs from earlier approaches to sanitation which prescribed high initial standards in order to reduce the costs of operation and maintenance. These involved upfront hardware subsidies in order to induce people to use the latrines or toilets. However, instead of adoption, toilets were often either not used or else used for other purposes such as storage, and there were also problems of affordability. CLTS shifts scales of sanitation from the individual to the community by advocating not for individual household toilet construction but instead for ODF villages and communities. Community-scale sanitation is critical because even partial sanitation does not lead to minimizing the adverse effects of open defecation (see Kar 2005; Kar and Pasteur 2005; Kar and Chambers 2008).

Kamal Kar (a development consultant from India) pioneered CLTS in 2000 in north-west Bangladesh together with the Village Education Resource Centre (VERC), a partner of WaterAid Bangladesh. Kar, an agricultural and livestock scientist, used his background in participatory approaches to persuade the local non-governmental organization (NGO) to stop top-down toilet construction through subsidy. He advocated a change in institutional attitudes and the need to draw on intense local mobilization and facilitation to enable villagers to analyse their sanitation and waste situation and to bring about collective decision-making to stop open defecation.

---

4   A latrine usually refers to a direct pit, whereas a toilet has some kind of a water seal. I tend to use the term toilet in order to highlight the dignity of using a sanitary arrangement, regardless of its level of sophistication.

The case of CLTS is interesting because it spans a range of scales: from the most intimate – namely the human body and the daily cultural practices and understandings of shit and defecation – to the politics of how sanitation is or is not taken up in a range of institutional settings, from local village or district institutions to national ministries and global institutions seeking solutions to the global sanitation 'crisis'. It speaks to the wider themes in this volume by showing how these hydrosocial (or 'sanisocial') dynamics are multiscalar – ranging from the individual (the body) and community (public health) to the state (through programme incentives).

Since its inception in rural Bangladesh in 2000 the CLTS approach is now practised in approximately 50 countries. According to the CLTS Foundation, more than 85,000 villages around the world have reached ODF status, with over 25 million people benefiting directly or indirectly from improved health and sanitary conditions as a result of CLTS.[5]

CLTS has the makings of a development 'success story'. The 'proliferation of success' is usually referred to as 'scaling up', 'going big' or 'universal coverage over an indefinite period of time' (Deak 2008: 13). However, decisions around sanitation governance (like water governance) are deeply political across a range of scales. Scale matters in determining the long-term sustainability and viability of a 'successful' intervention such as CLTS. As CLTS has gone 'global' it has been constantly rescaled, and there is huge diversity around the range of organizational and institutional arrangements deployed in scaling up, raising challenges for ensuring sustainability and equity. As with every development intervention, there is a danger that accounts of success may be exaggerated, but through the CLTS case this chapter highlights the process and challenges of taking a successful local innovation to scale. The CLTS story offers many lessons on scaling up effectively, which include addressing the quality (of scaling up CLTS) versus quantity (i.e. counting toilets); institutional, environmental and social sustainability; inclusion and equity as well as addressing long-term risks and uncertainties across multiple scales. This chapter outlines the approach, its key principles and how it differs from conventional sanitation interventions, and discusses how and why CLTS has spread so rapidly around the globe. It then turns to the dynamics of scaling up in diverse contexts, and finally addresses the challenges of scaling up with quality while maintaining a focus on inclusion and sustainability.

The Approach

At the heart of CLTS lies the recognition that in the past many sanitation projects were unsuccessful in meeting their goals because they assumed that the provision of subsidized toilets would result in improved sanitation and hygiene. Unlike water provision – which often requires expensive, centrally managed, large-scale infrastructure – sanitation is largely about achieving changes in people's

---

5   http://www.cltsfoundation.org (accessed 11 June 2013).

behaviour and sanitation practices.[6] However, old habits die hard. It is difficult to give up the accustomed practice of shitting in one's favourite spot in the fields or by the river early in the morning for a pit, which could be small and smelly. Thus, it is important to focus on the behavioural issues at stake, as well as cultural habits and practices. CLTS is based on the premise that once people are convinced of the need for sanitation, they will construct their own toilets according to the resources available (financial, land, technology and so on). This approach does not require high subsidies for toilet construction from governments or external agencies, though it must be borne in mind that financial and institutional support is required for facilitation, monitoring, evaluation and mobilization.

CLTS focuses on building on individual or collective 'triggers' that promote behaviour change. The principle here is a 'sanitary mirror' that enables individuals to see the potential disease pathways and health risks associated with current practice. Important here also is how population density most likely plays into framing open defecation as unsanitary. In this case the politics of scale is also the politics of density: the more people in a defined area, the greater disease vectors and pathways. In earlier times when fewer people inhabited an area, disease vectors would be noticeably fewer. The ability to 'see' disease pathways leads to an ignition process that should result in collective behaviour change (see Kar 2005; Kar and Pasteur 2005; Kar and Chambers 2008).

CLTS uses participatory methods: community members analyse their own sanitation profile, including the extent of open defecation and the spread of faecal-oral contamination that adversely affects every one of them. This is believed to cause an upsurge of various emotions in the community, including feelings of shame, embarrassment and disgust. Community members are supposed to realize, collectively, the health consequences of open defecation. The realization that they are quite literally ingesting one another's shit mobilizes them to initiate collective local action to improve the sanitation situation in the community (Kar 2005; Kar and Pasteur 2005; Kar and Chambers 2008).

The CLTS process is often triggered by an informal talk with a few community members during a walk through the village (a 'transect walk'), the aim being to motivate the people to carry out a more substantial sanitation analysis involving the whole community. There are many different ways of initiating a discussion on open defecation and village sanitation, for example by visiting places where people defecate and raising questions like Whose shit is this?, or Who defecated in the open this morning? Throughout the facilitation process, local and crude words for 'shit' and 'shitting' are used rather than the more polite terms often used when discussing these taboo subjects. Other methods include calculating the amount of excrement produced in the village every day and mapping defecation areas. CLTS refrains from telling people what they should do. Instead, the process seeks to

---

    6   But of course infrastructure matters in sanitation too, especially with regard to waste management and sewage treatment particularly in urban and peri-urban areas where decentralized options are not always possible.

encourage innovative and locally driven solutions to address open defecation –
such as the construction of low-cost toilets using local materials.

Once individuals within the community have started to make changes in relation
to open defecation, facilitators can aid the process by fuelling their enthusiasm,
for example by telling them that if they achieved 100 per cent total sanitation and
stopped open defecation many people from outside and neighbouring villages would
visit their village to see the results. 'Ignition' takes place when a large majority in
the village decides to stop open defecation. Governments in many countries now
provide incentives and rewards once a village becomes ODF. Once a village has been
successfully 'triggered', changes can take place in a matter of days, weeks or months,
and can have a dramatic effect on individual and collective well-being. CLTS has
often also spread organically through local agents of change, which could include:

- CLTS 'natural leaders' who take their messages to neighbouring villages
  that are keen to emulate the achievements of a successful CLTS village;
- children who pass on the message to their friends at school;
- women who refuse to marry into a household without a toilet;
- religious leaders such as imams who promote cleanliness messages through
  their sermons.

This is why some people have called CLTS a 'self-spreading' movement (Deak
2008) (See Figures 13.1 and 13.2).

Figure 13.1   Toilet made with local materials in northwest Bangladesh

Figure 13.2   Woman constructing her own toilet in a CLTS village, Bangladesh

Sustaining Behavioural Change and Targeting the Poor

Governance is influenced greatly by the politics of scale. For sanitation, behavioural change at the individual level is of great importance. It is usually notoriously difficult to initiate and sustain, and many authors argue that there are very few examples of truly successful interventions where the measure of success is acceptable, affordable, effective, sustainable and generalizable (see Panter-Brick et al. 2006; Loevinsohn 1990; Howe et al. 2011; Mahbub 2011). This is why – unlike most of the water governance innovations discussed in this volume – changes in sanitation practices first need to take place at the individual and community level. While CLTS also struggles with issues concerning sustainability and inclusion (which will be discussed shortly), it is known to achieve results quicker than conventional approaches due to its insistence on collective behavioural change. The triggering exercise can motivate swift toilet construction, and the presence of spontaneous or 'natural' leaders or a dynamic local champion (e.g. a village head, health expert or enthusiastic administrator) can help galvanize energy in achieving ODF communities.

Unanticipated positive benefits to villages that become ODF also go beyond sanitation: for example changes in behaviour related to the storage and use of drinking water; hand-washing; the use of soap; and improved food hygiene (Mehta and Movik 2011). CLTS could fall into what is often considered to be 'radical' health education (Gastaldo 1997) through its focus on self-analysis, community empowerment and community action to end open defecation. Empowerment has been a key feature of the work of some CLTS implementers, and CLTS helps achieve this in a relatively short time in communities. The CARE project *Nijeder Janya Nijera* (We, For Ourselves) in Bangladesh aims to build solidarity through collective action, with the overall objective of helping local women to articulate their own vision of development and to strengthen their capacity to act in pursuit of their self-defined goals (Kanji et al. 2006). As sanitation activities progress, facilitators work on a well-being analysis of the community to gain a better sense of the livelihood strategies of various socio-economic groups within that community. Examples of initiatives that may follow on from CLTS activities include negotiating better wages, road repair, confronting corruption and pro-poor share-rearing of livestock.

Although CLTS's radical approach to tackling behavioural change has stimulated initial change, difficulties remain in sustaining the approach for several reasons. First, poor facilitation, verification and monitoring could contribute to a false sense of success. In many cases, 100 per cent ODF may never have been achieved in the first place due to weak monitoring and verification systems, the exaggeration of success, an overreliance on targets and flawed reward systems (especially in India). Second, there are many constraints faced by poor women and men alike in terms of resources, time and capacity with respect to their daily hygiene and sanitation practices (see Tabuchi 2002; Howe et al. 2011). In villages without much social cohesion and where special efforts have not been made to address the interests of the poor, a change in behaviour of the whole population may not be achievable: for example, children are scared of dark spaces and can fall into pits. Third, there is a tendency to lose sight of the role of water in the context of both livelihood strategies and in acting as a constraint towards toilet construction and use. In a village in Himachal Pradesh, women said it was impossible to continue using their toilets with such an unreliable water supply and with such a long walk to the stream. Dry toilets did not appeal to them culturally.

What about the poorest of the poor? CLTS has been both praised and damned due to its stance on subsidies. In India in particular there are highly charged debates around the role of subsidies in sanitation (Sanan 2011). CLTS advocates a 'no hardware subsidy' position because subsidies in the past have not led to local community ownership and toilet usage.[7] CLTS instead encourages people to help themselves and, if necessary, the rich contribute and help the poor (Kar and Chambers 2008). This position has been welcomed by those aware of the litany of unused toilets and of no significant increase in toilet use as a result of top-down campaigns in the 1980s and 1990s. Furthermore, as development specialists are

---

7   In practice, indirect forms of subsidy take place all the time. The collective reward to a village at the end of the intervention could be seen as a form of subsidy. Even the principle of the no upfront hardware subsidy is often bent in practice. For example, CLTS-inspired programmes in Bangladesh and India sometimes provide help to those below the poverty line to avoid elite capture.

aware, it is very difficult to target the poorest of the poor. Instead, many not-so-poor and more articulate and powerful individuals end up benefiting from any subsidy.

CLTS is sometimes considered to be 'anti-poor' by NGOs and many government officials. In part, this is due to an existing deeply entrenched subsidy regime in development projects and because critics feel that the rich will not cross-subsidize the poor, who will invariably lose out. The overenthusiastic embrace of communitarian values on the part of CLTS proponents could also appear to be rather naive because in reality the interests of the poor tend to be neglected. Invariably, in every so-called successful community some groups may be left out. They tend to be discriminated groups such disabled people, those from lower castes or minority communities, impoverished widows, female-headed households and so on. There are wider questions about the role of the state and how CLTS fits in with people's basic right to sanitation, which often calls for strong state action. Also it could imply a rural bias because in urban areas there is no way to implement CLTS –urban people cannot manage their waste disposal and sewage systems without strong state action and funding – and urban areas arguably have some of the most compelling sanitation problems.

CLTS discourses often tend to draw on a rather idealized notion of 'community', which in reality is usually conflict-ridden and moulded by gender, power and patron/client relations and inequalities. This need not only be in South Asia, which is riddled with caste inequalities, but also in parts of Africa where much power rests with chiefs. The community is rarely problematized in CLTS discourses, as has been done in the literature on community-based natural resource management and participatory development (see Guijt and Shah 1998). Based on extensive field research, I suggest that while CLTS proponents are certainly not anti-poor, in some cases marginalized people have been left out of CLTS programmes. This is because poverty has often prevented the most marginalized from constructing new toilets and/or rebuilding them after they collapse (see Haq and Bode 2011; Howe et al. 2011). However, doling out wide-scale subsidies and creating top-down target-driven approaches as in India is also no solution where 600 million people continue to defecate in the open (JMP 2013). Thus, while CLTS interventions (when they work) are more sustainable and empowering than top-down government, target-driven approaches, empirical research reveals that flexible arrangements are necessary to ensure that the poorest of the poor are not excluded. In other words, the poorest of the poor may need some additional help without which they will either never abandon open defecation or will revert to open defecation once their toilets can no longer be used.

Even though CLTS has moved away from the top-down expert-dominated behaviour change approach to 'participation', this does not mean that it totally avoids the exercise of control (Gastaldo 1997). Normalizing the new behaviour now takes places in a participatory way rather than through top-down education. Instead of professionals putting forward their views, community members can create new norms that should be used, and this could constitute a new form of control (ibid.). Control could take place through ostracizing groups. For example, in Ethiopia non-adopters are not allowed to participate in *Edir*, a key community organization for local well-being; and in rural Bangladesh fines are imposed, and children blow whistles and spy on those shitting in the open. The 'shaming' aspects of CLTS could also be a form of social control potentially harmful to marginalized people. However, multi-country research finds that sanctions, control and monitoring do not last very long (Mehta and Movik 2011). Rather, these techniques tend to be lifted either after the village attains ODF status or after the momentum of the programme has died down, which again highlights the challenge of sustaining behaviour change. Behaviour change is also an ongoing challenge in other resource management issues. For example, it is problematic in many certified and user-controlled green buildings, as once the buildings are certified, they are not monitored to ensure users are engaged in 'sustainable' practices.

Institutional Dynamics and the Politics of Scaling Up

While CLTS chimes well with debates on 'bottom-up' and grassroots or participatory approaches to development, clearly the state and various actors play important roles in scaling up. As described below, in many countries the state has played a key role and is often needed for large-scale impacts and institutionalization. CLTS demonstrates that there is tremendous diversity; in any given context NGOs may take the lead, or it may be an entirely state-driven process.

Since its emergence in rural Bangladesh in early 2000, CLTS has spread remarkably fast across Asia and subsequently to Africa, the Middle East and Latin America. This spread has been through both NGO and government processes, and its champions have been dynamic grassroots activists, state bureaucrats and members of NGOs and donor communities. The Water and Sanitation Programme (WSP) initially played an important role in enabling the spread of CLTS to neighbouring India and to Indonesia and parts of Africa; and UNICEF, arguably the major player among the relevant aid agencies, also turned around its policies and practices in 2008 to support CLTS and similar community-based approaches to sanitation. NGOs such as Plan and WaterAid have also played a crucial role, and CLTS is now being implemented in diverse ways in more than 50 countries.

The adoption of CLTS is a result of key individuals, organizations and priorities. For example, a major factor in its growth is its charismatic pioneer, Kamal Kar, who rolled out CLTS in many countries. Other key aspects include exposure visits between countries organized by the WSP and governments. These have served not only as learning opportunities but have also convinced governments, NGOs and others to try CLTS and have provided evidence that it can work. The UK's Department for International Development (DFID) played a key role in the uptake and spread of CLTS in South Asia, and UNICEF's contribution to the spread across Africa has been significant. International NGOs have also played an important role in sharing experience of CLTS with their different regional and country programmes. Good examples include Plan Region of Eastern and Southern Africa

(RESA), which has built on Plan's positive experiences with CLTS in Bangladesh; and WaterAid, which has facilitated exposure visits not only to Bangladesh but also between its various African programmes. Learning platforms such as the CLTS website and the Kolkata-based CLTS Foundation have also played an important role in allowing for exchanges and learning across different contexts, organizations and countries.[8] Regional conferences on sanitation in Asia and Africa have also served as platforms to launch CLTS and have facilitated learning between donors, government officials, researchers and practitioners.

While some 'universals' in CLTS exist – for example the community must lead the process and the entire community should be open defecation free (ODF) – it remains contextualist. Today there is tremendous diversity in CLTS approaches and practices around the world, and the contexts vary from country to country. To demonstrate this diversity of scaling up and spread, let us focus on the three countries where CLTS originally took root: Bangladesh, India and Indonesia.[9] In Bangladesh where CLTS originated, going to scale began with NGOs such as VERC – along with support from WaterAid, CARE, the Dhaka Ahsania Mission (DAM), Plan Bangladesh and others – before becoming part of a nationwide government campaign. A unique feature was the umbrella organization Dishari, a coalition between DAM, Plan, WaterAid and WSP that worked full time on CLTS implementation, coordinating efforts between local government and communities.

In India, CLTS is a purely state-driven effort and the context is the government's Total Sanitation Campaign (TSC). A unique feature is the Nirmal Gram Puraskar (NGP) award, which is given to rural local governments that achieve total sanitation and open defecation free status. However, the NGP can be seen as a 'perverse incentive' counteracting CLTS efforts, as it has led to other target-/toilet-driven top-down initiatives rather than community-led processes; and as already discussed, almost 60 per cent of the world's open defecators live in India.

In Indonesia, the prime mover has been the government, which piloted and implemented CLTS through its Water and Sanitation for Low Income Communities Phase 2 (WSLIC II) project in South Sumatra and West Java, funded by the World Bank and AusAID. The fact that the Ministry of Health championed the project has made a big difference. In addition, the WSP has been rolling out the Total Sanitation and Sanitation Marketing (TSSM) programme in East Java, which combines CLTS with sanitation marketing approaches.

Recognizing the variable institutional context per country is key to CLTS implementation. CLTS often begins as an NGO- or donor-driven process and is then gradually transferred to a regular government programme in the course of scaling up and out. Going to scale usually requires institutionalization processes and high-level support from government agencies and champions. Once CLTS becomes part of a national programme or campaign, donors or NGOs are

---

8   http://www.communityledtotalsanitation.org; http://www.cltsfoundation.org.

9   It should be noted that CLTS is largely a rural movement, except for a few scattered cases such as Kalyani and Nanded in India and in Nairobi.

required to change their roles from implementing agency to supporting agency. CLTS success is often due to the presence of high-profile champions within state agencies and institutions who spend considerable time on its promotion. These are often highly charismatic individuals, and when they move to other positions the momentum they have built can die down somewhat. Taking CLTS to scale also means that messages can be diluted and proper facilitation is compromised.

The success of CLTS often relies on finding an appropriate institutional home. Joshi (2011) found that in Indonesia and Ethiopia, the Ministry of Health proved to be an effective avenue to lead such an effort. Still, support from other government departments (e.g. finance, water resources, public works etc.) and non-governmental entities – in addition to communities – is necessary for the programme to succeed. Another challenge to CLTS is the frequent transfer of officials, which threatens the continuity of CLTS.

To enable the spread of CLTS, governments may introduce targets and reward systems which could lead to a false sense of achievement. There is also often pressure to disburse hardware subsidies which may not necessary lead to individual ownership of toilets. As discussed earlier, key challenges in going to scale remain verification, monitoring and evaluation. Largely the verification of success has tended to be arbitrary and good monitoring and follow-up systems are still required to ensure the sustainability of CLTS (Mehta and Movik 2011). This could take place through facilitators, local government or community leaders. In the drive to achieve targets, reward systems such as huge cash prizes to ODF communities can inflate indications of success and lead to capture by elites (as is often the case in India). It is also unclear whether or for how long any change in behaviour is sustained once the reward has been obtained.

Despite its emphasis on behavioural change, CLTS implementation through government programmes and NGO projects means that success is often still counted in terms of the number of toilets constructed. Thus there are trade-offs between the degree of institutionalization and the nature of CLTS as an inherently community-based approach (Priyono 2011). Messages about behaviour change and empowerment can sometimes get lost in the process, and indicators of CLTS success frequently revert to easily measurable quantities such as toilets. Governments and donors want and need to measure the progress that they have achieved and to demonstrate 'value for money', but this can compromise the overall quality and integrity of CLTS. CLTS demands a switch in mindset, with a focus on people rather than hardware such as toilets. Donors and government officials are often reluctant to embrace this change, and are still focused on the pressure to spend and disburse money rather than on key issues such as sustainability and behavioural change. The bureaucratic requirement to achieve targets and spend budgets wisely thus severely compromises the quality of CLTS and how it is taken to scale.

Socio-Political and Cultural Challenges

Community-Led Total Sanitation can be time-intensive, and its stated goal of community empowerment is often easier to achieve in smaller, homogenous villages handpicked by NGOs; in other words, it may be more difficult in heterogeneous communities. Empowerment may not necessarily be a goal in government-driven processes which often focus on targets. Many government-driven campaigns in India, Indonesia and Ethiopia do not involve intense social mobilization and facilitation. Here, extension workers from the district or community health workers might enter communities and provide training and directions. Such a diluted form of CLTS would probably not be different from top-down models of behavioural change. Many NGOs too might find that the quality of their facilitation and mobilization declines due to the compulsion of going to scale, which will compromise their use of intense participatory approaches in the field. There is thus the wider question of whether CLTS can be truly empowering when it goes to scale.

There are of course cultural and other challenges of moving CLTS across continents. For example, in many African countries South Asian notions of 'shaming' or using the word 'shit' may not be appropriate, and other more locally appropriate ways to ignite communities are required. Religious beliefs and practices also have an impact in terms of triggering and sustaining behaviour change and the choice of technology in subtle ways – e.g. Muslims leaders drawing on notions of purity before worship to promote ODF and CLTS in their communities. Overall though, the key messages of CLTS are universal enough and can be adapted to work across a range of cultural contexts. The massive spread and uptake of CLTS means that in practice there is no one 'pure' version and discursive battles regarding what CLTS is or is not are not uncommon among those who call themselves CLTS enthusiasts or proponents.[10]

A body of research has now demonstrated that CLTS also appears to be most successful when champions are present (at village or state level) and/or when local facilitation and mobilization are of high quality and time-intensive (Mehta and Movik 2011). CLTS takes off best in countries where training is sustained and of good quality, involving successful hands-on triggering in communities in real time (Kar 2010), and where there is general approval from the government and no history of individual hardware subsidy (e.g. Indonesia, Pakistan). At the community level, CLTS works best where communities are cohesive and efforts are made to address the interests of the poor and the marginalized. In the absence of these factors CLTS may not take off.

CLTS, Incertitude and Long-Term Environmental Impacts

In the rush to scale up CLTS, some crucial long-term risks can be ignored (see Movik 2011). Long-term change in behaviour leads to new practices which

---

10   See various chapters in Mehta and Movik (2011).

can have unknown impacts. For example, there is the risk of both surface and groundwater contamination due to the increased concentration of toilets in a small area (ibid.). Preliminary research in Maharashtra, India, indicated that CLTS could contaminate the groundwater if the toilets were not constructed properly (see Khale and Dyalchand 2001), but of course much depends on several contingent factors such as soil type, flow of groundwater, vegetation and precipitation. Often declarations and certifications of ODF are seen as an endpoint instead of the start of a new process. After the initial momentum dies out, local people can slip back to old patterns of open defecation. Thus, it is important to understand both post-ODF dynamics in CLTS communities and how and whether communities have moved up the sanitation ladder. Technology matters, and needs to be sustainable and appropriate to local situations. Finally, it is notoriously difficult to provide conclusive links between toilet construction and improved health outcomes. There are several intervening factors – including breastfeeding, maternal health, nutrition, groundwater quality, poverty, living conditions – which make causal linkages difficult. All these issues require reflection and some stepping back, and can be somewhat compromised in the current global momentum around CLTS.

Conclusion

This chapter has focused on several aspects of sanitation governance, which tends to have a different logic to water governance but bears important insights into how governance and the politics of scale influence each other. Sanitation projects do not carry the same links with power and prestige that water infrastructure ones do, and sanitation has long been regarded as the poor cousin of water. At the local level, toilets, when built, are often not used; and for the most part sanitation programmes have been top-heavy and have failed to make significant progress, thus making sanitation one of the most off-track Millennium Development Goals, especially in sub-Saharan Africa. In this respect, CLTS offers a new approach and has also succeeded in making 'shit' more 'sexy' for policymakers and NGOs. The concept has spread remarkably quickly in a short time and has the makings of a development success story.

The CLTS story also has important lessons for scaling up. It highlights how rescaling depends on a range of institutional, social, cultural and political factors; and, indeed, experiences of CLTS have been truly diverse in different contexts. However, it is important not to be totally seduced by the rapid uptake and scaling up of CLTS. In its second decade, attention needs to be paid to achieving long-term behavioural change, inclusion, and gender and social equity – scaling up with quality, institutional, environmental and social sustainability – as well as addressing both long-term risks and uncertainties across multiple scales.

References

BBC News. 2007. Sanitation 'best medical advance'. 18 January [Online] http://news.bbc.co.uk/1/hi/health/6275001.stm [accessed 19 August 2010].

Black, M. and Fawcett, B. 2008. *The Last Taboo: Opening the Door on the Global Sanitation Crisis*, London: Earthscan.

Cairncross, S. 2003. Water supply and sanitation: some misconceptions, *Tropical Medicine and International Health* 8(3), 193–5.

Chambers, R. 2009. *Going to Scale with Community-Led Total Sanitation: Reflections on Experience, Issues and Ways Forward.* IDS Practice Paper 1. Brighton: Institute of Development Studies.

Deak, A. 2008. *Taking Community-Led Total Sanitation to Scale: Movement, Spread and Adaption.* IDS Working Paper 298: Brighton: Institute of Development Studies.

Douglas, M. 1966. *Purity and Danger: An Analysis of Concepts of Pollution and Taboo.* New York: Praeger.

Esrey, S.A. 1996. Water, waste, and well-being: A multicountry study, *American Journal of Epidemiology* 143, 608–23.

Fewtrell L., Kaufmann R.B., Kay D., Enanoria W., Haller L. and Colford J.M. Jr. 2005. Water, sanitation, and hygiene interventions to reduce diarrhoea in less developed countries: A systematic review and meta-analysis, *Lancet Infectious Diseases* 1, 42–52.

Gastaldo, D. 1997. Is health education good for you? Re-thinking health education through the concept of bio-power. In A. Peterson and R. Bunton (eds), *Foucault: Health and Medicine.* London: Routledge, 113–33.

Guijt, I. and Shah, M.K. 1998. *The Myth of Community: Gender Issues in Participatory Development.* London: Intermediate Technology Publications.

Haq, A. and Bode, B. 2011. The challenges of facilitating CLTS. In L. Mehta and S. Movik (eds), *Shit Matters: The Potential for Community-Led Total Sanitation.* Rugby: Practical Action, 71–84.

Howes, M., Huda, E. and Naser, A. 2011. NGOs and the implementation of CLTS in Bangladesh: Selected case studies. In L. Mehta and S. Movik (eds), *Shit Matters: The Potential for Community-Led Total Sanitation.* Rugby: Practical Action, 53–69.

JMP (Joint Monitoring Programme). 2013. *JMP Report on Progress on Sanitation and Drinking Water, 2010 Update.* [Online] http://www.wssinfo.org/datamining/introduction.html [accessed 28 July 2010].

Joshi, A. 2011. CLTS in India and Indonesia: Institutions, incentives and politics. In L. Mehta and S. Movik (eds), *Shit Matters: The Potential for Community-Led Total Sanitation.* Rugby: Practical Action, 191–204.

Kanji, N., Bode, B. and Haq, A. 2006. *Nijeder Janyia Nijera (We for Ourselves): Strategic Impact Inquiry.* Bangladesh: CARE Bangladesh.

Kar, K. 2010. *Facilitating 'Hands-On' Training: Workshops for Community-Led Total Sanitation: A Trainers' Training Guide*. Geneva: CLTS Foundation/ Water Supply and Sanitation Collaborative Council (WSSCC).

Kar, K. 2005. *Practical Guide to Triggering Community-Led Total Sanitation (CLTS)*. Brighton: Institute of Development Studies.

Kar, K. and Chambers, R. 2008. *Handbook on Community-Led Total Sanitation*. London: Plan UK.

Kar, K. and Pasteur, K. 2005. *Subsidy or Self-Respect? Community-Led Total Sanitation: An Update on Recent Developments (including reprint of IDS Working Paper 184)*. IDS Working Paper 257. Brighton: Institute of Development Studies.

Khale, M and Dyalchand, A. 2011. The impact of rural sanitation on water quality and waterborne diseases. In L. Mehta and S. Movik (eds), *Shit Matters: The Potential of Community-Led Sanitation*. Rugby: Practical Action, 115–31.

Loevinsohn, B.P. 1990. Health education interventions in developing countries: A methodological review of published articles. *International Journal of Epidemiology*, 19, 788–94.

Mahbub, M. 2011. Exploring the social dynamics of CLTS in Bangladesh: The inclusion of children, women and vulnerable people. In L. Mehta and S. Movik (eds), *Shit Matters: The Potential for Community-Led Total Sanitation*. Practical Action Publishing, 39–51.

Mehta, L. 2011. Introduction. Why shit matters: Community-led total sanitation and the sanitation challenge for the 21st century. In L. Mehta and S. Movik (eds), *Shit Matters: The Potential of Community-Led Sanitation*, Rugby: Practical Action, 1–25.

Mehta, L. and Movik, S. 2014. Liquid dynamics: Challenges for sustainability in the water domain. *Wiley Interdisciplinary Reviews: Water*, 1(4), 369–84.

Mehta, L. and Movik, S. 2011 (eds). *Shit Matters: The Potential of Community-Led Total Sanitation*. Rugby: Practical Action.

Movik, S. 2011. The dynamics and sustainability of CLTS: Mapping challenges and pathways. In L. Mehta L and S. Movik (eds), *Shit Matters: The Potential of Community-Led Total Sanitation*, 231–45.

Panter-Brick, C., Clarke, S.E., Lomas, H., Pinder, M. and Lindsay, S.W. 2006. Culturally compelling strategies for behaviour change: A social ecology model and case study in malaria prevention. *Social Science and Medicine*, 62(11), 2810–25.

Peterson, A. and Bunton, R. 1997. *Foucault: Health and Medicine*, London: Routledge.

Priyoni, E. 2011. Institutional dimensions of scaling up CLTS in Indonesia. In L. Mehta and S. Movik (eds), *Shit Matters: The Potential for Community-Led Total Sanitation*. Rugby: Practical Action, 175–88.

Sanan, D. 2011. The CLTS story in India: The sanitation story of the Millennium. In L. Mehta and S. Movik (eds), *Shit Matters: The Potential for Community-Led Total Sanitation*. Rugby: Practical Action, 87–100.

Tabuchi, H. 2002. 'It's what's between your ears, not where you s(h)it': A critical analysis of discourses of health and hygiene. MPhil dissertation, University of Sussex.

UNDP. 2006. *Human Development Report*. New York: United Nations Development Programme.

WaterAid. 2007. *Community Led Total Sanitation (CLTS): An Evaluation of the WaterAid's CLTS Programme in Nigeria*. WaterAid.

Water Aid. 2009. *Sustainability and Equity Aspects of Total Sanitation Programmes: A Study of Recent WaterAid-Supported Programmes in Three Countries*. Global Synthesis Report, http://www.wateraid.org/documents/plugin_documents/clts_synthesis_report.pdf [accessed 20 August 2010].

WSP. 2004. *The Case for Marketing Sanitation: Field Note*. Nairobi: Water and Sanitation Program (World Bank).

WSP. 2009. *Global Scaling up Sanitation Project. Second Annual Progress Report: Indonesia, Tanzania and the States of Himachal Pradesh and Madhya Pradesh, India*. Washington DC: Water and Sanitation Program (World Bank).

Waterlines. 2009. Sustainable sanitation, *Waterlines* 28(4), October.

Zeitlyn, S. and Rowshan, R. 1997. Privileged knowledge and mothers' 'perceptions': The case of breast-feeding and insufficient milk in Bangladesh, *Medical Anthropology Quarterly*, 11(1), 56–68.

Chapter 14

Hydrosocial Governance and Agricultural Development in Semi-Arid Northwest China

Afton Clarke-Sather

Historically, the relationship between rainfall and the food peasants ate in the Zuli valley of northwest China was fairly straightforward.[1] Rain fell. It was absorbed by the soil *in situ*. Some of it evaporated. Some of it went to nourish the roots of crops. In general those crops – spring wheat, millet and pulses – fed those who tended them. The volume and timing of rainfall were the primary determinants of the success or failure of a harvest. However, over the past three decades this direct connection between rainfall and what people ate has been interrupted at several points by state-backed development interventions that have changed the way peasants relate to both agricultural water and food, and in the process rescaled the political, technical and economic institutions that mediate the relationship between people and water.

Three interventions have transformed how humans relate to agricultural water in the Zuli valley: state-backed irrigation; the introduction of cash crops suited to local hydro-climatological conditions, particularly potatoes; and the introduction of hybrid maize combined with plastic film mulches. What these three interventions share is an explicit aim to alter how peasants deal with shortages of agricultural water. Distinguishing between 'green' water and 'blue' water helps clarify how each of these interventions governed water (Falkenmark and Rockström 2006; Liu et al. 2009). Blue water is water that enters rivers or is pumped from the ground as groundwater. Green water is used *in situ* by plants, and re-enters the atmosphere through evapotranspiration. Green water generally does not enter discussions of water governance because we rarely see its biophysical manifestation. Yet green water accounts for 74 per cent of global water use by humans (Hoestra and Mekennon 2012), and its governance calls for greater scrutiny. This study examines how the management of green and blue water was rescaled between 1990 and 2010 in the Zuli valley (Figure 14.1).

That scalar processes of water governance relate differently to blue and green water resources is the first of four related arguments that this chapter will make. Second, in green water governance, the connection between the administrative

---

1   Throughout I will describe residents of the Zuli valley as both 'peasants' and 'farmers'. I use peasant because it is the direct translation of the Chinese word *nongmin* that residents of the Zuli valley use to describe themselves.

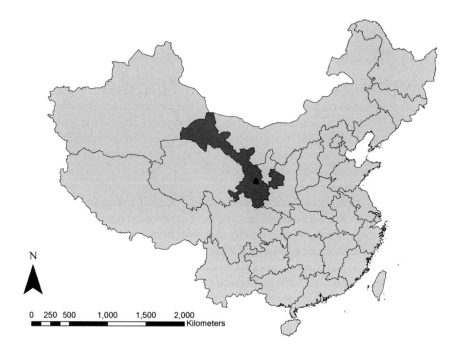

Figure 14.1   Map of the Zuli River valley, Gansu province, China

level policy intervention and the spatial extent of the social process being altered may not be aligned. In contrast, blue water resources in the case study have been rescaled to match the spatial extent of water governance with the territorial administration of water agencies. Third, rescalings of hydrosocial governance – again, particularly of green water resources – may involve simultaneously shifting water governance both up towards national institutions and down towards household institutions. Finally, the interventions that most profoundly rescaled hydrosocial governance are those that have not actively attempted to align water resources with a particular administrative level of governance. Instead, such rescalings have been born of contingency and expedience.

Background

Scale and Hydrosocial Governance

Throughout this study I discuss hydrosocial governance, rather than water governance, which I understand as the political mediation of humans' relationship to both blue and green water. In previous studies agricultural water governance has broadly been conceptualized as political elements of the allocation, distribution, of blue water resources (cf. Ostrom 1990; Dubash 2004; Baker 2008; Birkenholtz

2009). When turning our attention to green water governance in agriculture, it is instructive to look to the rubric of the hydrosocial cycle (Swyngedouw 1999; Bakker 2003; Linton 2010), which emphasizes that nature and society arc co-produced. When applied to agriculture, this approach shows that activities governing green water may be quite remote from the biophysical water used to grow crops.

As the work throughout this volume makes clear, scale has been a central yet contested concept in human geography over the past two decades, and has recently received increased scrutiny from scholars of water governance. While details of the recent debates surrounding the role of scale in human geography lie beyond the scope of this chapter, a central point of recent scholarship is that scale is not an ontologically pre-existing phenomenon, but is rather both socially and epistemologically constructed. This chapter takes as a point of engagement Moore's (2008) call to consider how scale is used, rather than what scale is. It shows how political actors actively *rescale* hydrosocial governance by shifting the scale at which both biophysical processes (i.e. basin management) and socioeconomic processes connecting humans and water occur. Rescaling hydrosocial governance also reconfigures power relations surrounding water, shifting who has access to and control of water resources.

Scale has several meanings, and the tensions between two of these meanings are central to this chapter. First, scale may refer to the administrative level of state governance (e.g. county, province). Although juridically constructed, administrative scales are actualized in political practice through state actors tasked with performing their jobs at those scales. Second, scale may describe the spatial extent of hydrosocial processes and relationships. This spatial extent may or may not be coincident with the administrative scale of state actors whose policies have created them.

Discussions of how scale is used in the water governance literature have generally examined blue water and have tended to take one of two approaches, both of which illustrate how rescaling water governance shifts power relationships. The first involves various forms of scaling up water governance, often as part of the 'state hydraulic paradigm' (Bakker 2003) associated with the high modernist ethos of the twentieth century (Scott 1998). Such studies examine how hydrosocial governance has been rescaled to match the administrative scale of state actors at the national (Swyngedouw 1999, 2007) and urban (Kaika 2006) levels. In such cases water is often physically moved to make the spatial extent of biophysical processes match the new scales of governance. The second approach involves scaling down governance by removing centralized power over water from the state actors and placing greater control at lower levels (Perreault 2005; Norman and Bakker 2009). Such devolution often attempts to match the scale of administrative governance to the spatial extent of biophysical processes (Cohen and Davidson 2011). This case study illustrates that in the governance of green water, rescaling may simultaneously move both up and down through contingent processes.

Hydrosocial Governance in China

The role of the state in managing water resources in China has long been central to conceptualizations of state power there, dating to Wittfogel's (1957) theory of Oriental Despotism. More recent scholars of water and the state have used the theory of fragmented authoritarianism (FA) to argue that while the Chinese state is authoritarian in nature, it is also divided into competing bureaucracies organized both vertically by function (*tiao*) and territorially by administrative level (*kuai*) (Lieberthal and Oksenberg 1990; Mertha 2008; Nickum 2010). The FA model of state power is an implicitly scalar one. *Kuai* can be conceptualized as administrative scales in the sense levels of territorial state governance. The FA model argues that state actors at different administrative levels will compete for relative power in social, political and economic processes. Outside the context of water, Shue (1990) and Oi (1991) have also illustrated how local governments in China compete with higher levels of administration. While the scales of governance (e.g. province, county) are socially constructed, their *effects* are quite real (see also Chapter 4). The FA model can then be understood in terms of Moore's argument that actors will aim to actively create scalar processes that benefit them. As state actors maximize resources at the scales where they operate, they may be viewed as creating *scaleness*.

A clear case of such scale making can be seen in blue water resources, which are governed through the functional bureaucracy (*tiao*) of the Ministry of Water Resources and its correlates at each level of government. State actors at each scale seek to expand and extend their control over water resources in ways that are congruent with the scalar configurations of state power (Lieberthal and Oksenberg 1990; Mertha 2008), a point I will later illustrate with respect to water irrigation. However, other functional ministries often have significant influence over water management as well. For example, the Ministry of Construction, which is charged with road building, has successfully opposed dam projects supported by the Ministry of Water Resources that would flood desirable bridge sites (Mertha 2008). I extend this literature by showing that when hydrosocial governance rather than water governance is considered, other functional bureaucracies, such as the Ministry of Agriculture, are involved at often competing scales.

Research Setting

The Zuli River valley, in eastern Gansu province, stretches approximately 80 km through the semi-arid Loess Plateau of the upper Yellow River basin. It is famous for two things: aridity and poverty. The Zuli valley lies on a 380 mm annual rainfall isopleth that divides rain-fed from irrigation agriculture in China (Wei et al. 2005). Due to the seasonal monsoon cycle of East Asia, 60 per cent of precipitation in the area falls between July and September, leaving crops vulnerable to drought early in the growing season (May and June) when water is most demanded by small grains (Wei et al. 2005). In addition to seasonal variation, the region experiences relatively high inter-annual variability in rainfall, making the success of crops unpredictable from one year to the next. Ground and surface water, outside a few areas detailed below, are also unusable for agriculture due to salinization. Because of these constraints, water is widely viewed as the limiting resource for agriculture in eastern Gansu, and is often linked to food (in)security. Over the past three decades, state actors have aimed to break this relationship through three distinct interventions that have changed the hydrosocial governance in agricultural production, the face of agriculture, in the Zuli valley: irrigation; the introduction of climate appropriate crops; and the introduction of maize.

Hydrosocial Interventions and Agrarian Change

I use *interventions* in this case study to mean policies and technologies, generally state-backed, that are intended to solve the problem of limited agricultural water. These interventions have included technologies to introduce new blue water sources; technologies to use water more efficiently; and policies to mediate the relationship between crop production and food. Each of the interventions discussed below has shifted the scale of hydrosocial governance by either shifting the scale at which biophysical water resources are managed, or through the introduction of socio-economic relationships at different scales that have direct bearing on how peasants relate to agricultural water.

Irrigation

Agricultural water governance is most often associated with blue water governance, particularly irrigation (Dubash 2004; Mollinga et al. 2007; Budds 2008; Perreault 2008; Birkenholtz 2009; Nickum 2010), and the Zuli valley is no exception. Irrigation projects in the valley can be divided into three different subtypes: basin-scale, groundwater and inter-basin.

In the late 1970s the Dingxi County Water Bureau (DCWB) implemented a basin-scale irrigation project in the Zuli valley. Following the failure of that project in the early 1990s due to siltation in seven of the eight reservoirs that constituted the project, the DCWB began a decentralized groundwater irrigation system in the upper reaches of the valley. Much smaller in scale, groundwater irrigation was initially used to support wheat, but later came to be used for commercial vegetable production. Finally, the Tao River Project – a major inter-basin transfer scheme, originally scheduled for completion in 2012 (Xinhua 2009) though presently at the time of writing – is promised as the panacea that will provide stable irrigation to the whole valley over the coming decades. Each of these irrigation systems aims to solve the problem of water scarcity in the Zuli valley by regulating blue water availability across larger spatial or temporal extents.

Potatoes: Going with Nature and the Seasons

The second major intervention in the agricultural hydrosocial relations of the Zuli valley has been the expansion of potatoes from part of a diversified cropping strategy into a cash crop. Growing potatoes does not require moving or altering blue water supplies in any way. Instead, potato agriculture solves the problem of water scarcity by attuning seasonal water demand to seasonal water availability. While summer grains (e.g. wheat) require water early in the growing season (May–June), potatoes require water later in the summer (July and August) (Shang 2007). With 60 per cent of annual precipitation in the area falling between July and September (Wei et al. 2005), potatoes seemed an ideal fit (Shang 2007; Yan 2008).

The introduction of potatoes can be understood as a deliberate form of hydrosocial governance to solve the problem of aridity in the Zuli valley's agriculture. In the late 1990s the local government began to formulate a plan to promote growing potatoes for the national market as a way to alleviate poverty in the region by solving the problem of aridity (Shang 2007; Yan 2008). The switch to potatoes was widely framed as adapting to the local weather conditions, with the slogan 'going with nature and the seasons' (*shunying tianshi*) (Shang 2007). Potato agriculture was promoted by a variety of state-backed interventions that created national markets for potatoes, including new marketing and storage facilities in two central towns and organized crop transportation to outside markets. These interventions introduced a new relationship to national scale markets that changed the ties between farmers and the food they ate.

Introduction of Maize

The final major intervention in agricultural hydrosocial relations has been the introduction of maize as an agricultural crop in the region. Maize is less labour-intensive and more profitable to grow than potatoes, but has not historically been grown in the region because peasants considered the possibility of crop failure too high. Since approximately 2005, however, three changes have facilitated the expansion of maize agriculture, each supported by state actors. First, plastic film mulches were introduced to retain soil moisture. Second, new varieties of maize were bred to be drought resistant. Finally, the arrival of maize was dependent upon the introduction of national and international markets for maize as a commodity.

The first change, thin plastic film mulches, biophysically intervenes in hydrosocial relations by preventing evaporation and by shifting that water use to productive transpiration – an example of 'vapour shift', which is a common green water management intervention (Hoff et al. 2010). In eastern Gansu, maize has historically suffered from crop failures early in the growing season (April–June). Plastic films allow the soil to retain enough moisture to last through a dry early summer (Li and Gong 2002). Mulches, which have been heavily subsidized by the local government, intervene in the maize agriculture by preventing the loss of soil moisture rather than the provision of water, and thus can be seen as a form of green water hydrosocial governance.

The second change that has facilitated maize agriculture in the Zuli River valley was the introduction of drought-resistant maize cultivars. Several drought-resistant maize varieties, the most prominent of which is called 'success ball' (*cheng dan*), have been introduced to the valley in the past decade. The choice of crops and seed varieties is an often underappreciated aspect of agricultural water governance, but the choices of crop varieties and cultivars may have profound impacts on green water use. Drought-resistant cultivars and plastic films enabled the creation of maize agriculture; but, like potatoes, maize has also required the introduction of markets at new scales to become a widespread crop.

The shift to maize agriculture, like potatoes, represents a green water strategy of hydrosocial governance. Plastic films, drought-resistant varieties and national markets are approaches that manage water *in situ* by more efficiently using soil moisture, rather than through the allocation or distribution of blue water.

The Result: Agricultural Hydrosocial Change

The three interventions presented above have facilitated a complete change in the nature of agriculture that is quite clear from responses to a 2010 survey of peasants in six villages in the Zuli Valley that asked how much land they dedicated to various crops in the past and present. Figure 14.2 illustrates the changes in the

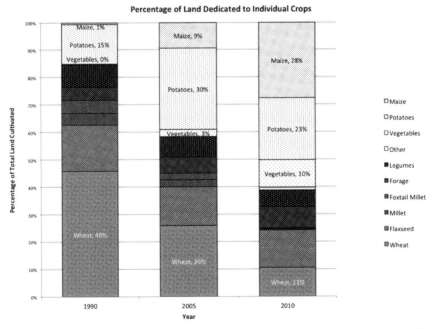

Figure 14.2 Percentage of land dedicated to crops in all villages in the Zuli valley study area

average percentage of each farmer's land dedicated to each crop across all of the surveyed villages. In 1990 the average household in the Zuli valley dedicated 85 per cent of its land to subsistence crops (defined as anything except potatoes, maize and vegetables) and 15 per cent to market crops (potatoes, maize and vegetables). While national markets exist for some of the crops grown on a subsistence basis (particularly wheat and legumes), their cultivation in this particular region has historically been mostly limited to subsistence-level production. By 2010, this allocation had changed to 60 per cent market crops and 40 per cent subsistence crops. The shift from subsistence to commercial crops was facilitated through the hydrosocial interventions detailed above. Each of these interventions also had the effect of rescaling agricultural hydrosocial governance by introducing new actors and new scalar power relationships.

Interventions and Rescaling

The three interventions described above – irrigation, climate-appropriate cash crops and maize agriculture – have rescaled both biophysical and social

Table 14. 1   Interventions in agricultural hydrosocial relations in the Zuli River valley

Intervention	Administrative Level of State Actor Making Decision	Spatial Extent of Social-Political Process	Green or Blue Water
Irrigation (basin-scale)	County Water Bureau	County/river valley	Blue
Irrigation (inter-basin)	Provincial Water Bureau	Multi-river basin	Blue
Irrigation (groundwater)	County Water Bureau (irrigation) Township government (cabbage marketing)	Very localized (irrigation) National (cabbage marketing)	Blue
Climate-appropriate cash crops	County government County Agriculture Ministry National Poverty Alleviation Office	National	Green
Maize agriculture	Township, county, and provincial agricultural authorities National Poverty Alleviation Office National seed-breeding infrastructure	Household (seed and planting decisions) National (commodity market integration)	Green

processes of water governance. Biophysically, irrigation shifted the scale of water governance from households to state-managed irrigation schemes. Socio-economically, the relationship between rainfall and food has come to be mediated by national markets, local government subsidies and a national infrastructure of plant breeding. Table 14.1 details the rescalings wrought by these policies.

Prior to the interventions discussed in this chapter, hydrosocial governance in the Zuli valley was primarily conducted at the household scale. There were few centralized irrigation systems, and none managed by the state. Agricultural water was managed as a green water resource: it was primarily used where it fell. Within these constraints, individual farmers made hydrosocial governance decisions that mitigated the risk of water shortage at different times of the year through a diverse cropping pattern that included crops demanding water in both the early and late summer growing season (roughly illustrated in the cropping pattern shown for 1990 in Figure 14.2). These governance decisions have been shifted to new scales as state actors introduced both blue and green water hydrosocial management cycles.

Irrigation

Irrigation projects in the Zuli valley have rescaled decisions about hydrosocial governance away from local households and towards scales coincident with the administrative level of the state actor developing the irrigation systems. In the process, agricultural water has been transformed from a green into a blue water resource. The introduction of irrigation marked the introduction of agricultural water as an abstract quantity that could be predicted, measured and allocated at new spatial extents. As Linton (2010) has pointed out, the abstraction of water – in the sense of making water into something calculable, measureable and interchangeable – was a central moment in the creation of modern water management. The quantification of water as a resource is not only an act of abstraction, but also abstraction *at a specific scale*. In the case of the Zuli valley, water has been abstracted as being either a basin-wide or a national resource.

Under basin scale irrigation (from the late 1970s to 1990), agricultural water went from being governed through household crop decisions to being governed at the scale of the river valley, a scale that was largely congruent with the administrative charge of the DCWB. The alignment of the spatial extent of hydrosocial governance and the territorial extent of the DCWB was driven by the model of state power at the time. Under the Chinese state's diffuse governance structure during the Maoist period, county level governments were encourage to operate autonomously from larger political organizations, resulting in a cellular structure with little incentive to operate across county boundaries (Shue 1988). The spatial extent of basin-scale irrigation in the Zuli valley followed this pattern, and was coincident with the territorial reach of the county water bureau.

The inter-basin Tao River Project (under construction at the time of writing in 2014) represents a similar rescaling, but on a much larger scale. This programme is a technologically intensive mega-project similar to those that have symbolized modernity and rescaled water governance towards centralized state actors the world over (Kaika 2006; Swyngedouw 2007). Under the Tao River Project, water is abstracted by state planners to the provincial level. The provincial-based engineers of the Tao basin transfer project conceptualized the water of the Tao River as a provincial resource that could be used to irrigate the Zuli basin as early as the 1950s, and construction was begun but was stopped during the difficulties of the Great Leap Forward at the end of that decade (Dikötter 2010). It was not until the 2000s that the provincial water ministry gained the technical and financial ability to convert the long-standing vision of water as a provincial resource, movable between basins, into a material reality.

Groundwater irrigation presents a slightly different case of rescaling. As with basin-scale irrigation, with groundwater irrigation agricultural water changed from a green water resource governed by households to a blue water resource governed by the DCWB. However, this irrigation scheme was conducted at a much smaller spatial extent than basin-scale or inter-basin irrigation (only about 700 acres total). Key informants in the DCWB expressed two primary reasons for the much smaller scale of groundwater irrigation. First, the DCWB views groundwater irrigation as something of a bridge solution until the Tao River Project can be completed. It allowed irrigation delivery systems to begin working while a long-term water source was still being developed. Second, the DCWB, acutely aware of the technical difficulties of large-scale projects, viewed groundwater irrigation as a programme that could be achieved in a realistic timeframe. Although the spatial extent of the project was much smaller than the territorial jurisdiction of the state institution governing water, its implementation was bounded by the technical constraints of the state actor.

When hydrosocial governance is considered more broadly, the development of groundwater irrigation involved additional state actors at different scales. Groundwater initially irrigated wheat, a subsistence crop, but by the late 2000s was redirected at cabbage, a cash crop. This shift toward irrigation water for cash crops arose from a deliberate policy decision made by the government of Neiguan, a neighbouring township in the upper valley not included in this study. Township leaders realized that the relatively cool and dry climate, along with new groundwater irrigation, made the upper valley well suited to cabbage production. The township's government built cold storage cellars that made Neiguan a centre for cabbage marketing in northwest China. While not directly involving water, these policy changes have profoundly influenced agricultural water management though more frequent irrigation. Although the state actor involved in promoting cabbage (Neiguan township) is of relatively low administrative level and limited territorial extent, its policies have spilled into other townships, shifting water management in administrative spaces it does not govern. In this case, the territorial jurisdiction of the state actor is quite different from the spatial extent of the hydrosocial processes it has created, a process we will see below with green water approaches to agricultural management.

Potatoes: National Markets as Hydrosocial Governance

As with cabbage, the introduction of climate-appropriate potato agriculture required a fundamental rescaling of how agricultural water related to peasants' food security that was primarily socio-economic. Potatoes have long been grown in the area as part of a household-scale hydrosocial governance strategy rooted in growing crops that demand water in both early and late summer. Commercial potato agriculture emphasizes growing a crop has late summer demand as a primary cash crop. With market potato agriculture, the previously direct link between rainfall and peasants' food security came to be mediated by national commodity markets, which are in turn supported by local state policies to promote trade. Potatoes are sold in national markets, and the wheat that peasants rely on for food is, in turn, purchased on a national market. Through the creation of national markets, a national-scale economic process mediated the relationship between agricultural water and food.

Integration with national markets was not an organic process, but rather the result of a series of specific policies of the county and prefecture governments, the agricultural ministry and national-scale poverty alleviation authorities. Each of these policies has introduced new scalar power relationships for peasants. First, integrating potatoes in a national market requires extensive transport networks. The Dingxi county government arranges several trains each year (approximately 40 in 2010) to transport the potato crop to cities in eastern China. Similarly, improved roads built over the last decade have made it economically feasible to ship potatoes to eastern cities by truck. Second, county and township governments have promoted storage and marketing. Several larger towns in the valley have built storage caves that are rented to vendors each autumn, and the prefecture and county governments organize two large potato markets located at railheads. Third, with national support, the county has been involved in breeding programmes to increase the quality, and therefore price, of local potatoes. Based on interviews in 2010, such varieties commanded a 10 per cent market premium. Each of these efforts has been supported by state actors – most notably the prefectural government, but also county and township officials – with the specific goal of solving the problem of aridity (Yan 2008), and as such can be thought of as green water interventions in the Zuli valley's agriculture.

The networks of potato trade that begin with peasants in the remote Zuli valley now stretch to commercial vegetable markets of eastern China. Peasants are now dependent on prices in national markets, not just rainfall, to eat. The markets that support this water-saving crop are national in their spatial extent, but the interventions that created them have been promoted by a variety of local-scale actors at the prefecture, county and township level. As in the case of cabbage agriculture, there is a scalar mismatch between administrative levels of state actors engaging in hydrosocial governance and the spatial extent of the hydrosocial processes being governed. Local state actors engage in policies locally that introduce national-scale hydrosocial relationships. Both cabbage and potato marketing illustrate another facet of hydrosocial governance in the Zuli valley: the rescaling of hydrosocial relationships has largely been a contingent processes, as state actors have identified solutions to the problem of aridity that are readily available. During the past 20 years, such solutions have often involved integration with national markets as a green water solution, including the most recent intervention, maize agriculture.

Maize and Multiple and Contingent Rescalings

Potatoes illustrate that rescalings of hydrosocial relationships are often based on the opportunities available to state actors, and the growth of maize has been a similarly contingent process. Two changes in the biophysical nature of maize have facilitated its expansion as a cash crop in the valley, and in the process rescaled water governance; both were promoted by state actors. First, the use of plastic film mulches has been subsidized by funds provided by central poverty alleviation authorities and distributed by township governments. The expansion of plastic film mulches has also been supported by extension efforts undertaken by the Dingxi County Agricultural Bureau.

The second biophysical shift that arose from a national actor was the introduction of drought-resistant seed varieties. Drought-resistant maize cultivars came to the valley through a national infrastructure of seed breeding and extension. While the state actors who have created drought-resistant cultivars are national in territorial extent, this seed-breeding infrastructure has enabled peasants to make much smaller-scale decisions about their own cultivation. These peasant-level decisions are made within a context of varying risk of crop failure from drought, different labour requirements and expected returns. Thus, with both films and seed breeding, state actors at a variety of larger territorial scales provide a framework through which hydrosocial decisions are made at the spatial extent of the household.

Finally, expansion of maize agriculture in the Zuli River valley has, like cabbage and potatoes, depended upon the introduction of national and local markets for maize. Interest in planting maize has been driven by a rapid rise in its price in recent years in China, due in large part to its role as an input in growing animal protein (both meat and eggs) demanded by increasingly prosperous urban residents. National markets for maize brought national-scale institutions to bear on the previous direct link between peasants and their staple foods, and facilitated the biophysical transformations in how agricultural water is used. Yet these national markets were created through the policies of the local state.

Maize in the Zuli valley illustrates a green water example of the multiple and contingent ways that hydrosocial governance may be rescaled. With film mulches and hybrid seeds, state actors at a variety of scales have altered the conditions under which peasants weigh the risks of drought against the costs of labour and possible profits. In doing so, national interventions have created much more localized shifts in hydrosocial governance. Simultaneously, national processes of market integration have increased the demand for maize, making it a feasible crop for peasants to grow. These processes of hydrosocial governance surrounding maize are divergent, rescaling governance both upwards (through national market integration) and downwards (through extension efforts).

Conclusions

Four conclusions with broader implications for the discussions of this book can be drawn from the example presented in this chapter. First, this case study illustrates that considerations of scale in hydrosocial governance may be attentive to green water governance as well as blue water governance. When considering green water, specific actions that constitute water governance may not be as proximate to biophysical as is the case of blue water governance, but are no less influential in how water is governed. For example, the introduction of commodity markets for maize and potatoes has changed how farmers make decisions surrounding agricultural green water. The governance interventions that facilitated maize and potatoes did not change who received what quantities of water, but has profoundly altered what peasants do with the water that is already available. While rescaling of the governance of blue water resources (e.g. basin-scale management) may be more readily linked to water governance, in this case study green water governance rescalings have had the most profound impact.

Second, the spatial extent of hydrosocial processes is often not coincident with the administrative level of the state actors undertaking the governance interventions from which such processes arose. This has been particularly apparent in green water governance. For example, governance intervention made at county and prefecture level has supported the promotion of potato agriculture but has entangled farmers in new commodity markets of national extent. In this case, the county-level government has engaged in a hydrosocial intervention that is national in its spatial extent.

Conversely, the expansion of maize agriculture has been facilitated by the interventions of state actors at the national scale for seed breeding, and at provincial, county and township levels for extension activities. Yet these activities have facilitated hydrosocial governance decisions that have been made at the spatial extent of the household. In the cases of irrigation (particularly inter-basin and basin-scale irrigation) the administrative level of state actors and the spatial extent of hydrosocial processes have been largely coincident. In this study, when scale as administrative level of governance and scale as spatial extent of process have coincided is in instances where water was managed as a blue water resource. Instances where water was managed as a green water resource, such as potato and maize agriculture, showed a divergence between level of administrative governance and territorial extent of hydrosocial process.

Third, state-backed governance interventions that rescale hydrosocial relations are not unidirectional, and may introduce new power relations at multiple scales simultaneously. Previous studies linking state development programmes to scale in water governance have tended to view changes in the scale of water governance as deliberate processes undertaken by state actors to move the scale at which water is managed: either upwards as part of a larger political process of modernization (Swyngedouw 1999, 2007; Kaika 2006) or downwards as a process of political devolution (Perreault 2005; Norman and Bakker 2009; Cohen and Davidson 2011). Yet the case study presented here illustrates that the rescaling of hydrosocial processes may introduce new social and power relationships in several directions at once. For example, maize agriculture brought national institutions to bear on water management in the Zuli valley, but in so doing expanded the opportunities of farmers to make decisions regarding their use of agricultural water at the spatial extent of the household.

Finally, these case studies illustrate that the role of rescaling in hydrosocial governance is *contingent*. The scales at which hydrosocial processes take place may or may not have been the deliberate choices of the state actors initiating them. State actors who have promoted potato and maize agriculture have introduced scalar relationships through national markets, but did not actively attempt to rescale how water was managed at a national level. Rather, in this case the introduction of potato markets, a process national in spatial extent, was the most expedient way of solving the local problem of aridity following the collapse of basin-scale irrigation in the 1990s. Similarly, the introduction of small-scale (100 acre) groundwater irrigation systems by the DCWB was a decision driven by what it viewed as achievable. Yet this small-scale introduction has embroiled farmers in national networks of cabbage trade promoted by yet another local government. In each instance, state actors have chosen governance interventions at the scales that are most convenient. By applying the fragmented authoritarianism framework which has been so productive in understanding the politics of large-scale water projects in China (Lieberthal and Oksenberg 1990; Mertha 2008) to small-scale changes in hydrosocial governance, particularly green water governance, we see that state-backed rescaling of hydrosocial relations is not necessarily deliberate, and is often contingent upon what opportunities are available to state actors. Conversely, the two instances of irrigation (basin-scale and inter-basin) where state actors attempt to govern water at the scale that coincided with their mandate – or in Moore's (2008) terminology attempt to create a scaleness of water management to match their administrative bailiwick – have been among the least successful. The dams of the basin-scale era languish unused, while the attempt to make water a provincial resource remains unfinished. Meanwhile, the green water projects of potato and maize agriculture have reshaped how peasants in the Zuli valley relate to the rain that sustains them.

References

Baker, J.M. 2008. *The Kuhls of Kangra: Community-Managed Irrigation in the Western Himalaya.* Seattle: University of Washington Press.

Bakker, K.J. 2003. *An Uncooperative Commodity: Privatizing Water in England and Wales.* New York: Oxford University Press.

Birkenholtz, T. 2009. Irrigated landscapes, produced scarcity, and adaptive social institutions in Rajasthan, India. *Annals of the Association of American Geographers* 99(1): 118–37.

Budds, J. 2008. Whose scarcity? The hydrosocial cycle and the changing waterscape of La Ligua river basin, Chile. In Goodman, M.K.; Boykoff, M.T. and Evered K.T. (eds), *Contentious Geographies: Environmental Knowledge, Meaning, Scale*, pp. 59–78. Aldershot: Ashgate.

Cohen, A. and Davidson, S. 2011. The watershed approach: Challenges, antecedents, and the transition from technical tool to governance unit. *Water Alternatives* 4(1): 1–14.

Dikötter, F. 2010. *Mao's Great Famine: The History of China's Most Devastating Catastrophe, 1958–1962.* New York: Walker.

Dubash, N. 2004. Water, markets, and embedded institutions in Western India. In Peet, R. and Watts, M. (eds), *Liberation Ecologies: Environment, Development, Social Movements*, pp. 218–43. London: Routledge.

Falkenmark, M. and J. Rockström, 2006. The new blue and green water paradigm: Breaking new ground for water resources planning and management. *Journal of Water Resources Planning and Management* 132(3): 129–32.

Hoekstra, A.Y. and Mekonnen, M.M. 2012. The water footprint of humanity. *Proceedings of the National Academy of Sciences* 109(9): 3232–7.

Hoff, H., Falkenmark, M., Gerten, D., Gordon, L., Karlberg, L. and Rockström, J. (2010). Greening the global water system. *Journal of Hydrology* 384(3–4): 177–86.

Kaika, M. 2006. Dams as symbols of modernization: The urbanization of nature between geographical imagination and materiality. *Annals of the Association of American Geographers* 96(2): 276–301.

Li, X.Y. and Gong, J.D. 2002. Effects of different ridge: Furrow ratios and supplemental irrigation on crop production in ridge and furrow rainfall harvesting system with mulches. *Agricultural Water Management* 54(3): 243–54.

Lieberthal, K. and Oksenberg, M. 1990. *Policy Making in China: Leaders, Structures, and Processes.* Princeton: Princeton University Press.

Linton, J. 2010. *What is Water? The History of a Modern Abstraction.* Vancouver: University of British Columbia Press.

Liu, J., Zehnder, A.J.B. and Yang, H. 2009. Global consumptive water use for crop production: The importance of green water and virtual water. *Water Resources Research* 45(5): W05428; DOI: 10.1029/2007WR006051.

Mertha, A. 2008. *China's Water Warriors: Citizen Action and Policy Change.* Ithaca: Cornell University Press.

Mollinga, P.P.. Meinzen-Dick, R.S. and Merrey, D.J. 2007. Politics, plurality and problemsheds: A strategic approach for reform of agricultural water resources management. *Development Policy Review* 25(6): 699–719.

Moore, A. 2008. Rethinking scale as a geographical category: From analysis to practice. *Progress in Human Geography* 32(2): 203–25.

Nickum, J. 2010. Water policy reform in China's fragmented hydraulic state: Focus on self-funded/managed irrigation and drainage districts. *Water Alternatives* 3(3): 537–51.

Norman, E. and Bakker, K. 2009. Transgressing scales: Water governance across the Canada–U.S. borderland. *Annals of the Association of American Geographers* 99(1): 99–117.

Oi, J.C. 1991. *State and Peasant in Contemporary China: The Political Economy of Village Government.* Berkeley: University of California Press.

Ostrom, E. 1990. *Governing the Commons: The Evolution of Institutions for Collective Action.* New York: Cambridge University Press.

Perreault, T. 2005. State restructuring and the scale politics of rural water governance in Bolivia. *Environment and Planning A* 37(2): 263–84.

Perreault, T. 2008. Custom and contradiction: Rural water governance and the politics of usos y costumbres in Bolivia's irrigators' movement. *Annals of the Association of American Geographers* 98(4): 834–54.

Scott, J.C. 1998. *Seeing Like a State: How Certain Schemes to Improve the Human Condition Have Failed.* New Haven: Yale University Press.

Shang, B. 2007. Dingxi potatoes go out. *People's Daily Online*, 3 April. http://www.cpad.gov.cn/data/2007/0403/article_333569.htm (accessed 29 February 2011).

Shue, V. 1990. *The Reach of the State: Sketches of the Chinese Body Politic.* Stanford: Stanford University Press.

Swyngedouw, E. 1999. Modernity and hybridity: Nature, regeneracionismo, and the production of the Spanish waterscape, 1890–1930. *Annals of the Association of American Geographers* 89(3): 443–65.

Swyngedouw, E. 2007. Technonatural revolutions: The scalar politics of Franco's hydro-social dream for Spain, 1939–1975. *Transactions of the Institute of British Geographers* 32(1): 9–28.

Wei, H., Li, J.L. and Liang, T.G. 2005. Study on the estimation of precipitation resources for rainwater harvesting agriculture in semi-arid land of China. *Agricultural Water Management* 71(1): 33–45.

Wittfogel, K.A. 1957. *Oriental Despotism: A Comparative Study of Total Power.* New Haven: Yale University Press.

Xinhua. 2009. The yin tao project: Gansu's dream of half a century. http://www.gs.xinhuanet.com/jdwt/yintaogc (accessed 29 February 2011).

Yan, Q.G. 2008. *Potato Smiles (tudou de weixiao).* Lanzhou, China: Duzhe.

Chapter 15

Performing Modernity: The Scalar Politics of Irrigation Development in Nepal

Margreet Zwarteveen and Janwillem Liebrand

Scales do not emanate from some pre-existing reality, but instead actively help to produce them. Scales divide, map and categorize; they are a way to help make sense of complexities by creating order. They demarcate, define, delineate and indeed proactively establish and produce the boundaries between what matters and what can be ignored. As many contributors to this volume (e.g. Sneddon and Fox; Budds) show, the choice of scales is often a matter of politics, reflecting interests and power. We add to this that it is also, and importantly, a matter of custom; it reflects, produces and protects traditions, territories and cultures, identities and social hierarchies. Particular scales belong to particular beliefs and communities; they quite literally help to produce these communities as well as the realities they believe in (or want to help create).

More specifically, the chapter is concerned with irrigation scales and the knowledge practices that produce them, investigating how these are linked to and help reproduce gendered decision-making processes and professional cultures to enact a specific reality. The question it sets out to answer is: which realities do irrigation data and scales enact or perform, and how are these related to the gendered professional identities and cultures of (members of) irrigation policy elites? We tell our story through a review of modern irrigation history and irrigation datasets, focusing on how scales are invoked by (and help reproduce) irrigation policy elites in Nepal.

Two theoretical concepts inform our argument. The first is that professions can be considered as cultures, in the sense that they consist of groups of people who share certain values and norms which are, for instance, expressed in behaviour and dress. These values and norms are constantly re-established through often ritualized procedures and practices. Gender is one important axis around and through which such professional cultures become articulated, with certain professions defining themselves as (and being seen as) more suited for men than for women (or vice versa). This gendering happens through mapping the characteristics of a profession onto a gender, a process which works to merge professional identities with gender identities by associating them with biology: men/women are 'naturally' better at doing certain things (cf. Butler 1990).

The second set of ideas that informs our analysis is that knowledge – in our case knowledge about irrigation realities – does not simply *describe* reality, but also tends to *enact* realities into being (Law 2009). In other words, we treat knowledge practices as performative. This stems from the idea that methods, like data collection on irrigation, tend to take on a life of their own, generating and enacting these realities. As a consequence, truths are not universal (Law and Mol 2001). Instead, the 'real' is only 'realized' in definite form within the networks of practices that enact or perform them. Enacted realities and identities are clearly gendered, and are importantly performed through the use of specific scalar definitions, boundaries and constructions.

Knowledge Practices as Performative

In policy reports or databases, numbers on irrigation development obtain the status of facts that reveal the state of the art in the sector. Professionals and members of policy elites use these facts as a basis for research and planning. Considering (scientific) data as 'facts' is based on the widely held assumption that reality has a definite form that is independent of the tools that are used to measure or count it. In this chapter, we adopt a different and less widespread view of science and scientific knowledge. We consider science and knowledge practices as performative: they enact realities as well as describe them (Law 2009: 239).

This of course immediately prompts questions about the ability to make any credible and plausible claim about anything. According to Bruno Latour, and many who have adopted his ideas, realities (and knowledge of realities) 'depend on practices that include or relate to a hinterland of other relevant practices' (Law 2009: 241). Sustainable knowledge rests in, and reproduces, more or less stable networks of relevant instruments, representations and the realities that these describe. This is what makes realities – together with the techniques and representations that enact them – seem stable, durable and reliable (Law 2009: 241–2). This also means that realities are only real within particular networks or systems of circulation. Truths, therefore, are not universal: they are only 'realized' in definite form within the networks of practices that perform them. We use these ideas to ask questions about the knowledge produced by irrigation policy elites in Nepal and, more specifically, about their use of scales and scalar ontologies.

The second theoretical cornerstone of this chapter is that knowledge practices do not just enact (or perform) realities, but also discipline and help form the (networks of) people producing them (cf. Butler 1990). In other words, we see specific ways of producing data as part of a larger range of cultural resources that members of a professional or academic community invoke to identify themselves. This theoretical idea can be traced, among a number of other sources, to Turner (1969), who posited that data (or knowledge) both *reflect* and *structure* the experience of those producing them (Turner 1969, 1974; Turner and Bruner 1986; John 2008). Following Turner, Butler (1990) used the term 'performativity', especially in relation to gender, to refer to a stylized repetition and reiteration of acts, whereas Schechner (2006) used the term 'cultural performance', more generally, to denote the outcome of restored behaviour. When applied to knowledge, cultural performance expresses the notion that the presentation of data or knowledge is always based on preconceived ideas (a culturally informed experience or hinterland) about what is considered real or important, and that such data in turn express and reproduce these preconceived ideas (enact or structure). Treating irrigation knowledge as performative thus casts it as a process of 'culture in the making' (cf. Turner and Bruner 1986).

Seen in this light, irrigation statistics are a ritual show, a stylized repetition of acts among members of global and national policy elites – an act that thus simultaneously enacts 'their' irrigation knowledge, 'their' professional cultures, as well as 'their' masculine genders. In analysing what irrigation knowledge is *performing*, it is important to keep in mind that the two performances identified above – let's call them the technical and cultural dimensions of performance – always go together; they are inseparable and happen simultaneously (McKenzie 2001).

Performing Modernity: Development of Irrigation in Nepal

Nepal's irrigation history can be traced as far back as 400 BC (DOI 2010; Whelpton 2005; Sharma 2004). Although there was some involvement of religious and royal rulers in constructing irrigation canals in the Tarai (or Terai), until the twentieth century the management of irrigation systems was largely done by farmers. More direct and 'modern' involvement of the Nepal government in the irrigation sector can be said to have started in the 1920s; but modern water development only gained particular momentum after 1947, when India became independent and democratic reform was in the air. It is around this time that high-level administrators in Nepal started proposing large-scale river basin projects, often modelled after the US Tennessee Valley Authority (TVA; see Chapter 4). The development of public irrigation systems was part of the modernization and territorialization politics of the autocratic Rana government, which sought to isolate and protect Nepal from the colonial expansion of British India, simultaneously protecting its own power (Whelpton 2005). After the Rana regime ended in 1951, the Ministry of Public Works and Transport developed a Department of Irrigation (DOI), then known as the Canal Department. At first, the department largely relied on financial and technical aid from India, fostering the new post-colonial relation between the countries (IAM 1964; Pradhan 1982).

'Modern' irrigation development and the establishment of the Canal Department were part of a concerted effort by the new government to disband the feudal agrarian system. Irrigation canals would not only increase agricultural production, but would also help fill the national treasury through the collection of water fees. In line with the TVA's hydraulic mission ideals, the construction of canals was also believed to catapult cultivators into the age of modernization – the sight of canals itself sufficient for peasants to abandon 'backward' agricultural practices – and win their hearts for the cause of the Nepalese nation.

This 'high modernist' vision of irrigation development set the scalar parameters for future irrigation debates and plans: it linked projected levels of agricultural production (based on assumptions of population growth and food requirements) on the one hand to irrigated area and particular irrigation projects on the other (see Figure 15.1). The figure shows the projected growth of agricultural productivity as

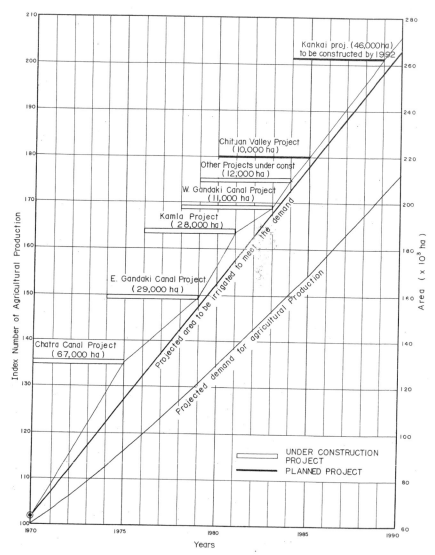

Figure 15.1   The irrigation engineering vision in Nepal

Source: HMG/N (1970: Figure XIII). Document obtained from the Agricultural Documentation Centre of the National Agricultural Research Council (NARC), Kathmandu, Nepal.

linearly related to the projected growth of the irrigated area expressed in hectares. The core of this vision is clear: *irrigation engineering* (or government support to irrigation projects) is critical to counter population growth and to facilitate progress and prosperity.

The specific use of scales inherent to this vision produces a number of hierarchies. First, and most importantly, it creates a temporal and spatial divide between 'developed' and 'non- (or under-)developed' areas, with the label of 'developed' (or 'modern') being reserved for public irrigation systems. All other areas, including those already irrigated, by definition suddenly become non-existent, 'backward' or in need of assistance. Over time, starting in the 1960s, members of irrigation policy elites mapped the complete territory of Nepal, dividing it into 'irrigable' and 'non-irrigable' areas (HMG/N 1970), thus creating a further hierarchy between regions based on their suitability for engineering assistance. The maps situated the most promising irrigable areas in Nepal in the ecological zone of the Tarai. Figure 15.2 presents an example of such a map, one that was produced for the second 'Master Plan for Irrigation Development in Nepal'.

A second important hierarchy created by the used scalar parameters is that between 'experts' and 'laypeople' (or ignorant, uneducated people) or between 'expert (scientific) knowledge' and 'indigenous' or farmers' knowledge. The vision of the hydraulic mission enacts irrigation as something that requires a very specific form of technical and scientific expertise: only systems that are designed, constructed (and perhaps managed) by scientifically trained (and publicly employed) engineers qualify as 'irrigation', whereas other systems represent backwardness and tradition and are therefore in need of upgrading or modernization. In South Asia (as in other places) this irrigation expertise evolved in and through specific ethnic, class and gender hierarchies (see Zwarteveen 2011).

In Nepal, the scalar ontologies that defined 'modern' irrigation development in the twentieth century continue to set the rough parameters for later plans, policies and projects. Yet, new economic and political realities increasingly blurred and questioned the dividing lines and hierarchies between 'developed' and 'non-developed' areas or between expert and indigenous knowledge. This started already in the 1980s, when the large-scale TVA-like projects became less popular because they were expensive and their performance was disappointing. In addition, the international oil crisis in the 1970s had worsened the terms of trade for primary agricultural production. Nepal felt the effects of this even more because of India's move to self-sufficiency in agriculture in the 1960s and 1970s (WECS 1981). The country could hardly meet its loan obligations. Decreasing levels of land productivity and stagnant or declining levels of food production helped to further decrease the popularity of capital-intensive, state-led irrigation development as a means to meet the needs of a rapidly growing population.

This signalled the beginning of a new neoliberal aid regime in Nepal, in which development came to be defined as 'meeting basic needs'. Through decentralization and cost-recovery, public expenditure had to be reduced. In irrigation this shift (next to policies to hand over public systems to farmers) also took the form of

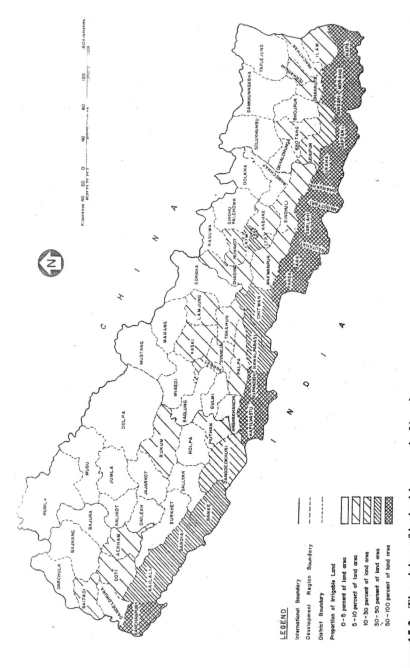

LEGEND

International Boundary
Development Region Boundary
District Boundary

Proportion of Irrigable Land

0 - 5 percent of land area
5 - 10 percent of land area
10 - 30 percent of land area
30 - 50 percent of land area
50 - 100 percent of land area

Figure 15.2   The vision of irrigable areas in Nepal
Source: DOI/WB/UNDP (1989: 88), from the library of CEMATS Consultants, Kupondole, Lalitpur, Nepal.

attention to the management and rehabilitation of community systems of farmers. Hence, and almost overnight, the Hill region of Nepal (the *Pahar*) was no longer seen as backward and 'non-engineerable', but instead became a potential area for technical intervention and support. So-called 'integrated rural development programmes' in the Hills abounded, which often included the rehabilitation of indigenous or 'farmer-managed irrigation systems' (FMIS) (Sharma 2004). Although large engineering projects remained on the irrigation agenda in the 1980s, FMIS became the new irrigation management model, with a focus on farmers' participation. In the 1990s, the first public systems in the Tarai were 'handed over' to users or administratively moulded into 'jointly managed' systems between the DOI and the newly established Water User Associations (WUAs) (Khanal 2003).

The adoption of participatory policies challenged the (need for) expertise and authority of the engineers at the DOI. To safeguard their position, therefore, engineers had to find new ways of reasserting their importance. They were reasonably successful in doing this, for instance through a concerted diversification of projects (groundwater projects and micro-irrigation infrastructure), all of which were deemed to require and depend on DOI input. Throughout its 60-year history and attendant changes, the DOI has succeeded in retaining its status and legitimacy as a technical organization that has provided the fundaments for agricultural growth and, therefore, national development.

Scalar Ontologies and Politics: Performing Territories and Identities

In Nepal, there is an abundance of irrigation data available at various government institutions, notably the DOI, the Department of Agriculture (DA), the Agricultural Development Bank of Nepal (ADB/N) and the Central Bureau of Statistics (CBS). In addition, the World Bank (WB) and the Asian Development Bank (ADB) periodically produce new 'agricultural development strategies' as part of their aid programmes, and these documents often contain a state of the art of the irrigation sector in Nepal (ADB 2012; DOI/WB/UNDP 1989).[1] Close inspection reveals that the steady production of irrigation reports among and between these organizations importantly relies on the circulation and recycling of existing sets of irrigation statistics. The datasets produced by foreign and national consultants under the auspices of the main irrigation authority in Nepal, the DOI, are particularly influential.

A review of these datasets and reports illustrates that they generate, and depend upon, a very particular professional community with a distinct identity and masculine culture. One specific example of this is the recently produced ADB report entitled 'Irrigated Agriculture and Water Resources Assessment Report' (ADB 2012). The list of people consulted for producing this report is

---

1   Funded by the World Bank under the United Nations Development Programme, and written by Canadian International Water and Energy (CIWEC) consultants and East Consult (Nepal).

revealing in terms of the composition of the professional irrigation community. Government staff, most notably male staff of the DOI, continue to constitute the largest proportion of experts, directly followed by representatives of various donor agencies. Civil engineering continues to be the main disciplinary background of water experts (DOI 2008). The core group for producing the report consisted of 16 high-caste Nepalese men and one American man. The other experts that were consulted were likewise mostly men – most of them from the higher castes, and some from North America or Europe. In all, there were only two female experts among the group of consulted people, one from Canada and one from the USA, both of them from donor organizations (ADB and WB).

The role of foreign aid and donor organizations in the irrigation sector has expanded in the last three decades, with each donor agency or development bank developing its own data requirements and specialized scalar terminologies. Current reports on irrigation in Nepal incorporate a great number of these scalar terms (ADB 2012), many of which are not very clearly defined. The vagueness and the multi-interpretability of the resulting data can be seen as a necessary by-product of 'making development' (Mosse 2005); vague definitions, empty columns and peculiar numbers in irrigation statistics express the strategic compromises and negotiated settlements between members of irrigation sector policy elites. They are, in other words, the outcome of ontological and scalar politics, expressing the multiplicity of interests, organizations and projects involved. This for instance explains why the numbers collected by the DOI on 'total irrigated area' before the 1980s mainly included public irrigation schemes in the Tarai, and often reflected the 'planned' irrigated area (in terms of developed infrastructure) rather than the 'actual' irrigated area (Liebrand 2010; Pradhan 2007; Shukla et al. 2002; Shukla and Sharma 1997). Also, the DOI at that time only included the surface irrigation systems with fixed head works in their count.[2] Yet, around 1980, an estimated 400,000 ha were irrigated by temporary stone and brushwood dams that were managed by farmers (WECS 1981; Pradhan 1989; Belbase 2010).[3]

Illustratively, the recognition of community irrigation systems by DOI engineers only happened under pressure from a coalition of cash-strapped national administrators and international aid and funding organizations in the early 1980s, which was accompanied by an international wave of critique on the engineering and construction focus of irrigation projects. Since that time, data collection by the DOI has included a category on 'non-government' or FMIS (WECS 1981; DOI/ WB/UNDP 1989; DOI/CERD 2007).

---

2   Personal communication with M. Belbase, who explained that the DOI initially did not count indigenous community systems because they did not have fixed head works.

3   Illustratively, this estimate was based on the land tax assessment records of the Ministry of Finance, an agency that aspires to tax every citizen in Nepal on an equal basis, and which had always registered land in four categories of productivity based on the availability of irrigation.

Likewise, the irrigation policy elites for a long time neglected the development of groundwater irrigation. The ADB/N had been involved in financing the implementation of shallow tube wells in the Tarai already since the 1970s, but this type of irrigation expansion did not count as irrigation according to the (implicit) definition of irrigation policy elites. This only changed when the second 'Master Plan for Irrigation Development in Nepal' for the 1990s identified ground water development in the Tarai as a promising short-term strategy to achieve rapid gains in food production (DOI/WB/UNDP 1989: xiv).

Table 15.1 shows the evolution of irrigation data in Nepal. It unsurprisingly expresses 'growth' in terms of an expansion of the irrigated area, but also illustrates that what counts as irrigated area is continually changing through the progressive addition of new categories. The data are subdivided according to the typical categorization of Nepal into three distinct geographical areas, the Tarai, the Hills and the Mountains.

Table 15.1   The evolution of irrigation statistics in Nepal

Year	Total irrigated area (ha)	Government systems (ha)	Farmer-managed irrigation systems (ha)		Groundwater (ha)	Non-conventional (ha)
		Tarai	Tarai	Hills and Mountains	Tarai	Tarai, Hills, Mountains
1961	31,900	31,900				
1970	117,500	117,500				
1972	180,000	180,000				
1980	267,000	267,000				
1981	875,000	-	458,000	150,000		
1988	1,019,000	350,000	-	-	61,000	
1990	1,216,605	547,605	-	-	-	
2006	1,252,406	314,521	416,184	229,532	278,158	13,011

Sources: Compilation of data from Biswas (1989), WECS (1981), DOI/WB/UNDP (1989) and DOI/CERD (2007).

To further examine how the irrigation policy elites construct realities through their use and presentation of data, we compared three irrigation datasets:

- the Database for Irrigation Development (DBID) in Nepal, developed by consultants of the Centre for Engineering Research and Development (CERD) under auspices of the DOI;

- the agricultural development strategy 'Irrigated Agriculture and Water Resources Assessment Report', a document prepared recently by the ADB in Nepal for the coming years (ADB 2012);
- the section on irrigation in the agricultural census of 2001 by the CBS (2006).[4]

The first two datasets can be seen to clearly enact a reality of the irrigation policy elites, whereas the CBS census performs a slightly different reality (see Table 15.2).

Table 15.2   Irrigation development realities in Nepal

Irrigation Scheme Type	Area (ha)		
	DOI/CERD 2007 (2005/06)	ADB 2012 (2005–11)	CBS 2006 (2001/02)
DOI project	314,521	314,521	*
Non-assisted FMIS	312,289	284,348	
Agency-assisted FMIS project, rehabilitation	295,258	298,665	
Agency-assisted FMIS project, new	38,169	38,650	
Total surface irrigation	*960,237*	*936,184*	*868,100*
DOI project/shallow tube well	53,964	139,992	**
DOI project/deep/medium tube well	34,455	39,075	
ADP Janakpur/shallow tube well	18,151	10,345	
ADP Janakpur/deep/medium tube well'	3,645	6,060	
ADB/N/shallow tube well	167,943	167,943	
Total groundwater irrigation	*278,158*	*363,415*	*238,800*
Mixed	–	–	14,600
Non-conventional project'	13,011	13,011	–
Other	–	–	46,900
Total other	*13,011*	*13,011*	*61,500*
Total	**1,251,406**	**1,312,610**	**1,168,400**

Notes: Irrigation scheme categories are taken from the Database for Irrigation Development (DOI/CERD 2007). *Listed as canal irrigation, distinguished as 'seasonal' and 'permanent'. **Listed as tube well/bore and pond/well irrigation.

4   The latest census of 2011/12 was not yet published at the time of writing this chapter.

Which realities do these data enact or perform? To answer this question we have traced the assumptions and scalar definitions that underpin them by identifying some of the contradictions and inconsistencies that emerge when comparing (and thus recontextualizing) the datasets, as well as by comparing them to those performed by farmers. We do this not to suggest any wrongdoing or ill-intentioned manipulation of data by the irrigation policy elites or the DOI. Nor do we intend to expose data collection methods or scales used as wrongly chosen. Rather, we intend to show that datasets enact very specific realities that may be real within the specific networks and contexts of the irrigation policy elites, but that fall apart in other networks and contexts (see Law 2009).

The first contradiction that the comparison of these datasets generates is a familiar one for irrigation experts, and has to do with the assessment of the irrigated area, in hectares. When asked, farmers in Nepal considered the 'irrigated area' to be a plot of land that is irrigated for rice cultivation in the monsoon, known as *khet*. Sometimes this land is also irrigated in winter and spring. The DBID uses the terms 'irrigated area' and 'culturable command area', but does not define them. Yet, it appears that the database refers to the 'net developed command area' rather than to the areas actually irrigated in any specific season: the numbers given in the DBID columns for 'net planned area', 'net developed command area' and 'irrigated command area' in the monsoon (or summer in the DBID) are often the same, whereas actual irrigated areas are likely different (and often lower).

The ADB report similarly defines the term 'irrigable area' as 'the area that *can be* irrigated in a given season; often *the maximum area* within an irrigation system that can be irrigated in a "normal" year' (ADB 2012: iii).[5] Thus, the area irrigated as specified by the term 'irrigated (command) area' refers to what is irrigated in the monsoon, which is the season in which farmers rely mostly on rainfall and only use supplementary irrigation. This particular ontological and scalar definition of 'irrigated area' thus shows the largest possible area as being irrigated. The definition thus helps in producing a reality that underscores the importance of irrigation experts in 'creating' development. It also reflects international practice, as for instance reflected in the AQUASTAT database constructed by the UN Food and Agricultural Organization (FAO).[6]

A related and second source of confusion stems from the term 'year-round irrigation', a key scalar category used by the DOI. It was first used in 1970 in the first Master Plan of Irrigation of Nepal, which defined it as two or more crops per year (HMG/N 1970). The ADB study cites the Agricultural Perspective Plan of 1995 to define year-round irrigation as a potential cropping intensity of at least 200 per cent for surface schemes (ADB 2012), which also means two or more crops per year. The term is not used by, and has no meaning for, farmers. As explained, in the monsoon farmers may not always use irrigation. In winter, the main crops (such as wheat and mustard in the Chitwan and Palpa districts, in the Tarai and

---

5   Emphasis added.
6   http://www.fao.org/nr/water/aquastat/main/index.stm.

the Hills respectively) rely on soil moisture or rain – except for rice, which needs irrigation (DOI/Nippon Koei/SILT 1990)[7] – but spring crops do rely mainly on irrigation. Hence, the size (and meaning) of 'irrigated area' changes throughout the year, depending on the availability of rain and the type of crop cultivated. The term 'year-round irrigation' thus enacts a specific reality of the irrigation policy elite, and not one of farmers. It is one in which the benefits of irrigation development (or rather the need for more irrigation development) appears as self-evident.

Although the term year-round irrigation seems synonymous with cropping intensity, there is an important difference: year-round irrigation does not link the number of cropping seasons per year to irrigation. This difference does the job of underscoring the need to build more surface irrigation systems, i.e. dams, reservoirs and canals. Hence, the ADB study (2012) refers to year-round irrigation only for *surface schemes*. In a similar fashion, CBS (2006) refers to 'permanent' irrigation for *canal systems*.

A third source of contradiction and confusion relates to the difficulty of precisely tracing the source of water, or the technology used for conveying water to fields. The databases suggest that each irrigation system is supplied by one water source, either surface or groundwater; that each irrigated area is serviced by just one source or system; and that farmers use just one source or system for irrigating their fields. This reality falls apart when recontextualized with the experiences of irrigating farmers or within the networks of the CBS. The CBS data do incorporate a category for 'mixed' and 'other' irrigation, accounting for a total area of 61,500 ha (see Table 15.2). This presumably covers areas that are irrigated by a mix of surface and groundwater through various technologies (e.g. a combination of canals, wells and natural flows).

Farmers in irrigated areas often combine and alternate different sources and systems. In times of drought, farmers use groundwater through shallow and deep tube wells in areas that are also served by a surface irrigation system (Gautam 2006). The command areas of FMIS in the Tarai sometimes rely on two sources of surface water, for instance because they have become part of the command areas of new public irrigation systems (Levine 1983). Two systems may also share one source of water (a small river or spring), for instance because the drain of one system is the source for the next system. Obviously, foreign and national irrigation specialists know about practices and situations of conjunctive water use (Gautam 2006). When asked, DOI engineers readily provided examples of it, and international organizations involved in irrigation policymaking regularly publish on conjunctive water use (ICID/FAO 1996; IWMI 2006; World Bank 2006). Yet, the reality of conjunctive and alternate uses of water from various sources and systems is not an enactment which serves the objectives of the irrigation policy elites, who prefer a more straightforward reality that allows clearly tracing them as generators of progress.

---

7   SILT consultancy (Nepal), prepared for Nippon Koei Co.

A fourth and last source of confusion relates to the distinction between FMIS and government-constructed irrigation systems. FMIS is a term to describe irrigation systems developed and managed by farmers (Martin and Yoder 1983; Coward and Levine 1987; Pradhan 1989). The DBID uses the term FMIS to denote existing surface irrigation systems, making a distinction between 'non-assisted FMIS' that do not rely on government resources and 'agency-assisted FMIS' that did receive government assistance (see Table 15.2). However, differentiating between the two forms of FMIS, as well as between FMIS and projects constructed by the DOI, is often less straightforward than this categorization suggests.

Many irrigation systems, especially those of less than 2,000 ha in the Tarai (Shukla and Sharma 1997; Khanal 2003), constructed by the government have been handed over to farmers and are (at least partially) managed by farmers who are organized into Water User Associations. (Shivakoti and Ostrom 2002). Yet, DOI engineers feel responsible for, and are keen to claim ownership over, the projects they constructed – which is why they prefer using the terms 'DOI project'/'surface irrigation' for such systems (see Table 15.2).

The reverse is also true: many FMIS have received several rounds of technical and financial government support, and have come to depend on the government. Whether these are or should be considered assisted or non-assisted FMIS or DOI projects is not easy to determine. Which label to apply reflects a fluctuating balance between donor pressure on the DOI to show ever-increasing levels of farmers' participation and the DOI's own desire to make its contributions and importance as visible as possible.

These sources of confusion about and inconsistencies in scalar parameters and ontological definitions illustrate that the available data on irrigation development in Nepal – about the extent to which irrigation has expanded or shrunk in terms of area and irrigation intensity in the last six decades – can be read both as enactments of desired realities, as expressions of the (cultural) aspirations of various professional organizations in the sector which produced them, most notably the DOI, and of the policy consensus at the time they were produced.

Conclusions

Looking at irrigation development in Nepal, we have approached scales produced by irrigation policy elites – and scalar ontologies and parameters – as performative: they do not simply describe 'the state of irrigation' in Nepal, but also perform a particular vision of development. This is a vision that consists of making water resources available for agriculture through the construction of sophisticated infrastructure and technology. It associates positivist science (and mathematics in particular) and modern technology with progress and civilization. The realities produced by irrigation datasets also enact the Nepal government, and more specifically the donor-supported Department of Irrigation, as the organization that is best equipped to help bring about this development. The policy elites (re-)produce maps and particular sets of technical, natural science and engineering data as (the most) reliable tools for representing and performing rural realities, thereby also endorsing the natural and engineering sciences as the preferred scientific languages and methods for understanding water.

All these (and probably more) realities are performed through, and happen because of, the simultaneous enactment of strong hierarchical distinctions between 'developed areas' and 'areas to be developed', and between 'experts' and 'laypeople'. Indeed, the ritualized act of using (and showing) irrigation statistics in policy deliberations *remakes* professional hierarchies. It also *re-enacts* hierarchies of Western domination and development aid, and existing differences of nationality, caste and gender. The effect is that an international donor elite of 'civilized' foreign male experts on the one hand and of high-caste consultants and state-employed male engineers on the other is continuously sustained and reproduced.

The enactments of irrigation realities by policy elites become more or less true, depending on how well they are connected to and embedded in national and international water policy and research networks. Shifts in the international water policy consensus or political-economic climate therefore may have the effect of making them less real by 'recontextualizing' them. This does not necessarily mean that these datasets, and the scalar assumptions they employ, are wrong or meaningless, but rather that the realities they enact are only alive in highly specific places (cf. Law 2009: 250), and are tied to specific histories and gendered professional cultures – most markedly the already noted masculine engineering one. Showing that scalar ontologies and parameters are tied to specific networks, histories and cultures supports what many feminist scholars (e.g. Haraway 1991) have long advocated: exposing claims to transcendence and universalism as false, thereby replacing the unity of science with a multiplicity that 'holds out the promise of distributed and heterogeneous politics of reals' (Law 2009: 251).

The datasets produced on the basis of these scalar ontologies are not particularly coherent; they leave room for (critical) questions and potentially allow for the enactment of alternative realities. This means that the reality performed by these datasets – as well as the masculinity of the irrigation policy elites that produce them and that they help sustain – may be powerful, but not totally hegemonic. There is, in other words, space for such 'conscious politics of reals', which importantly includes politics of scale; politics in which attempts are made to strengthen some realities while weakening others, or some systems of circulation rather than others (Law 2009). Our analysis suggests that such politics of 'reals' involve and are deeply tied to cultural and identity politics. They require challenging long-cherished knowledge traditions and epistemic identities – and the authorities and elites that these produce – as well as a deep interrogation of the social, cultural and gender hierarchies on which these are based and which they help sustain.

References

ADB. 2012. *Irrigated Agriculture and Water Resources Component*. Preparation of the Nepal agriculture water resources strategy. Manila: Asian Development Bank.

Belbase, Madhav. 2010. Challenges in financing irrigation systems. In: DOI, *Proceedings of the National Irrigation Seminar: Challenges in Irrigation Development and Management*, pp. 154–64. Department of Irrigation (DOI), 11–12 July, Kathmandu.

Biswas, Asit K. 1989. Irrigation in Nepal: Opportunities and constraints. *Journal of Irrigation and Drainage Engineering*, 115(6): 1051–64.

Butler, J. 1990. *Gender Trouble: Feminism and the Subversion of Identity*. London: Routledge

CBS. 2006. *Agricultural Monograph*. Kathmandu: Central Bureau of Statistics (CBS).

Coward, W. and G. Levine. 1987. Studies of farmer-managed irrigation systems: Ten years of cumulative knowledge and changing research priorities. In *Public Intervention in Farmer-Managed Irrigation Systems*, pp. 1–31. Digana Village via Kandy: International Irrigation Management Institute (IIMI).

DOI. 2008. *Human Resources Assessment of DOI*. Kathmandu: Department of Irrigation.

DOI. 2010. *Proceedings of the National Irrigation Seminar: Challenges in Irrigation Development and Management*. Department of Irrigation, 11–12 July, Kathmandu.

DOI/CERD. 2007. *Database for Irrigation Development in Nepal*. Department of Irrigation/Centre for Engineering Research and Development.

DOI/WB/UNDP. 1989. *Master Plan for Irrigation Development in Nepal*. Kathmandu: Department of Irrigation.

DOI/Nippon Koei/SILT. 1990. *Report on Inventory of Existing Farmer-Managed Irrigation Systems: East Rapti Irrigation Project*. Vol. 1. Kathmandu: Department of Irrigation.

Gautam R.S. 2006. *Incorporating Groundwater Irrigation: Technology Dynamics and Conjunctive Water Management in the Nepal Terai*. Hyderabad: Orient Longman.

Haraway, Donna J. 1991. *Simians, Cyborgs, and Women: The Reinvention of Nature*. New York: Routledge.

HMG/N. 1970. *Master Plan for Irrigation Development in Nepal*. Ministry of Water Resources. Kathmandu: Her Majesty's Government of Nepal.

IAM. 1964. *Brief Statistics of Indian Aid to Nepal*. Kathmandu: Indian Aid Mission.

ICID/FAO. 1996. *Irrigation Scheduling: From Theory to Practice*. Proceedings of the ICID/FAO workshop on irrigation scheduling. Rome, 12–13 September 1995. International Commission on Irrigation and Drainage/Food and Agricultural Organization.

IWMI. 2006. *Multiple-Use Water Services to Advance the Millennium Development Goals.* Research report 98. Colombo: International Water Management Institute.

Khanal, P.R. 2003. *Engineering Participation: The Processes and Outcomes of Irrigation Management Transfer in the Tarai of Nepal.* New Delhi: Orient Longman.

Law, J. 2009. Seeing like a survey. *Cultural sociology*, 3(2): 239–56.

Law, J. and A. Mol. 2001. Situating technoscience: An inquiry into spatialities. *Society and Space*, 19(5): 609–21.

Liebrand, J. 2010. Masculinities: A scale challenge in irrigation governance in Nepal. In: P. Pradhan, U. Gautam and N. Mangal Joshi (eds), *Dynamics of Farmer Managed Irrigation Systems: Socio-Institutional, Economic and Technical Contexts.* Proceedings of the 5th international seminar. Held on 25–26 March 2010, Kathmandu: Farmer Managed Irrigation Systems Promotion Trust.

Martin, E. and R. Yoder. 1983. Review of farmer-managed irrigation in Nepal. In: *Water Management in Nepal.* Proceedings of the seminar on water management issues, pp. 82–91. Her Majesty's Government of Nepal, Agricultural Project Services Centre (APROSC) and Agricultural Development Council (ADC). Held 31 July–2 August, Kathmandu.

McKenzie, J. 2001. *Perform or Else: From Discipline to Performance.* London: Routledge.

Mosse, D. 2005. *Cultivating Development: An Ethnography of Aid Policy and Practice.* London: Pluto.

Pradhan, B.B. 1982. *Participatory Irrigation Management: Medium Irrigation Project.* World Bank (WB) and Sir MacDonald and Partners Limited.

Pradhan, P. 2007. Twenty five years of FMIS study in Nepal. In: P. Pradhan et al. (eds), *Irrigation in Transition: Interacting with Internal and External Factors and Setting the Strategic Actions.* Proceedings of the 4th international seminar held on 6–7 November 2006, pp. 360–65. Kathmandu: Farmer Managed Irrigation Systems Promotion Trust

Pradhan, P. 1989. *A Comparative Study of 21 Farmer-Managed Irrigation Systems.* Colombo: International Irrigation Management Institute (IIMI).

Rising Nepal. 1967. Irrigation potentiality of Nepal. 29 March. National newspaper, Kathmandu.

St. John, G. (ed.). 2008. *Victor Turner and Contemporary Cultural Performance.* New York: Bergahn.

Turner, V. 1974. *Dramas, Fields and Metaphors: Symbolic Action in Human Society.* Ithaca: Cornell University Press.

Turner, V. 1969. *The Ritual Process: Structure and Anti-Structure.* Chicago: Aldine.

Turner, V. and E. Bruner (eds). 1986. *The Anthropology of Experience.* Urbana: University of Illinois Press.

Schechner, R. 2006. *Performance Studies: An Introduction.* 2nd edn. New York and London: Routledge.

Sharma, K.R. (ed.). 2004. *Irrigation Conditions, Visions and the Concept of Integrated Water Resources Management.* Kathmandu: Department of Irrigation.

Shivakoti, G. and E. Ostrom (eds). 2002. *Improving Irrigation Governance and Management in Nepal.* Oakland, CA: ICS Press.

Shukla, A., G.P. Shivakoti, P. Benjamin and E. Ostrom. 2002. Toward the future of irrigation governance and management in Nepal. In: G Shivakoti and E. Ostrom (eds). *Improving Irrigation Governance and Management in Nepal*, pp. 225–41. Oakland, CA: ICS Press.

Shukla, A. and K.R. Sharma. 1997. *Participatory Irrigation Management in Nepal: A Monograph on Evolution, Processes and Performance.* Kathmandu: Department of Irrigation.

Udas, P.B. and M. Zwarteveen. 2010. Can water professionals meet gender goals? A case study of the Department of Irrigation, Nepal. *Gender and Development*, 18(1): 87–97.

WECS. 1981. *Irrigation Sector Review.* Kathmandu: Water and Energy Commission Secretariat.

Whelpton, J. 2005. *A History of Nepal.* Cambridge: Cambridge University Press.

World Bank. 2006. Conjunctive use of groundwater and surface water. *Agricultural and Rural Development Notes*, 6 (February). Available at http://siteresources. worldbank.org/INTARD/Resources/Notes_Issue6_web.pdf.

Zwarteveen, M.Z. 2011. Questioning masculinities in water. *Economic and Political Weekly*, 46(18): 40–48.

Chapter 16

Indigenous Space, Scalar Politics and Water Governance in the Salish Sea Basin

Emma S. Norman[1]

In November 2005, the first annual Coast Salish Gathering was held at the Jamestown S'Klallam Tribal Center in Sequim, Washington. This Gathering brought together First Nation Chiefs, Tribal Chairs and Council members from around the Salish Sea region of North America. Invited delegates from Canadian and US governments and environmental organizations also participated in the dialogue with the tribal leaders in an attempt to address environmental issues of shared concern – particularly issues related to the protection of salmon habitats.

'It has been a long time since we have all come together as tribes', reflects Tom Sampson, a prominent Coast Salish elder and tribal leader on the first day of the Gathering in Jamestown S'Klallam (2005). 'The last five hundred years', he states solemnly, 'have not been great ones for our people.' The elder reminds the audience that the words spoken 'are the words from our ancestors' and that the purpose of the Gathering is 'to talk about the future of our children and the children yet to be born'.

The opening statement addressed several interrelated topics: tribal governance, ancestral rights, environmental degradation and the connectedness of the Coast Salish people. Although the words were spoken softly, they filled the long house in its entirety. Every one of the 200 participants listened intently as one of the most revered tribal leaders of the Coast Salish communities opened the discussions.

At the end of the three-day Gathering, the Coast Salish leaders committed their communities to finding solutions to pressing environmental issues in the Salish Sea region, particularly those related to protecting the waterways of critical salmon habitat. The leaders agreed that the most effective way to accomplish this

1   Many thanks to the Coast Salish Gathering members for allowing me to participate in the Gatherings, and to the Coast Salish tribes and bands – particularly staff at Swinomish and Tulalip, Department of Natural Resources – who reviewed this chapter and offered important insights. Thanks also to Tom Sampson, of the Tsartlip First Nation, for his earlier review, comments, and encouragement. Special thanks to Lummi Nation and Northwest Indian College, where my longstanding affiliation made much of this work possible. Earlier versions of this chapter were published in *Water Alternatives* (2012), 5(1): 138–60. An extended and revised version of this chapter also appears as chapter 6 in: Norman, E.S. 2015, *Governing Transboundary Waters: Canada, The United States and Indigenous communities* London: Routledge Press.

goal was to establish their own governing body and to speak with a unified voice. As a result, the leaders formed the annual Coast Salish Gatherings.

Through the development of the Gathering, the tribes and bands throughout Coast Salish territory have committed to working together to address shared environmental issues, drawing on a strong connection to their land, shared ancestors, and a commitment to the revitalization of their culture. As a group, they share the goal 'to protect the environment and natural resources of the Salish Sea for the sustainability of the Coast Salish peoples'. The Gathering represents more than 70 tribes and bands that span and pre-date the Canada–United States border, in the Coast Salish region encompassing approximately 72,000 square kilometres. However, the creation of the Salish governing body does not replace participation in other environmental forums; rather, it provides an organization designed for and by the Salish people that places the Coast Salish belief system at the forefront of the governance structure.

For the Coast Salish, the protection of the watercourses of the Salish Sea is a practical matter of preserving traditional lifeways. The bioaccumulative effects of pollution coupled with years of overharvesting have placed tremendous strain on the natural resources of the Salish Sea, thereby disrupting the political, economic and cultural fabric of many Coast Salish communities (Donatuto 2008). Understanding the importance of the Coast Salish Gatherings provides valuable insights into the scalar politics of transboundary water governance. That the new governance mechanisms are, at their foundation, based on Coast Salish territorial boundaries rather than institutions representing Canada or the US challenges implicit assumptions regarding constructions of scale, particularly in a postcolonial context.

This chapter explores the mechanisms that the indigenous leaders are using to challenge colonial scalar constructions and shows how, through methods such as critical cartography and strategic essentialism, Coast Salish communities are (re) creating a shared sense of identity congruent with traditional territory and that reinforces cultural values. As the other chapters in this book document, exploring scalar politics provides critical insights into the power dynamics often implicit in water governance – particularly for watercourses that transgress political boundaries. This case, which encompasses multiple jurisdictions and interpretations of spatial constructs, provides an interesting avenue to analyse scalar politics from the lens of transnational politics for indigenous communities because indigenous leaders are using shared cultural identities to challenge colonial boundary-drawing (see Figure 16.1).

Drawing the Line: Borders, Power and Indigenous Space

The delineation of the Canada–US border and its subsequent provinces, states and regions is part of the construction of a cultural landscape and identity built by culturally specific meanings. The centuries-old negotiation of territory that is

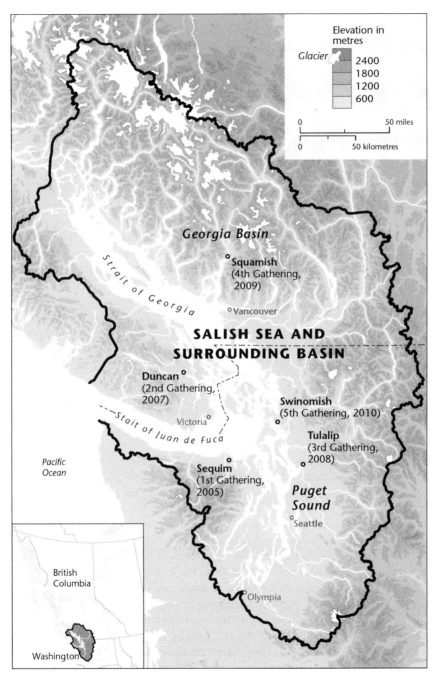

**Figure 16.1   Map of the Salish Sea basin and locations of Coast
Salish Gatherings**

Source: Original map. Cartography by Eric Leinberger, University of British Columbia.

now deemed Canada and the United States was part of a series of negotiations, disputes and treaties that defined and redefined territories as separate spaces. Although documenting the historical processes that defined the modern Canada–US border is beyond the scope of this chapter, it is important to acknowledge that the construction of political borders is part of wider geohistorical processes.

As Canada and the US built their cultural identities as bounded nations, the identities of the indigenous communities spanning the border were impacted by the changing political geography. The production of sovereign political systems in Canada and the US affected and continues to affect environmental governance – particularly access to and management of resources – for indigenous communities. The colonial political demarcation not only severed a cultural continuum that spanned and pre-dated the international border, but also created different national identities, rights to ownership of land, and land and resource policies that continue to impact indigenous communities (Boxberger 1989; Harris 2002). As the divergent political systems strengthened and developed national identities, indigenous communities whose traditional territory spanned the international divide became increasingly fragmented.

Shortly after the 1849 demarcation, yet another bounding of space occurred in North America. The establishment of the reserve system was a physical and political restructuring of indigenous communities which greatly impacted access to culturally relevant resources such as salmon and shellfish (Boxberger 1989; D.C. Harris 2000). A new tribal system was imposed on a cultural group based on family structures (Suttles 1974). As noted Coast Salish scholar Wayne Suttles (1960: 296) reflects, groups of villages in the Coast Salish region were linked by common dialect and traditions as 'tribes'. The creation of the reserve system in Canada (and reservations in the United States) significantly altered settlements, migration patterns and access to resources for the Salish communities (Boxberger 1993; Barman 1999; Miller 1997, 2006).

The political demarcations drastically changed participation in subsistence activities throughout Coast Salish territory, not only throughout Coast Salish territory but also wherever the indigenous communities would seek to harvest resources. Access to natural resources, including marine and freshwater resources, was regulated under divergent sets of codes, laws and principles. The implications of the changed governance structures post-contact are especially acute in the management of mobile marine resources, for example, salmon, that migrate between the newly demarcated borders. In many cases, the salmon spawn on one side of the international border and migrate to the other side during their adult life. This migration complicates treaty fishing rights and access during the harvest season. The access to, and distribution of, salmon are integral components of the societal makeup and identity of Coast Salish communities (Suttles 1964; Boxberger 1989). The shift from internally governed systems (pre-contact) to externally monitored systems (post-contact) has ongoing consequences and implications for cultural preservation and the preservation of intact family systems.

Beyond rights of access to marine resources for individual families, the political reorganization of the Salish Sea basin has had dramatic impacts on relationships between tribal members and nontribal members, and between tribes. For example, the contentious relationships – known as the 'salmon wars' in the Pacific Northwest (Findlay and Coates 2002; Brown 2005) – fuelled the shifting economic structures that supported competing for resources (as sources of cash) rather than cooperation for subsistence (Singleton 2002). Adding to the tensions are the extraterritorial impacts of environmental degradation on critical fish habitat (spawning grounds) and the negative impacts of global climate change on fish populations.

In the Coast Salish case (similar to other indigenous communities throughout the world), social restructuring adversely impacts the cultural fabric of the local population (White 1979; Thom 2009). As such, the Coast Salish Gatherings are not just about addressing environmental issues; rather, the governance structures have far-reaching goals that include language revitalization and self-determination. Thus, the work of the Gatherings is part of the process to reclaim and rebuild some of the internal control of decision-making and governance. It is also about strengthening the individual tribes and bands to think beyond the limits (geographic, economic, political etc.) that were placed on them during colonial times.

The Coast Salish Gatherings are deliberate attempts to rebuild the cultural structures and characteristics of its communities. This work is achieved, in part, through the 'scaling up' of individual bands and tribes to a singular nation. In this case, the process of reconstructing the scale based on wider Coast Salish territory is occurring through the employment of techniques such as strategic essentialism, performativity and counter-mapping.

Tools for Rescaling: Strategic Essentialism, Performativity and Counter-Mapping

Strategic essentialism is a concept that is often used in postcolonial studies to theorize citizen group unification. The term was coined by Spivak to describe a strategy that nationalities, ethnic and minority groups, can use to present themselves as unified. Although significant differences may exist between individual members of these groups, the process of 'essentializing' the group members to represent a singular (and simplified) group identity has proven a successful technique to achieve goals (Spivak 1987, 1988, 1996; Guha and Spivak 1998). The Coast Salish case is an example of a cultural group whose membership represents a diverse range of bands, tribes and family. Yet, the communities recognize that strengthening the Coast Salish connections helps to negotiate with external agencies, which ultimately supports the shared goals of cultural revitalization of individual tribes and bands.

Similarly, techniques such as performance theory (Mountz 2010) and counter-mapping (Harris and Hazen 2006; Sparke 1998, 2000, 2006) are documented strategies for activists to reimagine and recreate new space. 'Performance theory' is an analytic to help describe and understand the production of scales and scalar hierarchies (Mountz 2010). This theory helps us understand how performance, discourses and practice can help create (or recreate) new geopolitical scales (Brown and Purcell 2005; Kaiser and Nikiforova 2008; Harris and Alatout 2010; Cohen and Harris 2013).

In addition, cartographic tools such as 'counter-mapping' can be used to present physical spaces as unified. Increasingly, indigenous activist movements have successfully employed tools of counter-mapping to assert rights over land (see Wainwright and Bryan 2009 for examples in South America). In the Salish region, this occurred as a visualization of the Salish Sea (see Rose-Redwood 2011), which was used for 20 years by environmental groups and indigenous communities, prior to the official naming of the Salish Sea according to the records of Canada and the United States (Norman 2012, 2013). Counter-mapping has also been used for the creation of the treaty groups of First Nation Chiefs, Tribal Chairs and others mentioned above (Sparke 1998; Thom 2005, 2010) and is integral to the processes of creating – and sustaining – the Coast Salish Gatherings. These three performative and discursive techniques help to actively rescale a region, challenge colonial boundaries, and also work towards goals of self-governance.

Challenging Bounded Space: Rethinking Citizenry

Analysing the Coast Salish Gatherings as a governance mechanism provides three entry points into understanding how reconstructed borders (and reimagined scales of governance) might usefully inform water governance. First, governance mechanisms like the Coast Salish Gathering can socially reconstruct a new geographic region (the Salish Sea basin), thereby challenging and disrupting imposed nation-state borders and facilitating more coordinated water governance across jurisdictions.

Second, the development of the Coast Salish Gathering is motivated by a concern for the social and cultural implications of a degraded physical environment, and is achieved by reconnecting (politically, socially and culturally) with bands and tribes spanning the nation-state borders and increasing capacity for improved water governance throughout the Salish Sea basin.

Finally, the development of governance mechanisms based on traditional protocol can help reinforce goals of self-governance and self-determination, as has been articulated by scholars such as Deloria and Lytle (1984), Deloria and Wilkins (1999), Little Bear (2000) and Wilkinson (1987). Improved self-governance and empowerment will lead to greater capacity to carry out effective water governance throughout the basin.

Critical Scalar Construction: The Development of the Coast Salish Gathering

Understanding the context in which the Gathering was developed provides insights into the construction (or reconstruction) of a shared identity and the importance of including cultural politics in analyses of borders, water governance and scale. This story shows the deliberate intent to rescale governance by 'scaling up' identities from individual bands and tribes to the collective Coast Salish Nation. The conscious effort to unify groups on either side of the border draws simultaneously on historical connectedness and the shared desire to address issues of environmental degradation. In so doing, the members of the Gathering are rejecting scales of governance that bifurcate the Coast Salish community (based on the nation-state system) and adopting a scale of governance reflective of traditional Coast Salish geographies (the Salish Sea basin).

As Sampson explained at the 2008 Coast Salish Gathering held in Tulalip, Washington: 'When [former Premier of British Columbia] Harcourt asked how we communicated with each other, we said, 'Ceremonies bring us together. We have our agreement, we have our drum." The Drum Declaration, signed during one of the original meetings, outlines the inherent right to the lands, waters and resources within the Coast Salish traditional territories (see Figure 16.2 and Box 16.1). This declaration is important for a number of reasons. First, it states that these rights have existed since time immemorial. Second, it specifically outlines the territory of the Coast Salish region. Third, it commits the Salish Nations to govern these resources for future generations with the spirit of sovereignty as a connected nation:

> We declare and affirm our Inalienable Right of Aboriginal Title of Aboriginal Rights to the Lands, the Mountains, the Minerals, the Trees, the Lakes, the Rivers, the Streams, the Air, and other Resources on our Land. We, Declare that our Aboriginal title and rights have existed from time Immemorial, Exists at the present time and shall exist for ALL Future TIME. We, Declare unto ourselves that Sovereignty is Inherent in our NATION.

As a connected nation, inherent rights and title to the land, water and resources are articulated. The signatories articulate their vision, territory and membership. This process is central to the rescaling process that includes aligning themselves under a reconnected nation and agreeing to common terms.

Signing the Drum Declaration serves as a symbol of the leaders' commitment to ongoing cooperation throughout the Salish Nation. As one leader reflected, 'Signing the drum was one of the best things that we have done. I believe there is cause again to reaffirm that relationship.' 'After all', he continued, 'that continuity lies in the heart and minds of our people.' The drum continues to serve an important role in the Salish Gatherings.

Uniting individual bands and tribes under a singular Nation (represented as a singular drum that declares and asserts the rights of a Nation) serves as a discursive tool towards the 'performance' (and actualization) of unification. These connections are reaffirmed every year, as the Coast Salish Gatherings rotate between communities, displayed prominently at the meetings and referenced frequently throughout the Gatherings.

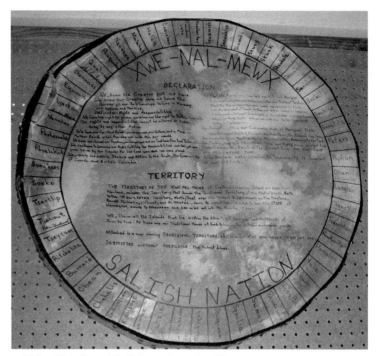

Figure 16.2   The Coast Salish Declaration Drum

Source: Photo by E. Norman, Coast Salish Gathering, Tulalip, Washington, 2008.

Self-Determination and Governance

Furthermore, the Gatherings place the Salish people at the locus of power for the management and protection of their natural environment. This organizational structure reinforces a governance model in which Salish people govern the resources for their community. The Gatherings serve as a place for the community leaders to identify key priority areas for the Salish Nation – these priority areas are then brought back to the communities and integrated into localized efforts. In addition, the Gatherings serve as an important place for information exchange and reaffirmation and revitalization of shared identity. They keep the momentum for the work ahead, and keep the goals aligned.

A growing number of scholars have written extensively on the need for indigenous communities to reclaim their governance mechanisms, breaking away from systems that perpetuate a dependence on federal governments (Deloria and Lytle 1984; Wilkinson 1987; Little Bear 2000; Wildcat 2011). For example, Deloria and Lytle (1984: viii) write:

> Citizens and tribal members often chafe at regulations and restrictions, not realizing that the burgeoning population has created a need for government to serve large numbers of people in a rather impersonal way. Some means

Box 16.1   Text of the Coast Salish Declaration Drum

XWE-NAL-MEWX: Salish Nation

DECLARATION

We know the Creator put us here. We know our Creator gave us laws that govern all our relationships to live in harmony with nature and mankind, defined our rights and responsibilities. We have the right to govern ourselves and the right to self-determination. Our rights and responsibilities cannot be altered or taken away by another Nation. We have spiritual beliefs, our languages, our culture, and a place on Mother Earth which provides us with all our needs.

We have maintained our freedom, our languages, and our traditions from time immemorial.

We continue to exercise our rights fulfilling the responsibilities and obligations given to us by the Creator for the land upon which we were placed. We, openly and publicly declare and affirm to the people, the governments of Canada and British Columbia:

That the Xwe-nal-mewx have held and still hold Aboriginal title to all the lands, waters and resources within our traditional territories. That the Xwe-nal-mewx have never rendered any agreement or Treaty with the Government of Canada, Britain, and British Columbia concerning the occupation, settlement, sovereignty or jurisdiction over our Lands except those treaties entered into with the British Government prior to Confederation.

We declare and affirm our Inalienable Right of Aboriginal Title of Aboriginal Rights to the lands, the mountains, the minerals, the trees, the lakes, the rivers, the streams, the air, and other resources on our Land. We, declare that our Aboriginal title and rights have existed from time immemorial, exists at the present time and shall exist for all future time. We, declare unto ourselves that sovereignty is inherent in our Nation.

TERRITORY

The territory of the XWE-NAL-MEWX of Southern Vancouver Island and Lower West Mainland, includes the territory that bounds the traditional territory of the MUTHA'LEMEXH, North the YEQW'LWTHTAX Territory, and NL'AKAPAX, down to Jenatchee, in what now the state of Washington, across to Aberdeen and 250 miles out into the Pacific Ocean.

We, claim all the Islands that lie with the Straits of Georgia and the Straits of Juan De Fuca: As these are our traditional homes of food gathering, for cultural and economic needs.

Attached is a map showing ABORIGINAL TERRITORY of Claim for XWE-NAL-MEWX NATIONS and SUBMITTED WITHOUT PREJUDICE: The Actual Lines.

must be found to humanize social and political institutions once again. Here
traditional Indian customs, if properly incorporated in the functions and mission
of government, can prove effective and important.

The spirit of these words come through at the Coast Salish Gatherings, which are
organized carefully – both in structure and language – to preserve and revitalize
Coast Salish cultural practices. Unlike other transboundary environmental
meetings, the Gathering does not immediately delve into policy talks and action
items. Rather, the organizers design the entire first day of the Gathering to 'rekindle
the relationship of Coast Salish First Nations and Tribes through traditional
practices' (CSG 2010).[2] The programme for the Tulalip Gathering outlined the
significance of this first day:

> The ceremonies are an important traditional process that is valuable in unifying
> the Gathering and will include the introduction and honor of the Coast Salish
> leadership's gallant triumphs that support the efforts to protect our aboriginal
> rights.

Through an intricate web of ceremony, blessings and introductions, the participants
at a Gathering become 'mentally and spiritually prepared' to participate in the
coming days' policy talks. The Gathering achieves this by following protocol such
as blessing the four corners, calling of witnesses and praying for the participants
and their families. 'This is important work', as one Salish leader noted, and 'we
all need to be fully present – in mind and body – to do the work for our ancestors
and children'. After the ceremonies and blessings, the remaining days are open
for introductions and testimony. For example, in the Tulalip Gathering members,[3]
elected officials, invited guests, veterans and elders each had the opportunity to
introduce themselves and reflect on the purpose of the meeting. Introductions
often included the delegate's English and Salish name, the tribe or band they
represented, and a declaration that they recognized and honoured the traditional
territory of the host tribe.

The Gatherings also follow traditional longhouse etiquette. The use of the
traditional Coast Salish language throughout the conference underscores (and
embodies) the desire for cultural preservation, and is used as a way to challenge
former practices of cultural dominance and forced assimilation. The deliberate
planning for the Gathering helped achieve many of its goals: employing innovative
strategies to transcend the political geographies of imposed borderlands to reach
cultural and environmental goals.

---

2   The preceding Gatherings in Duncan, BC (2007), Tulalip, WA (2008), Squamish,
BC (2009) and Swinomish, WA (2010) also followed this protocol.

3   Largely comprising tribal chiefs and band leaders and elected officials, such as
tribal chairs.

The Material Impacts of a Fixed Border: Governing across a Colonial Construction of Space

Although the Coast Salish communities identify themselves as a connected group, the realities of border crossing serve as harsh reminders of the politics of occupation and colonially constructed space. In fact, many Coast Salish people do not recognize the border as a matter of principle. Some even go as far as not declaring US or Canadian citizenship when crossing the border, choosing rather to self-identify by family or tribe.

Testimonies of participants attending the Jamestown and Tulalip Gatherings reflect the hardships of the border and the ongoing impacts of political fragmentation on resource management. At the Gatherings, participants provided testimony on the continued impacts of, consternation for and resistance to their bordered homeland. In discussions, the border – or 'the line', as it is commonly called by Coast Salish community members – was described by many as something that needed to be overcome. The demarcation of this line was often viewed as something that was separating their communities: 'Like the Great Wall of China, [the border] is separating us.' In addition, the further bounding of land and people through reserves/reservations was also voiced as a major concern. As one elder from the northern Coast Salish territory indicated: 'Our people once controlled over 600,000 [square] miles of ancestral land and now we live on reservations and they expect us to plan for the future of our children on small plots of land.' In addition, the physical passage through the border evoked strong emotions related to identity and power: 'Having to state, "I'm American" or "I'm Canadian" isn't right. "No!" I say to the guard, "I am Coast Salish!"'

The testimony also reflects that the Gathering provides a sense of (re) connectedness, allowing families that span the border to come together. Several of the participants voiced this as an opportunity to reconnect with family and community throughout Coast Salish territory: 'We are able to bring together our relatives. That border separates us, but we are connected in many, many ways.' The recognition that this was an opportunity to reunify and strengthen their voice was also noted: 'We need to speak with one voice. We need to continue to build upon that foundation of shared history. That is what we are doing. We are learning to speak with one voice again.' This quote is an example of how strategic essentialism is employed to push forward goals associated with a unified Coast Salish Nation – both in terms of self-determination and the capacity to serve as stewards of the shared natural environment.

In the discussions, the border was often linked to wider issues of natural resource management. As one participant reflected, 'Natural resources bring us together. It bothers me that we have to *compete* for natural resources because we have always worked together. The way the system is now, we are set up against each other.' The above statements capture a central driver of the establishment of the Gathering. They also reinforce observations by Thom (2010) on the changing fabric of Coast Salish community and the efforts to reconfigure strategically for a common purpose. Historically, Salish communities worked collectively to ensure adequate provisions for all family members. Intricate socioeconomic networks based on trade and ceremony helped in the distribution of wealth and basic resources throughout the extended communities (Boxberger 1993; Kennedy 1993; Suttles 1960).

Performing Unity and Counter-Mapping

In an effort to mitigate the historical (and contemporary) divisiveness of the constructed international border, the organizers of the Gathering employed strategic exercises to help reinforce cultural connections. In addition, they use discursive tools (i.e. maps, media coverage, literature) to empower communities and reframe governance structures. For example, the facilitator of the Tulalip Gathering suggested that during the introductions every Council member add the phrase 'And I am Coast Salish' after their name. As the leaders affirmed their status, the powerful words became increasingly impassioned: 'I *am* Coast Salish ... We are the same.' Some delegates uttered their statements with such passion that applause, cheers and whoops would spontaneously erupt. This 'performance' of unity helped align the material and the symbolic concept of a (re)connected community. Interestingly, this exercise plays on the very successful ad campaign that used the patriotic phrase 'I am Canadian' to sell their product (Molson beer) (see Seiler 2002).

This exercise was also a way of establishing consensus. By repeatedly emphasizing the connectedness of the community, the aim was to rewrite the discourse of a fragmented community. As one participant of the Gathering reflected, the affirmations remind the delegates that 'regardless of which side of the border our relatives happened to land, we are all interconnected'. As Coast Salish leader, Tom Sampson, further explained:

> You might ask what we did today ... We are learning to trust each other again. There are no hidden agendas. If we agree as to who we are, we are able to protect who we are. It is up to you to reach back and remember the works of our ancestors and bring it forward. We have to bring hope and life to our children.

Although the tribes and bands had and continue to have their own priorities, the intricate relationships and shared connection to the land are important components of the creation of the Gathering and of the dedication to address the environmental issues facing their respective communities and the Salish Nation as a whole – particularly the decline in salmon.

In addition to re-establishing cultural continuity, the Gathering provides the space for the Coast Salish leaders to collaborate and speak with one voice. Establishing consensus within the Salish communities serves an important purpose. It helps prioritize issues and strategically organize efforts to tackle increasingly complex and multijurisdictional environmental issues. The ongoing dialogue between the Gathering members helps to identify these critical areas. The objective is clearly stated in the literature put forth by the organizers:

> The objective of the Gathering was to provide a forum for Tribal and First Nation leaders to collaborate on environmental issues and share that information with governmental policy makers to assist them in making more protective and culturally sensitive decisions concerning the future of this richly endowed, yet fragile, region that we share, the Salish Sea. (CSG 2008)

With a unified voice, the representatives of the Gathering have committed to meeting a series of goals. For example, through the development of an environmental action plan, the participants aim to 'Conserve and restore the Salish Sea ecosystem to a level that ensures the sustainability of the Coast Salish People and our cultural lifeways' (CSG 2008). A number of priorities are identified in the plan, including the provision of adequate clean air, water and land to sustain and protect the health of the Coast Salish people. These priorities represent the general pairing of environmental and cultural protection in the contemporary Coast Salish governance model. They also highlight how protecting water resources (both marine and freshwater) directly supports subsistence, cultural and economic activities.

Establishing consensus among the Coast Salish tribes and bands also helps in coordinating with external agencies. The regional director of the United States Environmental Protection Agency expressed this point of view at the Tulalip Gathering: 'The more unified your voice, the more support we can give you.' The director further explained that although the department is 'sensitive to the needs of individual bands and tribes, establishing a common position aids in the navigation through large bureaucratic systems'. Thus, the creation of a unified voice among Salish communities and a (re)constructed space serve important roles both internally and externally.

Representative of this shift is a recent collaboration between Coast Salish communities and the United States Geological Survey (USGS) to conduct water quality sampling on the annual tribal canoe journey. The USGS describes the partnership as a 'blending of science and tradition', and the organizers laud the project as a unique new multijurisdictional partnership:

> In an exciting new partnership between the Coast Salish (Indigenous peoples of the Salish Sea ecoregion) and the USGS, members of western Washington Tribes and British Columbia First Nations will measure water quality in Puget Sound and the Strait of Georgia during the Tribal Journey, the annual summer canoe voyage. The project will provide a snapshot of current water quality conditions and data that can be compared with future measurements along successive journeys. This information is important to improve management of ancestral waters that are experiencing environmental decline. (USGS 2008)

Indicative of this coordinated project, the USGS website provides a link to the water quality sites and real-time information on the data collection (as well as video clips of the daily progress of the canoe journey).[4] This is, perhaps, one of the first of many tangible (and positive) outcomes of the creation of the Council in terms of multijurisdictional collaboration. The partnership has occurred on an annual basis since 2008, with increased participation and collaboration reported by the participants.

Discussion and Conclusion

This chapter has explored the politics of scale of water governance in a postcolonial context through the analysis of the Coast Salish Gatherings. This case provides an example of how collective rights (treaty and Aboriginal) are being scaled up from individual 'tribe' or 'band' to 'Nation', and contributes to the nascent discussions of politics of scale within water governance, complementing other critical scholarship on rescaling of water governance found in this volume. In addition, the chapter responds to a call from political geographers and border scholars to look more closely at how power is mobilized at the site of the border (Paasi 2003, 2009; Agnew 2007; Popescu 2011). I argue that including cultural politics in the investigations of borders, environmental governance and scale provides greater nuance to understanding water as a socionatural hybrid. This is important particularly – but not solely – in a postcolonial context. This call for greater inclusion of cultural politics in transboundary governance contributes to earlier insights put forth by critical scholars Don Mitchell (2000) and Kay Anderson (2007).

This case is particularly noteworthy given that the governance structure presents an apparent contradiction: it is both transnational (as it spans the Canada–US border) and national (as it represents a singular Salish Nation). The enactment of the Gathering thereby serves as a counter-narrative to a bordered geography by emphasizing the connectedness of their communities, rather than the differences in national identities. The Coast Salish efforts to employ strategic essentialism and counter-mapping are in line with other documented efforts within political geography to construct or reconstruct scale that is meaningful to the user (Harris and Hazen 2006).

There is a growing movement within indigenous communities to reclaim traditional governance processes (Norman 2014). As John Waterhouse, Director of the Yukon River Inter-tribal Watershed Council and participant of the Jamestown Gathering, aptly noted, 'We are the ones that we are waiting for.' This case study provides a starting point to evaluate larger issues of efficacy and power in tribal reorganization across state boundaries. Further research, however, is needed to continue evaluation of these efforts. Overall, my research finds that the aggregation of historically connected tribes and bands for the shared benefit

---

4   See http://wa.water.usgs.gov/projects/coastsalish.

of environmental protection and cultural reunification is a first step in reclaiming space and reconstructing traditional governance mechanisms.

This chapter marks a deliberate effort to include the cultural politics of the border in investigations of transboundary environmental governance. I suggest that investigating how the administrative structures and physical boundaries of water governance are both socially constructed and politically mobilized provides for a more nuanced approach to discussions of transboundary environmental governance. Including a critical discussion of the cultural politics of borders (and border making) helps to identify, and thereby address, more effectively the power dynamics constituted through postcolonial constructions of space and hydrosocial networks.

References

Agnew, J.C. 2007. No borders, no nations: Making Greece in Macedonia. *Annals of the Association of American Geographers* 97(2): 398–422.

Anderson, K. 2007. *Race and the Crisis of Humanism*. London: Routledge.

Barman, J. 1999. What a difference a border makes: Aboriginal racial intermixture in the Pacific Northwest. *Journal of the West* 38(3): 14–20.

Brown, D. 2005. *Salmon Wars: The Battle for the West Coast Salmon Fishery*. Madeira Park, BC: Harbour Publishing.

Brown, J.C. and Purcell, M. 2005. There's nothing inherent about scale: Political ecology, the local trap, and the politics of development in the Brazilian Amazon. *Geoforum* 36(5): 607–24.

Boxberger, D. 1989. *To Fish in Common: The Ethnohistory of Lummi Indian Salmon Fishing*. Seattle: University of Washington Press.

Boxberger, D. 1993. Lightning boldts and sparrow wings: A comparison of native fishing rights in British Columbia and Washington State. *Native Studies* 9(1): 1–13.

Cohen, A. and Harris, L.M. 2014. Watersheds as 'natural' governance units in the Canadian context. In Glass, M. and Rose-Redwood, R. (eds), *Performativity, Politics, and the Production of Social Space*. New York: Routledge.

CSG (Coast Salish Gathering). 2008. *Coast Salish Gathering Program*. Tulalip, WA.

CSG. 2010. *Coast Salish Gathering Program*. Swinomish, WA, http://www.coastsalishgathering.com (accessed 15 September 2010).

Deloria, V. and Lytle, C.M. 1984. *The Nations Within: The Past and Future of American Indian Sovereignty*. New York: Pantheon.

Deloria, V. and Wilkins, D.E. 1999. *Tribes, Treaties, and Constitutional Tribulations*. Austin: University of Texas Press.

Donatuto, J. 2008. When seafood feeds the spirit yet poisons the body: Developing health indicators for risk assessment in a Native American fishing community. PhD thesis. University of British Columbia, Vancouver.

Findlay, J.M. and Coates, K.S. 2002. *Parallel Destinies: Canadian-American Relations West of the Rockies*. Seattle: University of Washington Press.

Guha, R. and Spivak, G.C. (eds). 1988. *Selected Subaltern Studies*. New York: Oxford University Press.

Harris, C. 2000. *the resettlement of british columbia: essays on Colonialism and Geographic Change*. Vancouver: University of British Columbia Press.

Harris, C. 2002. *Making Native Space: Colonialism, Resistance, and Reserves in British Columbia*. Vancouver: University of British Columbia Press.

Harris, D.C. 2000. Territoriality, aboriginal rights and the Heiltuk spawn-on-kelp fishery. *University of British Columbia Law Review* 34(1): 195–238.

Harris, D.C. 2001. *Fish, Law, and Colonialism: The Legal Capture of Salmon in British Columbia*. Toronto: University of Toronto Press.

Harris, L. and Hazen, H. 2006. Power of maps: (Counter)-mapping for conservation. *ACME: An International E-Journal of Critical Geographies* 4(1): 99–130.

Harris, L.M. and Alatout, S. 2010. Negotiating hydro-scales, forging states: Comparison of the upper Tigris/Euphrates and Jordan River basins. *Political Geography*, 29(3): 148–56.

Kaiser, R. and Nikiforova, E. 2008. The performativity of scale: The social construction of scale effects in Narva, Estonia. *Environment and Planning D* 26(3): 537–62.

Kennedy, D. 1993. Looking for tribes in all of the wrong places: An examination of the central Cost Salish coastal environment. MA thesis. University of British Columbia, Vancouver.

Little Bear, L. 2000. Jagged worldviews colliding. In Battiste, M. (ed), *Reclaiming Indigenous Voice and Vision*, pp. 77–85. Vancouver: University of British Columbia Press.

Miller, B. 1997. The 'really real' border and the divided Salish community. *BC Studies: The British Columbian Quarterly* 112: 63–79.

Miller, B. 2006. Conceptual and practical boundaries: West coast Indians/First Nations and the border of contagion in the post-9/11 era. In Evans, S. (ed.), *The Borderlands of the American and Canadian Wests: Essays on Regional History of the Forty-Ninth Parallel*, pp. 49–66. Lincoln: University of Nebraska Press.

Mitchell, Don. 2000. *Cultural Geography: A Critical Introduction*. Malden, MA: Blackwell.

Mountz, A. 2010. Refugees – performing distinction: The paradoxical positionings of the displaced. In Cresswell, T. and Merriman, P. (eds), *Geographies of Mobilities: Practices, Spaces, Subjects*, pp. 255–70. Farnham: Ashgate.

Nadasdy, P. 2004. *Hunters and Bureaucrats: Power, Knowledge, and Aboriginal-State Relations in the Southwest Yukon*. Vancouver: University of British Columbia Press.

Norman, E.S. 2015. *Governing Transboundary Waters: Canada, the United States, and Indigenous Communities*. London: Routledge.

Norman, E.S. 2013 Who's counting? Spatial politics, ecocolonisation, and the politics of calculation in Boundary Bay, *Area* 45(2): 179–87.

Norman, E.S. 2012. Cultural politics and transboundary resource governance in the Salish Sea. *Water Alternatives* 5(1): 138–60.

Paasi, A. 2003. Region and place: Regional identity in question. *Progress in Human Geography* 27(4): 475–85.

Paasi, A. 2009. The resurgence of the 'region' and 'regional identity': Theoretical perspectives and empirical observations on regional dynamics in Europe. *Review of International Studies* 35: 121–46.

Phare, M.-A. 2009. *Denying the Source: The Crisis of First Nations Water Rights*. Calgary: Rocky Mountain Books.

Popescu, G. 2011. *Bordering and Ordering the Twenty-First Century*. New York: Rowman and Littlefield.

Rose-Redwood, R. 2011. Rethinking the agenda of political toponymy. *ACME: An International E-Journal for Critical Geographies* 10(1): 34–41.

Seiler, R.M. 2002. Selling patriotism/selling beer: The case of the 'I AM CANADIAN!' commercial. *American Review of Canadian Studies* 32(1): 45–66.

Singleton, S. 2002. Collaborative environmental planning in the American West: The good, the bad and the ugly. *Environmental Politics* 11(3): 54–75.

Sparke, M. 1998. A map that roared and an original atlas: Canada, cartography, and the narration of nation. *Annals of the Association of American Geographers* 88(3): 463–95.

Sparke, M. 2000. Excavating the future in Cascadia: Geoeconimcs and the imagined geographies of a cross-border region. *BC Studies: The British Columbian Quarterly* 127: 5–44.

Sparke, M.B. 2006. A neoliberal nexus: Economy, security and the biopolitics of citizenship on the border. *Political Geography* 25(2): 151–80.

Spivak, G.C. 1987. *In Other Worlds: Essays in Cultural Politics*: London: Methuen.

Spivak, G.C. 1988. Can the subaltern speak? In Nelson, C. and Grossberg, L. (eds), *Marxism and the Interpretation of Culture*, pp. 271–313. Urbana: University of Illinois Press.

Spivak, G.C. 1996. *The Spivak Reader: Selected Works of Gayatri Chakravorty Spivak*. London: Routledge.

Suttles, W. 1960. Affinal ties, subsistence, and prestige among the Coast Salish. *American Anthropologist* 62(2): 296–305.

Suttles, W. 1974. *Coast Salish and Western Washington Indians: The Economic Life of the Coast Salish of Haro and Rosario Straits*. New York: Garland.

Thom, B. 2005. Coast Salish sense of place: Dwelling, meaning, power, property, and territory in the Coast Salish world. PhD thesis, McGill University, Montreal.

Thom, B. 2009. The paradox of boundaries in Coast Salish territories. *Cultural Geographies* 16(2): 179-205.

Thom, B. 2010. The anathema of aggregation: Towards 21st-century self-government in the Coast Salish world. *Anthropoligica* 52(1): 33–48.

USGS. 2008. Coast Salish water quality monitoring project. http://www.usgs.gov/features/coastsalish (accessed 10 January 2012).

Wainwright, J. and Bryan, J. 2009. Cartography, territory, property: Postcolonial reflections on indigenous counter-mapping in Nicaragua and Belize. *Cultural Geographies* 16(2): 153–78.

White, R. 1979. *Land Use, Environment, and Social Change: The Shaping of Island County*. Washington, DC: University of Washington Press.

Wilkinson, C.F. 1987. *American Indians, Time, and the Law: Native Societies in a Modern Constitutional Democracy*. New Haven: Yale University Press.

Wildcat, D. 2011. *Red Alert: Saving the Planet with Indigenous Knowledge*. Golden, CO: Fulcrum.

Chapter 17

Conclusion: Negotiating Water Governance

Christina Cook, Alice Cohen and Emma S. Norman

We use the term 'negotiating' in two ways. The first relates to developing agreements between parties, which speak to the power dynamics and political institutions at the heart of many of the issues discussed in the chapters. The second definition refers to negotiating as a balancing act, as a way of fitting together the pieces of the water governance puzzle: environmental health, human health, domestic and international political agendas and so on. In each context and locale, the water governance puzzle pieces will be different, and together they will form a picture of unique challenges that demand unique solutions. Likewise, each chapter of the volume demonstrates the particularities of water governance challenges and solutions; lessons about balancing issues and actor concerns can be learned from different cases, but ultimately there is no 'one size fits all' answer to governing water: it will always be a negotiation.

Why the Politics of Scale Matter in Negotiating Water Governance

As discussed in the introduction, water governance is far from straightforward. Water's fluidity means it crosses boundaries of all kinds – political, social and ecological – and it comes in various forms: ground, surface, fresh and marine. It is the only substance on earth that occurs naturally as a liquid, a solid and a gas. Resource decision-making is nearly always political, and perhaps even more so in the case of water resources because water is non-substitutable and necessary for life itself. Decisions made about water access and allocation are often made some distance from the physical resource and, typically, as part of wider geopolitical processes.

This volume draws on a growing literature on water governance, and an established literature on scale, to advance both by recognizing that decision-making with respect to water is often, implicitly, a decision about scale and its related politics. In other words, the volume shows that understanding scale as more than a container within which decisions are made opens up conceptual space. Mobilizing scale as relational and fluid – so that scale does not merely exist 'out there' but is also understood as constructed – is central to developing critical understandings of our hydrosocial world.

The main argument of this volume is thus that negotiating water governance – in both senses of the term – requires explicit consideration of the politics of scale.

We root this argument in three interrelated points which form the basis for the three parts that structure the volume:

1. that the watershed scale cannot be taken for granted as a natural and apolitical scale;
2. that the historical legacies of water governance can inform current decision-making, including efforts to rescale water governance; and
3. that scales can be used as political tools.

In arguing for the importance of understanding the politics of scale to negotiating water governance, we contribute to critiques of nirvana concepts such as Integrated Water Resources Management (IWRM), the watershed scale and public participation. Each of these three concepts has value in the debates on water governance, but none is a panacea: there is no silver bullet that will resolve the challenges of water governance.

Theoretical Contributions of this Volume

Our argument brings together two literatures – scale and water governance. Specifically, we asked the contributors to consider the following questions:

- What does water management and governance scholarship gain by looking through a scalar lens?
- What does the scalar literature gain by looking through a water lens?

The chapters in this volume provide a variety of answers to these two central questions that we grouped into three main themes. First, exploring scale in water governance demonstrates the importance of the materiality of water – i.e. as flowing, heavy, non-substitutable and essential – in attempts to rescale its governance. The physical properties of water are especially important given that rescaling initiatives are often undertaken to address a 'scalar mismatch' (Cumming et al. 2006) between decision-making spaces or scales – i.e. political boundaries – and putatively natural ones. Looking at efforts to rescale water governance shows the fluidity and complexity of rescaling processes, and reveals that rescaling is never without consequence.

Several of the chapters suggest that the scalar literature can be enriched through explicit consideration of spaces which are *prima facie* non-jurisdictional, such as watersheds. Arguments in favour of broadening rescaling debates to include putatively natural scales emerge clearly in Part I, where Cohen (Chapter 2), Sneddon and Fox (Chapter 3) and Vogel (Chapter 4) each challenge the notion of the watershed as a natural and politically neutral geographic space. Other authors contest the narrow articulation of scale as jurisdiction by exploring power dynamics in complex socio-environmental issues such resource extraction (Budds, Chapter

12); lack of adequate sanitation (Mehta, Chapter 13); increased flooding due to global climate change (Warner et al., Chapter 5); agricultural demands (Clarke-Sather, Chapter 14); and ecosystem losses such as fisheries (Norman, Chapter 16).

A second (related) way in which the volume advances scalar scholarship is by exploring the social, political and ecological effects of rescaling, which here we take to mean a shift in the physical space under consideration in particular governance arrangements. Policy shifts toward centralization, decentralization and watersheds are all examples of rescaling; and although the drivers of rescaling have been the subject of some study in recent years,[1] the effects – and particularly the ecological effects – of rescaled decision-making remain undertheorized (Cohen and McCarthy 2014). Positing constructed scales as sites of political resistance (Chapter 3), identity affirmation (Chapter 16) or regionalist politics (Chapter 6) are all new ways in which we can understand the kinds of effects that rescaled decision-making can have.

Additionally, a number of chapters address the second question – how is water governance literature enriched by looking through a scalar lens? – by applying scalar concepts about the political dimensions of scale to recent water governance reforms. Several chapters explore how governance reforms address changing hydrosocial environments (Cook, Chapter 7 and Furlong, Chapter 8), while others show that discussions of sovereignty and territoriality are integral to the discussions of rescaling. In Chapter 4, Vogel explores the interaction between conventional and hydrological spaces of governance in US river basins; Thiel (Chapter 6) examines rescaling and decentralization in the implementation of the EU Water Framework Directive in Spain; Johnson (Chapter 10) considers the effect of the implementation of the same directive on the reconfiguration of the European Union; and Norman (Chapter 16) investigates rescaling in a postcolonial context in the Salish Sea of North America. Two contributions study the use of performativity to rescale a region: Zwarteveen and Liebrand (Chapter 15) explore the creation of borders by elites (performance) that reframed Nepalese scales of irrigation; and Norman (Chapter 16) examines rescaling performed through reconstructed traditional ties based on precolonial networks.

Third, looking at water governance through a scalar lens directly challenges water governance practices that often assume fixity of scale. Specifically, this volume challenges some of the most axiomatic assumptions in twenty-first century water management: namely, the objectivity and desirability of watershed-scale governance and the desirability of increasingly integrated modes of water-related decision-making. In other words, by drawing out the explicitly scalar dimensions of water governance the work presented here challenges us to think critically about the rationales and outcomes of understood 'best practices' for water governance. Water is essential to life, and its role as a commodity implicates it in nearly every

---

1   For a more thorough treatment of drivers, effects, and instances of rescaled governance, see, for example, Brenner (1999, 2003), Brenner and Theodore (2002), Cohen (2012), Gibbs and Jonas (2001), Leitner (2004) and Leitner et al. (2002).

resource management issue; but water need not be fixed at the centre. We can recognize it as a constant flowing component; and we can recognize that water's flowing nature challenges our governance institutions.

Moreover, many of the volume's contributions work to deepen contemporary understandings of the political dimensions of scale and water by exploring the ways in which specific scales have been used as political tools. Vogel (Chapter 4), for example, investigates different river basin-scale initiatives in recent decades and explores the ways in which outcomes mirror broader trends such as the state-hydraulic paradigm (in the case of the Tennessee Valley Authority). Similarly, Perramond (Chapter 10) explores the implications of multiple views (and enactments) of scale in New Mexico. Sneddon and Fox (Chapter 3) analyse how the Mekong basin, as a construction of American politics, has led to a sense of shared identity and, more recently, created a site of political resistance.

Toward (Re)Solving Water Governance

In addition to supporting the volume's central argument – that consideration of the politics of scale is critical in negotiating water governance – the chapters reflect on three questions that permeate the water governance literature:

- How and why does water governance fragment across sectors and governmental departments?
- How can we govern shared waters more effectively?
- How do politics and power mediate water governance?

The answers the chapters provide to these questions buttress our contention that each particular water governance challenge will demand a unique approach in which scale will figure prominently.

The chapters in Part I challenge the assumption that watersheds are a more effective (however defined) scale for water governance than jurisdictional boundaries, to show that rescaling rarely resolves water governance challenges. Cohen unpacks the watershed scale to suggest that the construction and use of watersheds has political impacts, and that rescaling alone does not necessarily lead to expected outcomes. Sneddon and Fox distil the narratives associated with the Mekong river basin to show how politics and power are critical to water governance not only for reasons that are well documented elsewhere (see Swyngedouw 2004, 2009) but also for how they (re)construct watersheds as sites of political identity and resistance.

In her chapter on parcelling out the benefits of river basins, Vogel reviews outcomes in three US river basins to find that water governance fragments across sectors and governments in different ways in different basins. In the low-lying Netherlands, Warner et al. look broadly at water governance to include threats of inundation from the sea. Their chapter shows that politics – including a sense of crisis and insecurity – can contribute to the scaling or rescaling of water governance. Thiel finds that, in Spain, a putative rescaling to the European Union under its Water Framework Directive has manifested as ascendant regional water governance. On the whole, Part I confirms that the politics of watershed governance play out uniquely in different countries and regions.

Part II of the volume looks beyond the watershed at processes and impacts of rescaling water governance. The chapters here examine the production and mobilization of scale in water governance. Cook's historical review of Ontario water governance shows that rescaling is not new, but rather an established practice. Rescaling may attempt to address fragmentation of water governance and improve governance efficacy; and it is frequently a venue of political contests. In her examination of water supply reform in Ontario, Furlong finds that rescaling obscures the positionalities within a perceived homogenous scale and the complex politics of water governance. In their chapter on south Texas water technologies, Jepson and Brannstrom discover that governments controlled and permitted water technologies as a 'scale-specific political strategy' for control of water governance. In New Mexico, Perramond finds that rescaling – from the individual to the community and from one identity to another – changes the applicable law and, in turn, the rights to water that can be claimed. In his chapter on the EU Water Framework Directive, Johnson argues that the directive's rescaling of water governance has reterritorialized environmental governance across the EU, perhaps leading to less fragmentation and more effective water governance at the scale of the federation. Together, the chapters of Part II show that water governance may indeed be rescaled (including to and from the watershed scale), but that the politics of scale cannot be escaped.

Part III examines the politics and power in water governance using the concepts of waterscapes and hybrid constructs. In her chapter on resource extraction, Budds mobilizes the concept of waterscapes to examine the changing hydrosocial relations in Andean communities. Her analysis showed that the mining industry and the waterscape (re)produce each other in the midst of the politics of resource extraction. Mehta's chapter highlighted a key fragmentation of water governance that is often simply accepted (and frequently ignored): the separate governance of water and sanitation. She focuses on the successes of Community-Led Total Sanitation in Bangladesh to show the challenges of scaling up a local solution to reach more communities.

In his chapter on agricultural hydrosocial relations in northwest China, Clarke-Sather examines a variety of state responses to the absence or scarcity of water. These state interventions – from different crops to new technologies – demonstrated the interconnectedness of local water governance and global political economy. Zwarteveen and Liebrand excavate the use of scale in irrigation development in Nepal; they find that the elites that control irrigation data imbue that data with a particular vision for development that impacts the subsequent production of data. In her chapter on the Salish Sea in the Pacific, Norman examined the performativity of scale to establish postcolonial, indigenous, hydrosocial networks. There, rescaling has reduced some fragmentation – breaking down the political boundary of the 49th parallel – and shifted power networks in Salish Sea governance.

Part III shows that using the concept of waterscapes or hybrid constructs to examine the relationship between the politics of scale and water governance can reveal embedded connections. The insights of the chapters in this volume as a whole, arrived at by bringing scale and water governance into conversation, serve to reveal the complexity that characterizes water governance and its negotiations.

Future Research Directions

Throughout this volume, we encourage (perhaps challenge) readers to think beyond the fixity of traditional notions of water governance and the politics of scale. The concept of negotiation played a central role in this project; as authors showed how 'slippery' water governance is, they articulated and negotiated theoretical debates regarding scale. This volume sought to stretch our thinking about water governance and the politics of scale; however, questions remain. What opportunities exist in this new conceptual space at the intersection of the politics of scale and water governance? Can academics help articulate the role of individuals in larger hydrosocial networks? If so, how?

Certainly, we need to continue to connect the work of academics from different disciplines. This includes incorporating contemporary work on gender and poverty and making more explicit links between health and water. Room remains – both theoretically and in the practice of water governance – to think critically about how the politics of scale produce and reinforce particular governance systems. In international relations, for example, the nation-state framework continues to provide a dominant narrative which informs governance patterns and systems – despite ongoing calls for reframing (see Furlong 2006). Governance systems that reify national boundaries through, for example, the repeated citation of particular waterways as 'transboundary' are a prime example of this phenomenon at work (Norman 2015). Works in postcolonial studies and cultural geography attempt to unsettle these dominant narratives by showing counter-narratives of governance regimes – particularly for indigenous communities living on borderlands (Norman 2015) and with greater attention to gender politics (Harris 2009). These projects that work to unsettle constructed scales and bordered spaces continue to reveal the normalized power dynamics that are often hidden in governance institutions.

Beyond the theoretical, though, the discussions in this book show the possibilities for application. For example, sanitation has noticeably been absent in the discussions of water governance and the politics of scale; more discussion in more places on the 'dirtier' business of water governance is greatly needed, in our opinion. Mehta (Chapter 13) provides a good starting point from which to engage in discussions related to choices of the 'the body' and 'the individual' and to consider impacts on the collective in public health debates and feminist geographies. Interesting possibilities emerge when the 'invisible' is made visible, and may reveal implications for the world's most vulnerable populations.

The volume also reinforces the need to be discerning of governance frameworks. Scalar politics tell us that voices are silenced through the construction of particular governance frameworks as 'normal'. Those often silenced voices are critically important to include in water governance, for reasons both ethical and pragmatic. Here, a key question might be: What techniques can we use to unsettle exploitative patterns of resource use? Work on answering this question has begun. For example, indigenous groups along the North American borderland – particularly in the Salish Sea, the Yukon River basin, and the Great Lakes basin – have created inter-tribal councils to address issues of shared waters, while also working on wider goals of decolonization, self-determination and self-governance (Norman 2015). Moreover, connecting academic work with practitioner expertise and everyday human experience may help to further articulate questions for future exploration and negotiation.

Lastly, to what extent can our conclusions be applied to other elements of the environment? Indeed, even the term 'environment' itself implies the non-human – an implication with which water scholars (including Budds and Mehta in this volume) have taken issue as they work to understand the ways in which water flows through both human and non-human systems. Nevertheless, we suggest that although the scalar politics of water are undertheorized, they may remain better understood than other non-human resources.

Negotiating From Here

Together the chapters in this volume support the need for a scale-sensitive approach to water governance, and converge on arguments that support a framework for decision-making that is explicit about its inclusion of scalar considerations (see also Padt et al. 2014). The volume works to unsettle the privileging of any scale as a best practice for water governance, and advocates for the importance of examining power and politics in processes of rescaling in water governance.

Importantly, governance refers to *process* and not *outcome*. Thus, engaging in governance reform (of the type described throughout this volume) does not necessarily guarantee a particular set of results. Thinking of water governance as a *negotiated process* opens conceptual and practical space to unsettle exploitative patterns and supplant them with structures that can support social and ecological equity, which are goals at the heart of many water governance initiatives at their outset. As the diverse contributions in this book remind us, the politics of scale matter.

References

Brenner, N. 1999. Globalisation as reterritorialisation: The re-scaling of urban governance in the European Union. *Urban Studies*, 36(3), 431–51.

Brenner, N. 2003. Metropolitan institutional reform and the rescaling of state space in contemporary Western Europe. *European Urban and Regional Studies*, 10(4), 297–324.

Brenner, N. and Theodore, N. 2002. Cities and the geographies of 'actually existing neoliberalism'. *Antipode*, 34(3), 349–79.

Cohen, A. 2012. Rescaling environmental governance: Watersheds as boundary objects at the intersection of science, neoliberalism, and participation. *Environment and Planning A*, 44(9), 2207–24.

Cohen, A. and McCarthy, J. 2014. Reviewing rescaling: Strengthening the case for environmental considerations. *Progress in Human Geography*, 7 March, doi: 10.1177/0309132514521483.

Cumming, G.S., Cumming, D.H. and Redman, C.L. 2006. Scale mismatches in social-ecological systems: Causes, consequences, and solutions. *Ecology and Society*, 11(1), 14.

Furlong, K. 2006. Hidden theories, troubled waters: International relations, the 'territorial trap', and the Southern African development community's transboundary waters. *Political Geography*, 25(4), 438–58.

Gibbs, D. and Jonas, A.E.G. 2001. Rescaling and regional governance: The English Regional Development Agencies and the environment. *Environment and Planning C*, 19(2), 269–88.

Harris, L. 2009. Gender and emergent water governance: Comparative overview of neoliberalized natures and gender dimensions of privatization, devolution and marketization. *Gender, Place and Culture*, 16(4), 387–408.

Leitner, H. 2004. The politics of scale and networks of spatial connectivity: Transnational interurban networks and the rescaling of political governance in Europe. In: Sheppard, E. and McMaster, R. (eds), *Scale and Geographic Inquiry: Nature, Society, and Method*. Oxford: Blackwell, pp. 236–55.

Leitner, H., Pavlik, C. and Sheppard, E. 2002. Networks, governance, and the politics of scale: Inter-urban networks and the European Union. In: Herod, A. and Wright, M.W. (eds), *Geographies of Power: Placing Scale*. Malden, MA: Blackwell, pp. 274–98.

Norman, E.S. 2015. *Governing Transboundary Waters: Canada, the United States, and Indigenous Communities*. London: Routledge.

Padt, F., Opdam, P., Polman, N. and Termeer, C. (eds). 2014. *Scale-Sensitive Governance of the Environment*. Chichester: Wiley Blackwell.

Swyngedouw, E. 2004. *Social Power and the Urbanization of Water: Flows of Power*. New York: Oxford University Press.

Swyngedouw, E. 2009. The political economy and political ecology of the hydro-social cycle. *Journal of Contemporary Water Research and Education*, 142(1), 55–60.

Index